P9-DDX-558

THE MODERN LIBRARY
OF THE WORLD'S BEST BOOKS

Lives of the Most Eminent

Painters, Sculptors,

and Architects

Lives of the Most Eminent Painters, Sculptors, and Architects

BY

GIORGIO VASARI (16ᵀʰ Cent.)

Abridged from the translation by
GASTON DuC. DeVere

Edited, with an Introduction, by
ROBERT N. LINSCOTT

The Modern Library
NEW YORK

Random House IS THE PUBLISHER OF *The Modern Library*

BENNETT CERF · DONALD S. KLOPFER

Manufactured in the United States of America by H. Wolff

CONTENTS

Contents

INTRODUCTION

Recognizing that the names of very many architects, sculptors and painters, together with innumerable most beautiful works wrought by them, are being forgotten and destroyed; and wishing to defend them as much as in me lies from this second death, and to preserve them as long as possible in the memory of the living; and having spent much time in seeking them out and used the greatest diligence in discovering the native city, the origin and the actions of the craftsmen, and having with great labor drawn them from the tales of old men and from various records and writings, left by their heirs a prey to dust and food for worms; and finally, having received from this both profit and pleasure, I have judged it expedient, nay, rather, my duty, to make for them whatsoever memorial my weak talents and my small judgment may be able to make. In honor, then, of those who are already dead, and for the benefit of all the followers of these three most excellent arts, Architecture, Sculpture, and Painting, I will write the Lives of the craftsmen of each according to the times wherein they lived.

GIORGIO VASARI

ONE evening in the year 1546, Giorgio Vasari, a Florentine painter and architect, age thirty-five, an industrious and uninspired disciple of Michelangelo, was dining, during a visit to Rome, with his patron, the celebrated Cardinal Farnese. The company was distinguished, the conversation learned. Paolo Giovio, art critic and art lover, remarked on the need for a history of Italian painting from the days of Giotto. Turning to Vasari, the Cardinal suggested that he should undertake the task, adding, "whereby you would also advance the arts." Coming from such a source the suggestion was vir-

vii

tually a command; moreover Vasari had already collected much material on the subject. Overburdened though he was with commissions for the somewhat mediocre paintings that he turned out by the yard for princely patrons, he nevertheless found time by the end of the following year to complete most of the book and turn it over to a copyist. Three years later *Lives of the Most Eminent Painters, Sculptors, and Architects* was published in Florence. The time and the man had come together to produce a lasting work of literature and to record a great moment in the history of art: the high noon of the Italian Renaissance.

Until recently historians conceived of the Renaissance as a sudden rebirth, the dawn of a new day after the long night of the Middle Ages. Now it is regarded, not as an explosion, but as an evolution: a period of transition between the medieval and the modern world brought about by the interaction of many complex forces, economic, political, and religious. The first light of dawn had come as far back as the twelfth century. Since then, slowly and with many setbacks, greater security and increasing commerce had resulted in a more ample margin of the leisure and economic health that provide a climate in which the arts can flourish. By the fifteenth century, the revival of learning and the rediscovery of classical literature and philosophy had brought man a new concept of life, teaching him no longer to be haunted by fear of Hell and hope of Heaven, but to enjoy the visible world and the pleasures of the senses.

When man had learned to consider this world as his abode rather than as a mere place of passage, it was natural that his next step should be to inquire into its laws and limits. The spirit of discovery was abroad, the first stirrings of modern science. Copernicus gave man a new heaven, Columbus a new earth. And all these elements—the opening of trade routes, the increase in economic stability, the cult of the individual, the cultivation of the senses, and the sudden enlargement of the frontiers of knowledge—combined to fertilize the creative imagination and nourish the creative artist.

By its geographical situation and as inheritor of the traditions of Rome, Italy was first to feel the warmth of this cultural springtime. Painters, wearied of the stiff and lifeless style of the Byzantine artists, devised new techniques of perspective and accurate representation; art acquired mass appeal and prestige value so that cities and principalities competed with one another for the services of its most renowned practitioners. Here, in the sixteenth century, the plastic arts reached their pinnacle and found their perfect historian.

Giorgio Vasari was born at the height of the Italian Renaissance and lived well into the days of its decline. When the first edition of his book was published in 1550, Leonardo had been dead for thirty-six years, Raphael for thirty, and Michelangelo and Titian were in their seventies. The artists who had brought glory to themselves and immortality to their patrons were dead or aging, the splendor was fading, the high tide of creative fury had begun to ebb, the great days were passing. It was time for survey and appraisal. It was time, in other words, for Vasari.

Of this, Vasari himself was sublimely unaware. The course of art, as he saw it, was still onward and upward. Indeed, in his more hopeful moments, it is probable that he thought of himself as the not unworthy successor of Raphael and Michelangelo. Had he been told that the immortality he so complacently anticipated would come, not from his paintings nor from his buildings, but from his book, it would have seemed to him a jest in shocking taste.

The fact is that Vasari expressed himself glowingly on paper, frigidly on canvas. His writings are warm and alive, his paintings cold as death. Pen in hand instead of brush he became a superb journalist, an indefatigable note taker and collector of information, a tireless traveler and gossip—in short, a man supremely endowed by temperament and by opportunity to be the historian of Italian Renaissance art.

Pedantic critics have disparaged Vasari for his failure to note his sources of information, his free and easy way with facts, his uncritical acceptance of legend, his leisurely pace and his moral platitudes. But these are faults of the period rather than of the man, and are far outweighed by the fact that Vasari knew many of the men of whom he wrote, and saw most of the pictures he described; moreover his style was as vital and lively as the age in which he lived. His strong points and his weak are neatly summed up by Bernard Berenson:

"The Florentine masters," it has been said, "are the Dr. Johnsons of art: they are so much more fascinating in the pages of their Boswell than in their own works." . . . Some such view of Vasari would account for the hold he has not only on people who read him as literature, but upon students of art. . . . He abounds in contradictions; he makes long excursions on looplines to kick an enemy or to puff a friend . . . and yet one comes back to him with an ever increasing sense of his charm and fascination. He has this charm and fascination because he wrote down with the naiveté of an Herodotus the folk-lore, romance and gossip that had, in the course of centuries, gathered in profusion about the artists, a class of people who in Florence formed a more prominent and more self-conscious part of the community than they did in any other Italian city. Their fellow-townsmen, therefore, took the keenest imaginable interest in them both as a class and as individuals, and heard and repeated stories about them with that delight in personal anecdote which was the distinguishing mark of the Florentine populace and of their literature. It was for such a public that Vasari wrote, and this accounts for his method, and for his success. He had to be personal, gossipy and readable. His unerring sense of the readable made him arrange his material in a way that would catch the eye, no matter at what cost to mere veracity, and for that reason he succeeded where others failed. . . . Wherever Vasari speaks of what he has seen—and he saw nearly all the best work in Italy—and where he is not led astray by what might be called the false morn of journalism, he is a singularly warm, generous and appreciative critic. . . . Everything considered, his interpretation is still the best there is. For documents we must look elsewhere. But Vasari is still the unrivaled critic of Italian art, and one of the great prose writers of Italy.

Lacking perspective, as historians must when writing of contemporaries and immediate predecessors, Vasari included in his *Lives* many artists whose work is of secondary interest and importance today. Also, in dealing with artists whose work did not interest him or whom he knew only by hearsay, he was often cursory and sometimes dull. And, finally, many of his pages are given over to descriptions of works which no longer exist. These portions of his book are of value to students and to specialists in the field of art rather than the general public. Accordingly they have been omitted from this edition, which includes only the artists and works most interesting to present-day readers. And in order that attention might not frequently be diverted from text to footnotes, Vasari's minor errors have been left uncorrected.

The standard translation of the *Lives* was made in 1850 by Mrs. Jonathan Foster. Sixty-two years later a new translation was made by Gaston DuC. DeVere for the Medici Society of London. This was not only terser, livelier and more readable, but was also much closer to the spirit of the original. It is the DeVere translation that has been used in this edition with one modification. DeVere used Italian proper names throughout. For the convenience of readers of this book, artists' names have here been given as commonly used: Raphael, for example, instead of Raffaello, and Michelangelo instead of Michelagnolo; also, the Italian measurement, *braccio,* has been changed to feet at the rate of two feet to a *braccio.* On the other hand, the names of churches and buildings have been left in Italian with occasional footnotes, in the case of important buildings, for ease of identification; for example, S. Pietro, known to us as St. Peter's.

Readers who wish to examine the complete Vasari text are referred to the lavishly illustrated edition of the *Lives* published in ten quarto volumes for the Medici Society by Macmillan of London—provided they are fortunate enough to find a set, since it has long been out of print. Further information on the author will be found in the *Life of Vasari* by Robert W. Carden, published in America by Holt.

ROBERT N. LINSCOTT

GIOTTO

[The date of Giotto di Bondone's birth is unknown but he was active by 1300 and died in 1336.]

THAT very obligation which the craftsmen of painting owe to nature, who serves continually as model to those who are ever wresting the good from her best and most beautiful features and striving to counterfeit and to imitate her, should be owed, in my belief, to Giotto, painter of Florence, for the reason that, after the methods of good paintings and their outlines had lain buried for so many years under the ruins of the wars, he alone, although born among inept craftsmen, by the gift of God revived that art, which had come to a grievous pass, and brought it to such a form as could be called good. And truly it was a very great miracle that that age, gross and inept, should have had strength to work in Giotto in a fashion so masterly, that design, whereof the men of those times had little or no knowledge, was restored completely to life by means of him. And yet this great man was born at the village of Vespignano, in the district of Florence, fourteen miles distant from that city, from a father named Bondone, a tiller of the soil and a simple fellow. He, having had this son, to whom he gave the name Giotto, reared him conformably to his condition; and when he had come to the age of ten, he showed in all his actions, although childish still, a vivacity and readiness of intelligence much out of the ordinary, which rendered him dear not only to his father but to all those also who knew him, both in the village and beyond. Now Bondone gave some sheep into his charge, and he, going about the holding, now in one part and now in another, to

graze them, and impelled by a natural inclination to the art
of design, was for ever drawing, on stones, on the ground, or
on sand, something from nature, or in truth anything that
came into his fancy. Wherefore Cimabue, going one day on
some business of his own from Florence to Vespignano, found
Giotto, while his sheep were browsing, portraying a sheep
from nature on a flat and polished slab, with a stone slightly
pointed, without having learnt any method of doing this
from others, but only from nature; whence Cimabue, standing fast all in a marvel, asked him if he wished to go to live
with him. The child answered that, his father consenting, he
would go willingly. Cimabue then asking this from Bondone,
the latter lovingly granted it to him, and was content that he
should take the boy with him to Florence; whither having
come, in a short time, assisted by nature and taught by Cimabue, the child not only equaled the manner of his master, but
became so good an imitator of nature that he banished completely that rude Greek manner and revived the modern and
good art of painting, introducing the portraying well from
nature of living people, which had not been used for more
than two hundred years. If, indeed, anyone had tried it, he
had not succeeded very happily, nor as well by a great measure as Giotto, who portrayed among others, as is still seen
to-day in the Chapel of the Palace of the Podestà at Florence,
Dante Alighieri, a contemporary and his very great friend,
and no less famous as poet than was in the same times Giotto
as painter, so much praised by Messer Giovanni Boccaccio in
the preface to the story of Messer Forese da Rabatta and of
Giotto the painter himself. In the same chapel are the portraits, likewise by the same man's hand, of Ser Brunetto
Latini, master of Dante, and of Messer Corso Donati, a great
citizen of those times.

The first pictures of Giotto were in the chapel of the high
altar in the Badia of Florence, wherein he made many works
held beautiful, but in particular a Madonna receiving the
Annunciation, for the reason that in her he expressed vividly

the fear and the terror that the salutation of Gabriel inspired in Mary the Virgin, who appears, all full of the greatest alarm, to be wishing almost to turn to flight. By the hand of Giotto, likewise, is the panel on the high altar of the said chapel, which has been preserved there to our own day, and is still preserved there, more because of a certain reverence that is felt for the work of so great a man than for any other reason. And in S. Croce there are four chapels by the same man's hand: three between the sacristy and the great chapel, and one on the other side. In the first of the three, which is that of Messer Ridolfo de' Bardi, and is that wherein are the bell-ropes, is the life of S. Francis, in the death of whom a good number of friars show very naturally the expression of weeping. In the next, which is that of the family of Peruzzi, are two stories of the life of S. John the Baptist, to whom the chapel is dedicated; wherein great vivacity is seen in the dancing and leaping of Herodias, and in the promptness of some servants bustling at the service of the table. In the same are two marvelous stories of S. John the Evangelist—namely, when he brings Drusiana back to life, and when he is carried off into Heaven. In the third, which is that of the Giugni, dedicated to the Apostles, there are painted by the hand of Giotto the stories of the martyrdom of many of them. In the fourth, which is on the other side of the church, toward the north, and belongs to the Tosinghi and to the Spinelli, and is dedicated to the Assumption of Our Lady, Giotto painted her Birth, her Marriage, her Annunciation, the Adoration of the Magi, and when she presents Christ as a little Child to Simeon, which is something very beautiful, seeing that, besides a great affection that is seen in that old man as he receives Christ, the action of the child, stretching out its arms in fear of him and turning in terror toward its mother, could not be more touching or more beautiful. Next, in the death of the Madonna herself, there are the Apostles, and a good number of angels with torches in their hands, all very beautiful.

After these works, departing from Florence in order to go to finish in Assisi the works begun by Cimabue, in passing through Arezzo he painted in the Pieve the Chapel of S. Francesco, which is above the place of baptism; and on a round column, near a Corinthian capital that is both ancient and very beautiful, he portrayed from nature a S. Francis and a S. Dominic; and in the Duomo outside Arezzo he painted the Stoning of S. Stephen in a little chapel, with a beautiful composition of figures. These works finished, he betook himself to Assisi, a city of Umbria, being called thither by Fra Giovanni di Muro della Marca, then General of the Friars of S. Francis; where, in the upper church, he painted in fresco, under the gallery that crosses the windows, on both sides of the church, thirty-two scenes of the life and acts of S. Francis —that is, sixteen on each wall—so perfectly that he acquired thereby very great fame. And in truth there is seen great variety in that work, not only in the gestures and attitudes of each figure but also in the composition of all the scenes; not to mention that it enables us very beautifully to see the diversity of the costumes of those times, and certain imitations and observations of the things of nature. Among others, there is one very beautiful scene, wherein a thirsty man, in whom the desire for water is vividly seen, is drinking, bending down on the ground by a fountain with very great and truly marvelous expression, in a manner that it seems almost a living person that is drinking. There are also many other things there most worthy of consideration, about which, in order not to be tedious, I do not enlarge further. Let it suffice that this whole work acquired for Giotto very great fame, by reason of the excellence of the figures and of the order, proportion, liveliness, and facility which he had from nature, and which he had made much greater by means of study, and was able to demonstrate clearly in all his works. And because, besides that which Giotto had from nature, he was most diligent and went on ever thinking out new ideas and wresting them from nature, he well deserved to be called the disciple of nature and not of others. The aforesaid scenes being finished, he painted in the same place, but in the lower church, the upper part of the walls at the sides of the high altar, and all the four angles of the vaulting above in the place where lies the body of S. Francis; and all with inventions both fanciful and beautiful. In these pictures is the portrait of Giotto himself, very well made, and over the door of the sacristy, by the same man's hand and also in fresco, there is a S. Francis who is receiving the Stigmata, so loving and devout that to me it appears the most excellent picture that Giotto made in these works, which are all truly beautiful and worthy of praise.

Having finished, then, for the last, the said S. Francis, he returned to Florence, where, on arriving there, he painted, on a panel that was to be sent to Pisa, a S. Francis on the tremendous rock of La Vernia, with extraordinary diligence, seeing that, besides certain landscapes full of trees and cliffs, which was something new in those times, there are seen in the attitude of a S. Francis, who is kneeling and receiving the Stigmata with much readiness, a most ardent desire to receive them and infinite love toward Jesus Christ, who, being surrounded in the sky by seraphim, is granting them to him with an expression so vivid that anything better cannot be imagined. In the lower part of the same panel there are three very beautiful scenes of the life of the same Saint. This panel, which to-day is seen in S. Francesco in Pisa on a pillar beside the high altar, and is held in great veneration as a memorial of so great a man, was the reason that the Pisans, having just finished the building of the Campo Santo after the design of Giovanni, son of Niccola Pisano, as has been said above, gave to Giotto the painting of part of the inner walls, to the end that, since this so great building was all incrusted on the outer side with marbles and with carvings made at very great cost, and roofed over with lead, and also full of sarcophagi and ancient tombs once belonging to the heathens and brought to Pisa from various parts of the world, even so it might be adorned within, on the walls, with the noblest paintings. Having gone to Pisa, then, for this purpose, Giotto made in fresco, on the first part of a wall in that Campo Santo, six large stories of the most patient Job. This work acquired for him so great fame, both in that city and abroad, that Pope Benedict IX of Treviso sent one of his courtiers into Tuscany to see what sort of man was Giotto, and of what kind his works, having designed to have some pictures made in S. Pietro.* This courtier, coming in order to see Giotto and to hear what other masters there were in Florence excellent in painting and in mosaic, talked to many masters in Siena. Then, having received drawings from them, he came to Florence, and having gone into the shop of Giotto, who was working, declared to him the mind of the Pope and in what way it was proposed to make use of his labor, and at last asked him for some little drawing, to the end that he might send it to His Holiness. Giotto, who was most courteous, took a paper, and on that, with a brush dipped in red, holding his arm fast against his side in order to make a compass, with a turn of the hand he made a circle, so true in proportion and circumference that to behold it was a marvel. This done, he smiled and said to the courtier: "Here is your drawing." He, thinking he was being derided, said: "Am I to have no other drawing but this?" " 'Tis enough and to spare," answered Giotto. "Send it, together with the others, and you will see if it will be recognized." The envoy, seeing that he could get nothing else, left him, very ill-satisfied and wondering whether he had been fooled. All the same, sending to the Pope the other drawings and the names of those who had made them, he also sent that of Giotto, relating the method that he had followed in making his circle without moving his arm and without compasses. Wherefore the Pope and many courtiers that were versed in the arts recognized by this how much Giotto surpassed in excellence all the other painters of his time.

* St. Peter's.

The aforesaid Pope then made him come to Rome, where, honoring him much and appreciating his talents, he made him paint five scenes from the life of Christ in the apse of S. Pietro, and the chief panel in the sacristy, which were all executed by him with so great diligence that there never issued from his hands any more finished work in distemper. Wherefore he well deserved that the Pope, holding himself to have been well served, should cause to be given to him six hundred ducats of gold, besides granting him so many favors that they were talked of throughout all Italy.

The Pope, having seen these works, and the manner of Giotto pleasing him infinitely, ordered him to make scenes from the Old Testament and the New right round S. Pietro. By his hand, also, was the Navicella in mosaic that is over the three doors of the portico in the court of S. Pietro, which is truly marvelous and deservedly praised by all beautiful minds. Giotto then returned to his own country, having been abroad six years. But no long time after, by reason of the death of Pope Benedict IX, Clement V was created Pope in Perugia, and Giotto was forced to betake himself with that Pope to the place where he brought his Court, to Avignon, in order to do certain works there; and having gone there, he made, not only in Avignon but in many other places in France, many very beautiful panels and pictures in fresco, which pleased the Pontiff and the whole Court infinitely. Wherefore, the work dispatched, the Pope dismissed him lovingly and with many gifts, and he returned home no less rich than honored and famous; and among the rest he brought back the portrait of that Pope, which he gave afterwards to Taddeo Gaddi, his disciple. And this return of Giotto to Florence was in the year 1316. But it was not granted to him to stay long in Florence, because, being summoned to Padua by the agency of the Signori della Scala, he painted a very beautiful chapel in the Santo, a church built in those times. From there he went to Verona, where, for Messer Cane, he made certain pictures in his palace, and in particular the portrait of that lord; and a panel for the Friars of S. Francis. These works completed, in returning to Tuscany he was forced to stay in Ferrara, and he painted at the behest of those Signori d'Este, in their palace and in S. Agostino, some works that are still seen there to-day. Meanwhile, it coming to the ears of Dante, poet of Florence, that Giotto was in Ferrara, he so contrived that he brought him to Ravenna, where he was living in exile; and he caused him to make round the Church of S. Francesco, for the Signori da Polenta, some scenes in fresco that are passing good. Next, having gone from Ravenna to Urbino, there too he wrought some works. Then, chancing to pass through Arezzo, he could not but comply with the wish of Piero Saccone, who had been much his friend; wherefore he made for him in fresco, on a pillar in the principal chapel of the Vescovado, a S. Martin who has cut his cloak in half and is giving one part of it to a beggar, who is standing before him almost wholly naked. Then, having made for the Abbey of S. Fiore a large Crucifix painted in distemper on wood, which is to-day in the middle of that church, he returned finally to Florence, where, among many other works, he made some pictures in the Convent of the Nuns of Faenza, both in fresco and in distemper, that are not in existence to-day, by reason of the destruction of that convent. In the year 1322, likewise—Dante, very much his friend, having died in the year before, to his great sorrow —he went to Lucca, and at the request of Castruccio, then Lord of that city, his birthplace, he made a panel in S. Martino with a Christ in air and four Saints, Protectors of that city—namely, S. Peter, S. Regulus, S. Martin, and S. Paulinus—who appear to be recommending a Pope and an Emperor, who, according to what is believed by many, are Frederick of Bavaria and the Anti-Pope Nicholas V. Some, likewise, believe that Giotto designed the castle and fortress of Giusta, which is impregnable, at San Frediano, in the same city of Lucca.

Afterwards, Giotto having returned to Florence, Robert,

King of Naples, wrote to Charles, King of Calabria, his first-born son, who chanced to be in Florence, that he should send him Giotto to Naples at all costs, for the reason that, having finished the building of S. Chiara, a convent of nuns and a royal church, he wished that it should be adorned by him with noble paintings. Giotto, then, hearing himself summoned by a King so greatly renowned and famous, went more than willingly to serve him, and, on arriving, painted many scenes from the Old Testament and the New in some chapels of the said convent. And the scenes from the Apocalypse that he made in one of the said chapels are said to have been inventions of Dante; and this may be also true of those at Assisi, so greatly renowned, whereof there has been enough said above. And although Dante at that time was dead, they may have held discourse on these matters, as often comes to pass between friends.

For the Frati Umiliati of Ognissanti in Florence, Giotto painted a chapel and four panels, in one of which there was the Madonna, with many angels round her and the Child in her arms, and a large Crucifix on wood, whereof Puccio Capanna took the design and wrought many of them afterwards throughout all Italy, having much practice in the manner of Giotto. In the transept of the said church, when this book was printed the first time, there was a little panel in distemper painted by Giotto with infinite diligence, wherein was the death of Our Lady, with the Apostles round her and with a Christ who is receiving her soul into His arms. This work was much praised by the craftsmen of painting, and in particular by Michelangelo Buonarroti, who declared, as was said another time, that the quality of this painted story could not be more like to the truth than it is. This little panel, I say, having come into notice from the time when the book of these Lives was first published, was afterwards carried off by someone unknown, who, perhaps out of love for art and out of piety, it seeming to him that it was little esteemed, became, as said our poet, impious. And truly it was a miracle in those times that Giotto had so great loveliness in his painting, considering, above all, that he learnt the art in a certain measure without a master.

After these works, in the year 1334, on July 9, he put his hand to the Campanile of S. Maria del Fiore, whereof the foundation was a platform of strong stone, in a pit sunk forty feet deep from which water and gravel had been removed; upon this platform he made a good mass of concrete, that reached to the height of twenty-four feet above the first foundation, and the rest—namely, the other sixteen feet—he caused to be made of masonry. And at this beginning and foundation there officiated the Bishop of the city, who, in the presence of all the clergy and all the magistrates, solemnly laid the first stone. This work, then, being carried on with the said model, which was in the German manner that was in use in those times, Giotto designed all the scenes that were going into the ornamentation, and marked out the model with white, black, and red colors in all those places wherein the marbles and the friezes were to go, with much diligence. The circuit round the base was two hundred feet—that is, fifty feet for each side—and the height, two hundred and eighty-eight feet. And if that is true, and I hold it as of the truest, which Lorenzo di Cione Ghiberti has left in writing, Giotto made not only the model of this campanile, but also part of those scenes in marble wherein are the beginnings of all the arts, in sculpture and in relief. And the said Lorenzo declares that he saw models in relief by the hand of Giotto, and in particular those of these works; which circumstance can be easily believed, design and invention being father and mother of all these arts and not of one alone. This campanile was destined, according to the model of Giotto, to have a spire, or rather a pyramid, four-sided and one hundred feet high, as a completion to what is now seen; but, for the reason that it was a German idea and in an old manner, modern architects have never done aught but advise that it should not be made, the work seeming to be better as it is. For all these works Giotto was not only made citizen of Florence, but was given a pension of one hundred florins yearly by the Commune of Florence, which was something very great in those times; and he was made overseer over this work, which was carried on after him by Taddeo Gaddi, for he did not live so long as to be able to see it finished.

Afterwards, having gone again to Padua, besides many other works and chapels that he painted there, he made a Mundane Glory in the precincts of the Arena, which gained him much honor and profit. In Milan, also, he wrought certain works, that are scattered throughout that city and held most beautiful even to this day. Finally, having returned from Milan, no long time passed before he gave up his soul to God, having wrought so many most beautiful works in his life, and having been no less good as Christian than he was excellent as painter. He died in the year 1336, to the great grief of all his fellow-citizens—nay, of all those who had known him or even only heard his name—and he was buried, even as his virtues deserved, with great honor, having been loved by all while he lived, and in particular by the men excellent in all the professions, seeing that, besides Dante, of whom we have spoken above, he was much honored by Petrarch, both he and his works, so greatly that it is read in Petrarch's testament that he left to Signor Francesco da Carrara, Lord of Padua, among other things held by him in the highest veneration, a picture by the hand of Giotto containing a Madonna, as something rare and dear to him.

Giotto was very ingenious and humorous, and very witty in his sayings, whereof there is still vivid memory in Florence.

He was buried in S. Maria del Fiore, on the left side as you enter the church, where there is a slab of white marble in memory of so great a man.

LUCA DELLA ROBBIA

[*Luca di Simone di Marco della Robbia was born in
1399 or 1400 and died in 1482.*]

LUCCA DELLA ROBBIA, sculptor of Florence, was born in the
year 1399 in the house of his ancestors, which is in Florence,
below the Church of S. Barnaba; and therein he was honestly
brought up until he had learnt not only to read and write but
also to cast accounts, in so far as it was likely to be needful,
after the custom of most Florentines. And afterwards he
was placed by his father to learn the art of the goldsmith with
Leonardo di Ser Giovanni, who was then held the best master
of that art in Florence. Now, having learnt under this man to
make designs and to work in wax, Luca grew in courage and
applied himself to making certain things in marble and in
bronze, which, seeing that he succeeded in them well enough,
brought it about that he completely abandoned his business
of goldsmith and applied himself to sculpture, insomuch that
he did nothing but ply his chisel all day and draw all night;
and this he did with so great zeal, that, feeling his feet very
often freezing at night, he took to keeping them in a basket
full of shavings, such as carpenters strip from planks when
they shape them with the plane, in order to warm them without giving up his drawing. Nor do I marvel in any way at this,
seeing that no one ever became excellent in any exercise
whatsoever without beginning from his childhood to endure
heat, cold, hunger, thirst, and other discomforts; wherefore
those men are entirely deceived who think to be able, at their
ease and with all the comforts of the world, to attain to hon-

orable rank. It is not by sleeping but by waking and studying continually that progress is made.

Luca was barely fifteen years of age when he was summoned, together with other young sculptors, to Rimini, in order to make some figures and other ornaments in marble for Sigismondo di Pandolfo Malatesti, Lord of that city, who was then having a chapel made in the Church of S. Francesco, and a tomb for his wife, who had died. Luca had given an honorable proof of his knowledge in some bas-reliefs in this work, which are still seen there, when he was recalled by the Wardens of Works of S. Maria del Fiore to Florence, where, for the campanile of that church, he made five little scenes in marble, which are on the side that faces the church, and which were wanting, according to the design of Giotto, to go with that wherein are the Sciences and Arts, formerly made, as it has been said, by Andrea Pisano. In the first Luca made Donatus teaching grammar; in the second, Plato and Aristotle, standing for philosophy; in the third, a figure playing a lute, for music; in the fourth, a Ptolemy, for astrology; and in the fifth, Euclid, for geometry. These scenes, in perfection of finish, in grace, and in design, were far in advance of the two made, as it has been said, by Giotto, in one of which Apelles, standing for painting, is working with his brush, while in the other Phidias, representing sculpture, is laboring with his chisel. Wherefore the said Wardens of Works—who, besides the merits of Luca, were persuaded thereunto by Messer Vieri de' Medici, then a great citizen and a friend of the people, who loved Luca dearly—commissioned him, in the year 1405, to make the marble ornament for the organ which the Office of Works was then having made on a very grand scale, to be set up over the door of the sacristy of the said church. In certain scenes at the base of this work Luca made the singing choirs, chanting in various fashions; and he put so much zeal into this labor and succeeded so well therein, that, although it is thirty-two feet from the ground, one can see the swelling of the throats of the singers, the leader of the music beating with his hands on the shoulders of the smaller ones, and, in short, diverse manners of sounds, chants, dances, and other pleasing actions that make up the delight of music. Next, on the great cornice of this ornament Luca placed two figures of gilded metal—namely, two nude angels, wrought with a high finish, as is the whole work, which was held to be something very rare, although Donatello, who afterwards made the ornament of the other organ, which is opposite to the first, made his with much more judgment and mastery than Luca had shown, as will be told in the proper place; for Donatello executed that work almost wholly with bold studies and with no smoothness of finish, to the end that it might show up much better from a distance, as it does, than that of Luca, which, although it is wrought with good design and diligence, is nevertheless so smooth and highly finished that the eye, by reason of the distance, loses it and does not grasp it well, as it does that of Donatello, which is, as it were, only sketched.

To this matter craftsmen should pay great attention, for the reason that experience teaches us that all works which are to be viewed from a distance, whether they be pictures, or sculptures, or any other similar thing whatsoever, have more vivacity and greater force if they are made in the fashion of beautiful sketches than if they are highly finished; and besides the fact that distance gives this effect, it also appears that very often in these sketches, born in a moment from the fire of art, a man's conception is expressed in a few strokes, while, on the contrary, effort and too great diligence sometimes rob men of their force and judgment, if they never know when to take their hands off the work that they are making. And whosoever knows that all the arts of design, not to speak only of painting, are similar to poetry, knows also that even as poems thrown off by the poetic fire are the true and good ones, and better than those made with great effort, so, too, the works of men excellent in the arts of design are better when they are made at one sitting by the force of that fire,

than when they go about investigating one thing after another with effort and fatigue. And he who has from the beginning, as he should have, a clear idea of what he wishes to do,
ever advances resolutely and with great readiness to perfection.

But to return to Luca: the said work being finished and
giving great satisfaction, he was entrusted with the bronze
door of the said sacristy, which he divided into ten squares—
namely, five on either side, making the head of a man at
every corner of each square, in the border; and he varied the
heads one from another, making young men, old, and middle-
aged, some bearded and some shaven, and, in short, each one
beautiful of its kind in diverse fashions, so that the framework
of that door was beautifully adorned. Next, in the scenes in
the squares—to begin at the upper part—he made the Madonna with the Child in her arms, with most beautiful grace;
and in the one beside it, Jesus Christ issuing from the Sepulcher. Below these, in each of the first four squares, is the
figure of an Evangelist; and below these, the four Doctors of
the Church, who are writing in different attitudes. And the
whole of this work is so highly finished and polished that it
is a marvel, and gives us to know that it was a great advantage
to Luca to have been a goldsmith.

But since, on reckoning up after these works how much
there had come to his hand and how much time he spent in
making them, he recognized that he had gained very little and
that the labor had been very great, he resolved to abandon
marble and bronze and to see whether he could gather better
fruits from another method. Wherefore, reflecting that clay
could be worked easily and with little labor, and that it was
only necessary to find a method whereby works made with
it might be preserved for a long time, he set about investigating to such purpose that he found a way to defend them from
the injuries of time; for, after having made many experiments,
he found that by covering them with a coating of glaze, made
with tin, litharge, antimony, and other minerals and mixtures

fused together in a special furnace, he could produce this
effect very well and make works in clay almost eternal. For
this method of working, as being its inventor, he gained very
great praise, and all the ages to come will therefore owe him
an obligation.

Having then succeeded in this as much as he could desire,
he resolved that his first works should be those that are in
the arch over the bronze door which he had made for the
sacristy, below the organ of S. Maria del Fiore; and therein
he made a Resurrection of Christ, so beautiful for that time
that it was admired, when placed in position, as something
truly rare. Moved by this, the said Wardens of Works desired
that the arch over the door of the other sacristy, where Donatello had made the ornament of the other organ, should be
filled by Luca in the same manner with similar figures and
works in terra-cotta; wherefore Luca made therein a very
beautiful Jesus Christ ascending into Heaven.

Now, not being yet satisfied with this beautiful invention
—so lovely and so useful, above all for places where there
is water, and where, because of damp or other reasons, there
is no scope for paintings—Luca went on seeking further
progress, and, instead of making the said works in clay simply
white, he added the method of giving them color, with incredible marvel and pleasure to all. Wherefore the Magnificent Piero di Cosimo de' Medici, one of the first to commission Luca to fashion colored works in clay, caused him to
execute the whole of the round vaulting of a study in the
Palace—built, as it will be told, by his father Cosimo—with
various things of fancy, and likewise the pavement, which
was something singular and very useful for the summer. And
seeing that this method was then very difficult, and that many
precautions were necessary in the firing of the clay, it is certainly a marvel that Luca could execute these works with so
great perfection that both the vaulting and the pavement appear to be made, not of many pieces, but of one only. The
fame of these works spreading not only throughout Italy but

throughout all Europe, there were so many who desired them that the merchants of Florence, keeping Luca, to his great profit, continually at this labor, sent them throughout the whole world. And because he could not supply the whole, he took his brothers, Ottaviano and Agostino, away from the chisel, and set them to work on these labors, wherein the three of them together gained much more than they had done up to then with the chisel, for the reason that, besides those of their works that were sent to France and Spain, they also wrought many things in Tuscany; and in particular, for the said Piero de' Medici, in the Church of S. Miniato al Monte, the vaulting of the marble chapel, which rests on four columns in the middle of the church, and which they divided most beautifully into octagons. But the most notable work of this kind that ever issued from their hands was the vaulting of the Chapel of S. Jacopo, where the Cardinal of Portugal is buried, in the same church. In this, although it has no salient angles, they made the four Evangelists in four medallions at the corners, and the Holy Spirit in a medallion in the middle of the vaulting, filling the other spaces with scales which follow the curve of the vaulting and diminish little by little till they reach the center, insomuch that there is nothing better of that kind to be seen, nor anything built and put together with more diligence.

Next, in a little arch over the door of the Church of S. Piero Buonconsiglio, below the Mercato Vecchio, he made the Madonna with some angels round her, all very vivacious; and over a door of a little church near S. Piero Maggiore, in a lunette, he made another Madonna with some angels, which are held very beautiful. And in the Chapter-house of S. Croce, likewise, built by the family of the Pazzi under the direction of Pippo di Ser Brunellesco, he made all the glazed figures that are seen therein both within and without. And Luca is said to have sent some very beautiful figures in full-relief to the King of Spain, together with some works in marble. For Naples, also, he made in Florence the marble tomb for the infant brother of the Duke of Calabria, with many glazed ornaments, being assisted by his brother Agostino.

After these works, Luca sought to find a way of painting figures and scenes on a level surface of terra-cotta, in order to give long life to pictures, and made an experiment in a medallion which is above the shrine of the four saints outside Or San Michele, on the level surface of which, in five parts, he made the instruments and insignia of the Guilds of the Masters in Wood and Stone, with very beautiful ornaments. And he made two other medallions in the same place, in relief, in one of which, for the Guild of Apothecaries, he made a Madonna, and in the other, for the Mercatanzia, a lily on a bale, which has round it a festoon of fruits and foliage of various sorts, so well made, that they appear to be real and not of painted terra-cotta. In the Church of S. Brancazio, also, he made a tomb of marble for Messer Benozzo Federighi, Bishop of Fiesole, and Federighi himself lying on it, portrayed from nature, with three other half-length figures; and in the ornament of the pilasters of this work, on the level surface, he painted certain festoons with clusters of fruit and foliage, so lifelike and natural, that nothing better could be done in oil and on panel with the brush. Of a truth, this work is marvelous and most rare, seeing that Luca made the lights and shades in it so well, that it scarcely appears possible for this to be done by the action of fire. And if this craftsman had lived longer than he did, even greater works would have been seen to issue from his hands, since, a little before he died, he had begun to make scenes and figures painted on a level surface, whereof I once saw some pieces in his house, which lead me to believe that he would have easily succeeded in this, if death, which almost always snatches the best men away just when they are on the point of conferring some benefit on the world, had not robbed him of life before his time.

Luca, while passing from one method of work to another,

from marble to bronze, and from bronze to clay, did this not by reason of laziness or because he was, as many are, capricious, unstable, and discontented with his art, but because he felt himself drawn by nature to new things and by necessity to an exercise according to his taste, both less fatiguing and more profitable. Wherefore the world and the arts of design became the richer by a new, useful, and most beautiful art, and he gained immortal and everlasting glory and praise.

UCCELLO

[*Paolo di Dono, called Uccello, was born about
1397 and died in 1477.*]

PAOLO UCCELLO would have been the most gracious and
fanciful genius that was ever devoted to the art of painting,
from Giotto's day to our own, if he had labored as much at
figures and animals as he labored and lost time over the details of perspective; for although these are ingenious and
beautiful, yet if a man pursues them beyond measure he does
nothing but waste his time, exhausts his powers, fills his
mind with difficulties, and often transforms its fertility and
readiness into sterility and constraint, and renders his manner,
by attending more to these details than to figures, dry and
angular, which all comes from a wish to examine things too
minutely; not to mention that very often he becomes solitary,
eccentric, melancholy, and poor, as did Paolo Uccello. This
man, endowed by nature with a penetrating and subtle mind,
knew no other delight than to investigate certain difficult, nay,
impossible problems of perspective, which, although they
were fanciful and beautiful, yet hindered him so greatly in
the painting of figures, that the older he grew the worse he
did them. And there is no doubt that if a man does violence
to his nature with too ardent studies, although he may
sharpen one edge of his genius, yet nothing that he does appears done with that facility and grace which are natural to
those who put each stroke in its proper place temperately
and with a calm intelligence full of judgment, avoiding cer-

tain subtleties that rather burden a man's work with a certain labored, dry, constrained, and bad manner, which moves those who see it rather to compassion than to marvel; for the spirit of genius must be driven into action only when the intellect wishes to set itself to work and when the fire of inspiration is kindled, since it is then that excellent and divine qualities and marvelous conceptions are seen to issue forth.

Now Paolo was for ever investigating, without a moment's intermission, the most difficult problems of art, insomuch that he reduced to perfection the method of drawing perspectives from the ground-plans of houses and from the profiles of buildings, carried right up to the summits of the cornices and the roofs, by means of intersecting lines, making them foreshortened and diminishing toward the center, after having first fixed the eye-level either high or low, according to his pleasure. So greatly, in short, did he occupy himself with these difficulties, that he introduced a way, method, and rule of placing figures firmly on the planes whereon their feet are planted, and foreshortening them bit by bit, and making them recede by a proportionate diminution; which hitherto had always been done by chance. He discovered, likewise, the method of turning the intersections and arches of vaulted roofs; the foreshortening of ceilings by means of the convergence of the beams; and the making of round columns at the salient angle of the walls of a house in a manner that they curve at the corner, and, being drawn in perspective, break the angle and cause it to appear level. For the sake of these investigations he kept himself in seclusion and almost a hermit, having little intercourse with anyone, and staying weeks and months in his house without showing himself. And although these were difficult and beautiful problems, if he had spent that time in the study of figures, he would have brought them to absolute perfection; for even so he made them with passing good draftsmanship. But, consuming his time in these researches, he remained throughout his whole life more poor

than famous; wherefore the sculptor Donatello, who was
very much his friend, said to him very often—when Paolo
showed him fantastic devices on which he spent and wasted
his time—"Ah, Paolo, this perspective of thine makes thee
abandon the substance for the shadow; these are things that
are only useful to men who work at the inlaying of wood,
seeing that they fill their borders with chips and shavings,
with spirals both round and square, and with other similar
things."

The first pictures of Paolo were in fresco, in an oblong
niche painted in perspective, at the Hospital of Lelmo. In
S. Maria Maggiore he wrought an Annunciation in fresco,
wherein he made a building worthy of consideration, which
was something new and difficult in those times, seeing that it
was the first possessing any beauty of manner which was seen
by craftsmen, showing them with grace and proportion how
to manage the receding of lines, and how to give so great an
extent to a level space which is small and confined, that it
appears far distant and large; and when to this, with judgment and grace, men can add shadows and lights by means of
colors in their proper places, there is no doubt that they cause
an illusion to the eye, so that it appears that the painting is
real and in relief. And not being satisfied with this, he wished
to demonstrate even greater difficulties in some columns,
which, foreshortened in perspective, curve round and break
the salient angle of the vaulting wherein are the four Evangelists; which was held something beautiful and difficult, and,
in truth, in that branch of his profession Paolo was ingenious
and able.

In a cloister of S. Miniato outside Florence, also, he
wrought the lives of the Holy Fathers, chiefly in terra-verde,
and partly in color; wherein he paid little regard to effecting
harmony by painting with one color, as should be done in
painting stories, for he made the fields blue, the cities red,
and the buildings varied according to his pleasure; and in

this he was at fault, for something which is meant to represent stone cannot and should not be tinted with another color. It is said that while Paolo was laboring at this work, the Abbot who was then head of that place gave him scarcely anything to eat but cheese. Wherefore Paolo, having grown weary of this, determined, like the shy fellow that he was, to go no more to work there; whereupon the Abbot sent to look for him, and Paolo, when he heard friars asking for him, would never be at home, and if peradventure he met any couples of that Order in the streets of Florence, he would start running and flying from them with all his might. Now two of them, more curious than the rest and younger than Paolo, caught him up one day and asked him for what reason he did not return to finish the work that he had begun, and why he fled at the sight of a friar; and Paolo answered: "You have murdered me in a manner that I not only fly from you, but cannot show myself near any carpenters' shop or pass by one, and all because of the thoughtlessness of your Abbot, who, what with pies and with soups always made of cheese, has crammed so much cheese into me that I am in terror lest, being nothing but cheese, they may use me for making glue. And if it were to go on any longer, I would probably be no more Paolo, but cheese." The friars, leaving him with peals of laughter, told everything to the Abbot, who made him return to his work, and ordered him some other fare than cheese.

After this, he painted the dossal of S. Cosimo and S. Damiano in the Carmine, in the Chapel of S. Girolamo (of the Pugliesi). In the house of the Medici he painted some scenes on canvas and in distemper, representing animals; in these he ever took delight, and in order to paint them well he gave them very great attention, and, what is more, he kept ever in his house pictures of birds, cats, dogs, and every sort of strange animal whereof he could get the likeness, being unable to have them alive by reason of his poverty; and because he delighted in birds more than in any other kind, he was given the name of "Paolo of the Birds" (Paolo Uccelli).

Afterwards he was commissioned to paint some scenes in the cloister of S. Maria Novella; and the first, which are at the entrance from the church into the cloister, represent the Creation of the animals, with an infinite number and variety of kinds belonging to water, earth, and air. And since he was very fanciful and took great delight, as it has been said, in painting animals to perfection, he showed in certain lions, who are seeking to bite each other, the great ferocity that is in them, and swiftness and fear in some stags and fallow-deer; not to mention that the birds and fishes, with their feathers and scales, are most lifelike. He made there the Creation of man and of woman, and their Fall, with a beautiful manner and with good and careful execution. And in this work he took delight in making the trees with colors, which the painters of those times were not wont to do very well; and in the landscapes, likewise, he was the first among the old painters to make a name for himself by his work, executing them well and with greater perfection than the painters before him had done; although afterwards there came men who made them more perfect, for with all his labor he was never able to give them that softness and harmony which have been given to them in our own day by painting them in oil colors. It was enough for Paolo to go on, according to the rules of perspective, drawing and foreshortening them exactly as they are, making in them all that he saw—namely, plowed fields, ditches, and other minutenesses of nature—with that dry and hard manner of his; whereas, if he had picked out the best from everything and had made use of those parts only that come out well in painting, they would have been absolutely perfect. This labor finished, he worked in the same cloister below two stories by the hand of others; and lower down he painted the Flood, with Noah's Ark, wherein he put so great pains and so great art and diligence into the painting of the dead bodies, the tempest, the fury of the winds, the flashes of the lightning, the shattering of trees, and the terror of men, that it is beyond all description. Here, likewise, he made in perspective a cask that curves on every side, which was held something very beautiful, and also a pergola covered with grapes, the woodwork of which, composed of squared planks, goes on diminishing to a point; but here he was in error, since the diminishing of the plane below, on which the figures are standing, follows the lines of the pergola, and the cask does not follow these same receding lines; wherefore I marvel greatly that a man so accurate and diligent could make an error so notable. He made there also the Sacrifice, with the Ark open and drawn in perspective, with the rows of perches in the upper part, distributed row by row; these were the resting-places of the birds, many kinds of which are seen issuing and flying forth in foreshortening, while in the sky there is seen God the Father, who is appearing over the sacrifice that Noah and his sons are making; and this figure, of all those that Paolo made in this work, is the most difficult, for it is flying, with the head foreshortened, toward the wall, and has such force and relief that it seems to be piercing and breaking through it. Besides this, Noah has round him an infinite number of diverse animals, all most beautiful. In short, he gave to all this work so great softness and grace, that it is beyond comparison superior to all his others; wherefore it has been greatly praised from that time up to our own.

In S. Maria del Fiore, in memory of Giovanni Acuto,* an Englishman, Captain of the Florentines, who had died in the year 1393, he made in terra-verde a horse of extraordinary grandeur, which was held very beautiful, and on it the image of the Captain himself, in chiaroscuro and colored with terra-verde, in a picture twenty feet high on the middle of one wall of the church; where Paolo drew in perspective

* Sir John Hawkwood.

a large sarcophagus, supposed to contain the corpse, and over this he placed the image of him in his Captain's armor, on horseback. This work was and still is held to be something very beautiful for a painting of that kind, and if Paolo had not made that horse move its legs on one side only, which naturally horses do not do, or they would fall—and this perchance came about because he was not accustomed to ride, nor used to horses as he was to other animals—this work would be absolutely perfect.

In many houses of Florence there are many pictures in perspective by the hand of the same man, for the adornment of couches, beds, and other little things; and in Gualfonda, in particular, on a terrace in the garden which once belonged to the Bartolini, there are four battle scenes painted on wood by his hand, full of horses and armed men, with very beautiful costumes of those days; and among the men are portraits of Paolo Orsino, Ottobuono da Parma, Luca da Canale, and Carlo Malatesti, Lord of Rimini, all captains-general of those times. And these pictures, since they were spoilt and had suffered injury, were restored in our own day by the agency of Giuliano Bugiardini, who did them more harm than good.

Paolo was summoned to Padua by Donatello, when the latter was working there, and at the entrance of the house of the Vitali he painted some giants in terra-verde, which, as I have found in a Latin letter written by Girolamo Campagnola to Messer Leonico Tomeo, the philosopher, are so beautiful that Andrea Mantegna held them in very great account. Paolo wrought in fresco the Volta de' Peruzzi, with triangular sections in perspective, and in the angles of the corners he painted the four elements, making for each an appropriate animal—for the earth a mole, for the water a fish, for the fire a salamander, and for the air a chameleon, which lives on it and assumes any color. And because he had never seen a chameleon, he painted a camel, which is opening its mouth and swallowing air, and therewith filling its belly; and great, indeed, was his simplicity in making allusion by means of the name of the camel to an animal that is like a little dry lizard, and in representing it by a great uncouth beast.

Truly great were the labors of Paolo in painting, for he drew so much that he left to his relatives, as I have learnt from their own lips, whole chests full of drawings. But, although it is a good thing to draw, it is nevertheless better to make complete pictures, seeing that pictures have longer life than drawings. In our book of drawings there are many figures, studies in perspective, birds, and animals, beautiful to a marvel. Paolo, although he was an eccentric person, loved talent in his fellow-craftsmen, and in order that some memory of them might go down to posterity, he painted five distinguished men with his own hand on a long panel, which he kept in his house in memory of them. One was Giotto, the painter, standing for the light and origin of art; the second was Filippo di Ser Brunellesco, for architecture; Donatello, for sculpture; himself, for perspective and animals; and, for mathematics, Giovanni Manetti, his friend, with whom he often conferred and discoursed on the problems of Euclid.

It is said that having been commissioned to paint, over the door of S. Tommaso in the Mercato Vecchio, that Saint feeling for the wound in the side of Christ, Paolo put into that work all the effort that he could, saying that he wished to show therein the full extent of his worth and knowledge; and so he caused a screen of planks to be made, to the end that no one might be able to see his work until it was finished. Wherefore Donatello, meeting him one day all alone, said to him: "And what sort of work may this be of thine, that thou keepest it screened so closely?" And Paolo said in answer: "Thou shalt see it. Let that suffice thee." Donatello would not constrain him to say more, thinking to see some miracle, as usual, when the time came. Afterwards, chancing one morning to be in the Mercato Vecchio buying fruit, Donatello saw Paolo uncovering his work, whereupon he saluted him courteously, and was asked by Paolo himself, who was curious and anxious to hear his judgment on it, what he thought of that picture. Donatello, having studied the work long and well, exclaimed: "Ah, Paolo, thou oughtest to be covering it up, and here thou art uncovering it!" Whereupon Paolo was much aggrieved, feeling that he was receiving much more by way of blame than he expected to receive by way of praise for this last labor of his; and not having courage, lowered as he was, to go out any more, he shut himself up in his house, devoting himself to perspective, which kept him ever poor and depressed up to his death. And so, growing very old, and having but little contentment in his old age, he died in 1477, and was buried in S. Maria Novella.

He left a daughter, who had knowledge of drawing, and a wife, who was wont to say that Paolo would stay in his study all night, seeking to solve the problems of perspective, and that when she called him to come to bed, he would say: "Oh, what a sweet thing is this perspective!" And in truth, if it was sweet to him, it was not otherwise than dear and useful, thanks to him, to those who exercised themselves therein after his time.

GHIBERTI

*[Lorenzo di Cione Ghiberti, or di Bartoluccio, was
born in 1378 and died in 1455.]*

SINCE it is seldom that talent is not persecuted by envy, men
must continue to the best of their power, by means of the
utmost excellence, to assure it of victory, or at least to make
it stout and strong to sustain the attacks of that enemy; even
as Lorenzo di Cione Ghiberti, otherwise called di Bartoluccio,
was enabled to do both by his own merits and by fortune.
This man well deserved the honor of being placed before
themselves by the sculptor Donatello and by the architect
and sculptor Filippo Brunelleschi, both excellent craftsmen,
since they recognized, in truth, although instinct perchance
constrained them to do the contrary, that Lorenzo was a better master of casting than they were. This truly brought glory
to them, and confusion to many who, presuming on their
worth, set themselves to work and occupy the place due to
the talents of others, and, without producing any fruits themselves, but laboring a thousand years at the making of one
work, impede and oppress the knowledge of others with
malignity and with envy.

Lorenzo, then, was the son of Bartoluccio Ghiberti, and
from his earliest years learnt the art of the goldsmith from
his father, who was an excellent master and taught him that
business, which Lorenzo grasped so well that he became
much better therein than his father. But delighting much
more in the arts of sculpture and design, he would sometimes handle colors, and at other times would cast little figures in bronze and finish them with much grace. He also

delighted in counterfeiting the dies of ancient medals, and he portrayed many of his friends from the life in his time.

Now, while he was working with Bartoluccio and seeking to make progress in his profession, the plague came to Florence in the year 1400, as he himself relates in a book by his own hand wherein he discourses on the subject of art, which is now in the possession of the Reverend Maestro Cosimo Bartoli, a gentleman of Florence. To this plague were added civil discords and other troubles in the city, and he was forced to depart and to go in company with another painter to Romagna, where they painted for Signor Pandolfo Malatesti, in Rimini, an apartment and many other works, which were finished by them with diligence and to the satisfaction of that Lord, who, although still young, took great delight in matters of design. Meanwhile Lorenzo did not cease to study the arts of design, and to work in relief with wax, stucco, and other similar materials, knowing very well that these small reliefs are the drawing-exercises of sculptors, and that without such practice nothing can be brought by them to perfection. Now, when he had been no long time out of his own country, the pestilence ceased; wherefore the Signoria of Florence and the Guild of Merchants—since at that time sculpture had many excellent craftsmen, both foreign and Florentine— determined that there should be made, as it had been already discussed many times, the other two doors of S. Giovanni, a very ancient temple, indeed, the oldest in that city; and they ordained among themselves that instructions should be sent to all the masters who were held the best in Italy, to repair to Florence in order that their powers might be tested by a specimen scene in bronze, similar to one of those which Andrea Pisano had formerly made for the first door.

Word of this determination was written to Lorenzo, who was working at Pesaro, by Bartoluccio, urging him to return to Florence in order to give a proof of his powers, and saying that this was an occasion to make himself known and to demonstrate his genius, not to mention that he might gain such profit that neither the one nor the other of them would ever again need to labor at making earrings.

The words of Bartoluccio stirred the spirit of Lorenzo so greatly, that although Signor Pandolfo, with all his Court and the other painter, kept showing him the greatest favor, Lorenzo took leave of that lord and of the painter, and they, with great unwillingness and displeasure, allowed him to go, neither promises nor increase of payment availing to detain him, since to Lorenzo every hour appeared a thousand years until he could return to Florence. Having departed, therefore, he arrived safely in his own city. Many foreigners had already assembled and presented themselves to the Consuls of the Guild, by whom seven masters were elected out of the whole number, three being Florentines and the others Tuscans; and it was ordained that they should have an allowance of money, and that within a year each man should finish a scene in bronze by way of test, of the same size as those in the first door. And for the subject they chose the story of Abraham sacrificing his son Isaac, wherein they thought that the said masters should be able to show their powers with regard to the difficulties of their art, seeing that this story contained landscapes, figures both nude and clothed, and animals, while the foremost figures could be made in full-relief, the second in half-relief, and the third in low-relief.

The competitors for this work were Filippo di Ser Brunellesco, Donatello, and Lorenzo di Bartoluccio, all Florentines; Jacopo della Quercia of Siena, and Niccolò d'Arezzo, his pupil; Francesco di Valdambrina; and Simone da Colle, called Simone de' Bronzi. All these men promised before the Consuls that they would deliver their scenes finished within the said time; and each making a beginning with his own, with all zeal and diligence they exerted all their strength and knowledge in order to surpass one another in excellence, keeping their work hidden and most secret, lest they should copy each other's ideas. Lorenzo alone, who had Bartoluccio to guide him and to compel him to labor at many models before they resolved to adopt any one of them—Lorenzo alone was ever inviting the citizens, and sometimes any passing stranger who had some knowledge of the art, to see his work, in order to hear what they thought, and these opinions enabled him to execute a model very well wrought and without one defect. And so, when he had made the moulds and cast the work in bronze, it came out very well; whereupon, with his father Bartoluccio, he polished it with such love and patience that nothing could be executed or finished better. And when the time came for comparing the various works, his and those of the other masters were completely finished, and were given to the Guild of Merchants for judgment; but after all had been seen by the Consuls and by many other citizens, diverse opinions were expressed about them. Many foreigners had assembled in Florence, some painters, some sculptors, and others goldsmiths; and they were invited by the Consuls to give judgment on these works, together with the other men of that profession who lived in Florence. They numbered thirty-four in all, each well experienced in his own art. Now, although there were differences of opinion among them, some liking the manner of one man and some that of another, nevertheless they were agreed that Filippo di Ser Brunellesco and Lorenzo di Bartoluccio had composed and completed their scenes better and with a richer abundance of figures than Donatello had done in his, although in that one, also, there was grand design. In that of Jacopo della Quercia the figures were good, but they had no delicacy, although they were made with design and diligence. The work of Francesco di Valdambrina had good heads and was well finished, but was confused in the composition. That of Simone da Colle was a beautiful casting, because the doing of this was his art, but it had not much design. The specimen of Niccolò d'Arezzo, which was made with good mastery, had the figures squat and was badly finished. Only that scene which Lorenzo made as a specimen, which is still seen in the Audience Chamber of the Guild of Merchants, was in every part wholly

perfect. The whole work had design, and was very well composed. The figures had so graceful a manner, being made
with grace and with very beautiful attitudes, and the whole
was finished with so great diligence, that it appeared not made
by casting and polished with tools of iron, but blown with
the breath. Donatello and Filippo, seeing the diligence that
Lorenzo had used in his work, drew aside, and, conferring together, they resolved that the work should be given to Lorenzo, it appearing to them that thus both the public and the
private interest would be best served, and that Lorenzo, being a young man not more than twenty years of age, would
be able to produce by this exercise of his profession those
greater fruits that were foreshadowed by the beautiful scene
which he, in their judgment, had executed more excellently
than the others; saying that there would have been more sign
of envy in taking it from him, than there was justice in giving
it to him.

Beginning the work of that door, then, for that entrance
which is opposite to the Office of Works of S. Giovanni,
Lorenzo made for one part of it a large framework of wood,
of the exact size that it was to be, with mouldings, and with
the ornaments of the heads at the corners, round the various
spaces wherein the scenes were to be placed, and with those
borders that were to go round them. Having then made and
dried the mould with all diligence, he made a very great furnace (that I remember seeing) in a room that he had hired
opposite to S. Maria Nuova, where to-day there is the Hospital of the Weavers, on the spot that was called the Aia,
and he cast the said framework in bronze. But, as chance
would have it, it did not come out well; wherefore, having
realized the mischief, without losing heart or giving way to
depression, he promptly made another mould and cast it
again, without telling anyone about it, and it came out very
well. Whereupon he went on and continued the whole work
in this manner, casting each scene by itself, and putting it,
when finished, into its place. The arrangement of the scenes

was similar to that which Andrea Pisano had formerly made in the first door, which Giotto designed for him. He made therein twenty scenes from the New Testament; and below, in eight spaces similar to these, after the said scenes, he made the four Evangelists, two on each side of the door, and likewise the four Doctors of the Church, in the same manner; which figures are all different in their attitudes and their draperies. One is writing, another is reading, others are in contemplation, and all, being varied one from another, appear lifelike and very well executed; not to mention that in the framework of the border surrounding the scenes in squares there is a frieze of ivy leaves and other kinds of foliage, with mouldings between each; and on every corner is the head of a man or a woman in the round, representing prophets and sibyls, which are very beautiful, and demonstrate with their variety the excellence of the genius of Lorenzo.

This work was brought to that completion and perfection without sparing any labor or time that could be devoted to a work in bronze, seeing that the limbs of the nudes are most beautiful in every part; and in the draperies, although they hold a little to the old manner of Giotto's time, there is a general feeling that inclines to the manner of the moderns, and produces, in figures of that size, a certain very lovely grace. And in truth the composition of each scene is so well ordered and so finely arranged, that he rightly deserved to obtain that praise which Filippo had given him at the beginning—nay, even more. And in like manner he gained most honorable recognition among his fellow-citizens, and was consummately extolled by them and by the native and foreign craftsmen. The cost of this work, with the exterior ornaments, which are also of bronze, wrought with festoons of fruits and with animals, was 22,000 florins, and the bronze door weighed 34,000 *libbre*.

This work finished, it appeared to the Consuls of the Guild of Merchants that they had been very well served, and by reason of the praises given by all to Lorenzo they determined that he should make a statue of bronze, nine feet high, in memory of S. John the Baptist, on a pilaster outside Or San Michele, in one of the niches there—namely, the one facing the Cloth-dressers. This he began, nor did he ever leave it until he delivered it finished. It was and still is a work highly praised, and in it, on the mantle, he made a border of letters, wherein he wrote his own name. In this work, which was placed in position in the year 1414, there is seen the beginning of the good modern manner, in the head, in an arm which appears to be living flesh, in the hands, and in the whole attitude of the figure. He was thus the first who began to imitate the works of the ancient Romans, whereof he was an ardent student, as all must be who desire to do good work. And in the frontal of that shrine he tried his hand at mosaic, making therein a half-length prophet.

The fame of Lorenzo, by reason of his most profound mastery in casting, had now spread throughout all Italy and abroad, insomuch that Jacopo della Fonte, Vecchietto of Siena, and Donatello having made for the Signoria of Siena some scenes and figures in bronze that were to adorn the baptismal font of their Church of S. Giovanni, the people of Siena, having seen the works of Lorenzo in Florence, came to an agreement with him and caused him to make two scenes from the life of S. John the Baptist. In one he made S. John baptizing Christ, accompanying it with an abundance of figures, both nude and very richly draped; and in the other he made S. John being taken and led before Herod. In these scenes he surpassed and excelled the men who had made the others; wherefore he was consummately praised by the people of Siena, and by all others who have seen them.

The Masters of the Mint in Florence had a statue to make for one of those niches that are round Or San Michele, opposite to the Guild of Wool, and it was to be a S. Matthew, of the same height as the aforesaid S. John. Wherefore they allotted it to Lorenzo, who executed it to perfection; and it was much more praised than the S. John, for he made it more in the modern manner. This statue brought it about that the Consuls of the Guild of Wool determined that he should make in the same place, for the niche next to that, a statue likewise in bronze, which should be of the same proportions as the other two, representing S. Stephen, their Patron Saint. And he brought it to completion, giving a very beautiful varnish to the bronze; and this statue gave no less satisfaction than the other works already wrought by him.

The General of the Preaching Friars at that time, Maestro Lionardo Dati, wishing to leave a memorial of himself to his country in S. Maria Novella, where he had taken his vows, caused Lorenzo to construct a tomb of bronze, with himself lying dead thereon, portrayed from nature; and this tomb, which was admired and extolled, led to another being erected by Lodovico degli Albizzi and Niccolò Valori in S. Croce.

After these things, Cosimo and Lorenzo de' Medici, wishing to honor the bodies and relics of the three martyrs, Protus, Hyacinthus, and Nemesius, had them brought from the Casentino, where they had been held in little veneration for many years, and caused Lorenzo to make a sarcophagus of bronze, in the middle of which are two angels in bas-relief who are holding a garland of olive, within which are the names of those martyrs; and they caused the said relics to be put into the said sarcophagus, which they placed in the Church of the Monastery of the Angeli in Florence.

And by reason of this work, which succeeded very nobly, there came a wish to the Wardens of Works of S. Maria del Fiore to have a sarcophagus and tomb of bronze made to contain the body of S. Zanobi, Bishop of Florence. This tomb was seven feet in length, and two in height; and besides adorning it with diverse varied ornaments, he made therein on the front of the body of the sarcophagus itself a scene with S. Zanobi restoring to life a child which had been left in his charge by the mother, and which had died while she was on a pilgrimage. In a second scene is another child, who has been killed by a wagon, and also the Saint restoring to life one of the two servants sent to him by S. Ambrose, who had been left dead on the Alps; and the other is there, making lamentation in the presence of S. Zanobi, who, seized with compassion, said: "Go, he doth but sleep; thou wilt find him alive." And at the back are six little angels, who are holding a garland of elm leaves, within which are carved letters in memory and in praise of that Saint. This work he executed and finished with the utmost ingenuity and art, insomuch that it received extraordinary praise as something beautiful.

The while that the works of Lorenzo were every day adding luster to his name, by reason of his laboring and serving innumerable persons, working in bronze as well as in silver and gold, it chanced that there fell into the hands of Giovanni, son of Cosimo de' Medici, a very large cornelian containing the flaying of Marsyas by command of Apollo, engraved in intaglio; which cornelian, so it is said, once served the Emperor Nero for a seal. And it being something rare, by reason both of the size of the stone, which was very great, and of the marvelous beauty of the intaglio, Giovanni gave it to Lorenzo, to the end that he might make a gold ornament in relief round it; and he, after toiling at it for many months, finished it completely, making round it a work in relief of a beauty not inferior to the excellence and perfection of the intaglio on the stone; which work brought it about that he wrought many other things in gold and silver, which to-day are not to be found. For Pope Martin, likewise, he made a gold button which he wore in his cope, with figures in full-relief, and among them jewels of very great price—a very excellent work; and likewise a most marvelous miter of gold leaves in open-work, and among them many little figures in full-relief, which were held very beautiful. And for this work, besides the name, he acquired great profit from the liberality of that Pontiff. In the year 1439, Pope Eugenius came to Florence—where the Council was held—in order to unite the Greek Church with the Roman; and seeing the works of Lorenzo, and being no less pleased with his person than with the works themselves, he caused him to make a miter of gold, weighing fifteen *libbre,* with pearls weighing five *libbre* and a half, which, with the jewels set in the miter, were estimated at 30,000 ducats of gold. It is said that in this work were six pearls as big as filberts, and it is impossible to imagine, as was seen later in a drawing of it, anything more beautiful and bizarre than the settings of the jewels and the great variety of children and other figures, which served for many varied and graceful ornaments. For this work he received infinite favors from that Pontiff, both for himself and his friends, besides the original payment.

Florence had received so much praise by reason of the excellent works of this most ingenious craftsman, that the Consuls of the Guild of Merchants determined to commission him to make the third door of S. Giovanni, likewise in bronze. Now, in the door that he had made before, he had followed their directions and had made it with that ornament which goes round the figures, and which encircles the framework of both parts of the door, as in the one of Andrea Pisano; but on seeing how greatly Lorenzo had surpassed him, the Consuls determined to remove that of Andrea from its position in the center, and to place it in the doorway that is opposite to the Misericordia, and to commission Lorenzo to make a new door to be placed in the center, looking to him to put forth the greatest effort of which he was capable in that art. And they placed themselves in his hands, saying that they gave him leave to make it as he pleased, and in whatsoever manner he thought it would turn out as ornate, as rich, as perfect, and as beautiful as it could be made or imagined; nor was he to spare time or expense, to the end that, even as he had surpassed all other sculptors up to his own time, he might surpass and excel all his own previous works.

Lorenzo began the said work, putting therein all the knowledge that he could; wherefore he divided the said door into ten squares, five on each side, so that the spaces enclosing the scenes were two feet and a half in extent, and round them, to adorn the framework that surrounds the scenes, there are niches—upright, in that part of the door—containing figures in almost full-relief, twenty in number and all most beautiful.

In this work, both in detail and as a whole, it is seen how much the ability and the power of a craftsman in statuary can effect by means of figures, some being almost in the round, some in half-relief, some in bas-relief, and some in the lowest, with invention in the grouping of the figures, and extravagance of attitude both in the males and in the females; and by variety in the buildings, by perspectives, and by having likewise shown a sense of fitness in the gracious expressions of each sex throughout the whole work, giving to the old gravity, and to the young elegance and grace. And it may be said, in truth, that this work is in every way perfect, and that it is the most beautiful work which has ever been seen in the world, whether ancient or modern. And right truly does Lorenzo deserve to be praised, seeing that one day Michelangelo Buonarroti, having stopped to look at this work, and being asked what he thought of it, and whether these doors were beautiful, answered: "They are so beautiful that they would do well for the gates of Paradise": praise truly appropriate, and given by an able judge. And well indeed might Lorenzo complete them, seeing that from the age of twenty, when he began them, he worked at them for forty years, with labor beyond belief.

Lorenzo was assisted in finishing and polishing this work, after it was cast, by many men, then youths, who afterwards became excellent masters—namely, by Filippo Brunelleschi, Masolino da Panicale, and Niccolò Lamberti, goldsmiths; and by Parri Spinelli, Antonio Filarete, Paolo Uccello, Antonio del Pollaiuolo, who was then quite young, and many others, who, growing intimate together over that work, and conferring one with another, as men do when they work in company, gained no less advantage for themselves than they gave to Lorenzo. To him, besides the payment that he had from the Consuls, the Signoria gave a good farm near the Abbey of Settimo, and no long time elapsed before he was made one of the Signori, and honored with the supreme magistracy of the city; wherefore the Florentines deserve no less to be praised for their gratitude to him, than they deserve to be blamed for having been little grateful to other excellent men of their city.

Lorenzo applied himself, while he lived, to many things, and delighted in painting and in working in glass, and for S. Maria del Fiore he made the round windows that are round the cupola, excepting one, which is by the hand of Donatello—namely, the one wherein Christ is crowning Our Lady. Lorenzo likewise made the three that are over the principal door of the same S. Maria del Fiore, and all those of the chapels and of the tribunes, and also the rose-window in the façade of S. Croce. In Arezzo he made a window for the principal chapel of the Pieve, containing the Coronation of Our Lady, with two other figures, for Lazzaro di Feo di Baccio, a very rich merchant; but since they were all of Venetian glass, loaded with color, they make the places where they were put rather dark than otherwise. Lorenzo was chosen to assist Brunellesco, when the latter was commissioned to make the Cupola of S. Maria del Fiore, but he was afterwards relieved of the task.

The same Lorenzo wrote a book in the vulgar tongue, wherein he treated of many diverse matters, but in such wise that little profit can be drawn from it. Finally, being assailed by a grievous and continuous fever, he died, leaving immortal fame for himself by reason of the works that he made, and through the pens of writers; and he was honorably buried in S. Croce.

MASACCIO

[*Tommaso di Ser Giovanni di Simone Guido, called Masaccio, was born in 1401 and died, probably, in 1428.*]

IT is the custom of nature, when she makes a man very excellent in any profession, very often not to make him alone, but at the same time, and in the same neighborhood, to make another to compete with him, to the end that they may assist each other by their talent and emulation; which circumstance, besides the singular advantage enjoyed by the men themselves, who thus compete with each other, also kindles beyond measure the minds of those who come after that age, to strive with all study and all industry to attain to that honor and that glorious reputation which they hear highly extolled without ceasing in those who have passed away. And that this is true we see from the fact that Florence produced in one and the same age Filippo, Donatello, Ghiberti, Paolo Uccello, and Masaccio, each most excellent in his own kind, and thus not only swept away the rough and rude manners that had prevailed up to that time, but incited and kindled so greatly, by reason of the beautiful works of these men, the minds of those who came after, that the work of those professions has been brought to that grandeur and to that perfection which are seen in our own times. Wherefore, in truth, we owe a great obligation to those early craftsmen who showed to us, by means of their labors, the true way to climb to the greatest height; and with regard to the good manner of painting, we are indebted above all to Masaccio, seeing that he, as one desirous of acquiring fame, perceived that painting is nothing but the counterfeiting of all the things of nature, vividly and simply, with drawing and with colors, even as she produced them for us, and that he who attains to this most perfectly can be called excellent. This truth, I say, being recognized by Masaccio, brought it about that by means of continuous study he learnt so much that he can be numbered among the first who cleared away, in a great measure, the hardness, the imperfections, and the difficulties of the art, and that he gave a beginning to beautiful attitudes, movements, liveliness, and vivacity, and to a certain relief truly characteristic and natural; which no painter up to his time had ever done. And since he had excellent judgment, he reflected that all the figures that did not stand firmly with their feet in foreshortening on the level, but stood on tiptoe, were lacking in all goodness of manner in the essential points, and that those who make them thus show that they do not understand foreshortening. And although Paolo Uccello had tried his hand at this, and had done something, solving this difficulty to some extent, yet Masaccio, introducing many new methods, made foreshortenings from every point of view much better than any other who had lived up to that time. And he painted his works with good unity and softness, harmonizing the flesh-colors of the heads and of the nudes with the colors of the draperies, which he delighted to make with few folds and simple, as they are in life and nature. This has been of great use to craftsmen, and he deserves therefore to be commended as if he had been its inventor, for in truth the works made before his day can be said to be painted, while his are living, real, and natural, in comparison with those made by the others.

This man was born at Castello San Giovanni in Valdarno, and they say that one may still see there some figures made by him in his earliest childhood. He was a very absent-minded and careless person, as one who, having fixed his whole mind and will on the matters of art, cared little about himself, and still less about others. And since he would never give any manner of thought to the cares and concerns of the world, or even to clothing himself, and was not wont to recover his money from his debtors, save only when he was in the greatest straits, his name was therefore changed from Tommaso to Masaccio,* not, indeed, because he was vicious, for he was goodness itself, but by reason of his so great carelessness; and with all this, nevertheless, he was so amiable in doing the service and pleasure of others, that nothing more could be desired.

He began painting at the time when Masolino da Panicale was working on the Chapel of the Brancacci in the Carmine, in Florence, ever following, in so far as he was able, in the steps of Filippo and Donatello, although their branch of art was different, and seeking continually in his work to make his figures very lifelike and with a beautiful liveliness in the likeness of nature. And his lineaments and his painting were so modern and so different from those of the others, that his works can safely stand in comparison with any drawing and coloring of our own day. He was very zealous at his labors, and a marvelous master of the difficulties of perspective, as it is seen in a story painted by him with small figures, which is to-day in the house of Ridolfo del Ghirlandaio. In this story, besides a Christ who is delivering the man possessed by a devil, there are very beautiful buildings in perspective, drawn in a manner that they show at one and the same time both the inside and the outside, by reason of his having chosen the point of view, not of the front, but over the corners, as being more difficult. He sought more than any other master to make his figures nude and foreshortened, which was little done before his day. He had great facility in handling, and, as it has been said, he is very simple in his draperies.

There is a panel by his hand, wrought in distemper, where-

* Careless Tom, or Hulking Tom (not necessarily in disapproval).

in is a Madonna upon the lap of S. Anne, with the Child in her arms. This panel is to-day in S. Ambrogio in Florence, in the chapel that is beside the door that leads to the parlor of the nuns. In S. Maria Novella, he painted a Trinity in fresco, which is placed over the altar of S. Ignazio, with Our Lady on one side and S. John the Evangelist on the other contemplating Christ Crucified. On the sides are two figures on their knees, which, in so far as it can be determined, are portraits of the men who had the picture painted; but little is seen of them, for they have been covered with a gilt ornament. But the most beautiful thing, apart from the figures, is a barrel-shaped vaulting, drawn in perspective and divided into squares filled with rosettes, which are foreshortened and made to diminish so well that the wall appears to be pierced.

In the Church of the Carmine in Pisa, on a panel that is in a chapel in the transept, there is a Madonna with the Child, by his hand, and at her feet are certain little angels sounding instruments, one of whom, playing on a lute, is listening attentively to the harmony of that sound. On either side of the Madonna are S. Peter, S. John the Baptist, S. Julian, and S. Nicholas, all very lifelike and vivacious figures. In the predella below are scenes from the lives of those Saints, with little figures; and in the center are the three Magi offering their treasures to Christ. In this part are some horses portrayed from life, so beautiful that nothing better can be desired; and the men of the Court of those three Kings are clothed in various costumes that were worn in those times. And above, as an ornament for the said panel, there are, in several squares, many saints round a Crucifix. It is believed that the figure of a saint, in the robes of a Bishop and painted in fresco, which is in that church, beside the door that leads into the convent, is by the hand of Masaccio; but I hold it as certain that it is by the hand of Fra Filippo, his disciple.

Returning from Pisa to Florence, he wrought there a

panel containing a man and a woman, nude and of the size
of life, which is to-day in the Palla Rucellai Palace. Then, not
feeling at ease in Florence, and stimulated by his affection
and love for art, he determined to go to Rome, in order to
learn and to surpass others; and this he did. And having
acquired very great fame there, he painted for Cardinal San
Clemente a chapel in the Church of S. Clemente, wherein he
made in fresco the Passion of Christ, with the Thieves on
the Cross, and the stories of S. Catherine the martyr. He also
made many panels in distemper, which have been all lost or
destroyed in the troublous times of Rome; one being in the
Church of S. Maria Maggiore, in a little chapel near the
sacristy, wherein are four saints, so well wrought that they
appear to be in relief, and in the midst of them is S. Maria
della Neve, with the portrait from nature of Pope Martin,
who is tracing out the foundations of that church with a hoe,
and beside him the Emperor Sigismund II. Michelangelo and
I were one day examining this work, when he praised it much,
and then added that these men were alive in Masaccio's time.
To him, while Pisanello and Gentile da Fabriano were laboring in Rome for Pope Martin on the walls of the Church of
S. Gianni, these masters had allotted a part of the work, when
he returned to Florence, having had news that Cosimo de'
Medici, by whom he was much assisted and favored, had
been recalled from exile; and there he was commissioned to
paint the Chapel of the Brancacci in the Carmine, by reason
of the death of Masolino da Panicale, who had begun it; but
before putting his hand to this, he made, by way of specimen,
the S. Paul that is near the bell-ropes, in order to show the
improvement that he had made in his art. And he demonstrated truly infinite excellence in this picture, for in the head
of that Saint, who is Bartolo di Angiolino Angiolini portrayed from life, there is seen an expression so awful that
there appears to be nothing lacking in that figure save speech;
and he who has not known S. Paul will see, by looking at this

picture, his honorable Roman culture, together with the unconquerable strength of that most divine spirit, all intent on the work of the faith. In this same picture, likewise, he showed a power of foreshortening things viewed from below upwards which was truly marvelous, as may still be seen to-day in the feet of the said Apostle, for this was a difficulty that he solved completely, in contrast with the old rude manner, which, as I said a little before, used to make all the figures on tiptoe; which manner lasted up to his day, without any other man correcting it, and he, by himself and before any other, brought it to the excellence of our own day.

It came to pass, the while that he was laboring at this work, that the said Church of the Carmine was consecrated; and Masaccio, in memory of this, painted the consecration just as it took place, with terra-verde and in chiaroscuro, over the door that leads into the convent, within the cloister. And he portrayed therein an infinite number of citizens in mantles and hoods, who are following the procession, among whom he painted Filippo di Ser Brunellesco in wooden shoes, Donatello, Masolino da Panicale, who had been his master, Antonio Brancacci, who caused him to paint the chapel, Niccolò da Uzzano, Giovanni di Bicci de' Medici, and Bartolommeo Valori, who are all also portrayed by the hand of the same man in the house of Simon Corsi, a gentleman of Florence. He also painted there Lorenzo Ridolfi, who was at that time the ambassador of the Florentine Republic in Venice; and not only did he portray there the aforesaid gentlemen from the life, but also the door of the convent and the porter with the keys in his hand. This work, truly, shows great perfection, for Masaccio was so successful in placing these people, five or six to a file, on the level of that piazza, and in making them diminish to the eye with proportion and judgment, that it is indeed a marvel, and above all because we can recognize there the wisdom that he showed in making those men, as if they were alive, not all of one size, but with a certain discretion which distinguishes those who are short and stout from those who are tall and slender; while they are all standing with their feet firmly on one level, and so well foreshortened that they would not be otherwise in nature.

After this, returning to the work of the Chapel of the Brancacci, and continuing the stories of S. Peter begun by Masolino, he finished a part of them—namely, the story of the Chair, the healing of the sick, the raising of the dead, and the restoring of the cripples with his shadow as he was going to the Temple with S. John. But the most notable among them all is that one wherein S. Peter, at Christ's command, is taking the money from the belly of the fish, in order to pay the tribute, since (besides the fact that we see there in an Apostle, the last of the group, the portrait of Masaccio himself, made by his own hand with the help of a mirror, so well that it appears absolutely alive) we can recognize there the ardor of S. Peter in his questioning and the attentiveness of the Apostles, who are standing in various attitudes round Christ, awaiting his determination, with gestures so vivid that they truly appear alive. Wonderful, above all, is the S. Peter who, while he is laboring to draw the money from the belly of the fish, has his head suffused with blood by reason of bending down; and he is even more wonderful as he pays the tribute, for here we see his expression as he counts it, and the eagerness of him who is receiving it and looking at the money in his hand with the greatest pleasure. There, also, he painted the resurrection of the King's son, wrought by S. Peter and S. Paul; although by reason of the death of Masaccio the work remained unfinished, and was afterwards completed by Filippino. In the scene wherein S. Peter is baptizing, a naked man, who is trembling and shivering with cold among the others who are being baptized, is greatly esteemed, having been wrought with very beautiful relief and sweet manner; which figure has ever been held in reverence and admiration by all craftsmen, both ancient and modern. For this reason that chapel has been frequented continually up to our own day by innumerable draftsmen and masters; and there still are therein some heads so lifelike and so beautiful, that it may truly be said that no master of that age approached so nearly as this man did to the moderns. His labors therefore deserve infinite praise, and above all because he gave form in his art to the beautiful manner of our times. And that this is true is proved by the fact that all the most celebrated sculptors and painters, who have lived from his day to our own, have become excellent and famous by exercising themselves and studying in this chapel. But although the works of Masaccio have ever been in so great repute, it is nevertheless the opinion—nay, the firm belief—of many, that he would have produced even greater fruits in his art, if death, which tore him from us at the age of twenty-six, had not snatched him away from us so prematurely. But either by reason of envy, or because good things rarely have any long duration, he died in the flower of his youth, and that so suddenly, that there were not wanting people who put it down to poison rather than to any other reason.

BRUNELLESCHI

[*Filippo di Ser Brunelleschi was born in 1377 and died in 1446.*]

MANY men are created by nature small in person and in features, who have a mind full of such greatness and a heart of such irresistible vehemence, that if they do not begin difficult—nay, almost impossible—undertakings, and bring them to completion to the marvel of all who behold them, they have never any peace in their lives; and whatsoever work chance puts into their hands, however lowly and base it may be, they give it value and nobility. This is clearly seen in Filippo di Ser Brunelleschi, who was no less insignificant in person than Messer Forese da Rabatta and Giotto, but so lofty in intellect that it can be truly said that he was sent to us by Heaven in order to give new form to architecture, which had been out of mind for hundreds of years; for the men of those times had spent much treasure to no purpose, making buildings without order, with bad method, with sorry design, with most strange inventions, with most ungraceful grace, and with even worse ornament. And Heaven ordained, since the earth had been for so many years without any supreme mind or divine spirit, that Filippo should bequeath to the world the greatest, the most lofty, and the most beautiful building that was ever made in modern times, or even in those of the ancients, proving that the talent of the Tuscan craftsmen, although lost, was not therefore dead. Heaven adorned him, moreover, with the best virtues, among which was that of kindliness, so that no man was ever more benign or more amiable than he. In judgment he was free from passion, and when he saw worth and merit in others he would sacrifice his own advantage and the interest of his friends. He knew himself, he shared the benefit of his own talent with many, and he was ever succoring his neighbor in his necessities. He declared himself a capital enemy of vice, and a friend of those who practiced virtue. He never spent his time uselessly, but would labor to meet the needs of others, either by himself or by the agency of other men; and he would visit his friends on foot and ever succor them.

It is said that there was in Florence a man of very good repute, most praiseworthy in his way of life and active in his business, whose name was Ser Brunellesco di Lippo Lapi, who had had a grandfather called Cambio, who was a learned person and the son of a physician very famous in those times, named Maestro Ventura Bacherini. Now Ser Brunellesco, taking to wife a most excellent young woman from the noble family of the Spini, received, as part payment of her dowry, a house wherein he and his sons dwelt to the day of their death. This house stands opposite to one side of S. Michele Berteldi, in a close past the Piazza degli Agli. The while that he was occupying himself thus and living happily, in the year 1377 there was born to him a son, to whom he gave the name Filippo, after his own father, now dead; and he celebrated this birth with the greatest gladness possible. Thereupon he taught him in his childhood, with the utmost attention, the first rudiments of letters, wherein the boy showed himself so ingenious and so lofty in spirit that his brain was often in doubt, as if he did not care to become very perfect in them——nay, it appeared that he directed his thoughts on matters of greater utility——wherefore Ser Brunellesco, who wished him to follow his own vocation of notary, or that of his great-great-grandfather, was very much displeased. But seeing him continually investigating ingenious problems of art and mechanics, he made him learn arithmetic and writing, and then apprenticed him to the goldsmith's art with one his friend, to the end that he might learn design. And this gave great satisfaction to Filippo, who, not many years after beginning to learn and to practice that art, could set precious stones better than any old craftsman in that vocation. He occupied himself with niello and with making larger works, such as some figures in silver, whereof two, half-length prophets, are placed at the head of the altar of S. Jacopo in Pistoia; these figures, which are held very beautiful, were wrought by him for the Wardens of Works in that city; and he made works in bas-relief, wherein he showed that he had so great knowledge in his vocation that his intellect must needs overstep the bounds of that art. Wherefore, having made acquaintance with certain studious persons, he began to penetrate with his fancy into questions of time, of motion, of weights, and of wheels, and how the latter can be made to revolve, and by what means they can be set in motion; and thus he made some very good and very beautiful clocks with his own hand.

Not content with this, there arose in his mind a very great inclination for sculpture; and this took effect, for Donatello, then a youth, being held an able sculptor and one of great promise, Filippo began to be ever in his company, and the two conceived such great love for each other, by reason of the talents of each, that one appeared unable to live without the other. Whereupon Filippo, who was most capable in various ways, gave attention to many professions, nor had he practiced these long before he was held by persons qualified to judge to be a very good architect. He gave much attention to perspective, which was then in a very evil plight by reason of many errors that were made therein; and in this he spent much time, until he found by himself a method whereby it might become true and perfect—namely, that of tracing it with the ground-plan and profile and by means of intersecting lines, which was something truly most ingenious and useful to the art of design. In this he took so great delight that he drew with his own hand the Palace, the Piazza, and the Loggia of the Signori, together with the roof of the Pisani and all the buildings that are seen round that Piazza; and these works were the means of arousing the minds of the other craftsmen, who afterwards devoted themselves to this with great zeal. He taught it, in particular, to the painter Masaccio, then a youth and much his friend, who did him credit in this art that Filippo showed him, as it is apparent from the buildings in his works. Nor did he refrain from teaching it even to those who worked in tarsia, which is the art of inlaying colored woods; and he stimulated them so greatly that he was the source of a good style and of many useful changes that were made in that craft, and of many excellent works wrought both then and afterwards, which have brought fame and profit to Florence for many years.

Now Messer Paolo dal Pozzo Toscanelli, returning from his studies, and chancing one evening to be at supper in a garden with some of his friends, invited Filippo, who, hearing him discourse on the mathematical arts, formed such an intimacy with him that he learnt geometry from Messer Paolo; and although Filippo had no learning, he reasoned so well in every matter with his instinct, sharpened by practice and experience, that he would many times confound him. And so he went on to give attention to the study of the Christian Scriptures, never failing to be present at the disputations and preachings of learned persons, from which he gained so much advantage, by reason of his admirable memory, that the aforesaid Messer Paolo was wont to extol him and to say that in hearing Filippo argue he appeared to be hearing a new S. Paul. He also gave much attention at this time to the works of Dante, which he understood very well with regard to the places described and their proportions, and he would avail himself of them in his conversations, quoting them often in making comparisons. He did naught else with his thoughts but invent and imagine ingenious and difficult things; nor could he ever find an intellect more to his satisfaction than that of Donatello, with whom he was ever holding familiar discourse, and they took pleasure in one another and would confer together over the difficulties of their vocation.

Now in those days Donatello had finished a Crucifix of wood, which was placed in S. Croce in Florence, below the scene of the child being restored to life by S. Francis, painted by Taddeo Gaddi, and he wished to have the opinion of Filippo about this work; but he repented, for Filippo answered that he had placed a ploughman on the Cross; whence there arose the saying, "Take wood and make one thyself," as it is related at length in the Life of Donatello. Whereupon Filippo, who would never get angry, whatever might be said to him, although he might have reason for anger, stayed in seclusion for many months until he had finished a Crucifix of wood of the same size, so excellent, and wrought with so much art, design, and diligence, that Donatello—whom he had sent to his house ahead of himself, as it were to surprise him, for he did not know that Filippo had made such a work—having an apron full of eggs and other things for their common dinner, let it fall as he gazed at the work, beside himself with marvel at the ingenious and masterly manner that Filippo had shown in the legs, the trunk, and the arms of the said figure, which was so well composed and united together that Donatello, besides admitting himself beaten, proclaimed it a miracle. This work is placed to-day in S. Maria Novella, between the Chapel of the Strozzi and that of the Bardi da Vernia, and it is still very greatly extolled by the moderns.

After these things, in the year 1401, now that sculpture had risen to so great a height, it was determined to reconstruct the two bronze doors of the Church and Baptistery of S. Giovanni, since, from the death of Andrea Pisano to that day, they had not had any masters capable of executing them. This intention being, therefore, communicated to those sculptors who were then in Tuscany, they were sent for, and each man was given a provision and the space of a year to make one scene; and among those called upon were Filippo and Donatello, each of them being required to make one scene by himself, in competition with Lorenzo Ghiberti, Jacopo della Fonte, Simone da Colle, Francesco di Valdambrina, and Niccolò d'Arezzo. These scenes, being finished in the same year and being brought together for comparison, Filippo and Donatello were not satisfied with any save with that of Lorenzo, and they judged him to be better qualified for that work than themselves and the others who had made the other scenes. And so with good reasons they persuaded the Consuls to allot the work to Lorenzo, showing that thus both the public and the private interest would be best served; and this was indeed the true goodness of friendship, excellence without envy, and a sound judgment in the knowledge of their own selves, whereby they deserved more praise than if they had executed the work to perfection. Happy spirits! who, while they were assisting one another, took delight in praising the labors of others. How unhappy are those of our own day, who, not sated with injuring each other, burst with envy while rending others.

The commission being given to Lorenzo Ghiberti, Filippo and Donatello, who were together, resolved to depart from Florence in company and to live for some years in Rome, to the end that Filippo might study architecture and Donatello sculpture; and this Filippo did from his desire to be superior both to Lorenzo and to Donatello, in proportion as architecture is held to be more necessary for the practical needs of men than sculpture and painting. After he had sold a little farm that he had at Settignano, they departed from Florence and went to Rome, where, seeing the grandeur of the buildings and the perfection of the construction of the temples, Filippo would stand in amaze like a man out of his mind. And so, having made arrangements for measuring the cornices and taking the ground-plans of those buildings, he and Donatello kept laboring continually, sparing neither time nor expense. There was no place, either in Rome or in the Campagna without, that they left unvisited, and nothing of the good that they did not measure, if only they could find it. And since Filippo was free from domestic cares, he gave himself over body and soul to his studies, and took no thought for eating or sleeping, being intent on one thing only—namely, architecture, which was now dead (I mean the good ancient Orders, and not the barbarous German, which was much in use in his time). And he had in his mind two vast conceptions, one being to restore to light the good manner of architecture, since he believed that if he could recover it he would leave behind no less a name for himself than Cimabue and Giotto had done; and the other was to find a method, if he could, of raising the Cupola of S. Maria del Fiore in Florence, the difficulties of which were such that after the death of Arnolfo Lapi there had been no one courageous enough to think of raising it without vast expenditure for a wooden framework. Yet he did not impart this his invention to Donatello or to any living soul, nor did he rest in Rome till he had considered all the difficulties connected with the Ritonda, wondering how the vaulting was raised. He had noted and drawn all the ancient vaults, and was for ever studying them; and if peradventure they had found pieces of capitals, columns, cornices, and bases of buildings buried underground, they would set to work and have them dug out, in order to examine them thoroughly. Wherefore a rumor spread through Rome, as they passed through the streets, going about carelessly dressed, so that they were called the "treasure-seekers," people believing that they were persons who studied geomancy in order to discover treasure; and this was because they had one day found an ancient earthenware vase full of medals. Filippo ran short of money and contrived to make this good by setting jewels of price for certain goldsmiths who were his friends; and thus he was left alone in Rome, for Donatello returned to Florence, while he, with greater industry and labor than before, was for ever investigating the ruins of those buildings. Nor did he rest until he had drawn every sort of building—round, square, and octagonal temples, basilicas, aqueducts, baths, arches, colosseums, amphitheaters, and every temple built of bricks, from which he copied the methods of binding and of clamping with ties, and also of encircling vaults with them; and he noted the ways of making buildings secure by binding the stones together, by iron bars, and by dovetailing; and, discovering a hole hollowed out under the middle of each great stone, he found that this was meant to hold the iron instrument wherewith the stones are drawn up; and this he reintroduced and brought into use afterwards. He then distinguished the different Orders one from another—Doric, Ionic, and Corinthian; and so zealous was his study that his intellect became very well able to see Rome, in imagination, as she was when she was not in ruins. At length the air of that city gave Filippo a slight indisposition, wherefore, being advised by his friends to try a change of air, he returned to Florence. There many buildings had suffered by reason of his absence; and for these, on his arrival, he gave many designs and much advice.

In 1417 a congress of architects and engineers of the country was summoned by the Wardens of Works of S. Maria del Fiore and by the Consuls of the Guild of Wool, to discuss methods for raising the cupola. Among these appeared Filippo, giving it as his advice that it was necessary, not to raise the fabric directly from the roof according to the design of Arnolfo, but to make a frieze thirty feet in height, with a large round window in the middle of each of its sides, since not only would this take the weight off the supports of the tribunes, but it would become easier to raise the cupola; and models were made in this way, and were put into execution. Filippo, being restored to health after some months, was standing one morning in the Piazza di S. Maria del Fiore with Donatello and other craftsmen, when they began to talk of antiquities in connection with sculpture, and Donatello related how, when he was returning from Rome, he had made the journey through Orvieto, in order to see that marble façade of the Duomo, a work greatly celebrated, wrought by the hands of diverse masters and held to be something notable in those times; and how, in passing afterwards by Cortona, he entered the Pieve and saw a very beautiful ancient sarcophagus, whereon there was a scene in marble—a rare thing then, when there had not been unearthed that abundance which has been found in our own day. And as Donatello went on to describe the method that the master of that work had used in its execution, and the finish that was to be seen therein, together with the perfection and the excellence of the workmanship, Filippo became fired with an ardent desire to see it, and went off on foot just as he was, in his mantle, cap, and wooden shoes, without saying where he was going, and allowed himself to be carried to Cortona by the devotion and love that he bore to art. And having seen the sarcophagus, and being pleased with it, he made a drawing of it with the pen, and returned with that to Florence, without Donatello or any other person knowing that he had been away, for they thought he must have been drawing or inventing something.

Having thus returned to Florence, he showed him the drawing of the sarcophagus, which he had made with great patience, whereat Donatello marveled not a little, seeing how much love Filippo bore to art. After this he stayed many months in Florence, where he kept making models and machines in secret, all for the work of the cupola, exchanging jokes the while with his fellow-craftsmen and going very often, for recreation, to assist Lorenzo Ghiberti in polishing some part of his doors. But hearing that there was some talk of providing engineers for the raising of the cupola, and being taken one morning with the idea of returning to Rome, he went there, thinking that he would be in greater repute and would be more sought from abroad than he would be if he stayed in Florence. When he was in Rome, therefore, the work came to be considered, and so, too, the great acuteness of his intellect, for he had shown in his discourse such confidence and such courage as had not been found in the other masters, who, together with the builders, were standing paralyzed and helpless, thinking that no way of raising the cupola could ever be found, nor beams to make a bridge strong enough to sustain the framework and the weight of so great an edifice; and having determined to make an end of the matter, they wrote to Filippo in Rome, praying him to come to Florence. He, desiring nothing better, returned with great readiness; and the Wardens of Works of S. Maria del Fiore and the Consuls of the Guild of Wool, assembling on his arrival, explained to Filippo all the difficulties, from the greatest to the smallest, which were being raised by the masters, who were in his presence at the audience together with them. Whereupon Filippo spoke these words: "My Lords the Wardens, there is no doubt that great enterprises ever present difficulties in their execution, and if any ever did so, this of yours presents them, and even greater than perchance you are aware of, for the reason that I do not know whether even the ancients ever raised a vault so tremendous as this will be; and although I have often pondered over the framework necessary both within and without, and how it may be possible to work at it securely, I have never been able to come to any resolution, and I am aghast no less at the breadth than at the height of the edifice, for the reason that, if it could be made round, we might use the method used by the Romans in raising the dome over the Pantheon in Rome, that is, the Ritonda, whereas here we must follow the eight sides, and bind the stones together with ties and by dovetailing them, which will be something very difficult. But remembering that this is a temple consecrated to God and to the Virgin, I am confident, since this is being done in memory of her, that she will not fail to infuse knowledge where it is lacking, and to give strength, wisdom, and genius to him who is to be the author of such a work. But how can I help you in this matter, since the task is not mine? I tell you, indeed, that if the work fell to me, I would have resolution and courage enough to find the method whereby the vault might be raised without so many difficulties; but as yet I have given no thought to it, and you would have me tell you the method! And when at last your Lordships determine to have it raised, you will be forced not only to make trial of me, for I do not think myself able to be the sole adviser in so great a matter, but also to spend money and to ordain that within a year and on a fixed day many architects shall come to Florence, not merely Tuscans and Italians, but Germans, French, and of every other nation; and to propose this work to them, to the end that, after discussing and deciding among so many masters, it may be begun, being entrusted to him who shall give the most direct proof of ability or possess the best method and judgment for such an undertaking. Nor could I give you other counsel or a better plan than this."

The plan and the counsel of Filippo pleased the Consuls and the Wardens of Works, but they would have liked him in the meanwhile to have made a model and to have given thought to the matter. But he showed that he cared nothing for it; nay, taking leave of them, he said that he had received letters soliciting him to return to Rome. Whereupon the Consuls, perceiving that their prayers and those of the Wardens did not avail to detain him, caused many of his friends to entreat him; but Filippo would not give way, and one morning (on May 26, 1417) the Wardens decreed him a present of money, which is found entered to the credit of Filippo in the books of the Office of Works; and all this was to conciliate him. But he, steadfast in his resolution, took his departure none the less from Florence and returned to Rome, where he studied continuously for that undertaking, making arrangements and preparing himself for the completion of the work, thinking, as was true, that no other than himself could carry it out. And as for his counsel that new architects should be summoned, Filippo had advanced it for no other reason but that they might serve to prove the greatness of his own intellect, and not because he thought that they would be able to vault that tribune or to undertake such a charge, which was too difficult for them. And thus much time was consumed before those architects arrived from their countries, whom they had caused to be summoned from afar by means of orders given to Florentine merchants who dwelt in France, in Germany, in England, and in Spain, and who were commissioned to spend any sum of money, if only they could obtain the most experienced and able intellects that there were in those regions from the Princes of those countries, and send them to Florence.

By the year 1420, all these ultramontane masters were finally assembled in Florence, and likewise those of Tuscany and all the ingenious craftsmen of design in Florence; and so Filippo returned from Rome. They all assembled, therefore, in the Office of Works of S. Maria del Fiore, in the presence of the Consuls and of the Wardens, together with a select body of the most ingenious citizens, to the end that these might hear the mind of each master on the question and might decide on a method of vaulting this tribune. Having called them, then, into the audience, they heard the minds of all, one by one, and the plan that each architect had devised for that work. And a fine thing it was to hear their strange and diverse opinions about the matter, for the reason that some said that piers must be built up from the level of the ground, which should have the arches turned upon them and should uphold the wooden bridges for sustaining the weight; others said that it was best to make the cupola of sponge-stone, to the end that the weight might be less; and many were agreed that a pier should be built in the center, and that the cupola should be raised in the shape of a pavilion, like that of S. Giovanni in Florence. Nor were there wanting men who said that it would have been a good thing to fill it with earth mingled with small coins, to the end that, when it had been raised, anyone who wanted some of that earth might be given leave to go and fetch it, and thus the people would carry it away in a moment without any expense. Filippo alone said that it could be raised without so much woodwork, without piers, without earth, without so great expenditure on so many arches, and very easily without any framework.

It appeared to the Consuls, who were expecting to hear of some beautiful method, and to the Wardens of Works and to all those citizens, that Filippo had talked like a fool; and deriding him with mocking laughter, they turned away, bidding him talk of something else, seeing that this was the plan of a madman, as he was. Whereupon Filippo, feeling himself affronted, answered: "My Lords, rest assured that it is not possible to raise the cupola in any other manner than this; and although you laugh at me, you will recognize, unless you mean to be obstinate, that it neither must nor can be done in any other way. And it is necessary, if you wish to erect it in the way that I have thought of, that it should be turned with the curve of a quarter-acute arch, and made double, one vault within, and the other without, in such wise that a man may be able to walk between the one and the other. And over the corners of the angles of the eight sides the fabric must be bound together through its thickness by dovetailing the stones, and its sides, likewise, must be girt round with oaken ties. And it is necessary to think of the lights, the staircases, and the conduits whereby the rain water may be able to run off; and not one of you has remembered that you must provide for the raising of scaffoldings within, when the mosaics come to be made, together with an infinite number of difficulties. But I, who see the vaulting raised, know that there is no other method and no other way of raising it than this that I am describing." And growing heated as he spoke, the more he sought to expound his conception, to the end that they might understand it and believe in it, the greater grew their doubts about his proposal, so that they believed in him less and less, and held him to be an ass and a babbler. Whereupon, having been dismissed several times and finally refusing to go, he was carried away bodily from the audience by their servants, being thought to be wholly mad; and this affront was the reason that Filippo could afterwards say that he did not dare to pass through any part of the city, for fear lest someone might say: "There goes that madman."

The Consuls remained in the Audience Chamber all confused, both by the difficult methods of the original masters and by this last method of Filippo's, which they thought absurd, for it appeared to them that he would ruin the work in two ways: first, by making the vaulting double, which would have made it enormous and unwieldy in weight; and secondly, by making it without a framework. On the other hand, Filippo, who had spent so many years in study in order to obtain the commission, knew not what to do and was often tempted to leave Florence. However, wishing to prevail, he was forced to arm himself with patience, having insight enough to know that the brains of the men of that city did not abide very firmly by any one resolution. Filippo could have shown a little model that he had in his possession, but he did not wish to show it, having recognized the small intelligence of the Consuls, the envy of the craftsmen, and the instability of the citizens, who favored now one and now another, according as it pleased each man best; and I do not marvel at this, since every man in that city professes to know as much in these matters as the experienced masters know, although those who truly understand them are but few; and let this be said without offense to those who have the knowledge. What Filippo, therefore, had not been able to achieve before the tribunal, he began to effect with individuals, talking now to a Consul, now to a Warden, and likewise to many citizens; and showing them part of his design, he induced them to determine to allot this work either to him or to one of the foreigners. Wherefore the Consuls, the Wardens of Works, and those citizens, regaining courage, assembled together, and the architects disputed concerning this matter, but all were overcome and conquered by Filippo with many arguments; and here, so it is said, there arose the dispute about the egg, in the following manner. They would have liked Filippo to speak his mind in detail, and to show his model, as they had shown theirs; but this he refused to do, proposing instead to those masters, both the foreign and the native, that whosoever could make an egg stand upright on a flat piece of marble should build the cupola, since thus each man's intellect would be discerned. Taking an egg, therefore, all those masters sought to make it stand upright, but not one could find the way. Whereupon Filippo, being told to make it stand, took it graciously, and, giving one end of it a blow on the flat piece of marble, made it stand upright. The craftsmen protested that they could have done the same; but Filippo answered, laughing, that they could also have raised the cupola, if they had seen the model or the design. And so it was resolved that he should be commissioned to carry out this work, and he was told that he must give fuller information about it to the Consuls and the Wardens of Works.

Going to his house, therefore, he wrote down his mind on a sheet of paper as clearly as he was able, to give to the tribunal, in the following manner: "Having considered the difficulties of this structure, Magnificent Lords Wardens, I find that it is in no way possible to raise the cupola perfectly round, seeing that the surface above, where the lantern is to go, would be so great that the laying of any weight thereupon would soon destroy it. Now it appears to me that those architects who have no regard for the durability of their structures, have no love of lasting memorials, and do not even know why they are made. Wherefore I have determined to turn the inner part of this vault in pointed sections, following the outer sides, and to give to these the proportion and the curve of the quarter-acute arch, for the reason that this curve, when turned, ever pushes upwards, so that, when it is loaded with the lantern, both will unite to make the vaulting durable. At the base it must be seven and one half feet in thickness, and it must rise pyramidically, narrowing from without, until it closes at the point where the lantern is to be; and at this junction the vaulting must be two and one half feet in thickness. Then on the outer side there must be another vault, which must be five feet thick at the base, in order to protect the inner one from the rain. This one must also diminish pyramidically in due proportion, so that it may come together at the foot of the lantern, like the other, in such wise that at the summit it may be a foot and a third in thickness. At each angle there must be a buttress, making eight in all: and in the middle of every side there must be two buttresses, making sixteen in all: and between the said angles, on every side, both within and without, there must be two buttresses, each eight feet thick at the base. The two said vaults, built in the form of a pyramid, must rise together in equal proportion up to the height of the round window closed by the lantern. There must then be made twenty-four buttresses with the said vaults built round them, and six arches of grey-stone blocks, stout and long, and well braced with irons, which must be covered with tin; and over the said blocks there must be iron ties, binding the said vaulting to its buttresses. The first part of the masonry, up to the height of ten and a half feet, must be solid, leaving no vacant space, and then the buttresses must be continued and the two vaults separated. The first and second courses at the base must be strengthened throughout with long blocks of grey-stone laid horizontally across them, in such wise that both vaults of the cupola may rest on the said blocks. At the height of every eighteen feet in the said vaults there must be little arches between one buttress and another, with thick ties of oak, to bind together the said buttresses, which support the inner vault; and then the said ties of oak must be covered with plates of iron, for the sake of the staircases. The buttresses must be all built of grey-stone and hard-stone, and all the sides of the cupola must be likewise of hard-stone and bound with the buttresses up to the height of forty-eight feet; and from there to the top the material must be brick, or rather, sponge-stone, according to the decision of the builder, who must make the work as light as he is able. A passage must be made on the outside above the windows, forming a gallery below, with an open parapet four feet in height, proportionately to those of the little tribunes below; or rather, two passages, one above the other, resting on a richly adorned cornice, with the upper passage uncovered. The rain water must flow from the cupola into a gutter of marble, eight inches wide, and must run off through outlets made of hard-stone below the gutter. Eight ribs of marble must be made at the angles in the outer surface of the cupola, of such thickness as may be required, rising two feet above the cupola, with a cornice above by way of roof, four feet wide, to serve as gable and eaves to the whole; and these ribs must rise pyramidically from their base up to the summit. The two vaults of the cupola must be built in the manner described above, without framework, up to the height of sixty feet, and from that point upwards in the manner recommended by those masters who will have the building of them, since practice teaches us what course to pursue."

Filippo, having finished writing all that is above, went in the morning to the tribunal and gave them that paper, which they studied from end to end. And although they could not grasp it all, yet, seeing the readiness of Filippo's mind, and perceiving that not one of the other architects had better ground to stand on—for he showed a manifest confidence in his speech, ever repeating the same thing in such wise that it appeared certain that he had raised ten cupolas—the Consuls, drawing aside, were minded to give him the work, saying only that they would have liked to see something to show how this cupola could be raised without framework, for they approved of everything else. To this desire fortune was favorable, for Bartolommeo Barbadori having previously resolved to have a chapel built in S. Felicita and having spoken of this to Filippo, the latter had put his hand to the work and had caused that chapel to be vaulted without framework, at the right hand of the entrance into the church, where the holy-water basin is, also made by his hand. In those days, likewise, he caused another to be vaulted beside the Chapel of the High Altar in

S. Jacopo sopra Arno, for Stiatta Ridolfi; and these works were the means of bringing him more credit than his words. And so the Consuls and the Wardens of Works, being assured by the writing and by the work that they had seen, gave him the commission for the cupola, making him principal superintendent by the vote with the beans. But they did not contract with him for more than twenty-four feet of the whole height, saying to him that they wished to see how the work succeeded, and that if it succeeded as well as he promised they would not fail to commission him to do the rest. It appeared a strange thing to Filippo to see so great obstinacy and distrust in the Consuls and Wardens, and, if it had not been that he knew himself to be the only man capable of executing the work, he would not have put his hand to it. However, desiring to gain the glory of its construction, he undertook it, and pledged himself to bring it to perfect completion. His written statement was copied into a book wherein the *provveditore* kept the accounts of the debtors and creditors for wood and marble, together with the aforesaid pledge; and they undertook to make him the same allowance of money as they had given up to then to the other superintendents.

The commission given to Filippo becoming known among the craftsmen and the citizens, some thought well of it and others ill, as it has ever been the case with the opinions of the populace, of the thoughtless, and of the envious. The while that the preparations for beginning to build were being made, a faction was formed among craftsmen and citizens, and they appeared before the Consuls and the Wardens, saying that there had been too much haste in the matter, and that such a work as this should not be carried out by the counsel of one man alone; that they might be pardoned for this if they had been suffering from a dearth of excellent masters, whereas they had them in abundance; and that it was not likely to do credit to the city, because, if some accident were to happen, as is wont to come to pass sometimes in buildings, they might be blamed, as persons who had laid too great a charge on one man, without considering the loss and the shame that might result to the public interest; wherefore it would be well to give Filippo a companion, in order to restrain his rashness.

Now Lorenzo Ghiberti had come into great repute, by reason of having formerly given proof of his genius in the doors of S. Giovanni; and that he was beloved by certain men who were very powerful in the Government was proved clearly enough, since, seeing the glory of Filippo waxing so great, they wrought on the Consuls and the Wardens so strongly, under the pretext of love and affection toward that building, that he was united to Filippo as his colleague in the work. How great were the despair and the bitterness of Filippo, on hearing what the Wardens had done, may be seen from this, that he was minded to fly from Florence; and if it had not been for Donatello and Luca della Robbia, who comforted him, he would have lost his reason. Truly impious and cruel is the rage of those who, blinded by envy, put into peril the honors and the beautiful works of others in their jealous emulation! It was no fault of theirs, in truth, that Filippo did not break his models into pieces, burn his designs, and throw away in less than half an hour all that labor which had occupied him for so many years. The Wardens at first made excuses to Filippo and exhorted him to proceed, saying that he himself and no other was the inventor and the creator of so noble a building; but at the same time they gave the same salary to Lorenzo as to Filippo. The work was pursued with little willingness on the part of Filippo, who saw that he must endure the labors that it entailed, and must then divide the honor and the fame equally with Lorenzo. Making up his mind, however, that he would find means to prevent Lorenzo from continuing very long in the work, he went on pursuing it in company with him, in the manner suggested by the writing given to the Wardens. Meanwhile, there arose in the mind of Filippo the idea of making such a model as had not yet been made; wherefore, having put his hand to this, he had it wrought by one Bartolommeo, a carpenter, who lived near the studio. In this model, which had all the exact proportions measured to scale, he made all the difficult parts, such as staircases both lighted and dark, and every sort of window, door, tie, and buttress, together with a part of the gallery. Lorenzo, hearing of this, wished to see it, but Filippo refused to let him, whereupon he flew into a rage and ordered another model to be made for himself, to the end that he might not appear to be drawing his salary for nothing and to be of no account in the work. With regard to these models, Filippo was paid fifty *lire* and fifteen *soldi* for his, as we see from an order in the book of Migliori di Tommaso, whereas three hundred *lire* are entered as paid to Lorenzo Ghiberti for the labor and expense of his model, more in consequence of the friendship and favor that he enjoyed than of any profit or need that the building had of it.

This torment lasted before the eyes of Filippo until 1426, the friends of Lorenzo calling him the inventor equally with Filippo; and this annoyance disturbed the mind of Filippo so greatly that he was living in the utmost restlessness. Now, having thought of various new devices, he determined to rid himself entirely of Lorenzo, recognizing that he was of little account in the work. Filippo had already raised the cupola right round, what with the one vault and the other, to the height of twenty-four feet, and he had now to place upon them the ties both of stone and of wood; and as this was a difficult matter, he wished to discuss it with Lorenzo, in order to see if he had considered this difficulty. And he found Lorenzo so far from having thought of such a matter, that he replied that he referred it to Filippo as the inventor. Lorenzo's answer pleased Filippo, since it appeared to him that this was the way to get him removed from the work, and to prove that he did not possess that intelligence which was claimed for him by his friends, and to expose the favor that had placed him in that position. Now the masons engaged on the work were at a standstill, waiting to be told to begin the part above the twenty-four feet, and to make the vaults and bind them with ties. Having begun the drawing in of the cupola toward the top, it was necessary for them to make the scaffoldings, to the end that the masons and their laborers might be able to work without danger, seeing that the height was such that merely looking down brought fear and terror into the stoutest heart. The masons and the other master-builders were standing waiting for directions as to the ties and the scaffoldings; and since no decision was made either by Lorenzo or by Filippo, there arose a murmuring among the masons and the other master-builders, who saw no signs of the solicitude that had been shown before; and because, being poor people, they lived by the work of their hands, and suspected that neither one nor the other of the architects had enough courage to carry the work any further, they went about the building occupying themselves, to the best of their knowledge and power, with filling up and finishing all that had as yet been built.

One morning Filippo did not appear at the work, but bound up his head and went to bed, and caused plates and cloths to be heated with great solicitude, groaning continually and pretending to be suffering from colic. The master-builders, who were standing waiting for orders as to what they were to do, on hearing this, asked Lorenzo what they were to go on with: but he replied that it was for Filippo to give orders, and that they must wait for him. There was one who said, "What, dost thou not know his mind?" "Yes," answered Lorenzo, "but I would do nothing without him"; and this he said to excuse himself, because, not having seen the model of Filippo, and having never asked him what method he intended to follow, he would never commit himself in talking of the matter, in order not to appear ignorant, and would always make a double-edged answer, the more so as he knew that he was employed in the work against the will of Filippo. The illness of the latter having already lasted for more than two days, the *provveditore* and many of the master-masons went to see him and asked him repeatedly to tell them what they were to do. And he replied, "You have Lorenzo, let him do something"; nor could they get another word out of him. Whereupon, this becoming known, there arose discussions and very adverse judgments with regard to the work: some saying that Filippo had gone to bed in his vexation at finding that he had not the courage to raise the cupola, and that he was repenting of having meddled with the matter; while his friends defended him, saying that his anger, if anger it was, came from the outrage of having been given Lorenzo as colleague, but that his real trouble was colic, caused by fatiguing himself overmuch at the work. Now, while this noise was going on, the building was at a standstill, and almost all the work of the masons and stonecutters was suspended; and they murmured against Lorenzo, saying, "He is good enough at drawing the salary, but as for directing the work, not a bit of it! If we had not Filippo, or if he were ill for long, what would the other do? Is it Filippo's fault that he is ill?" The Wardens of Works, seeing themselves disgraced by this state of things, determined to go and find Filippo; and after arriving and sympathizing with him first about his illness, they told him in how great confusion the building stood and what troubles his illness had brought upon them. Whereupon Filippo, speaking with great heat both under the cloak of illness and from love of the work, replied, "Is not that Lorenzo there? Can he do nothing? And I marvel at you as well." Then the Wardens answered, "He will do naught without thee"; and Filippo retorted, "But I could do well without him." This retort, so acute and double-edged, was enough for them, and they went their way, convinced that Filippo was ill from nothing but the desire to work alone. They sent his friends, therefore, to get him out of bed, with the intention of removing Lorenzo from the work. Wherefore Filippo returned to the building, but, seeing that Lorenzo was still strongly favored and that he would have his salary without any labor whatsoever, he thought of another method whereby he might disgrace him and demonstrate conclusively his little knowledge in that profession; and he made the following discourse to the Wardens in the presence of Lorenzo: "My Lords the Wardens of Works, if the time that is lent to us to live were as surely ours as the certainty of dying, there is no doubt whatsoever that many things which are begun would be completed instead of remaining unfinished. The accident of this sickness from which I have suffered might have cut short my life and put a stop to the work; wherefore I have thought of a plan whereby, if I should ever fall sick again, or Lorenzo, which God forbid, one or the other may be able to pursue his part of the work. Even as your Lordships have divided the salary between us, let the work also be divided, to the end that each of us, being spurred to show his knowledge, may be confident of acquiring honor and profit from our Republic. Now there are two most difficult things which have to be put into execution at the present time: one is the making of the scaffoldings to enable the masons to do their work, which have to be used both within and without the building, where they must support men, stones, and lime, and sustain the crane for lifting weights, with other instruments of that kind; the other is the chain of ties which has to be placed above the twenty-four feet, surrounding and binding together the eight sides of the cupola, and clamping the framework together, so that it may bind and secure all the weight that is laid above, in such a manner that the weight may not force it out or stretch it, and that the whole structure may rest firmly on its own basis. Let Lorenzo, then, take one of these two works, whichever he may think himself best able to execute; and I will undertake to accomplish the other without difficulty, to the end that no more time may be lost." Hearing this, Lorenzo was forced for the sake of his honor to accept one of these tasks, and, although he did it very unwillingly, he resolved to take the chain of ties, as being the easier, relying on the advice of the masons and on the remembrance that in the vaulting of S. Giovanni in Florence there was a chain of stone ties, where-from he might take a part of the design, if not the whole. And so one put his hand to the scaffoldings and the other to the ties, and each carried out his work. The scaffoldings of Filippo were made with so great ingenuity and industry, that the very opposite opinion was held in this matter to that which many had previously conceived, for the builders stood on them, working and drawing up weights, as securely as if they had been on the surface of the ground; and the models of the said scaffoldings were preserved in the Office of Works. Lorenzo had the chain of ties made on one of the eight sides with the greatest difficulty; and when it was finished, the Wardens caused Filippo to look at it. To them he said nothing, but he discoursed thereon with some of his friends, saying that it was necessary to have some form of fastening different from that one, and to apply it in a better manner than had been done, and that it was not strong enough to withstand the weight that was to be laid above, for it did not bind the masonry together firmly enough; adding that the supplies given to Lorenzo, as well as the chain that he had caused to be made, had been simply thrown away. The opinion of Filippo became known, and he was charged to show what was the best way of making such a chain. Whereupon, having already made designs and models, he immediately showed them, and when they had been seen by the Wardens and the other masters, it was recognized into what great error they had fallen by favoring Lorenzo; and wishing to atone for this error and to show that they knew what was good, they made Filippo overseer and superintendent of the whole construction for life, saying that nothing should be done in that work without his command. And as a proof of approbation they gave him one hundred florins, and voted him an allowance of one hundred florins a year as a provision for life. Wherefore, giving orders for the building to be pushed on, he pursued it with such scrupulous care and so great attention, that not a stone could be put into place without his having wished to see it.

Lorenzo, on the other hand, finding himself vanquished, and, as it were, put to shame, was favored and assisted by his friends so powerfully that he went on drawing his salary, claiming that he could not be dismissed until three years had passed.

Filippo was for ever making, on the slightest occasion, designs and models of stages for the builders and of machines for lifting weights. But this did not prevent certain malicious persons, friends of Lorenzo, from putting Filippo into despair by spending their whole time in making models in opposition to his, insomuch that some were made by one Maestro Antonio da Verzelli and other favored masters, and were brought into notice now by one citizen and now by another, demonstrating their inconstancy, their little knowledge, and their even smaller understanding, since, having perfection in their grasp, they brought forward the imperfect and the useless.

The ties were now finished right round the eight sides, and the masons, being encouraged, were laboring valiantly; but being pressed more than usual by Filippo, and resenting certain reprimands received with regard to the building and other things that were happening every day, they had conceived a grievance against him. Wherefore, moved by this and by envy, the foremen leagued themselves together into a faction and declared that the work was laborious and dangerous, and that they would not build the cupola without great payment—although their pay had been raised higher than usual—thinking in this way to take vengeance on Filippo and to gain profit for themselves. This affair displeased the Wardens and also Filippo, who, having pondered over it, made up his mind one Saturday evening to dismiss them all. They, seeing themselves dismissed and not knowing how the matter would end, were very evilly disposed; but on the following Monday Filippo set ten Lombards to work, and by standing ever over them and saying, "Do this here," and, "Do that there," he taught them so much in one day that they worked there for many weeks. The masons, on the other hand, seeing themselves dismissed, deprived of their work, and thus disgraced, and having no work as profitable as this, sent mediators to Filippo, saying that they would willingly return, and recommending themselves to him as much as they were able. Filippo kept them for many days in suspense as to his willingness to take them back; then he reinstated them at lower wages than they had before; and thus where they thought to gain they lost, and in taking vengeance on Filippo they brought harm and disgrace on themselves.

The murmurings were now silenced, and meanwhile, on seeing that building being raised so readily, men had come to recognize the genius of Filippo; and it was already held by those who were not prejudiced that he had shown such courage as perchance no ancient or modern architect had shown in his works. This came to pass because he brought out his model, wherein all could see how much thought he had given to the planning of the staircases and of the lights both within and without, in order that no one might be injured in the darkness by reason of fear, and how many diverse balusters of iron he had placed where the ascent was steep, for the staircases, arranging them with much consideration. Besides this, he had even thought of the irons for fixing scaffoldings within, in case mosaics or paintings had ever to be wrought there; and in like manner, by placing the different kinds of water conduits, some covered and some uncovered, in the least dangerous positions, and by duly accompanying these with holes and diverse apertures, to the end that the force of the winds might be broken and that neither exhalations nor the tremblings of the earth might be able to do any harm, he showed how great assistance he had received from his studies during the many years that he stayed in Rome. And in addition, when men considered what he had done in the way of dovetailing, joining, fixing, and binding together the stones, it made them marvel and tremble to think that one single mind should have been capable of all that the mind of Filippo had proved itself able to execute. So greatly did his powers continue to increase that there was nothing, however difficult and formidable, that he did not render easy and simple; and this he showed in the lifting of weights by means of counterweights and wheels, so that one ox could raise what six pairs could scarcely have raised before.

The building had now risen to such a height that it was a very great inconvenience for anyone who had climbed to the top to descend to the ground, and the builders lost much time in going to eat and drink, and suffered great discomfort in the heat of the day. Filippo therefore made arrangements for eating-houses with kitchens to be opened on the cupola, and for wine to be sold there, so that no one had to leave his labor until the evening, which was convenient for the men and very advantageous for the work. Seeing the work making great progress and succeeding so happily, Filippo had grown so greatly in courage that he was continually laboring, going in person to the furnaces where the bricks were being shaped and demanding to see the clay and to feel its consistency, and insisting on selecting them with his own hand when baked, with the greatest diligence. When the stonecutters were working at the stones, he would look at them to see if they showed flaws and if they were hard, and he would give the men models in wood or wax, or made simply out of turnips; and he would also make iron tools for the smiths. He invented hinges with heads, and hinge-hooks, and he did much to facilitate architecture, which was certainly brought by him to a perfection such as it probably had never enjoyed among the Tuscans.

Seeing that the two vaults were beginning to close in on the round window where the lantern was to rise, it now remained to Filippo (who had made many models of clay and of wood for both the one and the other in Rome and in Florence, without showing them) to make up his mind finally which of these he would put into execution. Wherefore, having determined to finish the gallery, he made diverse designs, which remained after his death in the Office of Works; but they have since been lost by reason of the negligence of those officials. In our own day, to the end that the whole might be completed, a part of it was made on one of the eight sides, but by the advice of Michelagnolo Buonarroti it was abandoned and not carried further, because it clashed with the original plan. Filippo also made with his own hand a model for the lantern; this was octagonal, with proportions in harmony with those of the cupola, and it turned out very beautiful in invention, variety, and adornment. He made therein the staircase for ascending to the ball, which was something divine, but, since Filippo had stopped up the entrance with a piece of wood let in below, no one save himself knew of this staircase. And although he was praised and had now overcome the envy and the arrogance of many, he could not prevent all the other masters who were in Florence from setting themselves, at the sight of this model, to make others in various fashions, and finally a lady of the house of Gaddi had the courage to compete with the one made by Filippo. But he, meanwhile, kept laughing at their presumption, and when many of his friends told him that he should not show his model to any craftsmen, lest they should learn from it, he would answer that there was but one true model and that the others were of no account. Some of the other masters had used some of the parts of Filippo's model for their own, and Filippo, on seeing these, would say, "The next model that this man makes will be my very own." Filippo's model was infinitely praised by all; only, not seeing therein the staircase for ascending to the ball, they complained that it was defective. The Wardens determined, none the less, to give him the commission for the said work, but on the condition that he should show them the staircase. Whereupon Filippo, removing the small piece of wood that there was at the foot of the model, showed in a pilaster the staircase that is seen at the present day, in the form of a hollow blow-pipe, having on one side a groove with rungs of bronze, whereby one ascends to the top, putting one foot after another. And because he could not live long enough, by reason of his old age, to see the lantern finished, he left or-

ders in his testament that it should be built as it stood in the
model and as he had directed in writing; protesting that otherwise the structure would collapse, since it was turned with
the quarter-acute arch, so that it was necessary to burden it
with this weight in order to make it stronger. He was not able
to see this edifice finished before his death, but he raised it
to the height of several feet, and caused almost all the marbles
that were going into it to be well wrought and prepared; and
the people, on seeing them prepared, were amazed that it
should be possible for him to propose to lay so great a weight
on that vaulting. It was the opinion of many ingenious men
that it would not bear the weight, and it appeared to them
great good-fortune that he had carried it so far, and a tempt-
ing of Providence to burden it so heavily. Filippo, ever laughing to himself, and having prepared all the machines and all
the instruments that were to be used in building it, spent all
his time and thought in foreseeing, anticipating, and providing for every detail, even to the point of guarding against the
chipping of the dressed marbles as they were drawn up, insomuch that the arches of the tabernacles were built with
wooden protections; while for the rest, as it has been said,
there were written directions and models.

How beautiful is this building it demonstrates by itself.
From the level of the ground to the base of the lantern it is
three hundred and eight feet in height; the body of the lantern is seventy-two feet; the copper ball, eight feet; the cross,
sixteen feet; and the whole is four hundred and four feet. And
it can be said with confidence that the ancients never went
so high with their buildings, and never exposed themselves to
so great a risk as to try to challenge the heavens, even as this
structure truly appears to challenge them, seeing that it rises
to such a height that the mountains round Florence appear
no higher. And it seems, in truth, that the heavens are envious of it, since the lightning keeps on striking it every day.

The Church of S. Lorenzo had been begun in Florence at
this time by order of the people of that quarter, who had

made the Prior superintendent of that building. This person made profession of much knowledge in architecture, and was ever amusing himself therewith by way of pastime. And they had already begun the building by making piers of brick, when Giovanni di Bicci de' Medici, who had promised the people of that quarter and the Prior to have the sacristy and a chapel made at his own expense, invited Filippo one morning to dine with him, and after much discourse asked him what he thought of the beginning of S. Lorenzo. Filippo was constrained by the entreaties of Giovanni to say what he thought, and being compelled to speak the truth, he criticized it in many respects, as something designed by a person who had perchance more learning than experience of buildings of that sort. Whereupon Giovanni asked Filippo if something better and more beautiful could be made: to which Filippo replied, "Without a doubt, and I marvel that you, being the chief in the enterprise, do not devote a few thousand crowns to building a body of a church with all its parts worthy of the place and of so many noble owners of tombs, who, seeing it begun, will proceed with their chapels to the best of their power; above all, because there remains no memorial of us save walls, which bear testimony for hundreds and thousands of years to those who built them." Giovanni, encouraged by the words of Filippo, determined to build the sacristy and the principal chapel, together with the whole body of the church, although only seven families were willing to cooperate, since the others had not the means: these seven were the Rondinelli, Ginori, Dalla Stufa, Neroni, Ciai, Marignolli, Martelli, and Marco di Luca, and these chapels were to be made in the cross. The sacristy was the first part to be undertaken, and afterwards the church, little by little. The other chapels along the length of the church came to be granted afterwards, one by one, to other citizens of the quarter. The roofing of the sacristy was not finished when Giovanni de' Medici passed to the other life, leaving behind him his son Cosimo, who, having a greater spirit than his father and delighting in memorials, caused this one to be carried on. It was the first edifice that he erected, and he took so great delight therein that from that time onwards up to his death he was for ever building. Cosimo pressed this work forward with greater ardor, and while one part was being begun, he would have another finished. Looking on the work as a pastime, he was almost always there, and it was his solicitude that caused Filippo to finish the sacristy, and Donatello to make the stucco-work, with the stone ornaments for those little doors and the doors of bronze. In the middle of the sacristy, where the priests don their vestments, he had a tomb made for his father Giovanni, under a great slab of marble supported by four little columns; and in the same place he made a tomb for his own family, separating that of the women from that of the men. In one of the two little rooms that are on either side of the altar in the said sacristy he made a well in one corner, with a place for a lavatory. In short, everything in this building is seen to have been built with much judgment. Giovanni and the others had arranged to make the choir in the middle, below the tribune; but Cosimo changed this at the wish of Filippo, who made the principal chapel—which had been designed at first as a smaller recess—so much greater, that he was able to make the choir therein, as it is at present. This being finished, there remained to be made the central tribune and the rest of the church; but this tribune, with the rest, was not vaulted until after the death of Filippo.

Filippo also designed a rich and magnificent palace for Messer Luca Pitti at a place called Ruciano, outside the Porta a San Niccolò in Florence, but this failed by a great measure to equal the one that he began in Florence for the same man, carrying it to the second range of windows, with such grandeur and magnificence that nothing more rare or more magnificent has yet been seen in the Tuscan manner. The doors of this palace are double, with the opening thirty-two feet in length and sixteen in breadth; the windows both of the first and second range are in every way similar to these doors, and the vaultings double; and the whole edifice is so masterly in design, that any more beautiful or more magnificent architecture cannot be imagined. The builder of this palace was Luca Fancelli, an architect of Florence, who erected many buildings for Filippo. This palace was bought not many years ago by the most Illustrious Lady Leonora di Toledo, Duchess of Florence, on the advice of the most Illustrious Lord Duke Cosimo, her consort; and she increased the grounds all round it so greatly that she made a very large garden, partly on the plain, partly on the top of the hill, and partly on the slope, filling it with all the sorts of trees both of the garden and of the forest, most beautifully laid out, and making most delightful little groves with innumerable sorts of evergreens, which flourish in every season; to say nothing of the waters, the fountains, the conduits, the fishponds, the fowling-places, the espaliers, and an infinity of other things worthy of a magnanimous prince, about which I will be silent, because it is not possible, without seeing them, ever to imagine their grandeur and their beauty. And in truth Duke Cosimo could have chanced upon nothing more worthy of the power and greatness of his mind than this palace, which might truly appear to have been erected by Messer Luca Pitti, from the design of Brunelleschi, for his most Illustrious Excellency. Messer Luca left it unfinished by reason of his cares in connection with the State, and his heirs, having no means wherewith to complete it, and being unwilling to let it go to ruin, were content to make it over to the Duchess, who was ever spending money on it as long as she lived, but not so much as to give hope that it would be soon finished. It is true, indeed, according to what I once heard, that she was minded to spend 40,000 ducats in one year alone, if she lived, in order to see it, if not finished, at least well on the way to completion. And because the model of Filippo has not been found, his Excellency has caused Bartolommeo Ammanati, an excellent sculptor and architect, to make another, according to which the work is being carried on; and a great part of the courtyard is already completed in rustic work, similar to the exterior. And in truth, if one considers the grandeur of this work, one marvels how the mind of Filippo could conceive so great an edifice, which is truly magnificent not only in the external façade, but also in the distribution of all the apartments. I say nothing of the view, which is most beautiful, and of the kind of theater formed by the most lovely hills that rise round the palace in the direction of the walls, because, as I have said, it would take too long to try to describe them in full, nor could anyone, without seeing this palace, imagine how greatly superior it is to any other royal edifice whatsoever.

One year the Lenten sermons in S. Spirito had been preached by Maestro Francesco Zoppo, who was then very dear to the people of Florence, and he had strongly recommended the claims of that convent, of the school for youths, and particularly of the church, which had been burnt down about that time. Whereupon the chief men of that quarter, Lorenzo Ridolfi, Bartolommeo Corbinelli, Neri di Gino Capponi, and Goro di Stagio Dati, with very many other citizens, obtained an order from the Signoria for the rebuilding of the Church of S. Spirito, and made Stoldo Frescobaldi *provveditore*. This man, by reason of the interest that he had in the old church, the principal chapel and the high altar of which belonged to his house, took very great pains therewith; nay, at the beginning, before the money had been collected from the taxes imposed on the owners of burial places and chapels, he spent many thousands of crowns of his own, for which he was repaid.

Now, after the matter had been discussed, Filippo was sent for and asked to make a model with all the features, both useful and honorable, that might be possible and suitable to a Christian church. Whereupon he urged strongly that the ground-plan of that edifice should be turned right round, because he greatly desired that the square should extend to the bank of the Arno, to the end that all those who passed that way from Genoa, from the Riviera, from the Lunigiana, and from the districts of Pisa and Lucca, might see the magnificence of that building. But since certain citizens objected, refusing to have their houses pulled down, the desire of Filippo did not take effect. He made the model of the church, therefore, with that of the habitation of the monks, in the form wherein it stands to-day. The length of the church was three hundred and twenty-two feet, and the width one hundred and eight feet, and it was so well planned, both in the ordering of the columns and in the rest of the ornaments, that it would be impossible to make a work richer, more lovely, or more graceful than that one. And in truth, but for the malevolence of those who are ever spoiling the beautiful beginnings of any work in order to appear to have more understanding than others, this would now be the most perfect church in Christendom.

Filippo was very humorous in his discourse and very acute in repartee, as he showed when he wished to hit at Lorenzo Ghiberti, who had bought a farm on Monte Morello, called Lepriano, on which he spent twice as much as he gained by way of income, so that he grew weary of this and sold it. Some one asked Filippo what was the best thing that Lorenzo had ever done, thinking perchance, by reason of the enmity between them, that he would criticize Lorenzo; and he replied, "The selling of Lepriano." Finally, having now grown very old—he was sixty-nine years of age—he passed to a better life on April 16, in the year 1446, after having exhausted himself greatly in making the works that enabled him to win an honored name on earth and to obtain a place of repose in Heaven. His death caused infinite grief to his country, which recognized and esteemed him much more when dead than it had done when he was alive; and he was buried with the most honorable obsequies and distinctions in S. Maria del Fiore, although his burial place was in S. Marco, under the pulpit opposite to the door, where there is a coat of arms with two fig leaves and certain green waves on a field of gold, because his family came from the district of Ferrara, that is, from Ficaruolo, a township on the Po, as it is shown by the leaves, which denote the place, and by the waves, which signify the river. He was mourned by innumerable brother-craftsmen, and particularly by the poorer among them, whom he was ever helping. Thus then, living the life of a Christian, he left to the world the sweet savor of his goodness and of his noble talents. It seems to me that it can be said for him that from the time of the ancient Greeks and Romans to our own there has been no rarer or more excellent master than Filippo; and he is all the more worthy of praise because in his times the German manner was held in veneration throughout all Italy and practiced by the old craftsmen, as it may be seen in innumerable edifices. He recovered the ancient mouldings and restored the Tuscan, Corinthian, Doric and Ionic Orders to their original forms.

DONATELLO

[*Donato di Niccolò di Betto Bardi, commonly known as
Donatello, was born, probably, in 1386 and died in 1466.*]

DONATO, who was called Donatello by his relatives and
wrote his name thus on some of his works, was born in
Florence in the year 1386. Devoting himself to the arts of
design, he was not only a very rare sculptor and a marvelous
statuary, but also a practiced worker in stucco, an able master of perspective, and greatly esteemed as an architect; and
his works showed so great grace, design, and excellence, that
they were held to approach more nearly to the marvelous
works of the ancient Greeks and Romans than those of any
other craftsman whatsoever. Wherefore it is with good reason
that he is ranked as the first who made a good use of the invention of scenes in bas-relief, which he wrought so well that
it is recognized from the thought, the facility, and the mastery that he showed therein, that he had a true understanding
of them, making them with a beauty far beyond the ordinary;
for not only did no craftsman in this period ever surpass him,
but no one even in our own age has equaled him.

Donatello was brought up from his early childhood in the
house of Ruberto Martelli, where, by his good qualities and
by his zealous talent, he won the affection not only of Martelli himself but of all that noble family. As a youth he
wrought many things, which were not held in great account,
by reason of their number; but what made him known for
what he was and gave him a name was an Annunciation in
grey-stone, which was placed close to the altar of the Chapel

of the Cavalcanti, in the Church of S. Croce in Florence. For this he made an ornament composed in the grotesque manner, with a base of varied intertwined work and a decoration of quadrantal shape, adding six boys bearing certain festoons, who appear to be holding one another securely with their arms in their fear of the height. But the greatest genius and art that he showed was in the figure of the Virgin, who, alarmed by the unexpected apparition of the Angel, is making a most becoming reverence with a sweet and timid movement of her person, turning with most beautiful grace toward him who is saluting her, in a manner that there are seen in her countenance that humility and gratitude which are due to one who presents an unexpected gift, and the more when the gift is a great one. Besides this, Donatello showed a masterly flow of curves and folds in the draperies of that Madonna and of the Angel, demonstrating with the suggestion of the nude forms below how he was seeking to recover the beauty of the ancients, which had lain hidden for so many years; and he displayed so great facility and art in this work, that nothing more could be desired, in fact, with regard to design, judgment, and mastery in handling the chisel.

In the same church, beside the scene painted by Taddeo Gaddi, he made a Crucifix of wood with extraordinary care; and when he had finished this, thinking that he had made a very rare work, he showed it to Filippo di Ser Brunelleschi, who was very much his friend, wishing to have his opinion. Filippo, whom the words of Donatello had led to expect something much better, smiled slightly on seeing it. Donatello, perceiving this, besought him by all the friendship between them to tell him his opinion; whereupon Filippo, who was most obliging, replied that it appeared to him that Donatello had placed a ploughman on the Cross, and not a body like that of Jesus Christ, which was most delicate and in all its parts the most perfect human form that was ever born. Donatello, hearing himself censured, and that more sharply than he expected, whereas he was hoping to be praised, replied, "If it were as easy to make this figure as to judge it, my Christ would appear to thee to be Christ and not a ploughman; take wood, therefore, and try to make one thyself." Filippo, without another word, returned home and set to work to make a Crucifix, without letting anyone know; and seeking to surpass Donatello in order not to confound his own judgment, after many months he brought it to the height of perfection. This done, he invited Donatello one morning to dine with him, and Donatello accepted the invitation. Whereupon, as they were going together to the house of Filippo, they came to the Mercato Vecchio, where Filippo bought some things and gave them to Donatello, saying, "Do thou go with these things to the house and wait for me there, I am coming in a moment." Donatello, therefore, entering the house and going into the hall, saw the Crucifix of Filippo, placed in a good light; and stopping short to study it, he found it so perfectly finished, that, being overcome and full of amazement, like one distraught, he spread out his hands, which were holding up his apron; whereupon the eggs, the cheese, and all the other things fell to the ground, and everything was broken to pieces. But he was still marveling and standing like one possessed, when Filippo came up and said with a laugh, "What is thy intention, Donatello, and what are we to have for dinner, now that thou hast upset everything?" "For my part," answered Donatello, "I have had my share for this morning: if thou must have thine, take it. But enough; it is thy work to make Christ and mine to make ploughmen."

In the Church of S. Giovanni in the same city Donatello made a tomb for Pope Giovanni Coscia, who had been deposed from the Pontificate by the Council of Constance. This tomb he was commissioned to make by Cosimo de' Medici, who was very much the friend of the said Coscia. He wrought therein with his own hand the figure of the dead man in gilded bronze, together with the marble statues of Hope and Charity that are there; and his pupil Michelozzo made the figure of Faith. In the same church, opposite to this work, there is a wooden figure by the hand of Donatello of S. Mary Magdalene in Penitence, very beautiful and excellently wrought, showing her wasted away by her fastings and abstinence, insomuch that it displays in all its parts an admirable perfection of anatomical knowledge. On a column of granite in the Mercato Vecchio there is a figure of Abundance in hard grey-stone by the hand of Donatello, standing quite by itself, so well wrought that it is consummately praised by craftsmen and by all good judges of art. The column on which this statue is placed was formerly in S. Giovanni, where there are the others of granite supporting the gallery within; it was removed and its place was taken by a fluted column, on which, in the middle of that temple, there once stood the statue of Mars which was taken away when the Florentines were converted to the faith of Jesus Christ. The same man, while still a youth, made a figure of the Prophet Daniel in marble for the façade of S. Maria del Fiore, and afterwards one of S. John the Evangelist seated, eight feet high, and clothed in a simple garment: which figure is much extolled. On one corner of the same place, on the side that faces toward the Via del Cocomero, there is an old man between two columns, more akin to the ancient manner than any other work that there is to be seen by the hand of Donatello, the head revealing the thoughts that length of years brings to those who are exhausted by time and labor. Within the said church, likewise, he made the ornament for the organ, which stands over the door of the old sacristy, with those figures so boldly sketched, as it has been said, that they appear to the eye to have actual life and movement. Wherefore it may be said of this man that he worked as much with his judgment as with his hands, seeing that many things are wrought which appear beautiful in the rooms where they are made, and afterwards, on being taken thence and set in another place, in a different light or at a greater height, present a different appearance, and turn out the contrary to what they appeared; whereas Donatello made his figures in such a manner, that in the room where he was working they did not appear half as good as they turned out to be in the positions where they were placed. For the new sacristy of the same church he made the design for those boys who uphold the festoons that go round the frieze, and likewise the design for the figures that were wrought in the glass of the round window which is below the cupola, namely, that one which contains the Coronation of Our Lady; which design is greatly superior to those of the other round windows, as it is clearly evident. For S. Michele in Orto in the said city he wrought the marble statue of S. Peter which is to be seen there, a most masterly and admirable figure, for the Guild of Butchers; and for the Guild of Linen-manufacturers he wrought the figure of S. Mark the Evangelist, which, after being commissioned to make it in company with Filippo Brunelleschi, he finished by himself with the consent of Filippo. This figure was wrought by Donatello with so great judgment that its excellence was not recognized, while it stood on the ground, by those who had no judgment, and the Consuls of that Guild were inclined to refuse to have it put into place; whereupon Donatello besought them to let him set it on high, saying that he wished to work on it and to show them a different figure as the result. His request being granted, he covered it up for a fortnight, and then uncovered it without having otherwise touched it, filling everyone with wonder.

For the Guild of Armorers he made a most spirited figure of S. George in armor, in the head of which there may be seen the beauty of youth, courage and valor in arms, and a proud and terrible ardor; and there is a marvelous suggestion of life bursting out of the stone. It is certain that no modern figure in marble has yet shown such vivacity and such spirit as nature and art produced in this one by means of the hand of Donatello. In the base that supports the shrine enclosing that figure he wrought in marble the story of the Saint killing the Dragon, in bas-relief, wherein there is a horse that is much esteemed and greatly extolled; and in the frontal he made a half-length figure of God the Father in bas-relief. Opposite to the church of the said oratory he wrought the marble shrine for the Mercatanzia, following the ancient Order known as Corinthian, and departing entirely from the German manner; this shrine was meant to contain two statues, but he refused to make them because he could not come to an agreement about the price. After his death these figures were made in bronze by Andrea del Verrocchio, as it will be told. For the main front of the Campanile of S. Maria del Fiore he wrought four figures in marble, ten feet in height, of which the two in the middle are portrayed from life, one being Francesco Soderini as a youth, and the other Giovanni di Barduccio Cherichini, now called Il Zuccone. The latter was held to be a very rare work and the most beautiful that Donatello ever made, and when he wished to take an oath that would command belief he was wont to say, "By the faith that I place in my Zuccone"; and the while that he was working on it, he would keep gazing at it and saying, "Speak, speak, plague take thee, speak!" Over the door of the campanile, on the side facing the Canon's house, he made Abraham about to sacrifice Isaac, with another Prophet; and these figures were placed between two other statues.

For the Signoria of that city he made a casting in metal which was placed under an arch of their Loggia in the Piazza, representing Judith cutting off the head of Holofernes; a work of great excellence and mastery, which, if one considers the simplicity of the garments and aspect of Judith on the surface, reveals very clearly below the surface the great spirit of that woman and the assistance given to her by God, even as one sees the effect of wine and sleep in the expression of

Holofernes, and death in his limbs, which have lost all life and are shown cold and limp. This work was so well executed by Donatello that the casting came out delicate and very beautiful, and it was afterwards finished so excellently that it is a very great marvel to behold. The base, likewise, which is a baluster of granite, simple in design, appears full of grace and presents an aspect pleasing to the eye. He was so well satisfied with this work that he deigned to place his name on it, which he had not done on the others; and it is seen in these words, "Donatelli opus." In the courtyard of the Palace of the said Signoria there is a life-size David, nude and in bronze. Having cut off the head of Goliath, he is raising one foot and placing it on him, holding a sword in his right hand. This figure is so natural in its vivacity and its softness, that it is almost impossible for craftsmen to believe that it was not moulded on the living form. This statue once stood in the courtyard of the house of the Medici, but it was transported to the said place on the exile of Cosimo. In our own day Duke Cosimo, having made a fountain on the spot occupied by this statue, had it removed, and it is being kept for a very large courtyard that he intends to make at the back of the palace, that is, where the lions formerly stood. In the hall where there is the clock of Lorenzo della Volpaia, on the left, there is a very beautiful David in marble; between his legs, under his feet, he has the head of the dead Goliath, and in his hand he holds the sling wherewith he slew him. In the first courtyard of the house of the Medici there are eight medallions of marble, wherein there are copies of ancient cameos and of the reverse sides of medals, with certain scenes, all made by him and very beautiful, which are built into the frieze between the windows and the architrave above the arches of the *loggie*. In like manner he restored an ancient statue of Marsyas in white marble, which was placed at the entrance of the garden; and a great number of ancient heads, which were placed over the doors, were restored and embellished by him with wings and diamonds (the emblem of Cosimo), wrought very well in stucco. He made a very lovely vessel of granite, which poured forth water, and he wrought a similar one, which also pours forth water, for the garden of the Pazzi in Florence. In the said Palace of the Medici there are Madonnas of marble and bronze made in bas-relief, besides some scenes in marble with most beautiful figures, marvelous in their flat-relief. So great was the love that Cosimo bore to the talent of Donatello that he kept him continually at work, and Donatello, on the other hand, bore so great love to Cosimo that he could divine his patron's every wish from the slightest sign, and obeyed him in all things.

It is said that a Genoese merchant caused Donatello to make a life-size head of bronze, which was very beautiful and also very light, because it had to be carried to a great distance; and that the commission for this work came to him through the recommendation of Cosimo. Now, when the head was finished and the merchant came to pay for it, it appeared to him that Donatello was asking too much; wherefore the matter was referred to Cosimo, who had the head carried to the upper court of the palace and placed between the battlements that overlook the street, to the end that it might be seen better. When Cosimo sought to settle the difference, he found the offer of the merchant very far from the demand of Donatello, and he turned round and said that it was too little. Whereupon the merchant, thinking it too much, said that Donatello had wrought it in a month or little more, and that this meant a gain of more than half a florin a day. Donatello, thinking this too much of an insult, turned round in anger and said to the merchant that in the hundredth part of an hour he would have been able to spoil the value of a year's labor; and giving the head a push, he sent it flying straightway into the street below, where it broke into a thousand pieces; saying to him that this showed that he was more used to bargaining for beans than for statues. Wherefore the merchant, regretting his meanness, offered to give him double the sum if he would make another; but neither his promises nor the entreaties of Cosimo could induce Donatello to make it again. In the houses of the Martelli there are many scenes in marble and in bronze; among others, a David six feet high, with many other works presented by him as a free gift to that family in proof of the devotion and love that he bore them; above all, a S. John of marble, made by him in the round and six feet high, a very rare work, which is to-day in the house of the heirs of Ruberto Martelli. With regard to this work, a legal agreement was made to the effect that it should be neither pledged, nor sold, nor given away, without heavy penalties, as a testimony and token of the affection shown by them to Donatello, and by him to them out of gratitude that he had learnt his art through the protection and the opportunities that he received from them.

He also made a tomb of marble for an Archbishop, which was sent to Naples and is in S. Angelo di Seggio di Nido; in this tomb there are three figures in the round that support the sarcophagus with their heads, and on the sarcophagus itself is a scene in bas-relief, so beautiful that it commands infinite praise. In the house of the Count of Matalone, in the same city, there is the head of a horse by the hand of Donatello, so beautiful that many take it for an antique. In the township of Prato he wrought the marble pulpit where the Girdle is shown, in which, in several compartments, he carved a dance of children so beautiful and so admirable, that he may be said to have demonstrated the perfection of his art no less in this work than in his others. To support this pulpit, moreover, he made two capitals of bronze, one of which is still there, while the other was carried away by the Spaniards who sacked that district.

It came to pass about this time that the Signoria of Venice, hearing of his fame, sent for him to the end that he might make the monument of Gattamelata in the city of Padua; wherefore he went there right willingly and made the bronze horse that is on the Piazza di S. Antonio, wherein are perceived the panting and neighing of the horse, with great spirit and pride, most vividly expressed by his art, in the figure of the rider. And Donatello proved himself such a master in the proportions and excellence of so great a casting, that he can truly bear comparison with any ancient craftsman in movement, design, art, proportion, and diligence; wherefore it not only astonished all who saw it then, but continues to astonish every person who sees it at the present day. The Paduans, moved by this, did their utmost to make him their fellow-citizen, and sought to detain him with every sort of endearment. In order to keep him in their midst, they commissioned him to make the stories of S. Anthony of Padua on the predella of the high altar in the Church of the Friars Minor, which are in bas-relief, wrought with so great judgment, that the most excellent masters of that art stand marveling and amazed before them, as they consider their beautiful and varied compositions, with the great abundance of extraordinary figures and diminishing perspectives. Very beautiful, likewise, are the Marys that he made on the altar-dossal, lamenting the Dead Christ. In the house of one of the Counts Capodilista he wrought the skeleton of a horse in wood, which is still to be seen to-day without the neck; wherein the various parts are joined together with so much method, that, if one considers the manner of this work, one can judge of the ingenuity of his brain and the greatness of his mind. In a convent of nuns he made a S. Sebastian in wood at the request of a chaplain, a Florentine, who was their friend and an intimate of his own. This man brought him a figure of that Saint that they had, old and clumsy, beseeching him to make the new one like it. Wherefore Donatello strove to imitate it in order to please the chaplain and the nuns, but, although he imitated it, clumsy as it was, he could not help showing in his own the usual excellence of his art. Together with this figure he made many others in clay and in stucco, and on one end of an old piece of marble that the said nuns had in their garden he carved a very beautiful Madonna. Throughout that whole city, likewise, there are innumerable works by his hand, by reason of which he was held by the Paduans to be a marvel and was praised by every man of understanding; but he determined to return to Florence, saying that if he remained any longer in Padua he would forget everything that he knew, being so greatly praised there by all, and that he was glad to return to his own country, where he would gain nothing but censure, since such censure would urge him to study and would enable him to attain to greater glory. Having departed from Padua, therefore, he returned by way of Venice, where, as a mark of his friendliness toward the Florentine people, he made them a present of a S. John the Baptist, wrought by him in wood with very great diligence and study, for their chapel in the Church of the Friars Minor. In the city of Faenza he carved a S. John and a S. Jerome in wood, which are no less esteemed than his other works.

Afterwards, having returned to Tuscany, he made a marble tomb, with a very beautiful scene, in the Pieve of Montepulciano, and a lavatory of marble, on which Andrea Verrocchio also worked, in the Sacristy of S. Lorenzo in Florence; and in the house of Lorenzo della Stufa he wrought some heads and figures that are very spirited and vivacious. Then, departing from Florence, he betook himself to Rome, in order to try to imitate the antiques to the best of his ability; and during this time, while studying these, he made a tabernacle of the Sacrament in stone, which is to be seen in S. Pietro at the present day. Passing through Siena on his way back to Florence, he undertook to make a door of bronze for the Baptistery of S. Giovanni; and he had already made the wooden model, and the wax moulds were almost finished and successfully covered with the outer mould, ready for the casting, when there arrived, on his way back from Rome, one Bernardetto di Mona Papera, a Florentine goldsmith and an intimate friend of Donatello, who wrought upon him so strongly both with words and in other ways, either for some business of his own or for some other reason, that he brought him back to Florence; wherefore that work remained unfinished, nay, not begun. There only remained in the Office of Works of the Duomo in that city a S. John the Baptist in bronze by his hand, with the right arm missing from the elbow downwards; and this Donatello is said to have done because he had not been paid in full.

Having returned to Florence, therefore, he wrought the Sacristy of S. Lorenzo in stucco for Cosimo de' Medici, making four medallions on the pendentives of the vault containing stories of the Evangelists, with grounds in perspective, partly painted and partly in bas-relief. And in the said place he made two very beautiful little doors of bronze in bas-relief, with the Apostles, Martyrs, and Confessors; and above these he made some flat niches, one containing a S. Laurence and a S. Stephen, and the other S. Cosimo and S. Damiano. He also designed the bronze pulpits that contain the Passion of Christ, a work displaying design, force, invention, and an abundance of figures and buildings; but these his old age prevented him from executing, and his pupil Bertoldo finished them and brought them to the utmost perfection. Over the door of S. Croce there is still to be seen a S. Louis wrought by him in bronze, ten feet high; for this someone criticized him, saying that it was stupid and perhaps the least excellent work that he had ever made, and he answered that he had made it so of set purpose, seeing that the Saint had been stupid to give up his throne and become a monk. The same man made the head of the wife of the said Cosimo de' Medici in bronze, and this head is preserved in the *guardaroba* of the Lord Duke Cosimo, wherein there are many other works in bronze and marble by the hand of Donatello.

The talent of Donatello was such, and he was so admirable in all his actions, that he may be said to have been one of the first to give light, by his practice, judgment, and knowledge, to the art of sculpture and of good design among the moderns; and he deserves all the more commendation, because in his day, apart from the columns, sarcophagi, and triumphal arches, there were no antiquities revealed above the earth. And it was through him, chiefly, that there arose in Cosimo de' Medici the desire to introduce into Florence the antiquities that were and are in the house of the Medici; all of which he restored with his own hand. He was most liberal, gracious, and courteous, and more careful for his friends than for himself; nor did he give thought to money, but kept his in a basket suspended by a cord from the ceiling, wherefore all his workmen and friends could take what they needed without saying a word to him. He passed his old age most joyously, and, having become decrepit, he had to be succored by Cosimo and by others of his friends, being no longer able to work. It is said that Cosimo, being at the point of death, recommended him to the care of his son Piero, who, as a most diligent executor of his father's wishes, gave him a farm at Cafaggiuolo, which produced enough to enable him to live in comfort. At this Donatello made great rejoicing, thinking that he was thus more than secure from the danger of dying of hunger; but he had not held it a year before he returned to Piero and gave it back to him by public contract, declaring that he refused to lose his peace of mind by having to think of household cares and listen to the importunity of the peasant, who kept pestering him every third day—now because the wind had unroofed his dovecote, now because his cattle had been seized by the Commune for taxes, and now because a storm had robbed him of his wine and his fruit. He was so weary and disgusted with all this, that he would rather die of hunger than have to think of so many things. Piero laughed at the simplicity of Donatello; and in order to deliver him from this torment, he accepted the farm (for on this Donatello insisted), and assigned him an allowance of the same value or more from his own bank, to be paid in cash, which was handed over to him every week in the due proportion owing to him; whereby he was greatly contented. Thus, as a servant and friend of the house of Medici, he lived happily and free from care for the rest of his life. When he had reached the age of eighty, however, he was so palsied that he could no longer work in any fashion, and took to spending all his time in bed in a poor little house that he had in the Via del Cocomero, near the Nunnery of S. Niccolò; where, growing worse from day to day and wasting away little by little, he died on December 13, 1466. He was buried in the Church of S. Lorenzo, near the tomb of Cosimo, as he had himself directed, to the end that his dead body might be near him, even as he had been ever near him in spirit when alive.

The world remained so full of Donatello's works, that it may be affirmed right truly that no craftsman ever worked more than he did. For, delighting in every kind of work, he put his hand to anything, without considering whether it was of little or of great value. Nevertheless it was indispensable to sculpture, this vast activity of Donatello in making figures in every kind of relief, full, half, low, and the lowest; because, whereas in the good times of the ancient Greeks and Romans it was by means of many that it became perfect, he alone by the multitude of his works brought it back to marvelous perfection in our own age. Wherefore craftsmen should trace the greatness of this art rather to him than to any man born in modern times, seeing that, besides rendering the difficulties of the art easy, in the multitude of his works he combined together invention, design, practice, judgment, and every other quality that ever can or should be looked for in a divine genius. Donatello was very resolute and ready, executing all his works with consummate facility, and he always accomplished much more than he had promised.

PIERO DELLA FRANCESCA

[The birth date of Pietro dei Franceschi, known as Piero della Francesca, is unknown but he was active by 1439 and died in 1492.]

TRULY unhappy are those who, laboring at their studies in order to benefit others and to make their own name famous, are hindered by infirmity and sometimes by death from carrying to perfection the works that they have begun. Such was the case with Piero della Francesca of Borgo a San Sepolcro, who, having been held a rare master of the difficulties of drawing regular bodies, as well as of arithmetic and geometry, was yet not able—being overtaken in his old age by the infirmity of blindness, and finally by the close of his life—to bring to light his noble labors and the many books written by him, which are still preserved in the Borgo, his native place. The very man who should have striven with all his might to increase the glory and fame of Piero, from whom he had learnt all that he knew, was impious and malignant enough to seek to blot out the name of his teacher, and to usurp for himself the honor that was due to the other, publishing under his own name, Fra Luca del Borgo, all the labors of that good old man, who, besides the sciences named above, was excellent in painting.

Piero was born in Borgo a San Sepolcro, which is now a city, although it was not one then; and he was called della Francesca after the name of his mother, because she had been left pregnant with him at the death of her husband, his father, and because it was she who had brought him up and assisted him to attain to the rank that his good fortune held out to him. Piero applied himself in his youth to mathematics, and although it was settled when he was fifteen years of age that he was to be a painter, he never abandoned this study; nay, he made marvelous progress therein, as well as in painting. He was employed by Guidobaldo Feltro the elder, Duke of Urbino, for whom he made many very beautiful pictures with little figures, which have been for the most part ruined on the many occasions when that state has been harassed by wars. Nevertheless, there were preserved there some of his writings on geometry and perspective, in which sciences he was not inferior to any man of his own time, or perchance even to any man of any other time; as is demonstrated by all his works, which are full of perspectives, and particularly by a vase drawn in squares and sides, in such a manner that the base and the mouth can be seen from the front, from behind, and from the sides; which is certainly a marvelous thing, for he drew the smallest details therein with great subtlety, and foreshortened the curves of all the circles with much grace. Having thus acquired credit and fame at that Court, he resolved to make himself known in other places; wherefore he went to Pesaro and Ancona, whence, in the very thick of his work, he was summoned by Duke Borso to Ferrara, where he painted many apartments in his palace, which were afterwards destroyed by Duke Ercole the elder in the renovation of the palace. Afterwards, being summoned to Rome, he painted two scenes for Pope Nicholas V in the upper rooms of his palace, in competition with Bramante of Milan; but these also were thrown to the ground by Pope Julius II.

His work in Rome finished, Piero della Francesca returned to the Borgo, where his mother had just died; and on the inner side of the central door of the Pieve he painted two saints in fresco, which are held to be very beautiful. In the Convent of the Friars of S. Augustine he painted the panel of the high altar, which was a thing much extolled; and he wrought in fresco a Madonna della Misericordia for a company, or rather, as they call it, a confraternity; with a Resurrection of Christ in the Palazzo de' Conservadori, which is held the best of all the works that are in the said city, and the best that he ever made.

Going from Loreto to Arezzo, Piero painted for Luigi Bacci, a citizen of Arezzo, the Chapel of the High Altar of S. Francesco, belonging to that family, the vaulting of which had been already begun by Lorenzo di Bicci. In this work there are Stories of the Cross, from that wherein the sons of Adam are burying him and placing under his tongue the seed of the tree from which there came the wood for the said Cross, down to the Exaltation of the Cross itself performed by the Emperor Heraclius, who, walking barefoot and carrying it on his shoulder, is entering with it into Jerusalem. Here there are many beautiful conceptions and attitudes worthy to be extolled; such as, for example, the garments of the women of the Queen of Sheba, executed in a sweet and novel manner; many most lifelike portraits from nature of ancient persons; a row of Corinthian columns, divinely well proportioned; and a peasant who, leaning with his hands on his spade, stands listening to the words of S. Helena—while the three Crosses are being disinterred—with so great attention, that it would not be possible to improve it. Very well wrought, also, is the dead body that is restored to life at the touch of the Cross, together with the joy of S. Helena and the marveling of the bystanders, who are kneeling in adoration. But above every other consideration, whether of imagination or of art, is his painting of Night, with an angel in foreshortening who is flying with his head downwards, bringing the sign of victory to Constantine, who is sleeping in a pavilion, guarded by a chamberlain and some men-at-arms who are seen dimly through the darkness of the night; and with his own light the angel illuminates the pavilion, the men-at-arms, and all the surroundings. This is done with very great thought, for Piero gives us to know in this darkness how important it is to copy things as they are and to ever take them from the true model; which he did so well that he enabled the moderns to attain, by following him, to that supreme perfection wherein art is seen in our own time. In this same story he represented most successfully in a battle fear, animosity, dexterity, vehemence, and all the other emotions that can be imagined in men who are fighting, and likewise all the incidents of battle, together with an almost incredible carnage, what with the wounded, the fallen, and the dead. In these Piero counterfeited in fresco the glittering of their arms, for which he deserves no less praise than he does for the flight and submersion of Maxentius painted on the other wall, wherein he made a group of horses in foreshortening, so marvelously executed that they can be truly called too beautiful and too excellent for those times. In the same story he made a man, half nude and half clothed in the dress of a Saracen, riding a lean horse, which reveals a very great mastery of anatomy, a science little known in his age. For this work, therefore, he well deserved to be richly rewarded by Luigi Bacci, whom he portrayed there in the scene of the beheading of a King, together with Carlo and others of his brothers and many Aretines who were then distinguished in letters; and to be loved and revered ever afterwards, as he was, in that city, which he had made so illustrious with his works.

In Perugia, also, he wrought many works that are still to be seen in that city; as, for example, a panel in distemper in the Church of the Nuns of S. Anthony of Padua, containing a Madonna with the Child in her lap, S. Francis, S. Elizabeth, S. John the Baptist, and S. Anthony of Padua. Above these is a most beautiful Annunciation, with an Angel that seems truly to have come out of Heaven; and, what is more, a row of columns diminishing in perspective, which is indeed beautiful. In the predella there are scenes with little figures, representing S. Anthony restoring a boy to life; S. Elizabeth saving a child that has fallen into a well; and S. Francis receiving the Stigmata.

Piero, as it has been said, was a very zealous student of art, and gave no little attention to perspective; and he had a very good knowledge of Euclid, insomuch that he understood all the best curves drawn in regular bodies better than any other geometrician, and the clearest elucidations of these matters that we have are from his hand. Now Maestro Luca del Borgo, a friar of S. Francis, who wrote about the regular geometrical bodies, was his pupil; and when Piero, after having written many books, grew old and finally died, the said Maestro Luca, claiming the authorship of these books, had them printed as his own, for they had fallen into his hands after the death of Piero.

Piero was much given to making models in clay, on which he spread wet draperies with an infinity of folds, in order to make use of them for drawing.

Piero became blind through an attack of catarrh at the age of sixty, and lived thus up to his death. His books are such that they have deservedly acquired for him the name of the best geometrician of his time.

FRA ANGELICO

[*Guido di Pietro da Mugello, known, as a monk, as Frate
Giovanni da Fiesole, and commonly called Fra Angelico,
was born some time after 1387 and died in 1455.*]

FRA GIOVANNI ANGELICO DA FIESOLE, who was known in
the world as Guido, was no less excellent as painter and
illuminator than he was upright as churchman, and for both
one and the other of these reasons he deserves that most honorable record should be made of him. This man, although
he could have lived in the world with the greatest comfort,
and could have gained whatever he wished, besides what he
possessed, by means of those arts, of which he had a very
good knowledge even in his youth, yet resolved, for his own
peace and satisfaction, being by nature serious and upright,
and above all in order to save his soul, to take the vows of
the Order of Preaching Friars; for the reason that, although
it is possible to serve God in all walks of life, nevertheless it
appears to some men that they can gain salvation in monasteries better than in the world. Now in proportion as this
plan succeeds happily for good men, so, on the contrary, it
has a truly miserable and unhappy issue for a man who takes
the vows with some other end in view.

There are some choral books illuminated by the hand of
Fra Giovanni in his Convent of S. Marco in Florence, so
beautiful that words are not able to describe them; and similar to these are some others that he left in S. Domenico da
Fiesole, wrought with incredible diligence. It is true, indeed,

that in making these he was assisted by an elder brother, who was likewise an illuminator and well practiced in painting.

Fra Giovanni was so greatly beloved for his merits by Cosimo de' Medici, that, after completing the construction of the Church and Convent of S. Marco, he caused him to paint the whole Passion of Jesus Christ on a wall in the chapter-house. Then, over certain lunettes in the first cloister, he made many very beautiful figures in fresco, and a Crucifix with S. Dominic at the foot, which is much extolled; and in the dormitory, besides many other things throughout the cells and on the surface of the walls, he painted a story from the New Testament, of a beauty beyond the power of words to describe. Particularly beautiful and marvelous is the panel of the high altar of that church; for, besides the fact that the Madonna rouses all who see her to devotion by her simplicity, and that the Saints that surround her are like her in this, the predella, in which there are stories of the martyrdom of S. Cosimo, S. Damiano, and others, is so well painted, that one cannot imagine it possible ever to see a work executed with greater diligence, or little figures more delicate or better conceived than these are.

In S. Domenico da Fiesole, likewise, he painted the panel of the high altar, which has been retouched by other masters and injured, perchance because it appeared to be spoiling. But the predella and the Ciborium of the Sacrament have remained in better preservation; and the innumerable little figures that are to be seen there, in a Celestial Glory, are so beautiful, that they appear truly to belong to Paradise, nor can any man who approaches them ever have his fill of gazing on them. In a chapel of the same church is a panel by his hand, containing the Annunciation of Our Lady by the Angel Gabriel, with features in profile, so devout, so delicate, and so well executed, that they appear truly to have been made rather in Paradise than by the hand of man; and in the landscape at the back are Adam and Eve, because of whom the

Redeemer was born from the Virgin. In the predella, also, there are some very beautiful little scenes.

But superior to all the other works that Fra Giovanni made, and the one wherein he surpassed himself and gave supreme proof of his talent and of his knowledge of art, was a panel that is beside the door of the same church, on the left hand as one enters, wherein Jesus Christ is crowning Our Lady in the midst of a choir of angels and among an infinite multitude of saints, both male and female, so many in number, so well wrought, and with such variety in the attitudes and in the expressions of the heads, that incredible pleasure and sweetness are felt in gazing at them; nay, one is persuaded that those blessed spirits cannot look otherwise in Heaven, or, to speak more exactly, could not if they had bodies; for not only are all these saints, both male and female, full of life and sweet and delicate in expression, but the whole coloring of that work appears to be by the hand of a saint or an angel like themselves; wherefore it was with very good reason that this excellent monk was ever called Fra Giovanni Angelico. Moreover, the stories of the Madonna and of S. Dominic in the predella are divine in their own kind; and I, for one, can declare with truth that I never see this work without thinking it something new, and that I never leave it sated.

In the Chapel of the Nunziata in Florence which Piero di Cosimo de' Medici caused to be built, he painted the doors of the press (in which the silver is kept) with little figures executed with much diligence. This father painted so many pictures, now to be found in the houses of Florentine citizens, that I sometimes stand marveling how one single man could execute so much work to such perfection, even in the space of many years. The pictures that are in the arch over the door of S. Domenico are also by the same man; and in the Sacristy of S. Trinita there is a panel containing a Deposition from the Cross, into which he put so great diligence, that it can

be numbered among the best works that he ever made. In
S. Francesco, outside the Porta a S. Miniato, there is an Annunciation; and in S. Maria Novella, besides the works already named, he painted with little scenes the Paschal candle
and some Reliquaries which are placed on the altar in the
most solemn ceremonies.

Over a door of the cloister of the Badia in the same city
he painted a S. Benedict, who is making a sign enjoining
silence. For the Linen-manufacturers he painted a panel that
is in the Office of their Guild; and in Cortona he painted a
little arch over the door of the church of his Order, and likewise the panel of the high altar. At Orvieto, on a part of the
vaulting of the Chapel of the Madonna in the Duomo, he
began certain prophets, which were finished afterwards by
Luca da Cortona. For the Company of the Temple in Florence he painted a Dead Christ on a panel; and in the Church
of the Monks of the Angeli he made a Paradise and a Hell
with little figures, wherein he showed fine judgment by making the blessed very beautiful and full of jubilation and celestial gladness, and the damned all ready for the pains of Hell,
in various most woeful attitudes, and bearing the stamp of
their sins and unworthiness on their faces. The blessed are
seen entering the gate of Paradise in celestial dance, and the
damned are being dragged by demons to the eternal pains
of Hell. This work is in the aforesaid church, on the right
hand as one goes toward the high altar, where the priest sits
when Mass is sung. For the Nuns of S. Piero Martire—who
now live in the Monastery of S. Felice in Piazza, which used
to belong to the Order of Camaldoli—he painted a panel with
Our Lady, S. John the Baptist, S. Dominic, S. Thomas, and
S. Peter Martyr, and a number of little figures. And in the
transept of S. Maria Nuova there may also be seen a panel
by his hand.

These many labors having made the name of Fra Giovanni
illustrious throughout all Italy, Pope Nicholas V sent for

him and caused him to adorn that chapel of his Palace in Rome wherein the Pope hears Mass with a Deposition from the Cross and some very beautiful stories of S. Laurence, and also to illuminate some books, which are most beautiful. In the Minerva he painted the panel of the high altar, and an Annunciation that is now set up against a wall beside the principal chapel. Now Fra Giovanni appeared to the Pope to be, as indeed he was, a person of most holy life, peaceful and modest; and, since the Archbishopric of Florence was at that time vacant, the Pope had judged him worthy of that rank; but the said friar, hearing this, implored His Holiness to find another man, for the reason that he did not feel himself fitted for ruling others, whereas his Order contained a brother most learned and well able to govern, a God-fearing man and a friend of the poor, on whom that dignity would be conferred much more fittingly than on himself. The Pope, hearing this and remembering that what he said was true, granted him the favor willingly; and thus the Archbishopric of Florence was given to Frate Antonino of the Order of Preaching Friars, a man truly very famous both for sanctity and for learning, and of such a character, in short, that he was deservedly canonized in our own day by Adrian VI.

Great excellence was that of Fra Giovanni, and a thing truly very rare, to resign a dignity and honor and charge so important, offered to himself by a Supreme Pontiff, in favor of the man whom he, with his singleness of eye and sincerity of heart, judged to be much more worthy of it than himself. Let the churchmen of our own times learn from this holy man not to take upon themselves charges that they cannot worthily carry out, and to yield them to those who are most worthy of them. Would to God, to return to Fra Giovanni (and may this be said without offense to the upright among them), that all churchmen would spend their time as did this truly angelic father, seeing that he spent every minute of his life in the service of God and in benefiting both the world and his neighbor.

Fra Giovanni was a man of great simplicity, and most holy in his ways; and his goodness may be perceived from this, that, Pope Nicholas V wishing one morning to entertain him at table, he had scruples of conscience about eating meat without leave from his Prior, forgetting about the authority of the Pontiff. He shunned the affairs of the world; and, living a pure and holy life, he was as much the friend of the poor as I believe his soul to be now the friend of Heaven. He was continually laboring at his painting, and he would never paint anything save Saints. He might have been rich, but to this he gave no thought; nay, he used to say that true riches consist only in being content with little. He might have ruled many, but he would not, saying that it was less fatiguing and less misleading to obey others. He had the option of obtaining dignities both among the friars and in the world, but he despised them, declaring that he sought no other dignity save that of seeking to avoid Hell and draw near to Paradise. And what dignity, in truth, can be compared to that which all churchmen, nay, all men, should seek, and which is to be found only in God and in a life of virtue? He was most kindly and temperate; and he lived chastely and withdrew himself from the snares of the world, being wont very often to say that he who pursued such an art had need of quiet and of a life free from cares, and that he whose work is connected with Christ must ever live with Christ. He was never seen in anger among his fellow-friars, which is a very notable thing, and almost impossible, it seems to me, to believe; and it was his custom to admonish his friends with a simple smile. With incredible sweetness, if any sought for works from him, he would say that they had only to gain the consent of the Prior, and that then he would not fail them. In short, this never to be sufficiently extolled father was most humble and modest in all his works and his discourse, and facile and devout in his pictures; and the Saints that he painted have more the air and likeness of Saints than those of any other man. It was his custom never to retouch or improve any of his pictures, but to leave them ever in the state to which he had first brought them; believing, so he used to say, that this was the will of God. Some say that Fra Giovanni would never have taken his brushes in his hand without first offering a prayer. He never painted a Crucifix without the tears streaming down his cheeks; wherefore in the countenances and attitudes of his figures one can recognize the goodness, nobility, and sincerity of his mind toward the Christian religion.

He died in 1455 at the age of sixty-eight, and was buried by his fellow-friars in the Minerva in Rome.

ALBERTI

[*Leon Battista Alberti was born 1404; died 1472.*]

VERY great is the advantage bestowed by learning, without
exception, on all those craftsmen who take delight in it, but
particularly on sculptors, painters, and architects, for it opens
up the way to invention in all the works that are made; not
to mention that a man cannot have a perfect judgment, be
his natural gifts what they may, if he is deprived of the com-
plemental advantage of being assisted by learning. And that
this is true is seen manifestly in Leon Battista Alberti, who,
having studied the Latin tongue, and having given attention
to architecture, to perspective, and to painting, left behind
him books written in such a manner, that, since not one of
our modern craftsmen has been able to expound these matters in writing, although very many of them in his own country have excelled him in working, it is generally believed—
such is the influence of his writings over the pens and speech
of the learned—that he was superior to all those who were
actually superior to him in work. Wherefore, with regard to
name and fame, it is seen from experience that writings have
greater power and longer life than anything else; for books
go everywhere with ease, and everywhere they command belief, if only they be truthful and not full of lies. It is no marvel, then, if the famous Leon Battista is known more for his
writings than for the work of his hands.

This man, born in Florence of the most noble family of
the Alberti, devoted himself not only to studying geography
and the proportions of antiquities, but also to writing, to

which he was much inclined, much more than to working. He was excellent in arithmetic and geometry, and he wrote ten books on architecture in Latin, which may now be read in a translation in the Florentine tongue made by the Reverend Maestro Cosimo Bartoli, Provost of S. Giovanni in Florence. He wrote three books on painting, now translated into the Tuscan tongue by Messer Lodovico Domenichi; he composed a treatise on traction and on the rules for measuring heights, as well as the books on the "Vita Civile," and some erotic works in prose and verse; and he was the first who tried to reduce Italian verse to the measure of the Latin.

Arriving at Rome in the time of Nicholas V, who had turned the whole of Rome upside down with his manner of building, Leon Battista, through the agency of Biondo da Forlì, who was much his friend, became intimate with that Pope, who had previously carried out all his building after the advice of Bernardo Rossellino, a sculptor and architect of Florence. This man, having put his hand to restoring the Pope's Palace and to certain works in S. Maria Maggiore, thenceforward, according to the will of the Pope, ever sought the advice of Leon Battista. Wherefore, using one of them as adviser and the other as executor, the Pope carried out many useful and praiseworthy works, such as the restoring of the conduit of the Acqua Vergine, which was in ruins; and there was made the fountain on the Piazza de' Trevi, with those marble ornaments that are seen there, on which are the arms of that Pontiff and of the Roman people.

Afterwards, having gone to Signor Sigismondo Malatesta of Rimini, he made for him the model of the Church of S. Francesco, and in particular that of the façade, which was made of marble; and likewise the side facing toward the south, which was built with very great arches and with tombs for the illustrious men of that city. In short, he brought that building to such a form that in point of solidity it is one of the most famous temples in Italy. Within it are six most beautiful chapels, one of which, dedicated to S. Jerome, is very ornate; and in it are preserved many relics brought from Jerusalem. In the same chapel are the tombs of the said Signor Sigismondo and of his wife, constructed very richly of marble in the year 1450; on one there is the portrait of Sigismondo himself, and in another part of the work there is that of Leon Battista.

After this, in the year 1457, when the very useful method of printing books was discovered by Johann Gutenberg the German, Leon Battista, working on similar lines, discovered a way of tracing natural perspectives and of effecting the diminution of figures by means of an instrument, and likewise the method of enlarging small things and reproducing them on a greater scale; all ingenious inventions, useful to art and very beautiful.

In Leon Battista's time Giovanni di Paolo Rucellai wished to build the principal façade of S. Maria Novella entirely of marble at his own expense, and he spoke of this to Leon Battista, who was very much his friend; and having received from him not only counsel, but the actual model, Giovanni resolved to have the work executed at all costs, in order to leave it behind him as a memorial of himself. A beginning having been made, therefore, it was finished in the year 1477, to the great satisfaction of all the city, which was pleased with the whole work, but particularly with the door, from which it is seen that Leon Battista took more than ordinary pains. For Cosimo Rucellai, likewise, he made the design for the palace which that man built in the street which is called La Vigna, and that for the loggia which is opposite to it. In the latter, having turned his arches over columns close together, both in the front and at the ends, since he wished to adhere to this plan and not to make one single arch, he had a certain space left over on each side; wherefore he was forced to make certain projections at the inner corners. And then, when he wished to turn the arch of the inner vaulting, having seen that he could not give it the shape of a half-circle, which would have been flat and awkward, he resolved to turn certain small arches at the corners from one projection to another; and this lack of judgment in design gives us to know clearly that practice is necessary as well as science, for the judgment can never become perfect unless science attains to experience by actual work.

It is said that the same man made the design for the house and garden of these Rucellai in the Via della Scala. This house is built with much judgment and very commodious, for, besides many other conveniences, it has two *loggie*, one facing south and the other west, both very beautiful, and made without arches on the columns, which is the true and proper method that the ancients used, for the reason that the architraves which are placed on the capitals of the columns lie level, whereas a four-sided thing like a curving arch cannot rest on a round column without the corners jutting out over space. The good method, therefore, demands that architraves should rest on columns, and that, when arches are to be turned, pilasters and not columns should be made.

For the same Rucellai Leon Battista made a chapel in the same manner in S. Pancrazio, which rests on great architraves placed on two columns and two pilasters, piercing the wall of the church below; which is a difficult thing, but safe; wherefore this work is one of the best that this architect ever made. In the middle of this chapel is a tomb of marble, wrought very well in the form of a rather long oval, and similar, as may be read on it, to the Sepulcher of Jesus Christ in Jerusalem.

About the same time Lodovico Gonzaga, Marquis of Mantua, wished to build the tribune and the principal chapel in the Nunziata, the Church of the Servi in Florence, after the design and model of Leon Battista; and pulling down a square chapel, old, not very large, and painted in the ancient manner, which stood at the head of the church, he built the said tribune in the bizarre and difficult form of a round temple surrounded by nine chapels, all curving in a round arch, and each within in the shape of a niche. Now, since the arches of the said chapels rest on the pilasters in front, the result is that the stone dressings of the arches, inclining toward the wall, tend to draw ever backwards in order to meet the said wall, which turns in the opposite direction according to the shape of the tribune; wherefore, when the said arches of the chapels are looked at from the side, it appears that they are falling backwards, and that they are clumsy, as indeed they are, although the proportions are correct, and the difficulties of the method must be remembered. Truly it would have been better if Leon Battista had avoided this method, for, although there is some credit for the difficulty of its execution, it is clumsy both in great things and in small, and it cannot have a good result. And that this is true of great things is proved by the great arch in front, which forms the entrance to the said tribune; for, although it is very beautiful on the outer side, on the inner side, where it has to follow the curve of the chapel, which is round, it appears to be falling backwards and to be extremely clumsy. This Leon Battista would perhaps not have done, if, in addition to science and theory, he had possessed practical experience in working; for another man would have avoided this difficulty, and would have rather aimed at grace and greater beauty for the edifice. The whole work is otherwise in itself very beautiful, bizarre, and difficult; and nothing save great courage could have enabled Leon Battista to vault that tribune in those times in the manner that he did. Being then summoned by the same Marquis Lodovico to Mantua, Leon Battista made for him the models of the Church of S. Andrea and of some other works; and on the road leading from Mantua to Padua there may be seen certain temples built after his manner. Many of the designs and models of Leon Battista were carried into execution by Salvestro Fancelli, a passing good architect and sculptor of Florence, who, according to the desire of the said Leon Battista, executed with judgment and extraordinary diligence all the works that he undertook in Florence. For those in Mantua he employed one Luca, a Florentine, who, living ever afterwards in that city and dying there, left his name— so Filarete tells us—to the family of the Luchi, which is still there to-day. It was no small good fortune for him to have friends who understood him and were able and willing to serve him, because architects cannot be always standing over their work, and it is of the greatest use to them to have a faithful and loving assistant; and if any man ever knew it, I know it very well by long experience.

In painting Leon Battista did not do great or very beautiful works, for the few by his hand that are to be seen do not show much perfection; nor is this to be wondered at, seeing that he devoted himself more to his studies than to draftsmanship. Yet he could express his conceptions well enough in drawing, as may be seen from some sketches by his hand that are in our book, in which there are drawn the Bridge of S. Angelo and the covering that was made for it with his design in the form of a loggia, for protection from the sun in summer and from the rain and wind in winter. This work he was commissioned to execute by Pope Nicholas V, who had intended to carry out many similar works throughout the whole of Rome; but death intervened to hinder him. There is a work of Leon Battista's in a little Chapel of Our Lady on the abutment of the Ponte alla Carraja in Florence— namely, an altar-predella, containing three little scenes with some perspectives, which he was much more able to describe with the pen than to paint with the brush. In the house of the Palla Rucellai family, also in Florence, there is a portrait of himself made with a mirror; and a panel with rather large figures in chiaroscuro. He also made a picture of Venice in perspective, with S. Marco, but the figures therein were executed by other masters; and this is one of the best examples of his painting that there are to be seen.

Leon Battista was a person of most honest and laudable ways, the friend of men of talent, and very open and courteous to all; and he lived honorably and like a gentleman—which he was—through the whole course of his life. Finally, having reached a mature enough age, he passed content and tranquil to a better life, leaving a most honorable name behind him.

FRA FILIPPO LIPPI

[Filippo di Tommaso Lippi, called Fra Filippo Lippi,
was born about 1406 and died in 1469.]

FRA FILIPPO DI TOMMASO LIPPI, a Carmelite, was born in
Florence in a street called Ardiglione, below the Canto alla
Cuculia and behind the Convent of the Carmelites. By the
death of his father Tommaso he was left a poor little orphan
at the age of two, with no one to take care of him, for his
mother had also died not long after giving him birth. He was
left, therefore, in the charge of one Mona Lapaccia, his aunt,
sister of his father, who brought him up with very great inconvenience to herself; and when he was eight years of age
and she could no longer support him, she made him a friar in
the aforesaid Convent of the Carmine. Living there, in proportion as he showed himself dexterous and ingenious in the
use of his hands, so was he dull and incapable of making any
progress in the learning of letters, so that he would never
apply his intelligence to them or regard them as anything
save his enemies. This boy, who was called by his secular
name of Filippo, was kept with others in the noviciate under
the discipline of the schoolmaster, in order to see what he
could do; but in place of studying he would never do anything
save deface his own books and those of the others with carica-
tures. Whereupon the Prior resolved to give him every opportunity and convenience for learning to paint. There was
then in the Carmine a chapel that had been newly painted by
Masaccio, which, being very beautiful, pleased Fra Filippo
so greatly that he would haunt it every day for his recreation;

and continually practicing there in company with many young men, who were ever drawing in it, he surpassed the others by a great measure in dexterity and knowledge, insomuch that it was held certain that in time he would do something marvelous. Nay, not merely in his maturity, but even in his early childhood, he executed so many works worthy of praise that it was a miracle. It was no long time before he wrought in terra-verde in the cloister, close to the Consecration painted by Masaccio, a Pope confirming the Rule of the Carmelites; and he painted pictures in fresco on various walls in many parts of the church, particularly a S. John the Baptist with some scenes from his life. And thus, making progress every day, he had learnt the manner of Masaccio very well, so that he made his works so similar to those of the other that many said that the spirit of Masaccio had entered into the body of Fra Filippo. On a pilaster in the church, close to the organ, he made a figure of S. Marziale which brought him infinite fame, for it could bear comparison with the works that Masaccio had painted. Wherefore, hearing himself so greatly praised by the voices of all, at the age of seventeen he boldly threw off his monastic habit.

Now, chancing to be in the March of Ancona, he was disporting himself one day with some of his friends in a little boat on the sea, when they were all captured together by the Moorish galleys that were scouring those parts, and taken to Barbary, where each of them was put in chains and held as a slave; and thus he remained in great misery for eighteen months. But one day, seeing that he was thrown much into contact with his master, there came to him the opportunity and the whim to make a portrait of him; whereupon, taking a piece of dead coal from the fire, with this he portrayed him at full length on a white wall in his Moorish costume. When this was reported by the other slaves to the master (for it appeared a miracle to them all, since drawing and painting were not known in these parts), it brought about his liberation from the chains in which he had been held for so long. Truly glorious was it for this art to have caused one to whom the power of condemnation and punishment was granted by law, to do the very opposite—nay, in place of inflicting pains and death, to consent to show friendliness and grant liberty! After having wrought some works in color for his master, he was brought safely to Naples, where he painted for King Alfonso, then Duke of Calabria, a panel in distemper for the Chapel of the Castle, where the guardroom now is.

After this there came upon him a desire to return to Florence, where he remained for some months. There he wrought a very beautiful panel for the high altar of the Nuns of S. Ambrogio, which made him very dear to Cosimo de' Medici, who became very much his friend for this reason. He also painted a panel for the Chapter-house of S. Croce, and another that was placed in the chapel of the house of the Medici, on which he painted the Nativity of Christ. For the wife of the said Cosimo, likewise, he painted a panel with the same Nativity of Christ and with S. John the Baptist, which was to be placed in the Hermitage of Camaldoli, in one of the hermits' cells, dedicated to S. John the Baptist, which she had caused to be built in proof of her devotion. And he painted some little scenes that were sent by Cosimo as a gift to Pope Eugenius IV, the Venetian; wherefore Fra Filippo acquired great favor with that Pope by reason of this work.

It is said that he was so amorous, that, if he saw any women who pleased him, and if they were to be won, he would give all his possessions to win them; and if he could in no way do this, he would paint their portraits and cool the flame of his love by reasoning with himself. So much a slave was he to this appetite, that when he was in this humor he gave little or no attention to the works that he had undertaken; wherefore on one occasion Cosimo de' Medici, having commissioned him to paint a picture, shut him up in his own house, in order that he might not go out and waste his time;

but after staying there for two whole days, being driven
forth by his amorous—nay, beastly—passion, one night he
cut some ropes out of his bed-sheets with a pair of scissors
and let himself down from a window, and then abandoned
himself for many days to his pleasures. Thereupon, since he
could not be found, Cosimo sent out to look for him, and
finally brought him back to his labor; and thenceforward
Cosimo gave him liberty to go out when he pleased, repenting greatly that he had previously shut him up, when he
thought of his madness and of the danger that he might run.
For this reason he strove to keep a hold on him for the future by kindnesses; and so he was served by Filippo with
greater readiness, and was wont to say that the virtues of
rare minds were celestial beings, and not slavish hacks.

For the Church of S. Maria Primerana, on the Piazza of
Fiesole, he painted a panel containing the Annunciation of
Our Lady by the Angel, which shows very great diligence,
and there is such beauty in the figure of the Angel that it appears truly a celestial thing. For the Nuns of the Murate he
painted two panels: one, containing an Annunciation, is
placed on the high altar; and the other is on an altar in the
same church, and contains stories of S. Benedict and S. Bernard. In the Palace of the Signoria he painted an Annunciation on a panel, which is over a door; and over another door
in the said Palace he also painted a S. Bernard. For the Sacristy of S. Spirito in Florence he executed a panel with the
Madonna surrounded by angels, and with saints on either
side—a rare work, which has ever been held in the greatest
veneration by the masters of these our arts. In the Chapel of
the Wardens of Works in S. Lorenzo he wrought a panel with
another Annunciation; with one for the Della Stufa Chapel,
which he did not finish. In Arezzo, by order of Messer Carlo
Marsuppini, he painted the panel of the Chapel of S. Bernardo for the Monks of Monte Oliveto, depicting therein
the Coronation of Our Lady, surrounded by many saints;

which picture has remained so fresh, that it appears to have been made by the hand of Fra Filippo at the present day. It was then that he was told by the aforesaid Messer Carlo to give attention to the painting of the hands, seeing that his works were much criticized in this respect; wherefore from that day onwards, in painting hands, Fra Filippo covered the greater part of them with draperies or with some other contrivance, in order to avoid the aforesaid criticism. In this work he portrayed the said Messer Carlo from the life.

Truly marvelous was the grace with which he painted, and very perfect the harmony that he gave to his works, for which he has been ever esteemed by craftsmen and honored by our modern masters with consummate praise; nay, so long as the voracity of time allows his many excellent labors to live, he will be held in veneration by every age. In Prato, near Florence, where he had some relatives, he stayed for many months, executing many works throughout that whole district in company with Fra Diamante, a friar of the Carmine, who had been his comrade in the noviciate. After this, having been commissioned by the Nuns of S. Margherita to paint the panel of their high altar, he was working at this when there came before his eyes a daughter of Francesco Buti, a citizen of Florence, who was living there as a ward or as a novice. Having set eyes on Lucrezia (for this was the name of the girl), who was very beautiful and graceful, Fra Filippo contrived to persuade the nuns to allow him to make a portrait of her for a figure of Our Lady in the work that he was doing for them. With this opportunity he became even more enamored of her, and then wrought upon her so mightily, what with one thing and another, that he stole her away from the nuns and took her off on the very day when she was going to see the Girdle of Our Lady, an honored relic of that township, being exposed to view. Whereupon the nuns were greatly disgraced by such an event, and her father, Francesco, who never smiled again, made every effort to recover her; but she, either through fear or for some other reason, refused to come back—nay, she insisted on staying with Filippo, to whom she bore a male child, who was also called Filippo, and who became, like his father, a very excellent and famous painter.

In S. Domenico, in the aforesaid Prato, there are two of his panels; and in the transept of the Church of S. Francesco there is a Madonna. In a courtyard of the Ceppo of Francesco di Marco, over a well, there is a little panel by the hand of the same man, containing the portrait of the said Francesco di Marco, the creator and founder of that holy place. In the Pieve of the said township, on a little panel over the side-door as one ascends the steps, he painted the Death of S. Bernard, by the touch of whose bier many cripples are being restored to health. In this picture are friars bewailing the death of their master, and it is a marvelous thing to see the beautiful expression of the sadness of lamentation in the heads, counterfeited with great art and resemblance to nature. Here there are draperies in the form of friars' gowns with most beautiful folds, which deserve infinite praise for their good design, coloring, and composition; not to mention the grace and proportion that are seen in the said work, which was executed with the greatest delicacy by the hand of Fra Filippo. The Wardens of Works for the said Pieve, in order to have some memorial of him, commissioned him to paint the Chapel of the High Altar in that place; and he gave great proof of his worth in that work, which, besides its general excellence and masterliness, contains most admirable draperies and heads. He made the figures therein larger than life, thus introducing to our modern craftsmen the method of giving grandeur to the manner of our own day. There are certain figures with garments little used in those times, whereby he began to incite the minds of men to depart from that simplicity which should be called rather old-fashioned than ancient. This work is in truth the most excellent of all his paintings, both for the reasons mentioned above, and because he made the figures somewhat larger than life, which encouraged those who came after him to give grandeur to their manner. So greatly was he esteemed for his excellent gifts, that many circumstances in his life that were worthy of blame were passed over in consideration of the eminence of his great talents. In this work he portrayed Messer Carlo, the natural son of Cosimo de' Medici, who was then Provost of that church, which received great benefactions from him and from his house.

In the year 1463, when he had finished this work, he painted a panel in distemper, containing a very beautiful Annunciation, for the Church of S. Jacopo in Pistoia, by order of Messer Jacopo Bellucci, of whom he made therein a most vivid portrait from the life. In the house of Pulidoro Bracciolini there is a picture by his hand of the Birth of Our Lady; and in the Hall of the Tribunal of Eight in Florence he painted in distemper a Madonna with the Child in her arms, on a lunette. In the house of Lodovico Capponi there is another picture with a very beautiful Madonna; and in the hands of Bernardo Vecchietti, a gentleman of Florence and a man of a culture and excellence beyond my power of expression, there is a little picture by the hand of the same man, containing a very beautiful S. Augustine engaged in his studies. Even better is a S. Jerome in Penitence, of the same size, in the *guardaroba* of Duke Cosimo; for if Fra Filippo was a rare master in all his pictures, he surpassed himself in the small ones, to which he gave such grace and beauty that nothing could be better, as may be seen in the predellas of all the panels that he painted. In short, he was such that none surpassed him in his own times, and few in our own; and Michelangelo has not only always extolled him, but has imitated him in many things.

For the Church of S. Domenico Vecchio in Perugia, also, he painted a panel that was afterwards placed on the high altar, containing a Madonna, S. Peter, S. Paul, S. Louis, and S. Anthony the Abbot. Messer Alessandro degli Alessandri, a Chevalier of that day and a friend of Filippo, caused him to paint a panel for the church of his villa at Vincigliata on the hill of Fiesole, containing a S. Laurence and other Saints, among whom he portrayed Alessandro and two sons of his.

Fra Filippo was much the friend of gay spirits, and he ever lived a joyous life. He lived honorably by his labors, spending extraordinary sums on the pleasures of love, in which he continued to take delight right up to the end of his life. He was requested by the Commune of Spoleto, through the mediation of Cosimo de' Medici, to paint the chapel in their principal church (dedicated to Our Lady), which he brought very nearly to completion, working in company with Fra Diamante, when death intervened to prevent him from finishing it. Some say, indeed, that in consequence of his great inclination for his blissful amours some relations of the lady that he loved had him poisoned.

Fra Filippo finished the course of his life in 1469, at the age of sixty-three, and left a will entrusting to Fra Diamante his son Filippo, a little boy of ten years of age, who learnt the art of painting from his guardian. Fra Diamante returned with him to Florence, carrying away three hundred ducats, which remained to be received from the Commune of Spoleto for the work done; with these he bought some property for himself, giving but a little share to the boy. Filippo was placed with Sandro Botticelli, who was then held a very good master; and the old man was buried in a tomb of red and white marble, which the people of Spoleto caused to be erected in the church that he had been painting.

His death grieved many friends, particularly Cosimo de' Medici, as well as Pope Eugenius, who offered in his lifetime to give him a dispensation, so that he might make Lucrezia, the daughter of Francesco Buti, his legitimate wife; but this he refused to do, wishing to have complete liberty for himself and his appetites.

GOZZOLI

*[Benozzo di Lese di Sandro, known as Benozzo Gozzoli,
was born in 1420 and died in 1497.]*

HE who pursues the path of excellence in his labors, although
it is, as men say, both stony and full of thorns, finds himself
finally at the end of the ascent on a broad plain, with all the
blessings that he has desired. And as he looks downwards
and sees the difficult and perilous way that he has come, he
thanks God for having brought him out safely, and with the
greatest contentment he blesses those labors that he has just
been finding so burdensome. And so, recompensed for his
past sufferings by the gladness of the happy present, he labors
without fatigue, in order to demonstrate to all who see him
how heat, cold, sweat, hunger, thirst, and all the other discomforts that are endured in the acquiring of excellence, deliver men from poverty, and bring them to that secure and
tranquil state in which, with so much contentment, Benozzo
Gozzoli enjoyed repose from his labors.

This man was a disciple of Fra Giovanni Angelico, by
whom he was loved with good reason; and by all who knew
him he was held to be a practiced master, very rich in invention, and very productive in the painting of animals, perspectives, landscapes, and ornaments. He wrought so many works
in his day that he showed that he cared little for other delights; and although, in comparison with many who surpassed
him in design, he was not very excellent, yet in this great mass
of work he surpassed all the painters of his age, for in such
a multitude of pictures he succeeded in making some that

were good. In his youth he painted a panel for the altar of the Company of S. Marco in Florence, and, in S. Friano, a picture of the passing of S. Jerome, which has been spoilt in restoring the façade of the church along the street. In the Chapel of the Palace of the Medici he painted the Story of the Magi in fresco. In the Araceli at Rome, in the Chapel of the Cesarini, he painted the stories of S. Anthony of Padua, wherein he made portraits from life of Cardinal Giuliano Cesarini and Antonio Colonna.

After returning from Rome to Florence, Benozzo went to Pisa, where he worked in the cemetery called the Campo Santo, which is beside the Duomo, covering the surface of a wall that runs the whole length of the building with stories from the Old Testament, wherein he showed very great invention. And this may be said to be a truly tremendous work, seeing that it contains all the stories of the Creation of the world from one day to another. After this come Noah's Ark and the inundation of the Flood, represented with very beautiful composition and an abundance of figures. Then there follow the building of the proud Tower of Nimrod, the burning of Sodom and the other neighboring cities, and the stories of Abraham, wherein there are some very beautiful effects to be observed, for the reason that, although Benozzo was not remarkable for the drawing of figures, yet he showed his art effectually in the Sacrifice of Isaac, for there he painted an ass foreshortened in such a manner that it seems to turn to either side, which is held something very beautiful. After this comes the Birth of Moses, together with all those signs and prodigies that were seen, up to the time when he led his people out of Egypt and fed them for so many years in the desert. To these he added all the stories of the Hebrews up to the time of David and his son Solomon; and in this work Benozzo displayed a spirit truly more than bold, for, whereas so great an enterprise might very well have daunted a legion of painters, he alone wrought the whole and brought it to perfection. Wherefore, he thus acquired very great fame.

Throughout this whole work there are scattered innumerable portraits from the life; but, since we have not knowledge of them all, I will mention only those that I have recognized as important, and those that I know by means of some record. In the scene of the Queen of Sheba going to visit Solomon there is the portrait of Marsilio Ficino among certain prelates, with those of Argiropolo, a very learned Greek, and of Batista Platina, whom he had previously portrayed in Rome; while he himself is on horseback, in the form of an old man shaven and wearing a black cap, in the fold of which there is a white paper, perchance as a sign, or because he intended to write his own name thereon.

In the same city of Pisa, for the Nuns of S. Benedetto a Ripa d'Arno, he painted all the stories of the life of that Saint; and in the building of the Company of the Florentines, which then stood where the Monastery of S. Vito now is, he wrought the panel and many other pictures. In the Duomo, behind the chair of the Archbishop, he painted a S. Thomas Aquinas on a little panel in distemper, with an infinite number of learned men disputing over his works, among whom there is a portrait of Pope Sixtus IV, together with a number of cardinals and many chiefs and generals of various Orders. This is the best and most highly finished work that Benozzo ever made.

In his youth, Benozzo also painted the altar of S. Bastiano in the Pieve of San Gimignano, opposite to the principal chapel; and in the Hall of the Council there are some figures, partly by his hand, and partly old works restored by him. For the Monks of Monte Oliveto, in the same territory, he painted a Crucifix and other pictures; but the best work that he made in that place was in the principal chapel of S. Agostino, where he painted stories of S. Augustine in fresco, from his conversion to his death.

Benozzo, wasted away at last by length of years and by

his labors, went to his true rest, in the city of Pisa, at the age of seventy-seven, and was honorably buried in the Campo Santo. Benozzo ever lived the well-ordered life of a true Christian, spending all his years in honorable labor. For this and for his good manner and qualities he was long looked upon with favor in that city.

JACOPO, GIOVANNI, AND
GENTILE BELLINI

*[Probably born, respectively, in 1400, about 1430, and
1429; died in 1464, 1516, and 1507.]*

ENTERPRISES that are founded on excellence, although their
beginnings often appear humble and mean, keep climbing
higher step by step, nor do they ever halt or take rest until
they have reached the supreme heights of glory: as could be
clearly seen from the poor and humble beginning of the
house of the Bellini, and from the rank to which it afterwards rose by means of painting.

Jacopo Bellini, a painter of Venice, having been a disciple
of Gentile da Fabriano, worked in competition with that
Domenico who taught the method of coloring in oil to Andrea
del Castagno; but, although he labored greatly to become excellent in that art, he did not acquire fame therein until after
the departure of Domenico from Venice. Then, finding himself in that city without any competitor to equal him, he kept
growing in credit and fame, and became so excellent that he
was the greatest and most renowned man in his profession.
And to the end that the name which he had acquired in painting might not only be maintained in his house and for his
descendants, but might grow greater, there were born to him
two sons of good and beautiful intelligence, strongly inclined
to the art: one was Giovanni, and the other Gentile, to whom
he gave that name in tender memory of Gentile da Fabriano,
who had been his master and like a loving father to him.

Now, when the said two sons had grown to a certain age, Jacopo himself with all diligence taught them the rudiments of drawing; but no long time passed before both one and the other surpassed his father by a great measure, whereat he rejoiced greatly, ever encouraging them and showing them that he desired them to do as the Tuscans did, who gloried among themselves in making efforts to outstrip each other, according as one after another took up the art: even so should Giovanni vanquish himself, and Gentile should vanquish them both, and so on in succession.

The first works that brought fame to Jacopo were the portraits of Giorgio Cornaro and of Caterina, Queen of Cyprus; a panel which he sent to Verona, containing the Passion of Christ, with many figures, among which he portrayed himself from the life; and a picture of the Story of the Cross, which is said to be in the Scuola of S. Giovanni Evangelista. All these works and many others were painted by Jacopo with the aid of his sons; and the last-named picture was painted on canvas, as it has been almost always the custom to do in that city, where they rarely paint, as is done elsewhere, on panels of the wood of that tree that is called poplar. This wood, which grows mostly beside rivers or other waters, is very soft, and admirable for painting on, for it holds very firmly when joined together with carpenters' glue. But in Venice they make no panels, and, if they do make a few, they use no other wood than that of the fir, of which that city has a great abundance by reason of the River Adige, which brings a very great quantity of it from Germany, not to mention that no small amount comes from Sclavonia. It is much the custom in Venice, then, to paint on canvas, either because it does not split and does not grow worm-eaten, or because it enables pictures to be made of any size that is desired, or because, as was said elsewhere, they can be sent easily and conveniently wherever they are wanted, with very little expense and labor. Be the reason what it may, Jacopo and Gentile, as was said above, made their first works on canvas.

To the last-named Story of the Cross Gentile afterwards added by himself seven other pictures, or rather, eight, in which he painted the miracle of the Cross of Christ, which the said Scuola preserves as a relic; which miracle was as follows. The said Cross was thrown, I know not by what chance, from the Ponte della Paglia into the Canal, and, by reason of the reverence that many bore to the piece of the Cross of Christ that it contained, they threw themselves into the water to recover it; but it was the will of God that no one should be worthy to succeed in grasping it save the Prior of that Scuola. Gentile, therefore, representing this story, drew in perspective, along the Grand Canal, many houses, the Ponte della Paglia, the Piazza di S. Marco, and a long procession of men and women walking behind the clergy; also many who have leapt into the water, others in the act of leaping, many half immersed, and others in other very beautiful actions and attitudes; and finally he painted the said Prior recovering the Cross. Truly great were the labor and diligence of Gentile in this work, considering the infinite number of people, the many portraits from life, the diminution of the figures in the distance, and particularly the portraits of almost all the men who then belonged to that Scuola, or rather, Confraternity. Last comes the picture of the replacing of the said Cross, wrought with many beautiful conceptions. All these scenes, painted on the aforesaid canvases, acquired a very great name for Gentile.

Afterwards, Jacopo withdrew to work entirely by himself, as did his two sons, each of them devoting himself to his own studies in the art. Of Jacopo I will make no further mention, seeing that his works were nothing out of the ordinary in comparison with those of his sons, and because he died not long after his sons withdrew themselves from him; and I judge it much better to speak at some length only of Giovanni and

Gentile. I will not, indeed, forbear to say that although these brothers retired to live each by himself, nevertheless they had so much respect for each other, and both had such reverence for their father, that each, extolling the other, ever held himself inferior in merit; and thus they sought modestly to surpass one another no less in goodness and courtesy than in the excellence of their art.

The first works of Giovanni were some portraits from the life, which gave much satisfaction, and particularly that of Doge Loredano—although some say that this was a portrait of Giovanni Mozzenigo, brother of that Piero who was Doge many years before Lordano. For the altar of S. Giobbe in the Church of that Saint, the same man painted a panel with good design and most beautiful coloring, in the middle of which he made the Madonna with the Child in her arms, seated on a throne slightly raised from the ground, with nude figures of S. Job and S. Sebastian, beside whom are S. Dominic, S. Francis, S. John, and S. Augustine; and below are three boys, sounding instruments with much grace. This picture was not only praised then, when it was seen as new, but it has likewise been extolled ever afterwards as a very beautiful work.

Certain noblemen, moved by the great praises won by these works, began to suggest that it would be a fine thing, in view of the presence of such rare masters, to have the Hall of the Great Council adorned with stories, in which there should be depicted the glories and the magnificence of their marvelous city—her great deeds, her exploits in war, her enterprises, and other things of that kind, worthy to be perpetuated by painting in the memory of those who should come after—to the end that there might be added, to the profit and pleasure drawn from the reading of history, entertainment both for the eye and for the intellect, from seeing the images of so many illustrious lords wrought by the most skilful hands, and the glorious works of so many noblemen right worthy of eternal memory and fame. And so Giovanni and Gentile, who kept on making progress from day to day, received the commission for this work by order of those who governed the city, who commanded them to make a beginning as soon as possible. And since these works of Giovanni, which are truly very beautiful, gave infinite satisfaction, arrangements were just being made to give him the commission to paint all the rest of that Hall, when, being now old, he died.

Now we must turn back a little and say that there are many other works to be seen by the hand of the same man. One is a panel which is now on the high altar of S. Domenico in Pesaro. In the Church of S. Zaccheria in Venice, in the Chapel of S. Girolamo, there is a panel of Our Lady and many saints, executed with great diligence, with a building painted with much judgment; and in the same city, in the Sacristy of the Friars Minor, called the "Cà Grande," there is another by the same man's hand, wrought with beautiful design and a good manner. There is likewise one in S. Michele di Murano, a monastery of Monks of Camaldoli; and in the old Church of S. Francesco della Vigna, a seat of the Frati del Zoccolo, there was a picture of a Dead Christ, so beautiful that it was highly extolled before Louis XI, King of France, whereupon he demanded it from its owners with great insistence, so that they were forced, although very unwillingly, to gratify his wish. In its place there was put another with the name of the same Giovanni, but not so beautiful or so well executed as the first; and some believe that this substitute was wrought for the most part by Girolamo Moretto, a pupil of Giovanni. The Confraternity of S. Girolamo also possesses a work with little figures by the same Bellini, which is much extolled. And in the house of Messer Giorgio Cornaro there is a picture, likewise very beautiful, containing Christ, Cleophas, and Luke.

In the aforesaid Hall he also painted, though not at the same time, a scene of the Venetians summoning forth from

the Monastery of the Carità a Pope—I know not which—
who, having fled to Venice, had secretly served for a long
time as cook to the monks of that monastery; in which
scene there are many portraits from the life, and other very
beautiful figures.

No long time after, certain portraits were taken to Turkey
by an ambassador as presents for the Grand Turk, which
caused such astonishment and marvel to that Emperor, that,
although pictures are forbidden among that people by the
Mahometan law, nevertheless he accepted them with great
good will, praising the art and the craftsman without ceasing;
and what is more, he demanded that the master of the work
should be sent to him. Whereupon the Senate, considering
that Giovanni had reached an age when he could ill endure
hardships, not to mention that they did not wish to deprive
their own city of so great a man, particularly because he was
then engaged on the aforesaid Hall of the Great Council,
determined to send his brother Gentile, believing that he
would do as well as Giovanni. Therefore, having caused
Gentile to make his preparations, they brought him safely in
their own galleys to Constantinople, where, after being presented by the Commissioner of the Signoria to Mahomet, he
was received very willingly and treated with much favor as
something new, above all after he had given that Prince a
most lovely picture, which he greatly admired, being well-
nigh unable to believe that a mortal man had within himself
so much divinity, so to speak, as to be able to represent the
objects of nature so vividly. Gentile had been there no long
time when he portrayed the Emperor Mahomet from the life
so well, that it was held a miracle. That Emperor, after having seen many specimens of his art, asked Gentile whether
he had the courage to paint his own portrait; and Gentile,
having answered "Yes," did not allow many days to pass before he had made his own portrait with a mirror, with such
resemblance that it appeared alive. This he brought to the

Sultan, who marveled so greatly thereat, that he could not but think that he had some divine spirit within him; and if it had not been that the exercise of this art, as has been said, is forbidden by law among the Turks, that Emperor would never have allowed Gentile to go. But either in fear of murmurings, or for some other reason, one day he summoned him to his presence, and after first causing him to be thanked for the courtesy that he had shown, and then praising him in marvelous fashion as a man of the greatest excellence, he bade him demand whatever favor he wished, for it would be granted to him without fail. Gentile, like the modest and upright man that he was, asked for nothing save a letter of recommendation to the most Serene Senate and the most Illustrious Signoria of Venice, his native city. This was written in the warmest possible terms, and afterwards he was dismissed with honorable gifts and with the dignity of Chevalier. Among other things given to him at parting by that Sovereign, in addition to many privileges, there was placed round his neck a chain wrought in the Turkish manner, equal in weight to 250 gold crowns, which is still in the hands of his heirs in Venice.

Departing from Constantinople, Gentile returned after a most prosperous voyage to Venice, where he was received with gladness by his brother Giovanni and by almost the whole city, all men rejoicing at the honors paid to his talent by Mahomet. Afterwards, on going to make his reverence to the Doge and the Signoria, he was received very warmly, and commended for having given great satisfaction to that Emperor according to their desire. And to the end that he might see in what great account they held the letters in which that Prince had recommended him, they decreed him a provision of 200 crowns a year, which was paid to him for the rest of his life. Gentile made but few works after his return; finally, having almost reached the age of eighty, and having executed the aforesaid works and many others, he passed to the other life, and was given honorable burial by his brother Giovanni in S. Giovanni e Paolo, in the year 1507.

Giovanni, thus bereft of Gentile, whom he had ever loved most tenderly, went on doing a little work, although he was old, to pass the time. And having devoted himself to making portraits from the life, he introduced into Venice the fashion that everyone of a certain rank should have his portrait painted either by him or by some other master; wherefore in all the houses of Venice there are many portraits, and in many gentlemen's houses one may see their fathers and grandfathers, up to the fourth generation, and in some of the more noble they go still farther back—a fashion which has ever been truly worthy of the greatest praise, and existed even among the ancients. Who does not feel infinite pleasure and contentment, to say nothing of the honor and adornment that they confer, at seeing the images of his ancestors, particularly if they have been famous and illustrious for their part in governing their republics, for noble deeds performed in peace or in war, or for learning or any other notable and distinguished talent? And to what other end, as has been said in another place, did the ancients set up images of their great men in public places, with honorable inscriptions, than to kindle in the minds of their successors a love of excellence and of glory?

Finally, Giovanni passed from this life, overcome by old age, leaving an eternal memorial of his name in the works that he had made both in his native city of Venice and abroad; and he was honorably buried in the same church and in the same tomb in which he had laid his brother Gentile to rest.

GHIRLANDAIO

[*Domenico di Tommaso di Currado Bigordi, called "Il Ghirlandaio," was born in 1449 and died in 1494.*]

DOMENICO DI TOMMASO DEL GHIRLANDAIO, who, from his talent and from the greatness and the vast number of his works, may be called one of the most important and most excellent masters of his age, was made by nature to be a painter; and for this reason, in spite of the opposition of those who had charge of him (which often nips the finest fruits of our intellects in the bud by occupying them with work for which they are not suited, and by diverting them from that to which nature inclines them), he followed his natural instinct, secured very great honor for himself and profit for his art and for his kindred, and became the great delight of his age. He was apprenticed by his father to his own art of goldsmith, in which Tommaso was a master more than passing good, for it was he who made the greater part of the silver votive offerings that were formerly preserved in the press of the Nunziata, and the silver lamps of the chapel, which were all destroyed in the siege of the city in the year 1529. Tommaso was the first who invented and put into execution those ornaments worn on the head by the girls of Florence, which are called *ghirlande;** whence he gained the name of Ghirlandaio, not only because he was their first inventor, but also because he made an infinite number of them, of a beauty so rare that none appeared to please save such as came out of his shop.

Being thus apprenticed to the goldsmith's art, but taking

* Garlands.

no pleasure therein, he was ever occupied in drawing. Endowed by nature with a perfect spirit and with an admirable and judicious taste in painting, although he was a goldsmith in his boyhood, yet, by devoting himself ever to design, he became so quick, so ready, and so facile, that many say that while he was working as a goldsmith he would draw a portrait of all who passed the shop, producing a likeness in a second; and of this we still have proof in an infinite number of portraits in his works, which show a most lifelike resemblance.

His first pictures were in the Chapel of the Vespucci in Ognissanti, where there is a Dead Christ with some saints, and a Misericordia over an arch, in which is the portrait of Amerigo Vespucci, who made the voyages to the Indies; and in the refectory of that place he painted a Last Supper in fresco. In S. Croce, on the right hand of the entrance into the church, he painted the Story of S. Paulino; wherefore, having acquired very great fame and coming into much credit, he painted a chapel in S. Trinita for Francesco Sassetti, with stories of S. Francis. This work was admirably executed by him, and wrought with grace, lovingness, and a high finish; and he counterfeited and portrayed therein the Ponte a S. Trinita, with the Palace of the Spini. On the first wall he depicted the story of S. Francis appearing in the air and restoring the child to life; and here, in those women who see him being restored to life—after their sorrow for his death as they bear him to the grave—there are seen gladness and marvel at his resurrection. He also counterfeited the friars issuing from the church behind the Cross, together with some gravediggers, to bury him, all wrought very naturally; and there are likewise other figures marveling at that event which give no little pleasure to the eye, among which are portraits of Maso degli Albizzi, Messer Agnolo Acciaiuoli, and Messer Palla Strozzi, eminent citizens often cited in the history of the city. On another wall he painted S. Francis, in the presence of the vicar, renouncing his inheritance from his father, Pietro

Bernardone, and assuming the habit of sackcloth, which he is girding round him with the cord. On the middle wall he is shown going to Rome and having his Rule confirmed by Pope Honorius, and presenting roses in January to that Pontiff. In this scene he depicted the Hall of the Consistory, with Cardinals seated around, and certain steps ascending to it, furnishing the flight of steps with a balustrade, and painting there some half-length figures portrayed from the life, among which is the portrait of the elder Lorenzo de' Medici, the Magnificent; and there he also painted S. Francis receiving the Stigmata. In the last he made the Saint dead, with his friars mourning for him, among whom is one friar kissing his hands —an effect that could not be rendered better in painting; not to mention that a Bishop in full robes, with spectacles on his nose, is chanting the prayers for the dead so vividly, that only the lack of sound shows him to be painted. In one of two pictures that are on either side of the panel he portrayed Francesco Sassetti on his knees, and in the other his wife, Monna Nera, with their children (but these last are in the aforesaid scene of the child being restored to life), and with certain beautiful maidens of the same family, whose names I have not been able to discover, all in the costumes and fashions of that age, which gives no little pleasure. Besides this, he made four Sibyls on the vaulting, and an ornament above the arch on the front wall outside the chapel, containing the scene of the Tiburtine Sibyl making the Emperor Octavian adore Christ, which is executed in a masterly manner for a work in fresco, with much vivacity and loveliness in the colors. To this work he added a panel wrought in distemper, also by his hand, containing a Nativity of Christ that should amaze any person of understanding, wherein he portrayed himself and made certain heads of shepherds, which are held to be something divine. Of this Sibyl and of other parts of this work there are some very beautiful drawings in our book, made in chiaroscuro, and in particular the view in perspective of the Ponte a S. Trinita.

For the Frati Ingesuati he painted a panel for their high altar, with certain Saints kneeling—namely, S. Giusto, Bishop of Volterra, who was the titular Saint of that church; S. Zanobi, Bishop of Florence; an Angel Raphael; a S. Michael, clad in most beautiful armor; and other saints. For this work Domenico truly deserves praise, for he was the first who began to counterfeit with colors certain trimmings and ornaments of gold, which had not been done up to that time; and he swept away in great measure those borders of gilding that were made with mordant or with bole, which were more suitable for church-hangings than for the work of good masters. More beautiful than all the other figures is the Madonna, who has the Child in her arms and four little angels round her. This panel, which is wrought as well as any work in distemper could be, was then placed in the church of those friars without the Porta a Pinti; but since that building, as will be told elsewhere, was destroyed, it is now in the Church of S. Giovannino, within the Porta S. Piero Gattolini, where there is the Convent of the aforesaid Ingesuati.

In the Church of Cestello he painted a panel—afterwards finished by his brothers David and Benedetto—containing the Visitation of Our Lady, with certain most charming and beautiful heads of women. In the Church of the Innocenti he painted the Story of the Magi on a panel in distemper, which is much extolled. In this are heads most beautiful in expression and varied in features, both young and old; and in the head of Our Lady, in particular, are seen all the dignity, beauty, and grace that art can give to the Mother of the Son of God. On the transept of the Church of S. Marco there is another panel, with a Last Supper in the guest-room, both executed with diligence; and in the house of Giovanni Tornabuoni there is a round picture with the Story of the Magi, wrought with diligence. In the Little Hospital, for the elder

Lorenzo de' Medici, he painted the story of Vulcan, in which many nude figures are at work with hammers making thunderbolts for Jove. And in the Church of Ognissanti in Florence, in competition with Sandro Botticelli, he painted a S. Jerome in fresco (which is now beside the door that leads to the choir), surrounding him with an infinite number of instruments and books, such as are used by the learned. The friars having occasion to remove the choir from the place where it stood, this picture, together with that of Sandro Botticelli, has been bound round with irons and transported without injury into the middle of the church, at the very time when these *Lives* are being printed for the second time. He also painted the arch over the door of S. Maria Ughi, and a little shrine for the Guild of Linen-manufacturers, and likewise a very beautiful S. George, slaying the Dragon, in the same Church of Ognissanti. And in truth he had a very good knowledge of the method of painting on walls, which he did with very great facility, although he was scrupulously careful in the composition of his works.

Being then summoned to Rome by Pope Sixtus IV to paint his chapel, in company with other masters, he painted there Christ calling Peter and Andrew from their nets, and the Resurrection of Jesus Christ, the greater part of which has since been spoilt in consequence of being over the door, on which it became necessary to replace an architrave that had fallen down. There was living in Rome at this same time Francesco Tornabuoni, a rich and honored merchant, much the friend of Domenico. This man, whose wife had died in childbirth, as is told in the Life of Andrea Verrocchio, desiring to honor her as became their noble station, had caused a tomb to be made for her in the Minerva; and he also wished Domenico to paint the whole wall against which this tomb stood, and likewise to make for it a little panel in distemper. On that wall, therefore, he painted four stories—two of S. John the Baptist and two of the Madonna—which brought him truly great praise at that time. And Francesco took so much pleasure in his dealings with Domenico, that, when the latter returned to Florence rich in honor and in gains, Francesco recommended him by letters to his relative Giovanni, telling him how well the painter had served him in that work, and how well satisfied the Pope had been with his pictures. Hearing this, Giovanni began to contemplate employing him on some magnificent work, such as would honor his own memory and bring fame and profit to Domenico.

Now it chanced that the principal chapel of S. Maria Novella (a convent of Preaching Friars), formerly painted by Andrea Orcagna, was injured in many parts by rain in consequence of the roof of the vaulting being badly covered. For this reason many citizens had wished to restore it, or rather, to have it painted anew; but the owners, who belonged to the family of the Ricci, had never consented to this, being unable to bear so great an expense themselves, and unwilling to allow others to do so, lest they should lose the rights of ownership and the distinction of the arms handed down to them by their ancestors. Giovanni, then, being desirous that Domenico should make him his memorial there, set to work in this matter, trying various ways; and finally he promised the Ricci to bear the whole expense himself, to give them some sort of recompense, and to have their arms placed in the most conspicuous and honorable place in that chapel. And so they came to an agreement, making a contract in the form of a very precise instrument according to the terms described above. Giovanni allotted this work to Domenico, with the same subjects as were painted there before; and they agreed that the price should be 1,200 gold ducats of full weight, with 200 more in the event of the work giving satisfaction to Giovanni. Thereupon Domenico put his hand to the work and labored without ceasing for four years until he had finished it—which was in 1485—to the very great satisfaction and contentment of Giovanni, who, while admitting that he had been well served, and confessing ingenuously that Domenico had earned the additional 200 ducats, said that he would be pleased if he would be satisfied with the original price. And Domenico, who esteemed glory and honor much more than riches, immediately let him off all the rest, declaring that he set much greater store on having given him satisfaction than on the matter of complete payment.

Giovanni afterwards caused two large coats of arms to be made of stone—one for the Tornaquinci and the other for the Tornabuoni—and placed on the pilasters outside the chapel, and in the arch he placed other arms belonging to that family, which is divided into various names and various arms—namely, in addition to the two already mentioned, those of the Ghiachinotti, Popoleschi, Marabottini, and Cardinali. And afterwards, when Domenico painted the altar-panel, he caused to be placed in the gilt ornament, under an arch, as a finishing touch to that panel, a very beautiful Tabernacle of the Sacrament, on the frontal of which he made a little shield a half a foot in length, containing the arms of the said owners —that is, the Ricci. And a fine jest it was at the opening of the chapel, for these Ricci looked for their arms with much ado, and finally, not being able to find them, went off to the Tribunal of Eight, contract in hand. Whereupon the Tornabuoni showed that these arms had been placed in the most conspicuous and most honorable part of the work; and although the others exclaimed that they were invisible, they were told that they were in the wrong, and that they must be content, since the Tornabuoni had caused them to be placed in so honorable a position as the neighborhood of the most Holy Sacrament. And so it was decided by that tribunal that they should be left untouched, as they may be seen to-day. Now, if this should appear to anyone to be outside the scope of the Life that I have to write, let him not be vexed, for it all flowed naturally from the tip of my pen. And it should serve, if for nothing else, at least to show how easily poverty falls a prey to riches, and how riches, if accompanied by discretion, achieve without censure anything that a man desires.

But to return to the beautiful works of Domenico: in that chapel, first of all, are the four Evangelists on the vaulting, larger than life; and, on the window-wall, stories of S. Dominic, S. Peter Martyr, S. John going into the Desert, the Madonna receiving the Annunciation from the Angel, and many patron saints of Florence on their knees above the window; while at the foot, on the right hand, is a portrait from life of Giovanni Tornabuoni, with one of his wife on the left, which are both said to be very lifelike. On the right-hand wall are seven scenes—six below, in compartments as large as the wall allows, and the last above, twice as broad as any of the others and bounded by the arch of the vaulting; and on the left-hand wall are also seven scenes from the life of S. John the Baptist.

The panel, which stands by itself, he executed in distemper, as he did the other figures in the six pictures. Besides the Madonna, who is seated in the sky with the Child in her arms, and the other saints who are round her, there are S. Laurence and S. Stephen, who are absolutely alive, with S. Vincent and S. Peter Martyr, who lack nothing save speech. It is true that a part of this panel remained unfinished in consequence of his death; but he had carried it so far on that there was nothing left to complete save certain figures on the back, where there is the Resurrection of Christ, with three figures in the other pictures, and the whole was afterwards finished by Benedetto and David Ghirlandaio, his brothers. This chapel was held to be a very beautiful work, grand, ornate, and lovely, through the vivacity of the colors, through the masterly finish in their application on the walls, and because very little retouching was done on the dry, not to mention the invention and the composition of the subjects. And in truth Domenico deserves the greatest praise on all accounts, particularly for the liveliness of the heads, which, being portrayed from nature, present to every eye most life-like effigies of many distinguished persons.

For the same Giovanni Tornabuoni, at his Villa of Casso Maccherelli, which stands on the River Terzolle at no great distance from the city, he painted a chapel which has since been half destroyed through being too near to the river; but the paintings, although they have been uncovered for many years, continually washed by rain and scorched by the sun, have remained so fresh that one might think they had been covered—so great is the value of working in fresco, when the work is done with care and judgment and not retouched on the dry. He also made many figures of Florentine Saints, with most beautiful adornments, in that hall of the Palace of the Signoria which contains the marvelous clock of Lorenzo della Volpaia. And so great was his love of working and of giving satisfaction to all, that he commanded his lads to accept any work that might be brought to his shop, even hoops for women's baskets, saying that if they would not do them he would paint them himself, to the end that none might leave the shop unsatisfied. But when household cares fell upon him he was troubled, and he therefore laid the charge of all expenditure on his brother David, saying to him, "Leave me to work, and do thou provide, for now that I have begun to understand the methods of this art, it grieves me that they will not commission me to paint the whole circuit of the walls of the city of Florence with stories"; thus revealing a spirit absolutely invincible and resolute in every action.

He is said to have been so accurate in draftsmanship, that, when making drawings of the antiquities of Rome, such as arches, baths, columns, colosseums, obelisks, amphitheaters, and aqueducts, he would work with the eye alone, without rule, compasses, or measurements; and after he had made them, on being measured, they were found absolutely correct, as if he had used measurements. He drew the Colosseum by the eye, placing at the foot of it a figure standing upright, from the proportions of which the whole edifice could be measured; this was tried by some masters after his death, and found quite correct.

Over a door of the cemetery of S. Maria Nuova he painted a S. Michael in fresco, clad in armor which reflects the light most beautifully—a thing seldom done before his day. At the Abbey of Passignano, a seat of the Monks of Vallombrosa, he wrought certain works in company with his brother David and Bastiano da San Gimignano. Here the two others, finding themselves poorly fed by the monks before the arrival of Domenico, complained to the Abbot, praying him to have them better served, since it was not right that they should be treated like bricklayers' laborers. This the Abbot promised to do, saying in excuse that it was due more to the ignorance of the monks who looked after strangers than to malice. Domenico arrived, but everything continued just the same; whereupon David, seeking out the Abbot once again, declared with due apologies that he was not doing this for his own sake but on account of the merits and talents of his brother. But the Abbot, like the ignorant man that he was, made no other answer. That evening, then, when they had sat down to supper, up came the stranger's steward with a board covered with bowls and messes only fit for a hangman, exactly the same as before. Thereupon David, flying into a rage, upset the soup over the friar, and, seizing the loaf that was on the table, fell upon him with it and belabored him in such a manner that he was carried away to his cell more dead than alive. The Abbot, who was already in bed, got up and ran to the noise, believing that the monastery was tumbling down; and finding the friar in a sorry plight, he began to upbraid David. Enraged by this, David bade him be gone out of his sight, saying that the talent of Domenico was worth more than all the pigs of Abbots like him that had ever lived in that monastery. Whereupon the Abbot, seeing himself in the wrong, did his utmost from that time onwards to treat them like the important men that they were.

This work finished, Domenico returned to Florence, where he painted a panel for Signor di Carpi, sending another to Rimini for Signor Carlo Malatesta, who had it placed in his chapel in S. Domenico. The latter panel was in distemper, with three very beautiful figures, and with little scenes below; and behind were figures painted to look like bronze, with very great design and art. Besides these, he painted two panels for the Abbey of S. Giusto, a seat of the Order of Camaldoli, outside Volterra; these panels, which are wondrously beautiful, he executed at the order of the Magnificent Lorenzo de' Medici, for the reason that the abbey was then held *"in commendam"* by his son Cardinal Giovanni de' Medici, who was afterwards Pope Leo. This abbey was restored not many years ago by the Very Reverend Messer Giovan Batista Bava of Volterra, who likewise held it *"in commendam,"* to the said Congregation of Camaldoli.

Being then summoned to Siena through the agency of the Magnificent Lorenzo de' Medici, Domenico undertook to adorn the façade of the Duomo with mosaics, Lorenzo acting as surety for him in this work to the extent of 20,000 ducats. And he began the work with much confidence and a better manner, but, being overtaken by death, he left it unfinished; even as, by reason of the death of the aforesaid Magnificent Lorenzo, there remained unfinished at Florence the Chapel of S. Zanobi, on which Domenico had begun to work in mosaic in company with the illuminator Gherardo. By the hand of Domenico is a very beautiful Annunciation in mosaic that is to be seen over that side door of S. Maria del Fiore which leads to the Servi; and nothing better than this has yet been seen among the works of our modern masters of mosaic. Domenico used to say that painting was mere drawing, and that the true painting for eternity was mosaic.

Just when Domenico was about to put his hand to some

very great works both in Pisa and in Siena, he fell sick of a
most grievous putrid fever, which cut short his life in five
days. As he lay ill, the Tornabuoni sent him a hundred ducats
of gold as a gift, proving their regard and particular friendship for Domenico in return for his unceasing labors in the
service of Giovanni and of his house.

Domenico enriched the art of painting by working in mosaic with a manner more modern than was shown by any of
the innumerable Tuscans who essayed it, as is proved by the
works that he wrought, few though they may be. Wherefore
he has deserved to be held in honor and esteem for such rich
and undying benefits to art, and to be celebrated with extraordinary praises after his death.

POLLAIUOLO

[*Antonio di Jacopo d'Antonio di Benci, called del
Pollaiuolo, was born between 1426 and 1433;
died in 1498.*]

MANY men begin in a humble spirit with unimportant works,
who, gaining courage from proficiency, grow also in power
and ability, in such a manner that they aspire to greater undertakings and almost reach Heaven with their beautiful
thoughts. Wherefore such men walk through this life to the
end with so much glory, that they leave marvelous memorials
of themselves to the world, as did Antonio Pollaiuolo, who
was greatly esteemed in his day for the rare acquirements
that he had made with his industry and labor.

This artist was born in the city of Florence, from a father
of humble station and no great wealth, who, recognizing by
many signs the good and acute intelligence of his son, but not
having the means to educate him in letters, apprenticed Antonio to the goldsmith's art under Bartoluccio Ghiberti, a
very excellent master in that calling at that time. Antonio,
then, being pushed on by Bartoluccio, not only learnt to set
jewels and to fire enamels on silver, but was also held the
best master of the tools of that art. Wherefore Lorenzo
Ghiberti, who was then working on the doors of S. Giovanni,
having observed the manner of Antonio, called him into that
work in company with many other young men, and set him
to labor on one of the festoons which he then had in hand.

On this Antonio made a quail which is still in existence, so
beautiful and so perfect that it lacks nothing but the power

of flight. Antonio, therefore, had not spent many weeks over this work before he was known as the best, both in design and in patient execution, of all those who were working there, and as more gifted and more diligent than any other. Whereupon, growing ever both in ability and in fame, he left Bartoluccio and Lorenzo, and opened a fine and magnificent goldsmith's shop for himself in the Mercato Nuovo in that city. And for many years he followed that art, never ceasing to make new designs, and executing in relief wax candles and other things of fancy, which in a short time caused him to be held—as he was—the first master of his calling.

There lived at the same time another goldsmith called Maso Finiguerra, who had an extraordinary fame, and deservedly, since there had never been seen any master of engraving and of niello who could make so great a number of figures as he could, whether in a small or in a large space; as is still proved by certain paxes in the Church of S. Giovanni in Florence, wrought by him with most minutely elaborated stories from the Passion of Christ. This man drew very well and in abundance, and in our book are many of his drawings of figures, both draped and nude, and scenes done in water-color. In competition with him Antonio executed certain scenes, in which he equaled him in diligence and surpassed him in design; wherefore the Consuls of the Guild of Merchants, seeing the excellence of Antonio, and remembering that there were certain scenes in silver to be wrought for the altar of S. Giovanni, such as it had ever been the custom for various masters to make at different times, determined among themselves that Antonio also should make some. This came to pass; and his works turned out so excellent, that they are recognized as the best among them all. These were the Feast of Herod and the Dance of Herodias; but more beautiful than anything else was the S. John that is in the middle of the altar, a work wrought wholly with the chasing-tool, and much extolled. For this reason he was commissioned by the said Consuls to make the candelabra of silver, each six feet in height, and the Cross in proportion; which work he brought to such perfection, with such an abundance of carving, that it has ever been esteemed a marvelous thing both by foreigners and by his countrymen. In this calling he took infinite pains, both with the works that he executed in gold and with those in enamel and silver. Among these are some very beautiful paxes in S. Giovanni, colored by the action of fire, which are such that they could be scarcely improved with the brush; and some of his marvelous enamels may be seen in other churches in Florence, Rome, and other parts of Italy. But many of the works of Pollaiuolo have been destroyed and melted down to meet the necessities of the city in times of war.

For this reason, recognizing that this art gave no long life to the labors of its craftsmen, and desiring to gain a more lasting memory, Antonio resolved to pursue it no longer. And so, his brother Piero being a painter, he associated himself with him in order to learn the methods of handling and using colors; but it appeared to him an art so different from the goldsmith's, that, if he had not been so hasty in resolving to abandon his own art entirely, it might well have been that he would never have brought himself to turn to the other. However, spurred by fear of shame rather than by hope of profit, in a few months he acquired a practical knowledge of coloring and became an excellent master. He associated himself entirely with Piero, and they made many pictures in company; among others, since they took great delight in color, a panel in oil in S. Miniato al Monte outside Florence, for the Cardinal of Portugal. On this panel, which was placed on the altar of his chapel, they painted S. James the Apostle, S. Eustace, and S. Vincent, which have been much extolled. Piero, in particular, painted certain prophets on the wall in oil (a method that he had learnt from Andrea del Castagno), in the corners of the angles below the architrave. In the Proconsulate Antonio made portraits from life of Messer Poggio, Secretary to the Signoria of Florence, who continued the History of Florence after Messer Leonardo d'Arezzo, and of Messer Giannozzo Manetti, a man of no small learning and repute, in the same place where other masters some time before had made portraits of Zanobi da Strada, a poet of Florence, Donato Acciaiuoli, and others. In the Chapel of the Pucci, in S. Sebastiano de' Servi, he painted the panel of the altar, which is a rare and excellent work, containing marvelous horses, nudes, and very beautiful figures in foreshortening, and S. Sebastian himself portrayed from life—namely, from Gino di Lodovico Capponi. This work received greater praise than any other that Antonio ever made, since, seeking to imitate nature to the utmost of his power, he showed in one of the archers, who is resting his crossbow against his chest and bending down to the ground in order to load it, all the force that a man of strong arm can exert in loading that weapon, for we see his veins and muscles swelling, and the man himself holding his breath in order to gain more strength. Nor is this the only figure wrought with careful consideration, for all the others in their various attitudes also demonstrate clearly enough the thought and the intelligence that he put into this work, which was certainly appreciated by Antonio Pucci, who gave him 300 crowns for it, declaring that he was barely paying him for the colors. It was finished in the year 1475.

Gaining courage from this, therefore, he painted at S. Miniato fra le Torri, outside the Gate, a S. Christopher twenty feet in height, a very beautiful work executed in a modern manner, the figure being better proportioned than any other of that size that had been made up to that time. In the Palace of the Signoria of Florence, at the Porta della Catena, he made a S. John the Baptist; and in the house of the Medici he painted for the elder Lorenzo three figures of Hercules in three pictures, each ten feet in height. The first of these, which is slaying Antaeus, is a very beautiful figure, in which the strength of Hercules as he crushes the other is seen most vividly, for the muscles and nerves of that figure are all strained in the struggle to destroy Antaeus. The head of Hercules shows the gnashing of the teeth so well in harmony with the other parts, that even the toes of his feet are raised in the effort. Nor did he take less pains with Antaeus, who, crushed in the arms of Hercules, is seen sinking and losing all his strength, and giving up his breath through his open mouth. The second Hercules, who is slaying the Lion, has the left knee pressed against its chest, and, setting his teeth and extending his arms, and grasping the Lion's jaws with both his hands, he is opening them and rending them asunder by main force, although the beast is tearing his arms grievously with its claws in self-defense. The third picture, wherein Hercules is slaying the Hydra, is something truly marvelous, particularly the serpent, which he made so lively and so natural in coloring that nothing could be made more lifelike. In that beast are seen venom, fire, ferocity, rage, and such vivacity, that he deserves to be celebrated and to be closely imitated in this by all good craftsmen.

For the Company of S. Angelo in Arezzo he executed an oil painting on cloth, with a Crucifix on one side, and on the other S. Michael in combat with the Dragon, as beautiful as any work that there is to be seen by his hand; for the figure of S. Michael, who is bravely confronting the Dragon, setting his teeth and knitting his brows, truly seems to have descended from Heaven in order to effect the vengeance of God against the pride of Lucifer, and it is indeed a marvelous work. He had a more modern grasp of the nude than the masters before his day, and he dissected many bodies in order to study their anatomy. He was the first to demonstrate the method of searching out the muscles, in order that they might have their due form and place in his figures, and he engraved on copper a battle of nude figures all girt round with a chain;

and after this one he made other engravings, with much better workmanship than had been shown by the other masters who had lived before him.

For these reasons, then, he became famous among craftsmen, and after the death of Pope Sixtus IV he was summoned by his successor, Pope Innocent, to Rome, where he made a tomb of metal for the said Innocent, wherein he portrayed him from nature, seated in the attitude of giving the Benediction; and this was placed in S. Pietro. That of the said Pope Sixtus, which was finished at very great cost, was placed in the chapel that is called by the name of that Pontiff. It stands quite by itself, with very rich adornments, and on it there lies an excellent figure of the Pope; and the tomb of Innocent stands in S. Pietro, beside the chapel that contains the Lance of Christ. It is said that the same man designed the Palace of the Belvedere for the said Pope Innocent, although, since he had little experience of building, it was erected by others. Finally, after becoming rich, Antonio died in 1498, and was buried in S. Pietro in Vincula.

Antonio left many disciples, among whom was Andrea Sansovino. He had a most fortunate life in his day, finding rich Pontiffs, and his own city at the height of its greatness and delighting in talent, wherefore he was much esteemed; whereas, if he had chanced to live in an unfavorable age, he would not have produced such fruits as he did, since troublous times are deadly enemies to the sciences in which men labor and take delight.

BOTTICELLI

[*Alessandro di Mariano Filipepi, called Sandro Botticelli,
was born in 1447 and died in 1510.*]

AT the same time with the elder Lorenzo de' Medici, the
Magnificent, which was truly a golden age for men of intellect, there also flourished one Alessandro, called Sandro after
our custom, and surnamed di Botticelli for a reason that we
shall see below. This man was the son of Mariano Filipepi,
a citizen of Florence, who brought him up with care, and
had him instructed in all those things that are usually taught
to children before they are old enough to be apprenticed to
some calling. But although he found it easy to learn whatever he wished, nevertheless he was ever restless, nor was he
contented with any form of learning, whether reading, writing, or arithmetic, insomuch that his father, weary of the
vagaries of his son's brain, in despair apprenticed him as a
goldsmith with a boon-companion of his own, called Botticelli, no mean master of that art in his day.

Now in that age there was a very close connection—nay,
almost a constant intercourse—between the goldsmiths and
the painters; wherefore Sandro, who was a ready fellow and
had devoted himself wholly to design, became enamored of
painting, and determined to devote himself to that. For this
reason he spoke out his mind freely to his father, who, recognizing the inclination of his brain, took him to Fra Filippo of
the Carmine, a most excellent painter of that time, with whom
he placed him to learn the art, according to Sandro's own
desire. Thereupon, devoting himself heart and soul to that

art, Sandro followed and imitated his master so well that Fra Filippo, growing to love him, taught him very thoroughly, so that he soon rose to such a rank as none would have expected for him.

While still quite young, he painted a figure of Fortitude in the Mercatanzia of Florence, among the pictures of Virtues that were wrought by Antonio and Piero del Pollaiuolo. For the Chapel of the Bardi in S. Spirito at Florence he painted a panel, wrought with diligence and brought to a fine completion, which contains certain olive trees and palms executed with consummate lovingness. He painted a panel for the Convertite Nuns, and another for those of S. Barnaba. In the transept of the Ognissanti, by the door that leads into the choir, he painted for the Vespucci a S. Augustine in fresco, with which he took very great pains, seeking to surpass all the painters of his time, and particularly Domenico Ghirlandaio, who had made a S. Jerome on the other side; and this work won very great praise, for in the head of that Saint he depicted the profound meditation and acute subtlety that are found in men of wisdom who are ever concentrated on the investigation of the highest and most difficult matters. This picture, as was said in the Life of Ghirlandaio, has this year (1564) been removed safe and sound from its original position.

Having thus come into credit and reputation, he was commissioned by the Guild of Porta Santa Maria to paint in S. Marco a panel with the Coronation of Our Lady and a choir of angels, which he designed and executed very well. He made many works in the house of the Medici for the elder Lorenzo, particularly a Pallas on a device of great branches, which spouted forth fire: this he painted of the size of life, as he did a S. Sebastian. In S. Maria Maggiore in Florence, beside the Chapel of the Panciatichi, there is a very beautiful Pietà with little figures. For various houses throughout the city he painted round pictures, and many female nudes, of which there are still two at Castello, a villa of Duke Cosimo's; one representing the birth of Venus, with those Winds and Zephyrs that bring her to the earth, with the Cupids; and likewise another Venus, whom the Graces are covering with flowers, as a symbol of spring; and all this he is seen to have expressed very gracefully. Round an apartment of the house of Giovanni Vespucci, now belonging to Piero Salviati, in the Via de' Servi, he made many pictures which were enclosed by frames of walnut-wood, by way of ornament and paneling, with many most lively and beautiful figures. In the house of the Pucci, likewise, he painted with little figures Boccaccio's tale of Nastagio degli Onesti in four square pictures of most charming and beautiful workmanship, and the Epiphany in a round picture. For a chapel in the Monastery of Cestello he painted an Annunciation on a panel.

At this time Sandro was commissioned to paint a little panel with figures a foot and a half in length, which was placed between two doors in the principal façade of S. Maria Novella, on the left as one enters the church by the door in the center. It contains the Adoration of the Magi, and wonderful feeling is seen in the first old man, who, kissing the foot of Our Lord, and melting with tenderness, shows very clearly that he has achieved the end of his long journey. The figure of this King is an actual portrait of the elder Cosimo de' Medici, the most lifelike and most natural that is to be found of him in our own day. The second, who is Giuliano de' Medici, father of Pope Clement VII, is seen devoutly doing reverence to the Child with a most intent expression, and presenting Him with his offering. The third, also on his knees, appears to be adoring Him and giving Him thanks, while confessing that He is the true Messiah; this is Giovanni, son of Cosimo.

It is not possible to describe the beauty that Sandro depicted in the heads that are therein seen, which are drawn in various attitudes, some in full face, some in profile, some in three-quarter face, others bending down, and others, again, in various manners; with different expressions for the young and the old, and with all the bizarre effects that reveal to us the perfection of his skill; and he distinguished the Courts of the three Kings one from another, insomuch that one can see which are the retainers of each. This is truly a most admirable work, and executed so beautifully, whether in coloring, drawing, or composition, that every craftsman at the present day stands in a marvel thereat. And at that time it brought him such great fame, both in Florence and abroad, that Pope Sixtus IV, having accomplished the building of the chapel of his palace in Rome, and wishing to have it painted, ordained that he should be made head of that work; whereupon he painted therein with his own hand the following scenes—namely, the Temptation of Christ by the Devil, Moses slaying the Egyptian, Moses receiving drink from the daughters of Jethro the Midianite, and likewise fire descending from Heaven on the sacrifice of the sons of Aaron, with certain Sanctified Popes in the niches above the scenes. Having therefore acquired still greater fame and reputation among the great number of competitors who worked with him, both Florentines and men of other cities, he received from the Pope a good sum of money, the whole of which he consumed and squandered in a moment during his residence in Rome, where he lived in haphazard fashion, as was his wont.

Having at the same time finished and unveiled the part that had been assigned to him, he returned immediately to Florence, where, being a man of inquiring mind, he made a commentary on part of Dante, illustrated the Inferno, and printed it; on which he wasted much of his time, bringing infinite disorder into his life by neglecting his work. Our artist was so ardent a partisan of Fra Girolamo Savonarola of Ferrara that he was thereby induced to desert his painting, and, having no income to live on, fell into very great distress. For this reason, persisting in his attachment to that party, and becoming a "Weeper" (as the members of the sect were then called), he abandoned his work; wherefore he ended in his old age by finding himself so poor, that, if Lorenzo de' Medici, for whom, besides many other things, he had done some work at the villa of Volterra, had not succored him the while that he lived, as did afterwards his friends and many excellent men who loved him for his talent, he would have almost died of hunger.

In S. Francesco, outside the Porta a San Miniato, there is a Madonna in a round picture by the hand of Sandro, with some angels of the size of life, which was held a very beautiful work. Sandro was a man of very pleasant humor, often playing tricks on his disciples and his friends; wherefore it is related that once, when a pupil of his who was called Biagio had made a round picture exactly like the one mentioned above, in order to sell it, Sandro sold it for six florins of gold to a citizen; then, finding Biagio, he said to him, "At last I have sold this thy picture; so this evening it must be hung on high, where it will be seen better, and in the morning thou must go to the house of the citizen who has bought it, and bring him here, that he may see it in a good light in its proper place; and then he will pay thee the money." "O, my master," said Biagio, "how well you have done." Then, going into the shop, he hung the picture at a good height, and went off. Meanwhile Sandro and Jacopo, who was another of his disciples, made eight caps of paper, like those worn by citizens, and fixed them with white wax on the heads of the eight angels that surrounded the Madonna in the said picture. Now, in the morning, up comes Biagio with his citizen, who had bought the picture and was in the secret. They entered the shop, and Biagio, looking up, saw his Madonna seated, not among his angels, but among the Signoria of Florence, with all those caps. Thereupon he was just about to begin to make an outcry and to excuse himself to the man who had bought it, when, seeing that the other, instead of complaining, was actually praising the picture, he kept silent himself. Finally, going with the citizen to his house, Biagio received his payment of six florins, the price for which his master had sold the picture; and then, returning to the shop just as Sandro and Jacopo had removed the paper caps, he saw his angels as true angels, and not as citizens in their caps. All in a maze, and not knowing what to say, he turned at last to Sandro and said: "Master, I know not whether I am dreaming, or whether this is true. When I came here before, these angels had red caps on their heads, and now they have not; what does it mean?" "Thou art out of thy wits, Biagio," said Sandro; "this money has turned thy head. If it were so, thinkest thou that the citizen would have bought the picture?" "It is true," replied Biagio, "that he said nothing to me about it, but for all that it seemed to me strange." Finally, all the other lads gathered round him and wrought on him to believe that it had been a fit of giddiness.

Another time a cloth-weaver came to live in a house next to Sandro's, and erected no less than eight looms, which, when at work, not only deafened poor Sandro with the noise of the treadles and the movement of the frames, but shook his whole house, the walls of which were no stronger than they should be, so that what with the one thing and the other he could not work or even stay at home. Time after time he besought his neighbor to put an end to this annoyance, but the other said that he both would and could do what he pleased in his own house; whereupon Sandro, in disdain, balanced on the top of his own wall, which was higher than his neighbor's and not very strong, an enormous stone, more than enough to fill a wagon, which threatened to fall at the slightest shaking of the wall and to shatter the roof, ceilings, webs, and looms of his neighbor, who, terrified by this danger, ran to Sandro, but was answered in his very own words —namely, that he both could and would do whatever he pleased in his own house. Nor could he get any other answer out of him, so that he was forced to come to a reasonable agreement and to be a good neighbor to Sandro.

It is also said that he had a surpassing love for all whom he saw to be zealous students of art; and that he earned much, but wasted everything through negligence and lack of management. Finally, having grown old and useless, and being forced to walk with crutches, without which he could not stand upright, he died, infirm and decrepit, and was buried in Ognissanti at Florence.

In the *guardaroba* of the Lord Duke Cosimo there are two very beautiful heads of women in profile by his hand, one of which is said to be the mistress of Giuliano de' Medici, brother of Lorenzo, and the other Madonna Lucrezia de' Tornabuoni, wife of the said Lorenzo. Sandro's drawings were extraordinarily good, and so many, that for some time after his death all the craftsmen strove to obtain some of them; and we have some in our book, made with great mastery and judgment.

VERROCCHIO

[*Andrea di Michele di Francesco Cione, called Verrocchio,
the name of the goldsmith to whom he was apprenticed,
was born in 1435 and died in 1488.*]

ANDREA DEL VERROCCHIO, a Florentine, was in his day a
goldsmith, a master of perspective, a sculptor, a woodcarver,
a painter, and a musician; but in the arts of sculpture and
painting, to tell the truth, he had a manner somewhat hard
and crude, as one who acquired it rather by infinite study
than by the facility of a natural gift. Even if he had been as
poor in this facility as he was rich in the study and diligence
that exalted him, he would have been most excellent in those
arts, which, for their highest perfection, require a union of
study and natural power. If either of these is wanting, a man
rarely attains to the first rank; but study will do a great deal,
and thus Andrea, who had it in greater abundance than any
other craftsman whatsoever, is counted among the rare and
excellent masters of our arts.

In his youth he applied himself to the sciences, particularly to geometry. Among many other things that he made
while working at the goldsmith's art were certain buttons for
copes, which are in S. Maria del Fiore at Florence; and he
also made larger works, particularly a cup, full of animals,
foliage, and other bizarre fancies, which is known to all
goldsmiths, and casts are taken of it; and likewise another,
on which there is a very beautiful dance of little children.
Having given a proof of his powers in these two works, he
was commissioned by the Guild of Merchants to make two

scenes in silver for the ends of the altar of S. Giovanni, from which, when put into execution, he acquired very great praise and fame.

There were wanting at this time in Rome some of those large figures of the Apostles which generally stood on the altar of the Chapel of the Pope, as well as certain other works in silver that had been destroyed; wherefore Pope Sixtus sent for Andrea and with great favor commissioned him to do all that was necessary in this matter, and he brought the whole to perfection with much diligence and judgment. Meanwhile, perceiving that the many antique statues and other things that were being found in Rome were held in very great esteem, insomuch that the famous bronze horse was set up by the Pope at S. Giovanni Laterano, and that even the fragments—not to speak of complete works—which were being discovered every day, were prized, Andrea determined to devote himself to sculpture. And so, completely abandoning the goldsmith's art, he set himself to cast some little figures in bronze, which were greatly extolled. Thereupon, growing in courage, he began to work in marble.

Having then returned to Florence with money, fame, and honor, he was commissioned to make a David of bronze, five feet in height, which, when finished, was placed in the Palace, with great credit to himself, at the head of the staircase, where the Catena was. The same Andrea made a half-length Madonna in half-relief, with the Child in her arms, in a marble panel, which was formerly in the house of the Medici, and is now placed, as a very beautiful thing, over a door in the apartment of the Duchess of Florence. He also made two heads of metal, likewise in half-relief; one of Alexander the Great, in profile, and the other a fanciful portrait of Darius; each being a separate work by itself, with variety in the crests, armor, and everything else. Both these heads were sent to Hungary by the elder Lorenzo de' Medici, the

Magnificent, to King Matthias Corvinus, together with many other things.

Having acquired the name of an excellent master by means of these works, above all through many works in metal, in which he took much delight, he made a tomb of bronze in S. Lorenzo, wholly in the round, for Giovanni and Pietro di Cosimo de' Medici, with a sarcophagus of porphyry supported by four corner-pieces of bronze, with twisted foliage very well wrought and finished with the greatest diligence. This tomb stands between the Chapel of the Sacrament and the Sacristy, and no work could be better done, whether wrought in bronze or cast; above all since at the same time he showed therein his talent in architecture, for he placed the said tomb within the embrasure of a window which is about ten feet in breadth and twenty in height, and set it on a base that divides the said Chapel of the Sacrament from the old Sacristy. And over the sarcophagus, to fill up the embrasure right up to the vaulting, he made a grating of bronze ropes in a pattern of *mandorle,* most natural, and adorned in certain places with festoons and other beautiful things of fancy, all remarkable and executed with much mastery, judgment, and invention.

Now Donatello had made for the Tribunal of Six of the Mercanzia that marble shrine which is now opposite to S. Michael, in the Oratory of Or San Michele, and for this there was to have been made a S. Thomas in bronze, feeling for the wound in the side of Christ; but at that time nothing more was done, for some of the men who had the charge of this wished to have it made by Donatello, and others favored Lorenzo Ghiberti. Matters stood thus as long as Donatello and Ghiberti were alive; but finally the said two statues were entrusted to Andrea, who, having made the models and moulds, cast them; and they came out so solid, complete, and well made, that it was a most beautiful casting. Thereupon, setting himself to polish and finish them, he brought them to that perfection which is seen at the present day, which could not be greater than it is, for in S. Thomas we see incredulity and a too great anxiety to assure himself of the truth, and at the same time the love that makes him lay his hand in a most beautiful manner on the side of Christ; and in Christ Himself, who is raising one arm and opening His raiment with a most spontaneous gesture, and dispelling the doubts of His incredulous disciple, there are all the grace and divinity, so to speak, that art can give to any figure. Andrea clothed both these figures in most beautiful and well-arranged draperies, which give us to know that he understood that art no less than did Donatello, Lorenzo, and the others who had lived before him; wherefore this work well deserved to be set up in a shrine made by Donatello, and to be ever afterwards held in the greatest price and esteem.

Now the fame of Andrea could not go further or grow greater in that profession, and he, as a man who was not content with being excellent in one thing only, but desired to become the same in others as well by means of study, turned his mind to painting. There are some drawings by his hand in our book, made with much patience and very great judgment, among which are certain heads of women, beautiful in expression and in the adornment of the hair, which Leonardo da Vinci was ever imitating for their beauty. In our book, also, are two drawings of horses with the due measures and protractors for reproducing them on a larger scale from a smaller, so that there may be no errors in their proportions. Among others, there is a design for a tomb made by him in Venice for a Doge, a scene of the Adoration of Christ by the Magi, and the head of a woman painted on paper with the utmost delicacy. He also made for Lorenzo de' Medici, for the fountain of his Villa at Careggi, a boy of bronze squeezing a fish, which the Lord Duke Cosimo has caused to be placed, as may be seen at the present day, on the fountain that is in the courtyard of his Palace; which boy is truly marvelous.

Afterwards, the building of the Cupola of S. Maria del Fiore having been finished, it was resolved, after much discussion, that there should be made the copper ball which, according to the instructions left by Filippo Brunelleschi, was to be placed on the summit of that edifice. Whereupon the task was given to Andrea, who made the ball eight feet high, and, placing it on a knob, secured it in such a manner that afterwards the cross could be safely erected upon it; and the whole work, when finished, was put into position with very great rejoicing and delight among the people. Truly great were the ingenuity and diligence that had to be used in making it, to the end that it might be possible, as it is, to enter it from below, and also in securing it with good fastenings, lest the winds might do it damage.

Andrea was never at rest, but was ever laboring at some work either in painting or in sculpture; and sometimes he would change from one to another, in order to avoid growing weary of working always at the same thing, as many do. Wherefore, he painted certain pictures; among others, a panel for the Nuns of S. Domenico in Florence, wherein it appeared to him that he had acquitted himself very well; whence, no long time after, he painted another in S. Salvi for the Monks of Vallombrosa, containing the Baptism of Christ by S. John. In this work he was assisted by Leonardo da Vinci, his disciple, then quite young, who painted therein an angel with his own hand, which was much better than the other parts of the work; and for that reason Andrea resolved never again to touch a brush, since Leonardo, young as he was, had acquitted himself in that art much better than he had done.

Now Cosimo de' Medici, having received many antiquities from Rome, had caused to be set up within the door of his garden, or rather, courtyard, which opens on the Via de'

Ginori, a very beautiful Marsyas of white marble, bound to a tree trunk and ready to be flayed; and his grandson Lorenzo, into whose hands there had come the torso and head of another Marsyas, made of red stone, very ancient, and much more beautiful than the first, wished to set it beside the other, but could not, because it was so imperfect. Thereupon he gave it to Andrea to be restored and completed, and he made the legs, thighs, and arms that were lacking in this figure out of pieces of red marble, so well that Lorenzo was highly satisfied and had it placed opposite to the other, on the other side of the door. This ancient torso, made to represent a flayed Marsyas, was wrought with such care and judgment that certain delicate white veins, which were in the red stone, were carved by the craftsman exactly in the right places, so as to appear to be little nerves, such as are seen in real bodies when they have been flayed; which must have given to that work, when it had its original finish, a most lifelike appearance.

The Venetians, meanwhile, wishing to honor the great valor of Bartolommeo da Bergamo, thanks to whom they had gained many victories, in order to encourage others, and having heard the fame of Andrea, summoned him to Venice, where he was commissioned to make an equestrian statue of that captain in bronze, to be placed on the Piazza di SS. Giovanni e Polo. Andrea, then, having made the model of the horse, had already begun to get it ready for casting in bronze, when, thanks to the favor of certain gentlemen, it was determined that Vellano da Padova should make the figure and Andrea the horse. Having heard this, Andrea broke the legs and head of his model and returned in great disdain to Florence, without saying a word. The Signoria, receiving news of this, gave him to understand that he should never be bold enough to return to Venice, for they would cut his head off; to which he wrote in answer that he would take good care not to, because, once they had cut a man's head off, it was not in their power to put it on again, and certainly not one like his own, whereas he could have replaced the head that he had knocked off his horse with one even more beautiful. After this answer, which did not displease those Signori, his payment was doubled and he was persuaded to return to Venice, where he restored his first model and cast it in bronze; but even then he did not finish it entirely, for he caught a chill by overheating himself during the casting, and died in that city within a few days. His death caused infinite grief to his friends and to his disciples, who were not few.

Andrea took much delight in casting in a kind of plaster which would set hard—that is, the kind that is made of a soft stone which is quarried in the districts of Volterra and of Siena and in many other parts of Italy. This stone, when burnt in the fire, and then pounded and mixed with tepid water, becomes so soft that men can make whatever they please with it; but afterwards it solidifies and becomes so hard, that it can be used for moulds for casting whole figures. Andrea, then, was wont to cast in moulds of this material such natural objects as hands, feet, knees, legs, arms, and torsos, in order to have them before him and imitate them with greater convenience. Afterwards, in his time, men began to cast the heads of those who died—a cheap method; wherefore there are seen in every house in Florence, over the chimney-pieces, doors, windows, and cornices, infinite numbers of such portraits, so well made and so natural that they appear alive.

MANTEGNA

[*Andrea Mantegna was born in 1431 and died in 1506.*]

How great is the effect of reward on talent is known to him
who labors valiantly and receives a certain measure of recompense, for he feels neither discomfort, nor hardship, nor
fatigue, when he expects honor and reward for them; nay,
what is more, they render his talent every day more renowned and illustrious. It is true, indeed, that there is not
always found one to recognize, esteem, and remunerate it as
that of Andrea Mantegna was recognized. This man was born
from very humble stock in the district of Mantua; and, although as a boy he was occupied in grazing herds, he was so
greatly exalted by destiny and by his merit that he attained to
the honorable rank of Chevalier, as will be told in the proper
place. When almost full grown he was taken to the city, where
he applied himself to painting under Jacopo Squarcione, a
painter of Padua, who took him into his house, and a little
time afterwards, having recognized the beauty of his intelligence, adopted him as his son. Now this Squarcione knew
that he himself was not the most able painter in the world;
wherefore, to the end that Andrea might learn more than he
himself knew, he made him practice much on casts taken
from ancient statues and on pictures painted upon canvas
which he caused to be brought from diverse places, particularly from Tuscany and from Rome. By these and other
methods, therefore, Andrea learnt not a little in his youth;
and the competition of Marco Zoppo of Bologna, Dario da
Treviso, and Niccolò Pizzolo of Padua, disciples of his mas-

ter and adoptive father, was of no small assistance to him, and a stimulus to his studies.

Now after Andrea, who was then no more than seventeen years of age, had painted the panel of the high altar of S. Sofia in Padua, which appears wrought by a mature and well-practiced master, and not by a youth, Squarcione was commissioned to paint the Chapel of S. Cristofano, which is in the Church of the Eremite Friars of S. Agostino in Padua; and he gave the work to the said Niccolò Pizzolo and to Andrea. Niccolò made therein a God the Father seated in Majesty between the Doctors of the Church, and these paintings were afterwards held to be in no way inferior to those that Andrea executed there. But Niccolò was ever under arms and had many enemies, and one day, when returning from work, was attacked and slain by treachery.

Andrea, thus left alone in the said chapel, painted the four Evangelists, which were held very beautiful. By reason of this and other works Andrea began to be watched with great expectation, and with hopes that he would attain to that success to which he actually did attain; wherefore Jacopo Bellini, the Venetian painter, father of Gentile and Giovanni, and rival of Squarcione, contrived to get him to marry his daughter, the sister of Gentile. Hearing this, Squarcione fell into such disdain against Andrea that they were enemies ever afterwards; and in proportion as Squarcione had formerly been ever praising the works of Andrea, so from that day onward did he ever decry them in public. Above all did he censure without reserve the pictures that Andrea had made in the said Chapel of S. Cristofano, saying that they were worthless, because in making them he had imitated the ancient works in marble, from which it is not possible to learn painting perfectly, for the reason that stone is ever from its very essence hard, and never has that tender softness that is found in flesh and in things of nature, which are pliant and move in various ways; adding that Andrea would have made those figures much better, and that they would have been more perfect, if he had given them the color of marble and not such a quantity of colors, because his pictures resembled not living figures but ancient statues of marble or other such-like things. This censure piqued the mind of Andrea; but, on the other hand, it was of great service to him, for, recognizing that Squarcione was in great measure speaking the truth, he set himself to portray living people, and made so much progress in this art, that, in a scene which still remained to be painted in the said chapel, he showed that he could wrest the good from living and natural objects no less than from those wrought by art. But for all this Andrea was ever of the opinion that the good ancient statues were more perfect and had greater beauty in their various parts than is shown by nature, since, as he judged and seemed to see from those statues, the excellent masters of old had wrested from living people all the perfection of nature, which rarely assembles and unites all possible beauty into one single body, so that it is necessary to take one part from one body and another part from another. In addition to this, it appeared to him that the statues were more complete and more thorough in the muscles, veins, nerves, and other particulars, which nature, covering their sharpness somewhat with the tenderness and softness of flesh, sometimes makes less evident, save perchance in the body of an old man or in one greatly emaciated; but such bodies, for other reasons, are avoided by craftsmen. And that he was greatly enamored of this opinion is recognized from his works, in which, in truth, the manner is seen to be somewhat hard and sometimes suggesting stone rather than living flesh. Be this as it may, in this last scene, which gave infinite satisfaction, Andrea portrayed Squarcione in an ugly and corpulent figure, lance and sword in hand. In the same work he portrayed the Florentine Noferi, son of Messer Palla Strozzi, Messer Girolamo della Valle, a most excellent physician, Messer Bonifazio Fuzimeliga, Doctor of

Laws, Niccolò, goldsmith to Pope Innocent VIII, and Baldassarre da Leccio, all very much his friends, whom he represented clad in white armor, burnished and resplendent, as
real armor is, and truly with a beautiful manner. He also
portrayed there the Chevalier Messer Bonramino, and a certain Bishop of Hungary, a man wholly witless, who would
wander about Rome all day, and then at night would lie down
to sleep like a beast in a stable; and he made a portrait of
Marsilio Pazzo in the person of the executioner who is cutting off the head of S. James, together with one of himself.
This work, in short, by reason of its excellence, brought him
a very great name.

The while that he was working on this chapel, he also
painted a panel, which was placed on the altar of S. Luca in
S. Justina, and afterwards he wrought in fresco the lunette
that is over the door of S. Antonino, on which he wrote his
name. In Verona he painted a panel for the altar of S. Cristofano and S. Antonio, and he made some figures at the corner of the Piazza della Paglia. In S. Maria in Organo, for the
Monks of Monte Oliveto, he painted the panel of the high
altar, which is most beautiful, and likewise that of S. Zeno.
And among other things that he wrought while living in Verona and sent to various places, one, which came into the
hands of an Abbot of Fiesole, his friend and relative, was a
picture containing a half-length Madonna with the Child in
her arms, and certain heads of angels singing, wrought with
admirable grace; which picture, now to be seen in the library
of that place, has been held from that time to our own to be
a rare thing.

Now, the while that he lived in Mantua, he had labored
much in the service of the Marquis Lodovico Gonzaga, and
that lord, who always showed no little esteem and favor
toward the talent of Andrea, caused him to paint a little
panel for the Chapel of the Castle of Mantua; in which panel
there are scenes with figures not very large but most beauti-

ful. In the same place are many figures foreshortened from
below upwards, which are greatly extolled, for although his
treatment of the draperies was somewhat hard and precise,
and his manner rather dry, yet everything there is seen to
have been wrought with much art and diligence. For the
same Marquis, in a hall of the Palace of S. Sebastiano in
Mantua, he painted the Triumph of Caesar, which is the best
thing that he ever executed. In this work we see, grouped
with most beautiful design in the triumph, the ornate and
lovely car, the man who is vituperating the triumphant Caesar, and the relatives, the perfumes, the incense, the sacrifices,
the priests, the bulls crowned for the sacrifice, the prisoners,
the booty won by the soldiers, the ranks of the squadrons,
the elephants, the spoils, the victories, the cities and fortresses
counterfeited in various cars, with an infinity of trophies
borne on spears, and a variety of helmets and body-armor,
head-dresses, and ornaments and vases innumerable; and in
the multitude of spectators is a woman holding the hand of
a boy, who, having pierced his foot with a thorn, is showing
it, weeping, to his mother, in a graceful and very lifelike
manner. Andrea, as I may have pointed out elsewhere, had
a good and beautiful idea in this scene, for, having set the
plane on which the figures stood higher than the level of the
eye, he placed the feet of the foremost on the outer edge and
outline of that plane, making the others recede inwards little
by little, so that their feet and legs were lost to sight in the
proportion required by the point of view; and so, too, with
the spoils, vases, and other instruments and ornaments, of
which he showed only the lower part, concealing the upper,
as was required by the rules of perspective; which same consideration was also observed with much diligence by Andrea
del Castagno in the Last Supper, which is in the Refectory
of S. Maria Nuova. Wherefore it is seen that in that age these
able masters set about investigating with much subtlety, and
imitating with great labor, the true properties of natural ob-

jects. And this whole work, to put it briefly, is as beautiful and as well wrought as it could be; so that if the Marquis loved Andrea before, he loved and honored him much more ever afterwards.

What is more, he became so famous thereby that Pope Innocent VIII, hearing of his excellence in painting and of the other good qualities wherewith he was so marvelously endowed, sent for him, even as he was sending for many others, to the end that he might adorn with his pictures the walls of the Belvedere, the building of which had just been finished. Having gone to Rome, then, greatly favored and recommended by the Marquis, who made him a Chevalier in order to honor him the more, he was received lovingly by that Pontiff and straightway commissioned to paint a little chapel that is in the said place. This he executed with diligence and love, and with such minuteness that the vaulting and the walls appear rather illuminated than painted; and the largest figures that are therein, which he painted in fresco like the others, are over the altar, representing the Baptism of Christ by S. John, with many people around, who are showing by taking off their clothes that they wish to be baptized. Among these is one who, seeking to draw off a stocking that has stuck to his leg through sweat, has crossed that leg over the other and is drawing the stocking off inside out, with such great effort and difficulty, that both are seen clearly in his face; which bizarre fancy caused marvel to all who saw it in those times. It is said that this Pope, by reason of his many affairs, did not pay Mantegna as often as he would have liked, and that therefore, while painting certain Virtues *in terretta* in that work, he made a figure of Discretion among the rest, whereupon the Pope, having gone one day to see the work, asked Andrea what figure that was; to which Andrea answered that it was Discretion; and the Pope added: "If thou wouldst have her suitably accompanied, put Patience beside her." The painter understood what the meaning of the

Holy Father was, and he never said another word. The work finished, the Pope sent him back to the Duke with much favor and honorable rewards.

The while that Andrea was working in Rome, he painted, besides the said chapel, a little picture of the Madonna with the Child sleeping in her arms; and within certain caverns in the landscape, which is a mountain, he made some stone-cutters quarrying stone for various purposes, all wrought with such delicacy and such great patience, that it does not seem possible for such good work to be done with the thin point of a brush. This picture is now in the possession of the most Illustrious Lord, Don Francesco Medici, Prince of Florence, who holds it among his dearest treasures.

In our book is a drawing by the hand of Andrea on a half-sheet of royal folio, finished in chiaroscuro, wherein is a Judith who is putting the head of Holofernes into the wallet of her Moorish slave-girl; which chiaroscuro is executed in a manner no longer used, for he left the paper white to serve for the light in place of white lead, and that so delicately that the separate hairs and other minute details are seen therein, no less than if they had been wrought with much diligence by the brush; wherefore in a certain sense this may be called rather a work in color than a drawing. The same man, like Pollaiuolo, delighted in engraving on copper; and, among other things, he made engravings of his own Triumphs, which were then held in great account, since nothing better had been seen.

One of the last works that he executed was a panel-picture for S. Maria della Vittoria, a church built after the direction and design of Andrea by the Marquis Francesco, in memory of the victory that he gained on the River Taro, when he was General of the Venetian forces against the French. In this panel, which was wrought in distemper and placed on the high altar, there is painted the Madonna with the Child seated on a pedestal; and below are S. Michelangelo, S. Anna, and

Joachim, who are presenting the Marquis—who is portrayed from life so well that he appears alive—to the Madonna, who is offering him her hand. Which picture, even as it gave and still continues to give universal pleasure, also satisfied the Marquis so well that he rewarded most liberally the talent and labor of Andrea, who, having been remunerated by Princes for all his works, was able to maintain his rank of Chevalier most honorably up to the end of his life.

Andrea built a very beautiful house in Mantua for his own use, which he adorned with paintings and enjoyed while he lived. Finally he died in 1506, at the age of seventy-five, and was buried with honorable obsequies in S. Andrea; and on his tomb stands his portrait in bronze.

Andrea was so kindly and praiseworthy in all his actions, that his memory will ever live, not only in his own country, but in the whole world. This master showed painters a much better method of foreshortening figures from below upwards, which was truly a difficult and ingenious invention; and he also took delight, as has been said, in engraving figures on copper for printing, a method of truly rare value, by means of which the world has been able to see not only the Bacchanalia, the Battle of Marine Monsters, the Deposition from the Cross, the Burial of Christ, and His Resurrection, with Longinus and S. Andrew, works by Mantegna himself, but also the manners of all the craftsmen who have ever lived.

PERUGINO

[*Pietro di Cristofano Vannucci, called Perugino after the town in which he lived, was probably born in 1445 and died in 1523.*]

How great a benefit poverty may be to men of genius, and how potent a force it may be to make them become excellent —nay, perfect—in the exercise of any faculty whatsoever, can be seen clearly enough in the actions of Pietro Perugino, who, flying from the extremity of distress at Perugia, and betaking himself to Florence in the desire to attain to some distinction by means of his talent, remained for many months without any other bed than a miserable chest to sleep in, turning night into day, and devoting himself with the greatest ardor to the unceasing study of his profession. And, having made a habit of this, he knew no other pleasure than to labor continually at his art, and to be for ever painting; for with the fear of poverty constantly before his eyes, he would do for gain such work as he would probably not have looked at if he had possessed the wherewithal to live. Riches, indeed, might perchance have closed the path on which his talent should advance toward excellence, no less effectually than poverty opened it to him, while necessity spurred him on in his desire to rise from so low and miserable a condition, if not to supreme eminence, at least to a rank in which he might have the means of life. For this reason he never took heed of cold, of hunger, of hardship, of discomfort, of fatigue, or of ridicule, if only he might one day live in ease and repose; ever saying, as it were by way of proverb, that after bad weather there must come the good, and that during the good men build the houses that are to shelter them when there is need.

But in order that the rise of this craftsman may be better known, let me begin with his origin, and relate that, according to common report, there was born in the city of Perugia, to a poor man of Castello della Pieve, named Cristofano, a son who was baptized with the name of Pietro. This son, brought up amid misery and distress, was given by his father as a shop-boy to a painter of Perugia, who was no great master of his profession, but held in great veneration both the art and the men who were excellent therein; nor did he ever cease to tell Pietro how much gain and honor painting brought to those who practiced it well, and he would urge the boy to the study of that art by recounting to him the rewards won by ancient and modern masters; wherefore he fired his mind in such a manner, that Pietro took it into his head to try, if only fortune would assist him, to become one of these. For this reason he was often wont to ask any man whom he knew to have seen the world, in what part the best craftsmen in that calling were formed; particularly his master, who always gave him one and the same answer—namely, that it was in Florence more than in any other place that men became perfect in all the arts, especially in painting, since in that city men are spurred by three things. The first is censure, which is uttered freely and by many, seeing that the air of that city makes men's intellects so free by nature, that they do not content themselves, like a flock of sheep, with mediocre works, but ever consider them with regard to the honor of the good and the beautiful rather than out of respect for the craftsman. The second is that, if a man wishes to live there, he must be industrious, which is naught else than to say that he must continually exercise his intelligence and his judgment, must be ready and adroit in his affairs, and, finally, must know how to make money, seeing that the territory of Florence is not so wide or abundant as to enable her to support at little cost all who live there, as can be done in countries that are rich enough. The third, which is perchance no less potent than the others, is an eager desire for glory and honor, which is generated mightily by that air in the men of all professions; and this desire, in all persons of spirit, will not let them stay content with being equal, much less inferior, to those whom they see to be men like themselves, although they may recognize them as masters—nay, it forces them very often to desire their own advancement so eagerly, that, if they are not kindly or wise by nature, they turn out evil-speakers, ungrateful, and unthankful for benefits. It is true, indeed, that when a man has learnt there as much as suffices him, he must, if he wishes to do more than live from day to day like an animal, and desires to become rich, take his departure from that place and find a sale abroad for the excellence of his works and for the repute conferred on him by that city, as the doctors do with the fame derived from their studies. For Florence treats her craftsmen as time treats its own works, which, when perfected, it destroys and consumes little by little.

Moved by these counsels, therefore, and by the persuasions of many others, Pietro came to Florence, minded to become excellent; and well did he succeed, for the reason that in those times works in his manner were held in very great price. He studied under the discipline of Andrea Verrocchio, and his first figures were painted outside the Porta a Prato, in the Nunnery of S. Martino, now in ruins by reason of the wars. In a few years, then, he came into such credit, that his works filled not only Florence and all Italy, but also France, Spain, and many other countries to which they were sent. Wherefore, his paintings being held in very great price and repute, merchants began to buy them up wholesale and to send them abroad to various countries, to their own great gain and profit.

For the Nuns of S. Chiara he painted a Dead Christ on a panel, with such lovely and novel coloring, that he made the craftsmen believe that he would become excellent and marvelous. In this work there are seen some most beautiful heads of old men, and likewise certain figures of the Marys, who, having ceased to weep, are contemplating the Dead Jesus with extraordinary awe and love; not to mention that he made therein a landscape that was then held most beautiful, because the true method of making them, such as it appeared later, had not yet been seen. It is said that Francesco del Pugliese offered to give to the aforesaid nuns three times as much money as they had paid to Pietro, and to have a similar one made for them by the same man's hand, but that they would not consent, because Pietro said that he did not believe he could equal it.

There were also many things by the hand of Pietro in the Convent of the Frati Gesuati, outside the Porta a Pinti; and since the said church and convent are now in ruins, none have been preserved save the panels, since those executed in fresco were thrown to the ground, together with the whole of that building, by reason of the siege of Florence, when the panels were carried to the Porta a S. Pier Gattolini, where a home was given to those friars in the Church and Convent of S. Giovannino. Now the two panels on the aforesaid partition-wall were by the hand of Pietro; and in one was Christ in the Garden, with the Apostles sleeping, in whom Pietro showed how well sleep can prevail over pains and discomforts, having represented them asleep in attitudes of perfect ease. In the other he made a Pietà—that is, Christ in the lap of Our Lady—surrounded by four figures no less excellent than any others in his manner; and, to mention only one thing, he made the Dead Christ all stiffened, as if He had been so long on the Cross that the length of time and the cold had reduced Him to this; wherefore he painted Him supported by John and the Magdalene, all sorrowful and weeping. In another panel he painted the Crucifixion, with the Magdalene, and, at the foot of the Cross, S. Jerome, S. John the Baptist, and the Blessed Giovanni Colombini, founder of that Order; all with infinite diligence. These three panels have suffered considerably, and they are all cracked in the dark parts and where there are shadows; and this comes to pass when the first coat of color, which is laid on the ground (for three coats of color are used, one over the other), is worked on before it is thoroughly dry; wherefore afterwards, with time, in the drying, they draw through their thickness and come to have the strength to make those cracks; which Pietro could not know, seeing that in his time they were only just beginning to paint well in oil.

By reason of these works, then, and many others, Pietro came into such repute that he was commissioned to paint a Dead Christ, with the Madonna and S. John, above the steps of the side door of S. Pietro Maggiore; and this he wrought in such a manner, that it has been preserved, although exposed to rain and wind, as fresh as if it had only just been finished by Pietro's hand. Truly intelligent was Pietro's understanding of color, both in fresco and in oil; wherefore all experienced craftsmen are indebted to him, for it is through him that they have knowledge of the lights that are seen throughout his works. He was then commissioned by Bernardino de' Rossi, a citizen of Florence, to paint a S. Sebastian to be sent into France, the price agreed on being one hundred gold crowns; but this work was sold by Bernardino to the King of France for four hundred gold ducats. At the command of Cardinal Caraffa of Naples he painted an Assumption of Our Lady, with the Apostles marveling round the tomb, for the high altar of the Piscopio; and for Abbot Simone de' Graziani of Borgo a San Sepolcro he executed a large panel, which was painted in Florence, and then borne to S. Gilio in the Borgo on the shoulders of porters, at very great expense. To S. Giovanni in Monte at Bologna he sent a panel with certain figures standing upright, and a Madonna in the sky.

Thereupon the fame of Pietro spread so widely throughout Italy and abroad, that to his great glory he was summoned to Rome by Pope Sixtus IV to work in his chapel in company with the other excellent craftsmen. There, in company with Don Bartolommeo della Gatta, Abbot of S. Clemente at Arezzo, he painted the scene of Christ giving the keys to S. Peter; and likewise the Nativity and Baptism of Christ, and the Birth of Moses, with the daughter of Pharaoh finding him in the little ark. And on the same wall where the altar is he painted a mural picture of the Assumption of Our Lady, with a portrait of Pope Sixtus on his knees. But these works were thrown to the ground in preparing the wall for the Judgment of the divine Michelangelo, in the time of Pope Paul III. On a vault of the Borgia Tower in the Papal Palace he painted certain stories of Christ, with some foliage in chiaroscuro, which had an extraordinary name for excellence in his time. For Sciarra Colonna, also, in the Palace of S. Apostolo, he painted a loggia and certain rooms.

These works brought him a very great sum of money; wherefore, having resolved to remain no longer in Rome, and having departed in good favor with the whole Court, he returned to his native city of Perugia, in many parts of which he executed panels and works in fresco; and, in particular, a panel-picture painted in oils for the Chapel of the Palace of the Signori, containing Our Lady and other saints. And for the Altar of the Sacrament, where there is preserved the ring with which the Virgin Mary was married, he painted the Marriage of the Virgin.

Afterwards he painted in fresco the whole of the Audience Chamber of the Exchange, adorning the compartments of the vaulting with the seven planets, drawn in certain cars by diverse animals, according to the old usage; on the wall opposite to the door of entrance he painted the Nativity and Resurrection of Christ, with a panel containing S. John the Baptist in the midst of certain other saints. The side walls he painted in his own manner: one with figures of Fabius Maximus, Socrates, Numa Pompilius, F. Camillus, Pythagoras, Trajan, L. Sicinius, the Spartan Leonidas, Horatius Cocles, Fabius Sempronius, the Athenian Pericles, and Cincinnatus.

On the other wall he made the Prophets, and the Sibyls, the Erythraean, the Libyan, the Tiburtine, the Delphic, and the others. Below each of the said figures he placed, in the form of a written motto, something said by them, and appropriate to that place. And in one of the ornaments he made his own portrait, which appears absolutely alive, and he wrote his own name below it.

After this, returning to Florence, he painted a S. Bernard on a panel for the Monks of Castello, and in the chapter-house a Crucifix, the Madonna, S. Benedict, S. Bernard, and S. John. And in S. Domenico da Fiesole, in the second chapel on the right hand, he painted a panel containing Our Lady and three figures, among which is a S. Sebastian worthy of the highest praise. Now Pietro had done so much work, and he always had so many works in hand, that he would very often use the same subjects; and he had reduced the theory of his art to a manner so fixed, that he made all his figures with the same expression. By that time Michelangelo Buonarroti had already come to the front, and Pietro greatly desired to see his figures, by reason of the praise bestowed on him by craftsmen; and seeing the greatness of his own name, which he had acquired in every place through so grand a beginning, being obscured, he was ever seeking to wound his fellow-workers with biting words. For this reason, besides certain insults aimed at him by the craftsmen, he had only himself to blame when Michelangelo told him in public that he was a clumsy fool at his art. But Pietro being unable to swallow such an affront, they both appeared before the Tribunal of Eight, where Pietro came off with little honor. Meanwhile the Servite Friars of Florence, wishing to have the altar-piece of their high altar painted by some famous master, had handed it over, by reason of the departure of Leonardo da Vinci, who had gone off to France, to Filippino; but he, when he had finished half of one of two panels that were to adorn the altar, passed from this life to the next; wherefore the friars, by reason of the faith that they had in Pietro, entrusted him with the whole work. It is said that when the work was unveiled, it received no little censure from all the new craftsmen, particularly because Pietro had availed himself of those figures that he had been wont to use in other pictures; with which his friends twitted him, saying that he had taken no pains, and that he had abandoned the good method of working, either through avarice or to save time. To this Pietro would answer: "I have used the figures that you have at other times praised, and which have given you infinite pleasure; if now they do not please you, and you do not praise them, what can I do?" But they kept assailing him bitterly with sonnets and open insults; whereupon, although now old, he departed from Florence and returned to Perugia.

It was ever Pietro's custom on his going and coming between the said Castello and Perugia, like a man who trusted nobody, to carry all the money that he possessed about his person. Wherefore certain men, lying in wait for him at a pass, robbed him, but at his earnest entreaty they spared his life for the love of God; and afterwards, by means of the services of his friends, who were numerous enough, he also recovered a great part of the money that had been taken from him; but none the less he came near dying of vexation. Pietro was a man of very little religion, and he could never be made to believe in the immortality of the soul—nay, with words in keeping with his head of granite, he rejected most obstinately every good suggestion. He placed all his hopes in the goods of fortune, and he would have sold his soul for money. He earned great riches; and he both bought and built houses in Florence, and acquired much settled property both at Perugia and at Castello della Pieve. He took a most beautiful young woman to wife, and had children by her; and he delighted so greatly in seeing her wearing beautiful head-dresses, both abroad and at home, that it is said that he would often tire her head with his own hand. Finally, having reached the age of seventy-eight, Pietro finished the course of his life at Castello della Pieve, where he was honorably buried, in the year 1523.

SIGNORELLI

*[Luca d' Egidio di Luca di Ventura Signorelli was born,
probably, in 1450 and died in 1523.]*

LUCA SIGNORELLI, an excellent painter, of whom, according
to the order of time, we have now to speak, was more famous
throughout Italy in his day, and his works were held in
greater price than has ever been the case with any other master at any time whatsoever, for the reason that in the works
that he executed in painting he showed the true method of
making nudes, and how they can be caused, although only
with art and difficulty, to appear alive. He was a pupil and
disciple of Piero della Francesca, and greatly did he strive in
his youth to imitate his master, and even to surpass him; and
the while that he was working with Piero at Arezzo, living in
the house of his uncle Lazzaro Vasari, as it has been told, he
imitated the manner of the said Piero so well that the one
could scarcely be distinguished from the other.

The first works of Luca were in S. Lorenzo at Arezzo,
where he painted the Chapel of S. Barbara in fresco in the
year 1472; and he painted for the Company of S. Caterina,
on cloth and in oil, the banner that is borne in processions,
and likewise that of the Trinità, although this does not appear
to be by the hand of Luca, but by Piero dal Borgo himself.

In Perugia he made many works; among others, a panel in
the Duomo for Messer Jacopo Vannucci of Cortona, Bishop
of that city; in which panel are Our Lady, S. Onofrio, S.
Ercolano, S. John the Baptist, and S. Stephen, with a most
beautiful angel, who is tuning a lute. At Volterra, over the
altar of a Company in the Church of S. Francesco, he painted

in fresco the Circumcision of Our Lord, which is considered beautiful to a marvel, although the Infant, having been injured by damp, was restored by Sodoma and made much less beautiful than before. And, in truth, it would be sometimes better to leave works half spoilt, when they have been made by men of excellence, rather than to have them retouched by inferior masters. In S. Margherita, a seat of the Frati del Zoccolo in his native city of Cortona, he painted a Dead Christ, one of the rarest of his works; and for the Company of the Gesù, in the same city, he executed three panels, of which the one that is on the high altar is marvelous, showing Christ administering the Sacrament to the Apostles, and Judas placing the Host into his wallet. For the high altar of the Capitular church he painted a panel with a most beautiful Assumption, and he designed the pictures for the principal round window of the same church.

Having gone from Siena to Florence in order to see both the works of those masters who were then living and those of many already dead, he painted for Lorenzo de' Medici certain nude gods on a canvas, for which he was much commended, and a picture of Our Lady with two little prophets *in terretta,* which is now at Castello, a villa of Duke Cosimo's. These works, both the one and the other, he presented to the said Lorenzo, who would never be beaten by any man in liberality and magnificence. He also painted a round picture of Our Lady, which is in the Audience Chamber of the Captains of the Guelph party—a very beautiful work. At Chiusuri in the district of Siena, the principal seat of the Monks of Monte Oliveto, he painted eleven scenes of the life and acts of S. Benedict on one side of the cloister. And from Cortona he sent some of his works to Montepulciano; to Foiano the panel which is on the high altar of the Pieve; and other works to other places in Valdichiana. In the Madonna, the principal church of Orvieto, he finished with his own hand the chapel that Fra Angelico had formerly begun there; in which chapel he painted all the scenes of the end of the world with bizarre and fantastic invention—angels, demons, ruins, earthquakes, fires, miracles of Antichrist, and many other similar things besides, such as nudes, foreshortenings, and many beautiful figures; imagining the terror that there shall be on that last and awful day. By means of this he encouraged all those who have lived after him, insomuch that since then they have found easy the difficulties of that manner; wherefore I do not marvel that the works of Luca were always very highly extolled by Michelangelo, nor that in certain parts of his divine Judgment, which he made in the chapel, he should have deigned to avail himself in some measure of the inventions of Luca, as he did in the angels, the demons, the division of the Heavens, and other things, in which Michelangelo himself imitated Luca's method, as all may see. In this work Luca portrayed himself and many of his friends; Niccolò, Paolo, and Vitelozzo Vitelli, Giovan Paolo and Orazio Baglioni, and others whose names are not known. In the Sacristy of S. Maria at Loreto he painted in fresco the four Evangelists, the four Doctors, and other saints, all very beautiful; and for this work he was liberally rewarded by Pope Sixtus.

It is said that a son of his, most beautiful in countenance and in person, whom he loved dearly, was killed at Cortona; and that Luca, heart-broken as he was, had him stripped naked, and with the greatest firmness of soul, without lamenting or shedding a tear, portrayed him, to the end that, whenever he might wish, he might be able by means of the work of his own hands to see that which nature had given him and adverse fortune had snatched away.

Being then summoned by the said Pope Sixtus to work in the chapel of his Palace in competition with many other painters, he painted therein two scenes, which are held the best among so many; one is Moses declaring his testament to the Jewish people on having seen the Promised Land, and the other is his death.

Finally, having executed works for almost every Prince in Italy, and being now old, he returned to Cortona, where, in those last years of his life, he worked more for pleasure than for any other reason, as one who, being used to labor, neither could nor would stay idle. In this his old age, then, he painted a panel for the Nuns of S. Margherita at Arezzo, and one for the Company of S. Girolamo, which was paid for in part by Messer Niccolò Gamurrini, Doctor of Laws and Auditor of the Ruota,* who is portrayed from life in that panel, kneeling before the Madonna, to whom he is being presented by a S. Nicholas who is in the same panel; there are also S. Donatus and S. Stephen, and lower down a nude S. Jerome, and a David who is singing to a psaltery; and also two prophets, who, as it appears from the scrolls that they have in their hands, are speaking about the Conception. This work was brought from Cortona to Arezzo on the shoulders of the men of that Company; and Luca, old as he was, insisted on coming to set it in place, and partly also in order to revisit his friends and relatives. And since he lodged in the house of the Vasari, in which I then was, a little boy eight years old, I remember that the good old man, who was most gracious and courteous, having heard from the master who was teaching me my first letters, that I gave my attention to nothing in lesson-time save to drawing figures, I remember, I say, that he turned to my father Antonio and said to him: "Antonio, if you wish little Giorgio not to become backward, by all means let him learn to draw, for, even were he to devote himself to letters, design cannot be otherwise than helpful, honorable, and advantageous to him, as it is to every gentleman." Then, turning to me, who was standing in front of him, he said: "Mind your lessons, little kinsman." He said many other things about me, which I withhold, for the reason that I know that I have failed by a great measure to justify the opinion which the good old man had of me. And since he heard, as was true, that the blood used to flow from my nose at that age in such quantities that this left me sometimes half dead, with infinite lovingness he bound a jasper

* A judicial court, the members of which sat in rotation.

round my neck with his own hand; and this memory of Luca will stay for ever fixed in my mind. The said panel set in place, he returned to Cortona, accompanied for a great part of the way by many citizens, friends, and relatives, as was due to the excellence of Luca, who always lived rather as a noble and a man of rank than as a painter.

About the same time a palace had been built for Cardinal Silvio Passerini of Cortona, half a mile beyond the city, by Benedetto Caporali, a painter of Perugia, who, delighting in architecture, had written a commentary on Vitruvius a short time before; and the said Cardinal determined to have almost the whole of it painted. Wherefore Benedetto, putting his hand to this with the aid of Maso Papacello of Cortona (who was his disciple and had also learnt not a little from Giulio Romano, as will be told), of Tommaso, and of other disciples and lads, did not cease until he had painted it almost all over in fresco. But the Cardinal wishing to have some painting by the hand of Luca as well, he, old as he was, and hindered by palsy, painted in fresco, on the altar-wall of the chapel of that palace, the scene of S. John the Baptist baptizing the Saviour; but he was not able to finish it completely, for while still working at it he died.

Luca was a man of most excellent character, true and loving with his friends, sweet and amiable in his dealings with every man, and, above all, courteous to all who had need of him, and kindly in teaching his disciples. He lived splendidly, and he took delight in clothing himself well. And for these good qualities he was ever held in the highest veneration both in his own country and abroad. His profound mastery of design, particularly in nudes, and his grace in invention and in the composition of scenes, opened to the majority of craftsmen the way to the final perfection of art, to which those men who followed were afterwards enabled to add the crown, of whom we are henceforward to speak.

LEONARDO DA VINCI

[Leonardo di Ser Piero d'Antonio di Ser Piero di Ser Guido da Vinci, called Leonardo da Vinci, was born in 1452 and died in 1519.]

THE greatest gifts are often seen, in the course of nature, rained by celestial influences on human creatures; and sometimes, in supernatural fashion, beauty, grace, and talent are united beyond measure in one single person, in a manner that to whatever such a one turns his attention, his every action is so divine, that, surpassing all other men, it makes itself clearly known as a thing bestowed by God (as it is), and not acquired by human art. This was seen by all mankind in Leonardo da Vinci, in whom, besides a beauty of body never sufficiently extolled, there was an infinite grace in all his actions; and so great was his genius, and such its growth, that to whatever difficulties he turned his mind, he solved them with ease. In him was great bodily strength, joined to dexterity, with a spirit and courage ever royal and magnanimous; and the fame of his name so increased, that not only in his lifetime was he held in esteem, but his reputation became even greater among posterity after his death.

Truly marvelous and celestial was Leonardo, the son of Ser Piero da Vinci; and in learning and in the rudiments of letters he would have made great proficience, if he had not been so variable and unstable, for he set himself to learn many things, and then, after having begun them, abandoned them. Thus, in arithmetic, during the few months that he studied it, he made so much progress, that, by continually suggesting doubts and difficulties to the master who was teaching him, he would very often bewilder him. He gave some little attention to music, and quickly resolved to learn to play the lyre, as one who had by nature a spirit most lofty and full of refinement: wherefore he sang divinely to that instrument, improvising upon it. Nevertheless, although he occupied himself with such a variety of things, he never ceased drawing and working in relief, pursuits which suited his fancy more than any other. Ser Piero, having observed this, and having considered the loftiness of his intellect, one day took some of his drawings and carried them to Andrea del Verrocchio, who was much his friend, and besought him straitly to tell him whether Leonardo, by devoting himself to drawing, would make any proficience. Andrea was astonished to see the extraordinary beginnings of Leonardo, and urged Ser Piero that he should make him study it; wherefore he arranged with Leonardo that he should enter the workshop of Andrea, which Leonardo did with the greatest willingness in the world. And he practiced not one branch of art only, but all those in which drawing played a part; and having an intellect so divine and marvelous that he was also an excellent geometrician, he not only worked in sculpture, making in his youth, in clay, some heads of women that are smiling, of which plaster casts are still being made, and likewise some heads of boys which appeared to have issued from the hand of a master; but in architecture, also, he made many drawings both of ground plans and of other designs of buildings; and he was the first, although but a youth, who suggested the plan of reducing the river Arno to a navigable canal from Pisa to Florence. He made designs of flour mills, fulling mills, and engines, which might be driven by the force of water: and since he wished that his profession should be painting, he studied much in drawing after nature, and sometimes in making models of figures in clay, over which he would lay soft pieces of cloth dipped in clay, and then set himself patiently to draw them on a certain kind of very fine Rheims cloth, or prepared linen: and he executed them in black and white with the point of his brush, so that it was a marvel, as some of them by his hand, which I have in our book of drawings, still bear witness; besides which, he drew on paper with such diligence and so well, that there is no one who has ever equaled him in perfection of finish; and I have one, a head drawn with the style in chiaroscuro, which is divine.

And there was infused in that brain such grace from God, and a power of expression in such sublime accord with the intellect and memory that served it, and he knew so well how to express his conceptions by draftsmanship, that he vanquished with his discourse, and confuted with his reasoning, every valiant wit. And he was continually making models and designs to show men how to remove mountains with ease, and how to bore them in order to pass from one level to another; and by means of levers, windlasses, and screws, he showed the way to raise and draw great weights, together with methods for emptying harbors, and pumps for removing water from low places, things which his brain never ceased from devising; and of these ideas and labors many drawings may be seen, scattered abroad among our craftsmen; and I myself have seen not a few. He even went so far as to waste his time in drawing knots of cords, made according to an order, that from one end all the rest might follow till the other, so as to fill a round; and one of these is to be seen in the form of an engraving, most difficult and beautiful, and in the middle of it are these words, "Leonardus Vinci Accademia." And among these models and designs, there was one by which he often demonstrated to many ingenious citizens, who were then governing Florence, how he proposed to raise the Temple of S. Giovanni in Florence, and place steps under it, without damaging the building; and with such strong reasons did he urge this, that it appeared possible although each man, after he had departed, would recognize for himself the impossibility of so vast an undertaking.

He was so pleasing in conversation, that he attracted to himself the hearts of men. And although he possessed, one might say, nothing, and worked little, he always kept servants and horses, in which latter he took much delight, and particularly in all other animals, which he managed with the greatest love and patience; and this he showed when often passing by the places where birds were sold, for, taking them with his own hand out of their cages, and having paid to those who sold them the price that was asked, he let them fly away into the air, restoring to them their lost liberty. For which reason nature was pleased so to favor him, that, wherever he turned his thought, brain, and mind, he displayed such divine power in his works, that, in giving them their perfection, no one was ever his peer in readiness, vivacity, excellence, beauty, and grace.

It is clear that Leonardo, through his comprehension of art, began many things and never finished one of them, since it seemed to him that the hand was not able to attain to the perfection of art in carrying out the things which he imagined; for the reason that he conceived in idea difficulties so subtle and so marvelous, that they could never be expressed by the hands, be they ever so excellent. And so many were his caprices, that, philosophizing of natural things, he set himself to seek out the properties of herbs, going on even to observe the motions of the heavens, the path of the moon, and the courses of the sun.

He was placed, then, as has been said, in his boyhood, at the instance of Ser Piero, to learn art with Andrea del Verrocchio, who was making a panel-picture of S. John baptizing Christ, when Leonardo painted an angel who was holding some garments; and although he was but a lad, Leonardo executed it in such a manner that his angel was much better than the figures of Andrea; which was the reason that Andrea would never again touch color, in disdain that a child should know more than he.

He was commissioned to make a cartoon for a door-hanging that was to be executed in Flanders, woven in gold and silk, to be sent to the King of Portugal, of Adam and Eve sinning in the Earthly Paradise; wherein Leonardo drew with the brush in chiaroscuro, with the lights in lead-white, a meadow of infinite kinds of herbage, with some animals, of which, in truth, it may be said that for diligence and truth to nature divine wit could not make it so perfect. In it is the fig tree, together with the foreshortening of the leaves and the varying aspects of the branches, wrought with such lovingness that the brain reels at the mere thought how a man could have such patience. There is also a palm tree which has the radiating crown of the palm, executed with such great and marvelous art that nothing save the patience and intellect of Leonardo could avail to do it. This work was carried no farther; wherefore the cartoon is now at Florence, in the blessed house of the Magnificent Ottaviano de' Medici, presented to him not long ago by the uncle of Leonardo.

It is said that Ser Piero da Vinci, being at his villa, was besought as a favor, by a peasant of his, who had made a buckler with his own hands out of a fig tree that he had cut down on the farm, to have it painted for him in Florence, which he did very willingly, since the countryman was very skilful at catching birds and fishing, and Ser Piero made much use of him in these pursuits. Thereupon, having had it taken to Florence, without saying a word to Leonardo as to whose it was, he asked him to paint something upon it. Leonardo, having one day taken this buckler in his hands, and seeing it twisted, badly made, and clumsy, straightened it by the fire, and, having given it to a turner, from the rude and clumsy thing that it was, caused it to be made smooth and even. And afterwards, having given it a coat of gesso, and having prepared it in his own way, he began to think what he could paint upon it, that might be able to terrify all who should come upon it, producing the same effect as once did the head of Medusa. For this purpose, then, Leonardo carried to a room of his own into which no one entered save himself alone, lizards great and small, crickets, serpents, butterflies, grasshoppers, bats, and other strange kinds of suchlike animals, out of the numbers of which, variously put together, he formed a great ugly creature, most horrible and terrifying, which emitted a poisonous breath and turned the air to flame; and he made it coming out of a dark and jagged rock, belching forth venom from its open throat, fire from its eyes, and smoke from its nostrils, in so strange a fashion that it appeared altogether a monstrous and horrible thing; and so long did he labor over making it, that the stench of the dead animals in that room was past bearing, but Leonardo did not notice it, so great was the love that he bore toward art. The work being finished, although it was no longer asked for either by the countryman or by his father, Leonardo told the latter that he might send for the buckler at his convenience, since, for his part, it was finished. Ser Piero having therefore gone one morning to the room for the buckler, and having knocked at the door, Leonardo opened to him, telling him to wait a little; and, having gone back into the room, he adjusted the buckler in a good light on the easel, and put to the window, in order to make a soft light, and then he bade him come in to see it. Ser Piero, at the first glance, taken by surprise, gave a sudden start, not thinking that that was the buckler, nor merely painted the form that he saw upon it, and, falling back a step, Leonardo checked him, saying, "This work serves the end for which it was made; take it, then, and carry it away, since this is the effect that it was meant to produce." This thing appeared to Ser Piero nothing short of a miracle, and he praised very greatly the ingenious idea of Leonardo; and then, having privately bought from a peddler another buckler, painted with a heart transfixed by an arrow, he presented it to the countryman, who remained obliged to him for it as long as he lived. Afterwards, Ser Piero sold the buckler of Leonardo secretly to some merchants in Florence, for a hundred ducats; and in a short time it came into the hands of the Duke of Milan, having been sold to him by the said merchants for three hundred ducats.

Leonardo then made a picture of Our Lady, a most excellent work, which was in the possession of Pope Clement VII; and, among other things painted therein, he counterfeited a glass vase full of water, containing some flowers, in which, besides its marvelous naturalness, he had imitated the dewdrops on the flowers, so that it seemed more real than the reality. For Antonio Segni, who was very much his friend, he made, on a sheet of paper, a Neptune executed with such careful draftsmanship that it seemed absolutely alive. In it one saw the ocean troubled, and Neptune's car drawn by sea-horses, with fantastic creatures, marine monsters and winds, and some very beautiful heads of sea-gods.

The fancy came to him to paint a picture in oils of the head of a Medusa, with the head attired with a coil of snakes, the most strange and extravagant invention that could ever be imagined; but since it was a work that took time, it remained unfinished, as happened with almost all his things. It is among the rare works of art in the Palace of Duke Cosimo, together with the head of an angel, who is raising one arm in the air, which, coming forward, is foreshortened from the shoulder to the elbow, and with the other he raises the hand to the breast.

It is an extraordinary thing how that genius, in his desire to give the highest relief to the works that he made, went so far with dark shadows, in order to find the darkest possible grounds, that he sought for blacks which might make deeper shadows and be darker than other blacks, that by their means he might make his lights the brighter; and in the end this method turned out so dark, that, no light remaining there, his pictures had rather the character of things made to represent an effect of night, than the clear quality of daylight; which all came from seeking to give greater relief, and to achieve the final perfection of art.

He was so delighted when he saw certain bizarre heads of men, with the beard or hair growing naturally, that he would follow one that pleased him a whole day, and so treasured him up in idea, that afterwards, on arriving home, he drew him as if he had had him in his presence. Of this sort there are many heads to be seen, both of women and of men, and I have several of them, drawn by his hand with the pen, in our book of drawings, which I have mentioned so many times; such was that of Amerigo Vespucci, which is a very beautiful head of an old man drawn with charcoal, and likewise that of Scaramuccia, Captain of the Gypsies, which afterwards came into the hands of M. Donato Valdambrini of Arezzo, Canon of S. Lorenzo, left to him by Giambullari.

He began a panel-picture of the Adoration of the Magi, containing many beautiful things, particularly the heads, which was in the house of Amerigo Benci, opposite the Loggia de' Peruzzi; and this, also, remained unfinished, like his other works.

It came to pass that Giovan Galeazzo, Duke of Milan, being dead, and Lodovico Sforza raised to the same rank, in the year 1494, Leonardo was summoned to Milan in great repute to the Duke, who took much delight in the sound of the lyre, to the end that he might play it: and Leonardo took with him that instrument which he had made with his own hands, in great part of silver, in the form of a horse's skull —a thing bizarre and new—in order that the harmony might be of greater volume and more sonorous in tone; with which he surpassed all the musicians who had come together there to play. Besides this, he was the best improviser in verse of his day. The Duke, hearing the marvelous discourse of Leonardo, became so enamored of his genius, that it was something incredible: and he prevailed upon him by entreaties to paint an altar-panel containing a Nativity, which was sent by the Duke to the Emperor.

He also painted in Milan, for the Friars of S. Dominic, at S. Maria delle Grazie, a Last Supper, a most beautiful and marvelous thing; and to the heads of the Apostles he gave such majesty and beauty, that he left the head of Christ unfinished, not believing that he was able to give it that divine air which is essential to the image of Christ. This work, remaining thus all but finished, has ever been held by the Milanese in the greatest veneration, and also by strangers as well; for Leonardo imagined and succeeded in expressing that anxiety which had seized the Apostles in wishing to know who should betray their Master. For which reason in all their faces are seen love, fear, and wrath, or rather, sorrow, at not being able to understand the meaning of Christ; which thing excites no less marvel than the sight, in contrast to it, of obstinacy, hatred, and treachery in Judas; not to mention that every least part of the work displays an incredible diligence, seeing that even in the tablecloth the texture of the stuff is counterfeited in such a manner that linen itself could not seem more real.

It is said that the Prior of that place kept pressing Leonardo, in a most importunate manner, to finish the work; for it seemed strange to him to see Leonardo sometimes stand half a day at a time, lost in contemplation, and he would have liked him to go on like the laborers hoeing in his garden, without ever stopping his brush. And not content with this, he complained of it to the Duke, and that so warmly, that he was constrained to send for Leonardo and delicately urged him to work, contriving nevertheless to show him that he was doing all this because of the importunity of the Prior. Leonardo, knowing that the intellect of that Prince was acute and discerning, was pleased to discourse at large with the Duke on the subject, a thing which he had never done with the

Prior: and he reasoned much with him about art, and made him understand that men of lofty genius sometimes accomplish the most when they work the least, seeking out inventions with the mind, and forming those perfect ideas which the hands afterwards express and reproduce from the images already conceived in the brain. And he added that two heads were still wanting for him to paint; that of Christ, which he did not wish to seek on earth; and he could not think that it was possible to conceive in the imagination that beauty and heavenly grace which should be the mark of God incarnate. Next, there was wanting that of Judas, which was also troubling him, not thinking himself capable of imagining features that should represent the countenance of him who, after so many benefits received, had a mind so cruel as to resolve to betray his Lord, the Creator of the world. However, he would seek out a model for the latter; but if in the end he could not find a better, he should not want that of the importunate and tactless Prior. This thing moved the Duke wondrously to laughter, and he said that Leonardo had a thousand reasons on his side. And so the poor Prior, in confusion, confined himself to urging on the work in the garden, and left Leonardo in peace, who finished only the head of Judas, which seems the very embodiment of treachery and inhumanity; but that of Christ, as has been said, remained unfinished. The nobility of this picture, both because of its design, and from its having been wrought with an incomparable diligence, awoke a desire in the King of France to transport it into his kingdom; wherefore he tried by all possible means to discover whether there were architects who, with cross-stays of wood and iron, might have been able to make it so secure that it might be transported safely; without considering any expense that might have been involved thereby, so much did he desire it. But the fact of its being painted on the wall robbed his Majesty of his desire; and the picture remained with the Milanese. In the same refectory, while he was working at the

Last Supper, on the end wall where is a Passion in the old manner, Leonardo portrayed the said Lodovico, with Massimiliano, his eldest son; and, on the other side, the Duchess Beatrice, with Francesco, their other son, both of whom afterwards became Dukes of Milan; and all are portrayed divinely well.

While he was engaged on this work, he proposed to the Duke to make a horse in bronze, of a marvelous greatness, in order to place upon it, as a memorial, the image of the Duke's father. And on so vast a scale did he begin it and continue it, that it could never be completed. And there are those who have been of the opinion (so various and so often malign out of envy are the judgments of men) that he began it with no intention of finishing it, because, being of so great a size, an incredible difficulty was encountered in seeking to cast it in one piece; and it might also be believed that, from the result, many may have formed such a judgment, since many of his works have remained unfinished. But, in truth, one can believe that his vast and most excellent mind was hampered through being too full of desire, and that his wish ever to seek out excellence upon excellence, and perfection upon perfection, was the reason of it. "The work was retarded by desire," as our Petrarch has said. And, indeed, those who saw the great model that Leonardo made in clay vow that they have never seen a more beautiful thing, or a more superb; and it was preserved until the French came to Milan with King Louis of France, and broke it all to pieces. Lost, also, is a little model of it in wax, which was held to be perfect, together with a book on the anatomy of the horse made by him by way of study.

He then applied himself, but with greater care, to the anatomy of man, assisted by and in turn assisting, in this research, Messer Marc' Antonio della Torre, an excellent philosopher, who was then lecturing at Pavia, and who wrote of this matter; and he was one of the first (as I have heard tell) that began to illustrate the problems of medicine with the doctrine of Galen, and to throw true light on anatomy, which up to that time had been wrapped in the thick and gross darkness of ignorance. And in this he found marvelous aid in the brain, work, and hand of Leonardo, who made a book drawn in red chalk, and annotated with the pen, of the bodies that he dissected with his own hand, and drew with the greatest diligence; wherein he showed all the frame of the bones; and then added to them, in order, all the nerves, and covered them with muscles; the first attached to the bone, the second that hold the body firm, and the third that move it; and beside them, part by part, he wrote in letters of an ill-shaped character, which he made with the left hand, backwards; and whoever is not practiced in reading them cannot understand them, since they are not to be read save with a mirror. Of these papers on the anatomy of man, a great part is in the hands of Messer Francesco da Melzo, a gentleman of Milan, who in the time of Leonardo was a very beautiful boy, and much beloved by him, and now is a no less beautiful and gentle old man; and he holds them dear, and keeps such papers together as if they were relics, in company with the portrait of Leonardo of happy memory; and to all who read these writings, it seems impossible that that divine spirit should have discoursed so well of art, and of the muscles, nerves, and veins, and with such diligence of everything. So, also, there are in the hands of a painter of Milan, certain writings of Leonardo, likewise in characters written with the left hand, backwards, which treat of painting, and of the methods of drawing and coloring. This man, not long ago, came to Florence to see me, wishing to print this work, and he took it to Rome, in order to put it into effect; but I do not know what may afterwards have become of it.*

And to return to the works of Leonardo; there came to

* This treatise on painting is included in *The Notebooks of Leonardo da Vinci,* now available in *The Modern Library.*

Milan, in his time, the King of France, wherefore Leonardo being asked to devise some bizarre thing, made a lion which walked several steps and then opened its breast, and showed it full of lilies.

In Milan he took for his assistant the Milanese Salai, who was most comely in grace and beauty, having fine locks, curling in ringlets, in which Leonardo greatly delighted; and he taught him many things of art; and certain works in Milan, which are said to be by Salai, were retouched by Leonardo.

He returned to Florence, where he found that the Servite Friars had entrusted to Filippino the painting of the panel for the high altar of the Nunziata; whereupon Leonardo said that he would willingly have done such a work. Filippino, having heard this, like the amiable fellow that he was, retired from the undertaking; and the friars, to the end that Leonardo might paint it, took him into their house, meeting the expenses both of himself and of all his household; and thus he kept them in expectation for a long time, but never began anything. In the end, he made a cartoon containing a Madonna and a S. Anne, with a Christ, which not only caused all the craftsmen to marvel, but, when it was finished, men and women, young and old, continued for two days to flock for a sight of it to the room where it was, as if to a solemn festival, in order to gaze at the marvels of Leonardo, which caused all those people to be amazed; for in the face of that Madonna was seen whatever of the simple and the beautiful can by simplicity and beauty confer grace on a picture of the Mother of Christ, since he wished to show that modesty and that humility which are looked for in an image of the Virgin, supremely content with gladness at seeing the beauty of her Son, whom she was holding with tenderness in her lap, while with most chastened gaze she was looking down at S. John, as a little boy, who was playing with a lamb; not without a smile from S. Anne, who, overflowing with joy, was beholding her earthly progeny become divine—ideas truly worthy of the brain and genius of Leonardo. This cartoon, as will be told below, afterwards went to France. He made a portrait of Ginevra d'Amerigo Benci, a very beautiful work; and abandoned the work for the friars, who restored it to Filippino; but he, also, failed to finish it, having been overtaken by death.

Leonardo undertook to execute, for Francesco del Giocondo, the portrait of Monna Lisa, his wife; and after toiling over it for four years, he left it unfinished; and the work is now in the collection of King Francis of France, at Fontainebleau. In this head, whoever wished to see how closely art could imitate nature, was able to comprehend it with ease; for in it were counterfeited all the minutenesses that with subtlety are able to be painted, seeing that the eyes had that luster and watery sheen which are always seen in life, and around them were all those rosy and pearly tints, as well as the lashes, which cannot be represented without the greatest subtlety. The eyebrows, through his having shown the manner in which the hairs spring from the flesh, here more close and here more scanty, and curve according to the pores of the skin, could not be more natural. The nose, with its beautiful nostrils, rosy and tender, appeared to be alive. The mouth, with its opening, and with its ends united by the red of the lips to the flesh tints of the face, seemed, in truth, to be not colors but flesh. In the pit of the throat, if one gazed upon it intently, could be seen the beating of the pulse. And, indeed, it may be said that it was painted in such a manner as to make every valiant craftsman, be he who he may, tremble and lose heart. He made use, also, of this device: Monna Lisa being very beautiful, he always employed, while he was painting her portrait, persons to play or sing, and jesters, who might make her remain merry, in order to take away that melancholy which painters are often wont to give to the portraits that they paint. And in this work of Leonardo's there was a smile so pleasing, that it was a thing more divine than human to behold; and it was held to be something marvelous, since the reality was not more alive.

By reason, then, of the excellence of the works of this most divine craftsman, his fame had so increased that all persons who took delight in art—nay, the whole city of Florence—desired that he should leave them some memorial, and it was being proposed everywhere that he should be commissioned to execute some great and notable work, whereby the commonwealth might be honored and adorned by the great genius, grace and judgment that were seen in the works of Leonardo. And it was decided between the Gonfalonier and the chief citizens, the Great Council Chamber having been newly built—the architecture of which had been contrived with the judgment and counsel of Giuliano da San Gallo, Simone Pollaiuoli, called Il Cronaca, Michelangelo Buonarroti, and Baccio D'Agnolo, as will be related with more detail in the proper places—and having been finished in great haste, it was ordained by public decree that Leonardo should be given some beautiful work to paint; and so the said hall was allotted to him by Piero Soderini, then Gonfalonier of Justice. Whereupon Leonardo, determining to execute this work, began a cartoon in the Sala del Papa, an apartment in S. Maria Novella, representing the story of Niccolò Piccinino, Captain of Duke Filippo of Milan; wherein he designed a group of horsemen who were fighting for a standard, a work that was held to be very excellent and of great mastery, by reason of the marvelous ideas that he had in composing that battle; seeing that in it rage, fury, and revenge are perceived as much in the men as in the horses, among which two with the forelegs interlocked are fighting no less fiercely with their teeth than those who are riding them do in fighting for that standard, which has been grasped by a soldier, who seeks by the strength of his shoulders, as he spurs his horse to flight, having turned his body backwards and seized the staff of the standard, to wrest it by force from the hands of four others, of whom two are defending it, each with one hand, and, raising their swords in the other, are trying to sever the staff; while an old soldier in a red cap, crying out, grips the staff with one hand, and, raising a scimitar with the other, furiously aims a blow in order to cut off both the hands of those who, gnashing their teeth in the struggle, are striving in attitudes of the utmost fierceness to defend their banner; besides which, on the ground, between the legs of the horses, there are two figures in foreshortening that are fighting together, and the one on the ground has over him a soldier who has raised his arm as high as possible, that thus with greater force he may plunge a dagger into his throat, in order to end his life; while the other, struggling with his legs and arms, is doing what he can to escape death.

It is not possible to describe the invention that Leonardo showed in the garments of the soldiers, all varied by him in different ways, and likewise in the helmet-crests and other ornaments; not to mention the incredible mastery that he displayed in the forms and lineaments of the horses, which Leonardo, with their fiery spirit, muscles, and shapely beauty, drew better than any other master. It is said that, in order to draw that cartoon, he made a most ingenious stage, which was raised by contracting it and lowered by expanding. And conceiving the wish to color on the wall in oils, he made a composition of so gross an admixture, to act as a binder on the wall, that, going on to paint in the said hall, it began to peel off in such a manner that in a short time he abandoned it, seeing it spoiling.

Leonardo had very great spirit, and in his every action was most generous. It is said that, going to the bank for the allowance that he used to draw every month from Piero Soderini, the cashier wanted to give him certain paper-packets of pence; but he would not take them, saying in answer, "I am no penny-painter." Having been blamed for cheating Piero Soderini, there began to be murmurings against him;

wherefore Leonardo so wrought upon his friends, that he got the money together and took it to Piero to repay him; but he would not accept it.

He went to Rome with Duke Giuliano de' Medici, at the election of Pope Leo, who spent much of his time on philosophical studies, and particularly on alchemy; where, forming a paste of a certain kind of wax, as he walked he shaped animals very thin and full of wind, and, by blowing into them, made them fly through the air, but when the wind ceased they fell to the ground. On the back of a most bizarre lizard, found by the vine-dresser of the Belvedere, he fixed, with a mixture of quicksilver, wings composed of scales stripped from other lizards, which, as it walked, quivered with the motion; and having given it eyes, horns, and beard, taming it, and keeping it in a box, he made all his friends, to whom he showed it, fly for fear. He used often to have the guts of a wether completely freed of their fat and cleaned, and thus made so fine that they could have been held in the palm of the hand; and having placed a pair of blacksmith's bellows in another room, he fixed to them one end of these, and blowing into them, filled the room, which was very large, so that whoever was in it was obliged to retreat into a corner; showing how, transparent and full of wind, from taking up little space at the beginning they had come to occupy much, and likening them to virtue. He made an infinite number of such follies, and gave his attention to mirrors; and he tried the strangest methods in seeking out oils for painting, and varnish for preserving works when painted.

He made at this time, for Messer Baldassarre Turini da Pescia, who was Datary to Pope Leo, a little picture of the Madonna with the Child in her arms, with infinite diligence and art; but whether through the fault of whoever primed the panel with gesso, or because of his innumerable and capricious mixtures of grounds and colors, it is now much spoilt. And in another small picture he made a portrait of a little boy, which is beautiful and graceful to a marvel; and both of them are now at Pescia, in the hands of Messer Giuliano Turini. It is related that, a work having been allotted to him by the Pope, he straightway began to distil oils and herbs, in order to make the varnish; at which Pope Leo said: "Alas! this man will never do anything, for he begins by thinking of the end of the work, before the beginning."

There was very great disdain between Michelangelo Buonarroti and him, on account of which Michelangelo departed from Florence, with the excuse of Duke Giuliano, having been summoned by the Pope to the competition for the façade of S. Lorenzo. Leonardo, understanding this, departed and went into France, where the King, having had works by his hand, bore him great affection; and he desired that he should color the cartoon of S. Anne, but Leonardo, according to his custom, put him off for a long time with words.

Finally, having grown old, he remained ill many months, and, feeling himself near to death, asked to have himself diligently informed of the teaching of the Catholic faith, and of the good way and holy Christian religion; and then, with many moans, he confessed and was penitent; and although he could not raise himself well on his feet, supporting himself on the arms of his friends and servants, he was pleased to take devoutly the most holy Sacrament, out of his bed. The King, who was wont often and lovingly to visit him, then came into the room; wherefore he, out of reverence, having raised himself to sit upon the bed, giving him an account of his sickness and the circumstances of it, showed withal how much he had offended God and mankind in not having worked at his art as he should have done. Thereupon he was seized by a paroxysm, the messenger of death; for which reason the King having risen and having taken his head, in order to assist him and show him favor, to the end that he might alleviate his pain, his spirit, which was divine, knowing that it could not have any greater honor, expired in the arms of the King.

The loss of Leonardo grieved beyond measure all those who had known him, since there was never any one who did so much honor to painting. With the splendor of his aspect, which was very beautiful, he made serene every broken spirit: and with his words he turned to yea, or nay, every obdurate intention. By his physical force he could restrain any outburst of rage: and with his right hand he twisted the iron ring of a doorbell, or a horseshoe, as if it were lead. With his liberality he would assemble together and support his every friend, poor or rich, if only he had intellect and worth. He adorned and honored, in every action, no matter what mean and bare dwelling; wherefore, in truth, Florence received a very great gift in the birth of Leonardo, and an incalculable loss in his death. In the art of painting, he added to the manner of coloring in oils a certain obscurity, whereby the moderns have given great force and relief to their figures. And in statuary, he proved his worth in the three figures of bronze that are over the door of S. Giovanni, on the side toward the north, executed by Giovan Francesco Rustici, but contrived with the advice of Leonardo; which are the most beautiful pieces of casting, the best designed, and the most perfect that have as yet been seen in modern days. By Leonardo we have the anatomy of the horse, and that of man even more complete. And so, on account of all his qualities, so many and so divine, although he worked much more by words than by deeds, his name and fame can never be extinguished.

GIORGIONE

[*Giorgio da Castelfranco, called Giorgione (Big George),
was born, probably, in 1477 and died in 1510.*]

At the same time when Florence was acquiring such fame by
reason of the works of Leonardo, no little adornment was
conferred on Venice by the talent and excellence of one of
her citizens, who surpassed by a great measure not only the
Bellini, whom the Venetians held in such esteem, but also
every other master who had painted up to that time in that
city. This was Giorgio, who was born at Castelfranco in the
territory of Treviso, in the year 1477, when the Doge was
Giovanni Mozzenigo, brother of Doge Piero. In time, from the
nature of his person and from the greatness of his mind,
Giorgio came to be called Giorgione; and although he was
born from very humble stock, nevertheless he was not otherwise than gentle and of good breeding throughout his whole
life. He was brought up in Venice, and took unceasing delight in the joys of love; and the sound of the lute gave him
marvelous pleasure, so that in his day he played and sang so
divinely that he was often employed for that purpose at
various musical assemblies and gatherings of noble persons.
He studied drawing, and found it greatly to his taste; and in
this nature favored him so highly, that he, having become
enamored of her beauties, would never represent anything in
his works without copying it from life; and so much was he
her slave, imitating her continuously, that he acquired the
name not only of having surpassed Giovanni and Gentile
Bellini, but also of being the rival of the masters who were

working in Tuscany and who were the creators of the modern manner. Giorgione had seen some things by the hand of Leonardo with a beautiful gradation of colors, and with extraordinary relief, effected, as has been related, by means of dark shadows; and this manner pleased him so much that he was for ever studying it as long as he lived, and in oil painting he imitated it greatly. Taking pleasure in the delights of good work, he was ever selecting, for putting into his pictures, the greatest beauty and the greatest variety that he could find. And nature gave him a spirit so benign, and with this, both in oil painting and in fresco, he made certain living forms and other things so soft, so well harmonized, and so well blended in the shadows, that many of the excellent masters of his time were forced to confess that he had been born to infuse spirit into figures and to counterfeit the freshness of living flesh better than any other painter, not only in Venice, but throughout the whole world.

In Florence, in the house of the sons of Giovanni Borgherini, there is a portrait by his hand of the said Giovanni, taken when he was a young man in Venice, and in the same picture is the master who was teaching him; and there are no two heads to be seen with better touches in the flesh-colors or with more beautiful tints in the shadows. In the house of Anton de' Nobili there is another head of a captain in armor, very lively and spirited, which is said to be one of the captains whom Consalvo Ferrante took with him to Venice when he visited Doge Agostino Barberigo. Giorgione made many other portraits which are scattered throughout many parts of Italy; all very beautiful, as may be believed from that of Leonardo Loredano, painted by Giorgione when Leonardo was Doge, which I saw exhibited on one Ascension day, when I seemed to see that most illustrious Prince alive. There is also one at Faenza, in the house of Giovanni da Castel Bolognese, an excellent engraver of cameos and crystals; which work, executed for his father-in-law, is truly divine, since there is such a harmony in the gradation of the colors that it appears to be rather in relief than painted.

Giorgione took much delight in painting in fresco, and one among many works that he executed was the whole of a façade of the Ca Soranzo on the Piazza di S. Polo; wherein, besides many pictures and scenes and other things of fancy, there may be seen a picture painted in oils on the plaster, a work which has withstood rain, sun, and wind, and has remained fresh up to our own day. There is also a Spring, which appears to me to be one of the most beautiful works that he painted in fresco, and it is a great pity that time has consumed it so cruelly. For my part, I know nothing that injures works in fresco more than the sirocco, and particularly near the sea, where it always brings a salt moisture with it.

There broke out at Venice, in the year 1504, in the House of the German Merchants by the Ponte del Rialto, a most terrible fire, which consumed the whole building and all the merchandise, to the very great loss of the merchants; wherefore the Signoria of Venice ordained that it should be rebuilt anew, and it was speedily finished with more accommodation in the way of living rooms, and with greater magnificence, adornment, and beauty. Thereupon, the fame of Giorgione having grown great, it was ordained after deliberation by those who had charge of the matter, that Giorgione should paint it in fresco with colors according to his own fancy, provided only that he gave proof of his genius and executed an excellent work, since it would be in the most beautiful place and most conspicuous site in the city. And so Giorgione put his hand to the work, but thought of nothing save of making figures according to his own fancy, in order to display his art, so that, in truth, there are no scenes to be found there with any order, or representing the deeds of any distinguished person, either ancient or modern; and I, for my part, have never understood them, nor have I found, for all the inquiries that I have made, anyone who understands them, for in one place there is a woman, in another a man, in diverse attitudes, while one has the head of a lion near him, and another an angel in the guise of a Cupid, nor can one tell what it may all mean. There is, indeed, over the principal door, which opens into the Merceria, a woman seated who has at her feet the severed head of a giant, almost in the form of a Judith; she is raising the head with her sword, and speaking with a German, who is below her; but I have not been able to determine for what he intended her to stand, unless, indeed, he may have meant her to represent Germany. However, it may be seen that his figures are well grouped, and that he was ever making progress; and there are in it heads and parts of figures very well painted, and most vivacious in coloring. In all that he did there he aimed at being faithful to nature, without any imitation of another's manner; and the work is celebrated and famous in Venice, no less for what he painted therein than through its convenience for commerce and its utility to the commonwealth.

He executed a picture of Christ bearing the Cross, with a Jew dragging him along, which in time was placed in the Church of S. Rocco, and which now, through the veneration that many feel for it, works miracles, as all may see. He worked in various places, such as Castelfranco, and throughout the territory of Treviso, and he made many portraits for Italian Princes; and many of his works were sent out of Italy, as things truly worthy to bear testimony that if Tuscany had a superabundance of craftsmen in every age, the region beyond, near the mountains, was not always abandoned and forgotten by Heaven.

It is related that Giorgione, at the time when Andrea Verrocchio was making his bronze horse, fell into an argument with certain sculptors, who maintained, since sculpture showed various attitudes and aspects in one single figure to one walking round it, that for this reason it surpassed painting, which only showed one side of a figure. Giorgione was of the opinion that there could be shown in a painted scene, without any necessity for walking round, at one single glance, all the various aspects that a man can present in many gestures—a thing which sculpture cannot do without a change of position and point of view, so that in her case the points of view are many, and not one. Moreover, he proposed to show in one single painted figure the front, the back, and the profile on either side, a challenge which brought them to their senses; and he did it in the following way. He painted a naked man with his back turned, at whose feet was a most limpid pool of water, wherein he painted the reflection of the man's front. At one side was a burnished cuirass that he had taken off, which showed his left profile, since everything could be seen on the polished surface of the piece of armor; and on the other side was a mirror, which reflected the other profile of the naked figure; which was a thing of most beautiful and bizarre fancy, whereby he sought to prove that painting does in fact, with more excellence, labor, and effect, achieve more at one single view of a living figure than does sculpture. And this work was greatly extolled and admired, as something ingenious and beautiful.

He also made a portrait from life of Caterina, Queen of Cyprus, which I once saw in the hands of the illustrious Messer Giovanni Cornaro. There is in our book a head colored in oils, the portrait of a German of the Fugger family, who was at that time one of the chief German merchants, which is an admirable work; together with other sketches and drawings made by him with the pen.

While Giorgione was employed in doing honor both to himself and to his country, and frequenting many houses in order to entertain his various friends with his music, he became enamored of a lady, and they took much joy, one with another, in their love. Now it happened that in the year 1510 she became infected with plague, without, however, knowing anything about it; and Giorgione, visiting her as usual, caught the plague in such a manner, that in a short time, at the age of thirty-four, he passed away to the other life, not without infinite grief on the part of his many friends, who loved him for his virtues, and great hurt to the world, which thus lost him. However, they could bear up against this hurt and loss, in that he left behind him two excellent disciples in Sebastiano, the Venetian, who afterwards became Friar of the Papal Signet-office at Rome, and Titian of Cadore, who not only equaled him, but surpassed him greatly.

CORREGGIO

*[Antonio Allegri da Correggio was born in 1494
and died in 1534.]*

I DO not wish to leave that country wherein our great mother
Nature, in order not to be thought partial, gave to the world
extraordinary men of that sort with which she had already
for many and many a year adorned Tuscany; among whom
was one endowed with an excellent and very beautiful genius,
by name Antonio da Correggio, a most rare painter, who
acquired the modern manner so perfectly, that in a few years,
what with his natural gifts and his practice in art, he became
a most excellent and marvelous craftsman. He was very timid
by nature, and with great discomfort to himself he was continually laboring at the exercise of his art, for the sake of his
family, which weighed upon him; and although it was a
natural goodness that impelled him, nevertheless he afflicted
himself more than was right in bearing the burden of those
sufferings which are wont to crush mankind. He was very
melancholy in his practice of art, a slave to her labors, and
an unwearying investigator of all the difficulties of her realm;
to which witness is borne by a vast multitude of figures in
the Duomo of Parma, executed in fresco and well finished,
which are to be found in the great tribune of the said church,
and are seen foreshortened from below with an effect of
marvelous grandeur.

Antonio was the first who began to work in the modern
manner in Lombardy; wherefore it is thought that if he, with
his genius, had gone forth from Lombardy and lived in Rome,
he would have wrought miracles, and would have brought

the sweat to the brow of many who were held to be great men in his time. For, his works being such as they are without his having seen any of the ancient or the best of the modern, it necessarily follows that, if he had seen them, he would have vastly improved his own, and, advancing from good to better, would have reached the highest rank. It may, at least, be held for certain that no one ever handled colors better than he, and that no craftsman ever painted with greater delicacy or with more relief, such was the softness of his flesh-painting, and such the grace with which he finished his works.

In the same place, also, he painted two large pictures executed in oils, in one of which, among other figures, there may be seen a Dead Christ, which was highly extolled. And in S. Giovanni, in the same city, he painted a tribune in fresco, wherein he represented Our Lady ascending into Heaven amidst a multitude of angels, with other saints around; as to which, it seems impossible that he should have been able, I do not say to express it with his hand, but even to conceive it in his imagination, so beautiful are the curves of the draperies and the expressions that he gave to those figures. Of these there are some drawings in our book, done in red chalk by his hand, with some very beautiful borders of little boys, and other borders drawn in that work by way of ornament, with various fanciful scenes of sacrifices in the ancient manner. And in truth, if Antonio had not brought his works to that perfection which is seen in them, his drawings (although they show excellence of manner, and the charm and practiced touch of a master) would not have gained for him among craftsmen the name that he has won with his wonderful paintings. This art is so difficult, and has so many branches, that very often a craftsman is not able to practice them all to perfection; for there have been many who have drawn divinely well, but have shown some imperfection in coloring, and others have been marvelous in coloring, but have not drawn half so well. All this depends on choice, and on the practice bestowed, in youth, in one case on drawing, in another on color. But since all is learnt in order to carry works to the height of perfection, which is to put good coloring, together with draftsmanship, into everything that is executed, for this reason Correggio deserves great praise, having attained to the height of perfection in the works that he colored either in oils or in fresco; as he did in the Church of the Frati de' Zoccoli di S. Francesco, in the same city, where he painted an Annunciation in fresco so well, that, when it became necessary to pull it down in making some changes in that building, those friars caused the wall round it to be bound with timber strengthened with iron, and, cutting it away little by little, they saved it; and it was built by them into a more secure place in the same convent.

He painted, also, over one of the gates of that city, a Madonna who has the Child in her arms; and it is an astounding thing to see the lovely coloring of this work in fresco, through which he has won from passing strangers, who have seen nothing else of his, infinite praise and honor. For S. Antonio, likewise in that city, he painted a panel wherein is a Madonna, with S. Mary Magdalene; and near them is a boy in the guise of a little angel, holding a book in his hand, who is smiling, with a smile that seems so natural that he moves whoever beholds him to smile also, nor can any person, be his nature ever so melancholy, see him without being cheered. There is also a S. Jerome; and the whole work is colored in a manner so wonderful and so astounding, that painters revere it for the marvel of its coloring, and it is scarcely possible to paint better.

In like manner, he executed square pictures and other paintings for many lords throughout Lombardy; and, among other works, two pictures in Mantua for Duke Federigo II, to be sent to the Emperor, a gift truly worthy of such a Prince. Giulio Romano, seeing these works, said that he had never seen any coloring that attained to such perfection. One was a naked Leda, and the other a Venus; both so soft in coloring, with the shadows of the flesh so well wrought, that they appeared to be not colors, but flesh. In one there was a marvelous landscape, nor was there ever a Lombard who painted such things better than he; and, besides this, hair so lovely in color, and executed in detail with such exquisite finish, that it is not possible to see anything better. There were also certain Loves, executed with beautiful art, who were making trial of their arrows, some of gold and some of lead, on a stone; and what lent most grace to the Venus was a clear and limpid stream, which ran among some stones and bathed her feet, but scarcely concealed any part of them, so that the sight of their delicate whiteness was a moving thing for the eye to behold. For which reason Antonio most certainly deserved all praise and honor during his lifetime, and the greatest glory from the lips and pens of men after his death.

In Modena, also, he painted a panel-picture of Our Lady, which is held in esteem by all painters, as the best picture in that city. In Bologna, likewise, in the house of the Ercolani, gentlemen of that city, there is a work by his hand, a Christ appearing to Mary Magdalene in the Garden, which is very beautiful. In Reggio there was a rare and most beautiful picture; and not long since, Messer Luciano Pallavigino, who takes much delight in noble paintings, passing through the city and seeing it, gave no thought to the cost, and, as if he had bought a jewel, sent it to his house in Genoa. At Reggio, likewise, is a panel containing a Nativity of Christ, wherein the splendor radiating from Him throws its light on the shepherds and all around on the figures that are contemplating Him; and among the many conceptions shown in that subject, there is a woman who, wishing to gaze intently at Christ, and not being able with her mortal sight to bear the light of His Divinity, which seems to be beating upon her with its rays, places a hand before her eyes; which is expressed so well that it is a marvel. Over the hut is a choir of angels singing, who are so well executed, that they appear rather to have rained down from Heaven than to have been made by the hand of a painter. And in the same city there is a little picture, a foot square, the rarest and most beautiful work that is to be seen by his hand, of Christ in the Garden, representing an effect of night, and painted with little figures; wherein the Angel, appearing to Christ, illumines Him with the splendor of his light, with such truth to nature, that nothing better can be imagined or expressed. Below, on a plain at the foot of the mountain, are seen the three Apostles sleeping, over whom the mountain on which Christ is praying casts a shadow, giving those figures a force which one is not able to describe. Far in the background, over a distant landscape, there is shown the appearing of the dawn; and on one side are seen coming some soldiers, with Judas. And although it is so small, this scene is so well conceived, that there is no work of the same kind to equal it either in patience or in study.

Many things might be said of the works of this master; but since, among the eminent men of our art, everything that is to be seen by his hand is admired as something divine, I will say no more. I have used all possible diligence in order to obtain his portrait, but, since he himself did not make it, and he was never portrayed by others, for he always lived in retirement, I have not been able to find one. He was, in truth, a person who had no opinion of himself, nor did he believe himself to be an able master of his art, contrasting his deficiencies with that perfection which he would have liked to achieve. He was contented with little, and he lived like an excellent Christian.

Antonio, like a man who was weighed down by his family, was anxious to be always saving, and he had thereby become as miserly as he could well be. Wherefore it is related that, having received at Parma a payment of sixty crowns in copper coins, and wishing to take them to Correggio to meet some demand, he placed the money on his back and set out to walk on foot; but, being smitten by the heat of the sun, which was very great, and drinking water to refresh himself,

he was seized by pleurisy, and had to take to his bed in a
raging fever, nor did he ever raise his head from it, but finished the course of his life at the age of forty, or thereabout.
He bestowed a very great gift on painting by his handling of
colors, which was that of a true master; and it was by means
of him that men's eyes were opened in Lombardy, where so
many beautiful intellects have been seen in painting, following him in making works worthy of praise and memory.
Thus, by showing them his treatment of hair, executed with
such facility, for all the difficulty of painting it, he taught
them how it should be painted; for which all painters owe him
an everlasting debt.

BRAMANTE

[*Donato d'Agnolo Bramante da Urbino was born, probably, in 1444 and died in 1514.*]

OF very great advantage to architecture, in truth, was the new method of Filippo Brunelleschi, who imitated and restored to the light, after many ages, the noble works of the most learned and marvelous ancients. But no less useful to our age was Bramante, in following the footsteps of Filippo, and making the path of his profession of architecture secure for all who came after him, by means of his courage, boldness, intellect, and science in that art, wherein he had the mastery not of theory only, but of supreme skill and practice. Nor could nature have created a more vigorous intellect, or one to exercise his art and carry it into execution with greater invention and proportion, or with a more thorough knowledge, than Bramante. But no less essential than all this was the election to the Pontificate, at that time, of Julius II, a Pope of great spirit, full of desire to leave memorials behind him. And it was fortunate both for us and for Bramante that he found such a Prince (a thing which rarely happens to men of great genius), at whose expense he might be able to display the worth of his intellect, and that mastery over difficulties which he showed in architecture. His ability was so universal in the buildings that he erected, that the outlines of the cornices, the shafts of the columns, the graceful capitals, the bases, the consoles and corners, the vaults, the staircases, the projections, and every detail of every Order of architecture, contrived from the counsel or model of this craftsman, never failed to astonish all who saw them. Wherefore it appears to me that the everlasting gratitude which is due to the ancients from the intellects that study their works, is also due from them to the labors of Bramante; for if the Greeks were the inventors of architecture, and the Romans their imitators, Bramante not only imitated what he saw, with new invention, and taught it to us, but also added very great beauty and elaboration to the art, which we see embellished by him at the present day.

He was born at Castel Durante, in the State of Urbino, of poor but honest parentage. In his boyhood, besides reading and writing, he gave much attention to arithmetic; but his father, who had need that he should earn money, perceiving that he delighted much in drawing, applied him, when still a mere boy, to the art of painting; whereupon Bramante gave much study to the works of Fra Bartolommeo, otherwise called Fra Carnovale da Urbino, who painted the panel-picture of S. Maria della Bella at Urbino. But since he always delighted in architecture and perspective, he departed from Castel Durante, and made his way to Lombardy, where he went now to one city, and now to another, working as best he could, but not on things of great cost or much credit, having as yet neither name nor reputation. For this reason he determined at least to see some noteworthy work, and betook himself to Milan, in order to see the Duomo. Having studied that building, and having come to know those engineers, he so took courage, that he resolved to devote himself wholly to architecture. Having therefore departed from Milan, he betook himself, just before the holy year of 1500, to Rome, where he was recognized by some friends, both from his own country and from Lombardy, and received a commission to paint, over the Porta Santa of S. Giovanni Laterano, which is opened for the Jubilee, the coat of arms of Pope Alexander VI, to be executed in fresco, with angels and other figures acting as supporters.

Bramante had brought some money from Lombardy, and he earned some more in Rome by executing certain works; and this he spent with the greatest economy, since he wished to be able to live independently, and at the same time, without having to work, to be free to take measurements, at his ease, of all the ancient buildings in Rome. And having put his hand to this, he set out, alone with his thoughts; and within no great space of time he had measured all the buildings in that city and in the Campagna without; and he went as far as Naples, and wherever he knew that there were antiquities. He measured all that was at Tivoli and in the Villa of Hadrian, and, as will be related afterwards in the proper place, made great use of it. The mind of Bramante becoming known in this way, the Cardinal of Naples, having noticed him, began to favor him. Whereupon, while Bramante was continuing his studies, the desire came to the said Cardinal to have the cloister of the Frati della Pace rebuilt in travertine, and he gave the charge of this cloister to Bramante, and he, desiring to earn money and to gain the good will of that Cardinal, set himself to work with all possible industry and diligence, and brought it quickly to perfect completion. And although it was not a work of perfect beauty, it gave him a very great name, since there were not many in Rome who followed the profession of architecture with such zeal, study, and resolution as Bramante.

At the beginning he served as under-architect to Pope Alexander VI for the fountain of Trastevere, and likewise for that which was made on the Piazza di S. Pietro.* He also took part, together with other excellent architects, when his reputation had increased, in the planning of a great part of the Palace of S. Giorgio, and of the Church of S. Lorenzo in Damaso, at the commission of Raffaello Riario, Cardinal of S. Giorgio, near the Campo di Fiore; which palace, whatever better work may have been executed afterwards, never-

* The Square of St. Peter's.

theless was and still is held, on account of its greatness, to be a commodious and magnificent habitation; and the building of this edifice was carried out by one Antonio Montecavallo. Bramante was consulted with regard to the enlargement of S. Jacopo degli Spagnuoli, on the Piazza Navona, and likewise in the deliberations for the building of S. Maria de Anima, which was afterwards carried out by a German architect. From his design, also, was the Palace of Cardinal Adriano da Corneto in the Borgo Nuovo, which was built slowly, and then finally remained unfinished by reason of the flight of that Cardinal; and in like manner, the enlargement of the principal chapel of S. Maria del Popolo was executed from his design.

These works brought him so much credit in Rome, that he was considered the best architect, in that he was resolute, prompt, and most fertile in invention; and he was continually employed by all the great persons in that city for their most important undertakings. Wherefore, after Julius II had been elected Pope, in the year 1503, he entered into his service. The fancy had taken that Pontiff to so transform the space that lay between the Belvedere and the Papal Palace, as to give it the aspect of a square theater, embracing a little valley that ran between the old Papal Palace and the new buildings that Innocent VIII had erected as a habitation for the Popes; and he intended, by means of two corridors, one on either side of this little valley, to make it possible to go from the Belvedere to the Palace under *loggie,* and also to go from the Palace to the Belvedere in the same way, and likewise, by means of various flights of steps, to ascend to the level of the Belvedere. Whereupon Bramante, who had very good judgment and an inventive genius in such matters, distributed two ranges of columns along the lowest part; first, a very beautiful Doric loggia, similar to the Colosseum of the Savelli (although, in place of half-columns, he used pilasters), and all built of travertine; and over this a second range of the Ionic

Order, full of windows, of such a height as to come to the level of the first-floor rooms of the Papal Palace, and to the level of those of the Belvedere; intending to make, afterwards, a loggia more than four hundred paces long on the side toward Rome, and likewise another on the side toward the wood, with which, one on either hand, he proposed to enclose the valley; into which, after it had been leveled, was to be brought all the water from the Belvedere; and for this a very beautiful fountain was to be made. Of this design, Bramante finished the first corridor, which issues from the Palace and leads to the Belvedere on the side toward Rome, except the upper loggia, which was to go above it. As for the opposite part, on the side toward the wood, the foundations, indeed, were laid, but it could not be finished, being interrupted by the death of Julius, and then by that of Bramante. His design was held to be so beautiful in invention, that it was believed that from the time of the ancients until that day, Rome had seen nothing better. But of the other corridor, as has been said, he left only the foundations, and the labor of finishing it has dragged on down to our own day, when Pius IV has brought it almost to completion.

Bramante also erected the head-wall of the Museum of ancient statues in the Belvedere, together with the range of niches; wherein were placed, in his life-time, the Laocoön, one of the rarest of ancient statues, the Apollo, and the Venus; and the rest of the statues were set up there afterwards by Leo X, such as the Tiber, the Nile, and the Cleopatra, with some others added by Clement VII; and in the time of Paul III and Julius III many important improvements were made, at great expense.

But to return to Bramante; he was very resolute, although he was hindered by the avarice of those who supplied him with the means to work, and he had a marvelous knowledge of the craft of building. This construction at the Belvedere was executed by him with extraordinary speed, and such was his eagerness as he worked, and that of the Pope, who would have liked to see the edifice spring up from the ground, without needing to be built, that the builders of the foundations brought the sand and the solid foundation-clay by night and let it down by day in the presence of Bramante, who caused the foundations to be made without seeing anything more of the work. This inadvertence was the reason that all his buildings have cracked, and are in danger of falling down, as did this same corridor, of which a piece one hundred and sixty feet in length fell to the ground in the time of Clement VII, and was afterwards rebuilt by Pope Paul III, who also had the foundations restored and the whole strengthened.

From his design, also, are many flights of steps in the Belvedere, varied according to their situations, whether high or low, in the Doric, Ionic, and Corinthian Orders—a very beautiful work, executed with extraordinary grace. And he had made a model for the whole, which is said to have been a marvelous thing, as may still be imagined from the beginning of the work, unfinished as it is. Moreover, he made a spiral staircase upon mounting columns, in such a way that one can ascend it on horseback; wherein the Doric passes into the Ionic, and the Ionic into the Corinthian, rising from one into the other; a work executed with supreme grace, and with truly excellent art, which does him no less honor than any other thing by his hand that is therein. This invention was copied by Bramante from S. Niccolò at Pisa.

For these reasons he was rightly held worthy by the aforesaid Pope, who loved him very dearly for his great gifts, to be appointed to the Office of the Papal Seal, for which he made a machine for printing Bulls, with a very beautiful screw. In the service of that Pontiff Bramante went to Bologna, in the year 1504, when that city returned to the Church; and he occupied himself, throughout the whole war against Mirandola, on many ingenious things of the greatest importance. He made many designs for ground-plans and

complete buildings, which he drew very well; and of such
there are some to be seen in our book, accurately drawn and
executed with very great art. He taught many of the rules of
architecture to Raphael of Urbino; designing for him, for
example, the buildings that Raphael afterwards drew in perspective in that apartment of the Pope wherein there is Mount
Parnassus; in which apartment he made a portrait of Bramante taking measurements with a pair of compasses.

The Pope resolved, having had the Strada Julia straightened out by Bramante, to place in it all the public offices and
tribunals of Rome, on account of the convenience which this
would bring to the merchants in their business, which up to
that time had always been much hindered. Wherefore Bramante made a beginning with the palace that is to be seen by
S. Biagio sul Tevere, wherein there is still an unfinished Corinthian temple, a thing of rare excellence. The rest of this
beginning is in rustic work, and most beautiful; and it is a
great pity that a work so honorable, useful, and magnificent,
which is held by the masters of the profession to be the most
beautiful example of design in that kind that has ever been
seen, should not have been finished. He made, also, in the
first cloister of S. Pietro a Montorio, a round temple of travertine, than which nothing more shapely or better conceived,
whether in proportion, design, variety, or grace, could be
imagined; and even more beautiful would it have been, if the
whole extent of the cloister, which is not finished, had been
brought to the form that is to be seen in a drawing by his
hand. He directed the building, in the Borgo, of the palace
which afterwards belonged to Raphael of Urbino, executed
with bricks and mould-castings, the columns and bosses being of the Doric Order and of rustic work—a very beautiful
work—with a new invention in the making of these castings.
He also made the design and preparations for the decoration
of S. Maria at Loreto, which was afterwards continued by
Andrea Sansovino; and an endless number of models for

palaces and temples, which are in Rome and throughout the States of the Church.

So sublime was the intellect of this marvelous craftsman, that he made a vast design for restoring and rearranging the Papal Palace. And so greatly had his courage grown, on seeing the powers and desires of the Pope rise to the level of his own wishes and genius, that, hearing that he was minded to throw the Church of S. Pietro to the ground, in order to build it anew, he made him an endless number of designs. And among those that he made was one that was very wonderful, wherein he showed the greatest possible judgment, with two bell-towers, one on either side of the façade, as we see it in the coins afterwards struck for Julius II and Leo X by Caradosso, a most excellent goldsmith, who had no peer in making dies, as may still be seen from the medal of Bramante, executed by him, which is very beautiful. And so, the Pope having resolved to make a beginning with the vast and sublime structure of S. Pietro, Bramante caused half of the old church to be pulled down, and put his hand to the work, with the intention that it should surpass, in beauty, art, invention, and design, as well as in grandeur, richness, and adornment, all the buildings that had been erected in that city by the power of the Commonwealth, and by the art and intellect of so many able masters; and with his usual promptness he laid the foundations, and carried the greater part of the building, before the death of the Pope and his own, to the height of the cornice, where are the arches to all the four piers; and these he turned with supreme expedition and art. He also executed the vaulting of the principal chapel, where the recess is, giving his attention at the same time to pressing on the building of the chapel that is called the Chapel of the King of France.

For this work he invented the method of casting vaults in wooden moulds, in such a manner that patterns of friezes and foliage, like carvings, come out in the plaster; and in the arches of this edifice he showed how they could be turned with flying scaffoldings, a method that we have since seen followed by Antonio da San Gallo. In the part that was finished by him, the cornice that runs right round the interior is seen to be so graceful, that no other man's hand could take away or alter anything from its design without spoiling it. It is evident from his capitals, which are of olive leaves within, and from all the Doric work on the outer side, which is extraordinarily beautiful, how sublime was the courage of Bramante, whereby, in truth, if he had possessed physical powers equal to the intellect that adorned his spirit, he would most certainly have achieved even more unexampled things than he did. This work, as will be related in the proper places, since his death and down to the present day, has been much mutilated by other architects, insomuch that it may be said that with the exception of four arches which support the tribune, nothing of his has remained there. For Raphael of Urbino and Giuliano da San Gallo, who carried on the work after the death of Julius II, together with Fra Giocondo of Verona, thought fit to begin to alter it; and after the death of those masters, Baldassarre Peruzzi, in building the Chapel of the King of France, in the transept on the side toward the Campo Santo, changed Bramante's design; and under Paul III Antonio da San Gallo changed it again entirely. Finally, Michelangelo Buonarroti, sweeping away the countless opinions and superfluous expenses, has brought it to such beauty and perfection as not one of those others ever thought of, which all comes from his judgment and power of design; although he said to me several times that he was only the executor of the design and arrangements of Bramante, seeing that he who originally lays the foundations of a great edifice is its true creator. Vast, indeed, seemed the conception of Bramante in this work, and he gave it a very great beginning, which, even if he had begun on a smaller scale, neither San Gallo nor the others, nor even Buonarroti, would have had enough power of design to increase, although they were able to diminish it; so immense, stupendous, and magnificent was this edifice, and yet Bramante had conceived something even greater.

It is said that he was so eager to see this structure making progress, that he pulled down many beautiful things in S. Pietro, such as tombs of Popes, paintings, and mosaics, and that for this reason we have lost all trace of many portraits of distinguished persons, which were scattered throughout that church, which was the principal church of all Christendom. He preserved only the altar of S. Pietro, and the old tribune, round which he made a most beautiful ornament of the Doric Order, all of peperino-stone, to the end that when the Pope came to S. Pietro to say Mass, he might be able to stand within it with all his Court and with the Ambassadors of the Christian Princes; but death prevented him from finishing it entirely, and the Sienese Baldassarre afterwards brought it to completion.

Bramante was a very merry and pleasant person, ever delighting to help his neighbor. He was very much the friend of men of ability, and favored them in whatever way he could; as may be seen from his kindness to the gracious Raphael of Urbino, most celebrated of painters, whom he brought to Rome. He always lived in the greatest splendor, doing honor to himself; and in the rank to which his merits had raised him, what he possessed was nothing to what he would have been able to spend. He delighted in poetry, and loved to improvise upon the lyre, or to hear others doing this: and he composed some sonnets, if not as polished as we now demand them, at least weighty and without faults. He was much esteemed by the prelates, and was received by an endless number of noblemen who made his acquaintance. In his lifetime he had very great renown, and even greater after his death, because of which the building of S. Pietro was interrupted for many years. He lived to the age of seventy, and he was borne to his tomb in Rome, with most honorable obsequies, by the Court of the Pope and by all the sculptors, architects, and painters. He was buried in S. Pietro, in the year 1514.

Very great was the loss that architecture suffered in the death of Bramante, who was the discoverer of many good methods wherewith he enriched that art, such as the invention of casting vaults, and the secret of stucco; both of which were known to the ancients, but had been lost until his time through the ruin of their buildings. And those who occupy themselves with measuring ancient works of architecture, find in the works of Bramante no less science and design than in any of the former; wherefore, among those who are versed in the profession, he can be accounted one of the rarest intellects that have adorned our age.

RAPHAEL

[*Raffaello Santi da Urbino was born in 1483
and died in 1520.*]

How bountiful and benign Heaven sometimes shows itself in
showering upon one single person the infinite riches of its
treasures, and all those graces and rarest gifts that it is wont
to distribute among many individuals, over a long space of
time, could be clearly seen in the no less excellent than
gracious Raphael of Urbino, who was endowed by nature
with all that modesty and goodness which are seen at times in
those who, beyond all other men, have added to their natural sweetness and gentleness the beautiful adornment of
courtesy and grace, by reason of which they always show
themselves agreeable and pleasant to every sort of person and
in all their actions. Him nature presented to the world, when,
vanquished by art through the hands of Michelangelo Buonarroti, she wished to be vanquished, in Raphael, by art and
character together. And in truth, since the greater part of the
craftsmen who had lived up to that time had received from
nature a certain element of savagery and madness, which, besides making them strange and eccentric, had brought it
about that very often there was revealed in them rather the
obscure darkness of vice than the brightness and splendor
of those virtues that make men immortal, there was right
good reason for her to cause to shine out brilliantly in
Raphael, as a contrast to the others, all the rarest qualities of
the mind, accompanied by such grace, industry, beauty, modesty, and excellence of character, as would have sufficed to
efface any vice, however hideous, and any blot, were it ever

so great. Wherefore it may be surely said that those who are the possessors of such rare and numerous gifts as were seen in Raphael of Urbino, are not merely men, but, if it be not a sin to say it, mortal gods; and that those who, by means of their works, leave an honorable name written in the archives of fame in this earthly world of ours, can also hope to have to enjoy in Heaven a worthy reward for their labors and merits.

Raphael was born at Urbino, a very famous city in Italy, at three o'clock of the night on Good Friday, in the year 1483, to a father named Giovanni de' Santi, a painter of no great excellence, and yet a man of good intelligence, well able to direct his children on that good path which he himself had not been fortunate enough to have shown to him in his boyhood. And since Giovanni knew how important it is to rear infants, not with the milk of nurses, but with that of their own mothers, no sooner was Raphael born, to whom with happy augury he gave that name at baptism, than he insisted that this his only child—and he had no more afterwards—should be suckled by his own mother, and that in his tender years he should have his character formed in the house of his parents, rather than learn less gentle or even boorish ways and habits in the houses of peasants or common people. When he was well grown, he began to exercise him in painting, seeing him much inclined to such an art, and possessed of a very beautiful genius: wherefore not many years passed before Raphael, still a boy, became a great help to Giovanni in many works that he executed in the state of Urbino. In the end, this good and loving father, knowing that his son could learn little from him, made up his mind to place him with Pietro Perugino, who, as he heard tell, held the first place among painters at that time. He went, therefore, to Perugia: but not finding Pietro there, he set himself, in order to lessen the annoyance of waiting for him, to execute some works in S. Francesco. When Pietro had returned from Rome, Giovanni, who was a gentle and well-bred person, formed a friendship with him, and, when the time appeared to have come, in the most adroit method that he knew, told him his desire. And so Pietro, who was very courteous and a lover of beautiful genius, agreed to have Raphael: whereupon Giovanni, going off rejoicing to Urbino, took the boy, not without many tears on the part of his mother, who loved him dearly, and brought him to Perugia, where Pietro, after seeing Raphael's method of drawing, and his beautiful manners and character, formed a judgment of him which time, from the result, proved to be very true.

It is a very notable thing that Raphael, studying the manner of Pietro, imitated it in every respect so closely, that his copies could not be distinguished from his master's originals, and it was not possible to see any clear difference between his works and Pietro's; as is still evident from some figures in a panel in S. Francesco at Perugia, which he executed in oils. These are a Madonna who has risen into Heaven, with Jesus Christ crowning her. This work is executed with truly supreme diligence; and one who had not a good knowledge of the two manners, would hold it as certain that it is by the hand of Pietro, whereas it is without a doubt by the hand of Raphael.

After this work, Pietro returning to Florence on some business of his own, Raphael departed from Perugia and went off with some friends to Città di Castello, where he painted a panel for S. Agostino in the same manner, and likewise one of a Crucifixion for S. Domenico, which, if his name were not written upon it, no one would believe to be a work by Raphael, but rather by Pietro. For S. Francesco, also in the same city, he painted a little panel-picture of the Marriage of Our Lady, in which one may recognize the excellence of Raphael increasing and growing in refinement, and surpassing the manner of Pietro. In this work is a temple drawn in perspective with such loving care, that it is a marvelous thing to see the difficulties that he was for ever seeking out in this branch of his profession.

Meanwhile, when he had acquired very great fame by following his master's manner, Pope Pius II had given the commission for painting the library of the Duomo at Siena to Pinturicchio; and he, being a friend of Raphael, and knowing him to be an excellent draftsman, brought him to Siena, where Raphael made for him some of the drawings and cartoons for that work. The reason that he did not continue at it was that some painters in Siena kept extolling with vast praise the cartoon that Leonardo da Vinci had made in the Sala del Papa of a very beautiful group of horsemen, to be painted afterwards in the Hall of the Palace of the Signoria, and likewise some nudes executed by Michelangelo Buonarroti in competition with Leonardo, and much better; and Raphael, on account of the love that he always bore to the excellent in art, was seized by such a desire to see them, that, putting aside that work and all thought of his own advantage and comfort, he went off to Florence.

Having arrived there, and being pleased no less with the city than with those works, which appeared to him to be divine, he determined to take up his abode there for some time; and thus he formed a friendship with some young painters, among whom were Ridolfo Ghirlandaio, Aristotile da San Gallo, and others, and became much honored in that city, particularly by Taddeo Taddei, who, being one who always loved any man inclined to excellence, would have him ever in his house and at his table. And Raphael, who was gentleness itself, in order not to be beaten in courtesy, made him two pictures, which incline to his first manner, derived from Pietro, but also to the other much better manner that he afterwards acquired by study, as will be related; which pictures are still in the house of the heirs of the said Taddeo.

Raphael also formed a very great friendship with Lorenzo Nasi; and for this Lorenzo, who had taken a wife about that time, he painted a picture in which he made a Madonna, and between her legs her Son, to whom a little S. John, full of joy, is offering a bird, with great delight and pleasure for both of them. In the attitude of each is a certain childlike simplicity which is wholly lovely, besides that they are so well colored, and executed with such diligence, that they appear to be rather of living flesh than wrought by means of color and draftsmanship; the Madonna, likewise, has an air truly full of grace and divinity; and the foreground, the landscapes, and in short all the rest of the work, are most beautiful. This picture was held by Lorenzo Nasi, as long as he lived, in very great veneration, both in memory of Raphael, who had been so much his friend, and on account of the dignity and excellence of the work; but afterwards, on August 9, in the year 1548, it met an evil fate, when, on account of the collapse of the hill of S. Giorgio, the house of Lorenzo fell down, together with the ornate and beautiful houses of the heirs of Marco del Nero, and other neighboring dwellings. However, the pieces of the picture being found among the fragments of the ruins, the son of Lorenzo, Batista, who was a great lover of art, had them put together again as well as was possible.

After these works, Raphael was forced to depart from Florence and go to Urbino, where, on account of the death of his mother and of his father Giovanni, all his affairs were in confusion. While he was living in Urbino, therefore, he painted for Guidobaldo da Montefeltro, then Captain of the Florentines, two pictures of Our Lady, small but very beautiful, and in his second manner, which are now in the possession of the most illustrious and excellent Guidobaldo, Duke of Urbino. For the same patron he painted a little picture of Christ praying in the Garden, with the three Apostles sleeping at some distance from Him. This painting is so highly finished, that a miniature could not be better, or in any way different; and after having been a long time in the possession of Francesco Maria, Duke of Urbino, it was then presented by the most illustrious Signora Leonora, his consort, to the Venetians Don Paolo Giustiniano and Don Pietro Quirini, hermits of the holy Hermitage of Camaldoli, who afterwards placed it, as a relic and a very rare thing, and, in a word, as a work by the hand of Raphael of Urbino, and also to honor the memory of that most illustrious lady, in the apartment of the Superior of that hermitage, where it is held in the veneration that it deserves.

Having executed these works and settled his affairs, Raphael returned to Perugia, where he painted a panel-picture of Our Lady, S. John the Baptist, and S. Nicholas, for the Chapel of the Ansidei in the Church of the Servite Friars. And in the Chapel of the Madonna in S. Severo, a little monastery of the Order of Camaldoli, in the same city, he painted in fresco a Christ in Glory, and a God the Father with angels round Him, and six saints seated, S. Benedict, S. Romualdo, S. Laurence, S. Jerome, S. Mauro, and S. Placido, three on either side; and on this picture, which was held at that time to be most beautiful for a work in fresco, he wrote his name in large and very legible letters. In the same city, also, he was commissioned by the Nuns of S. Anthony of Padua to paint a panel-picture of Our Lady, with Jesus Christ fully dressed, as it pleased those simple and venerable sisters, in her lap, and on either side of the Madonna S. Peter, S. Paul, S. Cecilia, and S. Catherine; to which two holy virgins he gave the sweetest and most lovely expressions of countenance and the most beautifully varied headdresses that are anywhere to be seen, which was a rare thing in those times. Above this panel, in a lunette, he painted a very beautiful God the Father, and in the predella of the altar three scenes with little figures, of Christ praying in the Garden, bearing the Cross (wherein are some soldiers dragging Him along with most beautiful movements), and lying dead in the lap of His Mother. This work is truly marvelous and devout; and it is held in great veneration by those nuns, and much extolled by all painters.

I will not refrain from saying that it was recognized, after he had been in Florence, that he changed and improved his manner so much, from having seen many works by the hands of excellent masters, that it had nothing to do with his earlier manner; indeed, the two might have belonged to different masters, one much more excellent than the other in painting.

Before he departed from Perugia, Madonna Atalanta Baglioni besought him that he should consent to paint a panel for her chapel in the Church of S. Francesco; but since he was not able to meet her wishes at that time, he promised her that, after returning from Florence, whither he was obliged to go on some affairs, he would not fail her. And so, having come to Florence, where he applied himself with incredible labor to the studies of his art, he made the cartoon for that chapel, with the intention of going, as he did, as soon as the occasion might present itself, to put it into execution.

While he was thus staying in Florence, Agnolo Doni—who was very careful of his money in other things, but willing to spend it, although still with the greatest possible economy, on works of painting and sculpture, in which he much delighted—caused him to make portraits of himself and of his wife; and these may be seen, painted in his new manner, in the possession of Giovan Battista, his son, in the beautiful and most commodious house that the same Agnolo built on the Corso de' Tintori, near the Canto degli Alberti, in Florence. For Domenico Canigiani, also, he painted a picture of Our Lady, with the Child Jesus welcoming a little S. John brought to Him by S. Elizabeth, who, as she holds him, is gazing with a most animated expression at a S. Joseph, who is standing with both his hands leaning on a staff, and inclines his head toward her, as though praising the greatness of God and marveling that she, so advanced in years, should have so young a child. And all appear to be amazed to see with how much feeling and reverence the two cousins, for all their tender age, are caressing one another; not to mention that every touch of color in the heads, hands, and feet seems to be living flesh rather than a tint laid on by a master of that art. This most noble picture is now in the possession of the heirs of the said Domenico Canigiani, who hold it in the estimation that is due to a work by Raphael of Urbino.

This most excellent of painters studied in the city of Florence the old works of Masaccio; and what he saw in those of Leonardo and Michelangelo made him give even greater attention to his studies, in consequence of which he effected an extraordinary improvement in his art and manner. While he was living in Florence, Raphael, besides other friendships, became very intimate with Fra Bartolommeo di San Marco, being much pleased with his coloring, and taking no little pains to imitate it: and in return he taught that good father the principles of perspective, to which up to that time the monk had not given any attention.

But at the very height of this friendly intercourse, Raphael was recalled to Perugia, where he began by finishing the work for the aforesaid Madonna Atalanta Baglioni in S. Francesco, for which, as has been related, he had made the cartoon in Florence. In this most divine picture there is a Dead Christ being borne to the Sepulcher, executed with such freshness and such loving care, that it seems to the eye to have been only just painted. In the composition of this work, Raphael imagined to himself the sorrow that the nearest and most affectionate relatives of the dead one feel in laying to rest the body of him who has been their best beloved, and on whom, in truth, the happiness, honor, and welfare of a whole family have depended. Our Lady is seen in a swoon; and the heads of all the figures are very gracious in their weeping, particularly that of S. John, who, with his hands clasped, bows his head in such a manner as to move the hardest heart to pity. And in truth, whoever considers the diligence, love, art, and grace shown by this picture, has great reason to marvel, for it amazes all who behold it, what with the air of the figures, the beauty of the draperies, and, in short, the supreme excellence that it reveals in every part.

This work finished, he returned to Florence, where he received from the Dei, citizens of that city, the commission for an altar-panel that was to be placed in their chapel in S. Spirito; and he began it, and brought the sketch very nearly to completion. At the same time he painted a picture that was afterwards sent to Siena, although, on the departure of Raphael, it was left with Ridolfo Ghirlandaio, to the end that he might finish a piece of blue drapery that was wanting. This happened because Bramante of Urbino, who was in the service of Julius II, wrote to Raphael, on account of his being distantly related to him and also his compatriot, that he had so wrought upon the Pope, who had caused some new rooms to be made (in the Vatican), that Raphael would have a chance of showing his worth in them. This proposal pleased Raphael: wherefore, abandoning his works in Florence, and leaving the panel for the Dei unfinished, in the state in which Messer Baldassarre da Pescia had it placed in the Pieve of his native city after the death of Raphael, he betook himself to Rome. Having arrived there, he found that most of the rooms in the Palace had been painted, or were still being painted, by a number of masters. To be precise, he saw that there was one room in which a scene had been finished by Piero della Francesca; Luca da Cortona had brought one wall nearly to completion; and Don Pietro della Gatta, Abbot of S. Clemente at Arezzo, had begun some works there. Bramantino, the Milanese, had likewise painted many figures, which were mostly portraits from life, and were held to be very beautiful. After his arrival, therefore, having been received very warmly by Pope Julius, Raphael began in the Camera della Segnatura a scene of the theologians reconciling Philosophy and Astrology with Theology: wherein are portraits of all the sages in the world, disputing in various ways. Standing apart are some astrologers, who have made various kinds of figures and characters of geomancy and astrology on some little tablets, which they send to the Evangelists by certain very beautiful angels; and these Evangelists are expounding them. Among them is Diogenes with his cup, lying on the steps, and lost in thought, a figure very well conceived, which, for its beauty and the characteristic negligence of its dress, is worthy to be extolled. There, also, are Aristotle and Plato, one with the Timaeus in his hand, the other with the Ethics; and round them, in a circle, is a great school of philosophers. Nor is it possible to express the beauty of those astrologers and geometricians who are drawing a vast number of figures and characters with compasses on tablets: among whom, in the figure of a young man, shapely and handsome, who is throwing out his arms in admiration, and inclining his head, is the portrait of Federigo II, Duke of Mantua, who was then in Rome. There is also a figure that is stooping to the ground, holding in its hand a pair of compasses, with which it is making a circle on a tablet: this is said to be the architect Bramante, and it is no less the man himself than if he were alive, so well is it drawn. Beside a figure with its back turned and holding a globe of the heavens in its hand, is the portrait of Zoroaster; and next to him is Raphael, the master of the work, who made his own portrait by means of a mirror, in a youthful head with an air of great modesty, filled with a pleasing and excellent grace, and wearing a black cap.

Nor is one able to describe the beauty and goodness that are to be seen in the heads and figures of the Evangelists, to whose countenances he gave an air of attention and intentness very true to life, and particularly in those who are writing. Thus, behind S. Matthew, who is copying the characters from the tablet wherein are the figures (which is held before him by an angel), and writing them down in a book, he painted an old man who, having placed a piece of paper on his knee, is copying all that S. Matthew writes down; and while intent on his work in that uncomfortable position, he seems to twist his head and his jaws in time with the motion of the pen. And in addition to the details of the conceptions, which are numerous enough, there is the composition of the whole scene, which is truly arranged with so much order and proportion, that he may be said to have given therein such a proof of his powers as made men understand that he was resolved to hold the sovereignty, without question, among all who handled the brush.

He also adorned this work with a view in perspective and with many figures, executed in such a sweet and delicate manner, that Pope Julius was induced thereby to cause all the scenes of the other masters, both the old and the new, to be thrown to the ground, so that Raphael alone might have the glory of all the labors that had been devoted to these works up to that time. The work of Giovanni Antonio Sodoma of Vercelli, which was above Raphael's painting, was to be thrown down by order of the Pope; but Raphael determined to make use of its compartments and grotesques. There were also some medallions, four in number, and in each of these he made a figure as a symbol of the scenes below, each figure being on the same side as the scene that it represented. Over the first scene, wherein he painted Philosophy, Astrology, Geometry, and Poetry making peace with Theology, is a woman representing Knowledge, who is seated on a throne that is supported on either side by a figure of the Goddess Cybele, each with those many breasts which in ancient times were the attributes of Diana Polymastes; and her dress is of four colors, standing for the four elements; from the head downwards there is the color of fire, below the girdle that of the sky, from the groin to the knees there is the color of earth, and the rest, down to the feet, is the color of water. With her, also, are some truly beautiful little boys. In another medallion, on the side toward the window that looks over the Belvedere, is a figure of Poetry, who is in the form of Polyhymnia, crowned with laurel, and holds an antique musical instrument in one hand, and a book in the other, and has her legs crossed. With a more than human beauty of expression in her countenance, she stands with her eyes uplifted toward Heaven, accompanied by two little boys, who are lively and spirited, and who make a group of beautiful variety both with her and with the others. On this side, over the aforesaid window, Raphael afterwards painted Mount Parnassus. In the third medallion, which is above the scene where the Holy Doctors are ordaining the Mass, is a figure of Theology, no less beautiful than the others, with books and other things round her, and likewise accompanied by little boys. And in the fourth medallion, over the other window, which looks out on the court, he painted Justice with her scales, and her sword uplifted, and with the same little boys that are with the others; of which the effect is supremely beautiful, for in the scene on the wall below he depicted the giving of the Civil and the Canon Law, as we will relate in the proper place.

In like manner, on the same ceiling, in the angles of the pendentives, he executed four scenes which he drew and colored with great diligence, but with figures of no great size. In one of these, that near the Theology, he painted the Sin of Adam, the eating of the apple, which he executed with a most delicate manner; and in the second, near the Astrology, is a figure of that science setting the fixed stars and planets in their places. In the next, that belonging to Mount Parnassus, is Marsyas, whom Apollo has caused to be bound to a tree and flayed; and on the side of the scene wherein the Decretals are given, there is the Judgment of Solomon, showing him proposing to have the child cut in half. These four scenes are all full of expression and feeling, and executed with excellent draftsmanship, and with pleasing and gracious coloring.

But now, having finished with the vaulting—that is, the ceiling—of that apartment, it remains for us to describe what he painted below the things mentioned above, wall by wall. On the wall toward the Belvedere, where there are Mount Parnassus and the Fount of Helicon, he made round that mount a laurel wood of darkest shadows, in the verdure of which one almost sees the leaves quivering in the gentle zephyrs; and in the air are vast numbers of naked Loves, most beautiful in feature and expression, who are plucking branches of laurel and with them making garlands, which they throw and scatter about the mount. Over the whole, in truth, there seems to breathe a spirit of divinity, so beautiful are the figures, and such the nobility of the picture, which makes whoever studies it with attention marvel how a human brain, by the imperfect means of mere colors, and by excellence of draftsmanship, could make painted things appear alive. Most lifelike, also, are those Poets who are seen here and there about the mount, some standing, some seated, some writing, and others discoursing, and others, again, singing or conversing together, in groups of four or six, according as it pleased him to distribute them. There are portraits from nature of all the most famous poets, ancient and modern, and some only just dead, or still living in his day.

On another wall he made a Heaven, with Christ, Our Lady, S. John the Baptist, the Apostles, the Evangelists, and the Martyrs, enthroned on clouds, with God the Father sending down the Holy Spirit over them all, and particularly over an endless number of saints, who are below, writing the Mass, and engaged in disputation about the Host, which is on the altar. In the air are four little children, who are holding open the Gospels. Anything more graceful or more perfect than these figures no painter could create, since those saints are represented as seated in the air, in a circle, and so well, that in truth, besides the appearance of life that the coloring gives them, they are foreshortened and made to recede in such a manner, that they would not be otherwise if they were in relief. Moreover, their vestments show a rich variety, with most beautiful folds in the draperies, and the expressions of the heads are more Divine than human; as may be seen in that of Christ, which reveals all the clemency and devoutness that Divinity can show to mortal men through the medium of painting. For Raphael received from nature a particular gift of making the expressions of his heads very sweet and gracious; of which we have proof also in the Madonna, who, with her hands pressed to her bosom, gazing in contemplation upon her Son, seems incapable of refusing any favor; not to mention that he showed a truly beautiful sense of fitness, giving a look of age to the expressions of the Holy Patriarchs, simplicity to the Apostles, and faith to the Mar-

tyrs. Even more art and genius did he display in the holy
Christian Doctors, in whose features, while they make disputation throughout the scene in groups of six or three or two,
there may be seen a kind of eagerness and distress in seeking
to find the truth of that which is in question, revealing this
by gesticulating with their hands, making various movements
of their persons, turning their ears to listen, knitting their
brows, and expressing astonishment in many different ways,
all truly well varied and appropriate; save only the four
Doctors of the Church, who, illumined by the Holy Spirit,
are unraveling and expounding, by means of the Holy Scriptures, all the problems of the Gospels, which are held up by
those little boys who have them in their hands as they hover
in the air.

On another wall, where the other window is, on one side,
he painted Justinian giving the Laws to the Doctors to be
revised; and above this, Temperance, Fortitude, and Pru-
dence. On the other side he painted the Pope giving the
Canonical Decretals; for which Pope he made a portrait from
life of Pope Julius, and, beside him, Cardinal Giovanni de'
Medici, who became Pope Leo, Cardinal Antonio di Monte,
and Cardinal Alessandro Farnese, who afterwards became
Pope Paul III, with other portraits.

The Pope was very well satisfied with this work; and in
order to make the paneling worthy of the paintings, he sent
to Monte Oliveto di Chiusuri, a place in the territory of Siena,
for Fra Giovanni da Verona, a great master at that time of
perspective-views in inlaid woodwork, who made there not
only the paneling right round, but also very beautiful doors
and seats, wrought with perspective-views, which brought
him great favor, rewards, and honor from the Pope.

Raphael's powers grew in such a manner, that he was
commissioned by the Pope to go on to paint a second room,
that near the Great Hall. And at this time, when he had
gained a very great name, he also made a portrait of Pope
Julius in a picture in oils, so true and so lifelike, that the por-

trait caused all who saw it to tremble, as if it had been the living man himself. This work is now in S. Maria del Popolo, together with a very beautiful picture of Our Lady, painted at the same time by the same master, and containing the Nativity of Jesus Christ, wherein is the Virgin laying a veil over her Son, whose beauty is such, both in the air of the head and in all the members, as to show that He is the true Son of God. And no less beautiful than the Child is the Madonna, in whom, besides her supreme loveliness, there may be seen piety and gladness. There is also a Joseph, who, leaning with both his hands on a staff, and lost in thoughtful contemplation of the King and Queen of Heaven, gazes with the adoration of a most saintly old man. Both these pictures are exhibited on days of solemn festival.

By this time Raphael had acquired much fame in Rome; but, although his manner was graceful and held by all to be very beautiful, and despite the fact that he had seen so many antiquities in that city, and was for ever studying, nevertheless he had not yet given thereby to his figures that grandeur and majesty which he gave to them from that time onward. For it happened in those days that Michelangelo made the terrifying outburst against the Pope in the chapel, of which we will speak in his Life; whence he was forced to fly to Florence. Whereupon Bramante, having the keys of the chapel, allowed Raphael, who was his friend, to see it, to the end that he might be able to learn the methods of Michelangelo. And that sight of it was the reason that Raphael straightway repainted, although he had already finished it, the Prophet Isaiah that is to be seen in S. Agostino at Rome, above the S. Anne by Andrea Sansovino; in which work, by means of what he had seen of Michelangelo's painting, he made the manner immeasurably better and more grand, and gave it greater majesty. Wherefore Michelangelo, on seeing afterwards the work of Raphael, thought, as was the truth, that Bramante had done him that wrong on purpose in order to bring profit and fame to Raphael.

Not long after this, Agostino Chigi, a very rich merchant of Siena, who was much the friend of every man of excellence, gave Raphael the commission to paint a chapel; and this he did because a short time before Raphael had painted for him in his softest manner, in a loggia of his palace, now called the Chigi, in the Trastevere, a Galatea in a car on the sea drawn by two dolphins, and surrounded by Tritons and many sea-gods. Raphael, then, having made the cartoon for that chapel, which is at the entrance of the Church of S. Maria della Pace, on the right hand as one goes into the church by the principal door, executed it in fresco, in his new manner, which was no little grander and more magnificent than his earlier manner. In this painting Raphael depicted some Prophets and Sibyls, before Michelangelo's chapel had been thrown open to view, although he had seen it; and in truth it is held to be the best of his works, and the most beautiful among so many that are beautiful, for in the women and children that are in it, there may be seen a marvelous vivacity and perfect coloring. And this work caused him to be greatly esteemed both in his lifetime and after his death, being the rarest and most excellent that Raphael executed in all his life.

Next, spurred by the entreaties of a Chamberlain of Pope Julius, he painted the panel for the high altar of the Araceli, wherein he made a Madonna in the sky, with a most beautiful landscape, a S. John, a S. Francis, and a S. Jerome represented as a Cardinal; in which Madonna may be seen a humility and a modesty truly worthy of the Mother of Christ; and besides the beautiful gesture of the Child as He plays with His Mother's hand, there is revealed in S. John that penitential air which fasting generally gives, while his head displays the sincerity of soul and frank assurance appropriate to those who live away from the world and despise it, and, in their dealings with mankind, make war on falsehood and speak out the truth. In the middle of the panel, below the Madonna, Raphael made a little boy standing, who is raising his head toward her and holding an inscription: than whom none better or more graceful could be painted, what with the beauty of his features and the proportionate loveliness of his person. And in addition there is a landscape, which is singularly beautiful in its absolute perfection.

Afterwards, going on with the apartments of the Palace, he painted a scene of the Miracle of the Sacramental Corporal of Orvieto, or of Bolsena, whichever it may be called. In this scene there may be perceived in the face of the priest who is saying Mass, which is glowing with a blush, the shame that he felt on seeing the Host turned into blood on the Corporal on account of his unbelief. With terror in his eyes, dumbfounded and beside himself in the presence of his hearers, he seems like one who knows not what to do; and in the gesture of his hands may almost be seen the fear and trembling that a man would feel in such a case. Round him Raphael made many figures, all varied and different, some serving the Mass, others kneeling on a flight of steps; and all, bewildered by the strangeness of the event, are making various most beautiful movements and gestures, while in many, both men and women, there is revealed a belief that they are to blame. Among the women is one who is seated on the ground at the foot of the scene, holding a child in her arms; and she, hearing the account that another appears to be giving her of the thing that has happened to the priest, turns in a marvelous manner as she listens to this, with a womanly grace that is very natural and lifelike. On the other side he painted Pope Julius hearing that Mass, a most marvelous work, wherein he made a portrait of Cardinal di San Giorgio, with innumerable others; and the window-opening he turned to advantage by making a flight of steps, in such a way that all the painting seems to be one whole: nay, it appears as if, were that window-space not there, the work would in nowise have been complete. Wherefore it may be truly credited to him that in the invention and composition of every kind of painted story, no one has ever been more dexterous, facile, and able than Raphael.

This he also proved in another scene in the same place, opposite to the last-named, of S. Peter in the hands of Herod, and guarded in prison by men-at-arms; wherein he showed such a grasp of architecture, and such judgment in the buildings of the prison, that in truth the others after him seem to have more confusion than he has beauty. For he was ever seeking to represent stories just as they are written, and to paint in them things gracious and excellent; as is proved in this one by the horror of the prison, wherein that old man is seen bound in chains of iron between the two men-at-arms, by the deep slumber of the guards, and by the dazzling splendor of the Angel, which, in the thick darkness of the night, reveals with its light every detail of the prison, and makes the arms of the soldiers shine resplendent, in such a way that their burnished luster seems more lifelike than if they were real, although they are only painted. No less art and genius are there in the action of S. Peter, when, freed from his chains, he goes forth from the prison, accompanied by the Angel, wherein one sees in the face of the Saint a belief that it is rather a dream than a reality; and so, also, terror and dismay are shown in some other armed guards outside the prison, who hear the noise of the iron door, while a sentinel with a torch in his hand rouses the others, and, as he gives them light with it, the blaze of the torch is reflected in all their armor; and all that its glow does not reach is illumined by the light of the moon. This composition Raphael painted over the window, where the wall is darkest; and thus, when you look at the picture, the light strikes you in the face, and the real light conflicts so well with the different lights of the night in the painting, that the smoke of the torch, the splendor of the Angel, and the thick darkness of the night seem to you to be wholly real and natural, and you would never say that it was all painted, so vividly did he express this difficult conception. In it are seen shadows playing on the armor, other shadows projected, reflections, and a vaporous glare from the lights, all executed with darkest shade, and so well, that it may be truly said that he was the master of every other master; and as an effect of night, among all those that painting has ever produced, this is the most real and most divine, and is held by all the world to be the rarest.

On one of the unbroken walls, also, he painted the Divine Worship and the Ark of the Hebrews, with the Candlestick; and likewise Pope Julius driving Avarice out of the Temple, a scene as beautiful and as excellent as the Night described above. Here, in some bearers who are carrying Pope Julius, a most lifelike figure, in his chair, are portraits of men who were living at that time. And while the people, some women among them, are making way for the Pope, so that he may pass, one sees the furious onset of an armed man on horseback, who, accompanied by two on foot, and in an attitude of the greatest fierceness, is smiting and riding down the proud Heliodorus, who is seeking, at the command of Antiochus, to rob the Temple of all the wealth stored for the widows and orphans. Already the riches and treasures could be seen being removed and taken away, when, on account of the terror of the strange misfortune of Heliodorus, so rudely struck down and smitten by the three figures mentioned above (although, this being a vision, they are seen and heard by him alone), behold, they are all dropped and upset on the ground, those who were carrying them falling down through the sudden terror and panic that had come upon all the following of Heliodorus. Apart from these may be seen the holy Onias, the High Priest, dressed in his robes of office, with his eyes and hands raised to Heaven, and praying most fervently, being seized with pity for the poor innocents who were thus nearly losing their possessions, and rejoicing at the help that he feels has come down from on high. Besides this, through a beautiful fancy of Raphael's, one sees many who have climbed on to the socles of the column-bases, and, clasping the shafts, stand looking in most uncomfortable attitudes; with a throng of people showing their amazement in many various ways, and awaiting the result of this event.

On the ceiling above these works, he then executed four scenes, God appearing to Abraham and promising him the multiplication of his seed, the Sacrifice of Isaac, Jacob's Ladder, and the Burning Bush of Moses: wherein may be recognized no less art, invention, draftsmanship, and grace, than in the other works that he painted.

While the happy genius of this craftsman was producing such marvels, the envy of fortune cut short the life of Julius II, who had fostered such abilities, and had been a lover of every excellent work. Whereupon a new Pope was elected in Leo X, who desired that the work begun should be carried on; and Raphael thereby soared with his genius into the heavens, and received endless favors from him, fortunate in having come upon a Prince so great, who had by the inheritance of blood a strong inclination for such an art. Raphael, therefore, thus encouraged to pursue the work, painted on the other wall the Coming of Attila to Rome, and his encounter at the foot of the Monte Mario with Leo III, who drove him away with his mere benediction. In this scene Raphael made S. Peter and S. Paul in the air, with swords in their hands, coming to defend the Church; and while the story of Leo III says nothing of this, nevertheless it was thus that he chose to represent it, perchance out of fancy, for it often happens that painters, like poets, go straying from their subject in order to make their work the more ornate, although their digressions are not such as to be out of harmony with their first intention. In those Apostles may be seen that celestial wrath and ardor which the Divine Justice is wont often to impart to the features of its ministers, charged with defending the most holy Faith; and of this we have proof in Attila, who is to be seen riding a black horse with white feet and a star on its forehead, as beautiful as it could be, for in an attitude of the utmost terror he throws up his head and turns his body in flight. There are other most beautiful horses, particularly a dappled jennet, which is ridden by a figure that has all the body covered with scales after the manner of a fish; which is copied from the Column of Trajan, wherein the figures have armor of that kind; and it is thought that such armor is made from the skins of crocodiles. There is Monte Mario, all aflame, showing that when soldiers march away, their quarters are always left a prey to fire. He made portraits from nature, also, in some mace-bearers accompanying the Pope, who are marvelously lifelike, as are the horses on which they are riding; and the same is true of the retinue of Cardinals, and of some grooms who are holding the palfrey on which rides the Pope in full pontificals (a portrait of Leo X, no less lifelike than those of the others), with many courtiers; the whole being a most pleasing spectacle and well in keeping with such a work, and also very useful to our art, particularly for those who have no such objects at their command.

At this same time he painted a panel containing Our Lady, S. Jerome robed as a Cardinal, and an Angel Raphael accompanying Tobias, which was placed in S. Domenico at Naples, in that chapel wherein is the Crucifix that spoke to S. Thomas Aquinas. For Signor Leonello da Carpi, Lord of Meldola, who is still alive, although more than ninety years old, he executed a picture that was most marvelous in coloring, and of a singular beauty, for it is painted with such force, and also with a delicacy so pleasing, that I do not think it is possible to do better. In the countenance of the Madonna may be seen such a divine air, and in her attitude such a dignity, that no one would be able to improve her; and he made her with the hands clasped, adoring her Son, who is seated on her knees, caressing a S. John, a little boy, who is adoring Him, in company with S. Elizabeth and Joseph. This picture was once in the possession of the very reverend Cardinal da Carpi, the son of the said Signor Leonello, and a great lover of our arts; and it should be at the present day in the hands of his heirs.

Afterwards, Lorenzo Pucci, Cardinal of Santi Quattro, having been created Grand Penitentiary, Raphael was favored by him with a commission to paint a panel for S. Giovanni in Monte at Bologna, which is now set up in the chapel wherein lies the body of the Blessed Elena dall' Olio: in which work it is evident how much grace, in company with art, could accomplish by means of the delicate hands of Raphael. In it is a S. Cecilia, who, entranced by a choir of angels on high, stands listening to the sound, wholly absorbed in the harmony; and in her countenance is seen that abstraction which is found in the faces of those who are in ecstasy. Scattered about the ground, moreover, are musical instruments, which have the appearance of being, not painted, but real and true; and such, also, are some veils that she is wearing, with vestments woven in silk and gold, and, below these, a marvelous hair-shirt. And in a S. Paul, who has the right arm leaning on his naked sword, and the head resting on the hand, one sees his profound air of knowledge, no less well expressed than the transformation of his pride of aspect into dignity. He is clothed in a simple red garment by way of mantle, below which is a green tunic, after the manner of the Apostles, and his feet are bare. There is also S. Mary Magdalene, who is holding in her hands a most delicate vase of stone, in an attitude of marvelous grace; turning her head, she seems full of joy at her conversion; and indeed, in that kind of painting, I do not think that anything better could be done. Very beautiful, likewise, are the heads of S. Augustine and S. John the Evangelist. Of a truth, other pictures may be said to be pictures, but those of Raphael life itself, for in his figures the flesh quivers, the very breath may be perceived, the pulse beats, and the true presentment of life is seen in them; on which account this picture gave him, in addition to the fame that he had already, an even greater name.

After this he also painted a little picture with small figures, which is likewise at Bologna, in the house of Count Vincenzio Ercolano, containing a Christ after the manner of Jove in Heaven, surrounded by the four Evangelists as Ezekiel describes them, one in the form of a man, another as a lion, the third an eagle, and the fourth an ox, with a little landscape below to represent the earth: which work, in its small proportions, is no less rare and beautiful than his others in their greatness.

To the Counts of Canossa in Verona he sent a large picture of equal excellence, in which is a very beautiful Nativity of Our Lord, with a daybreak that is much extolled, as is also the S. Anne, and, indeed, the whole work, which cannot be more highly praised than by saying that it is by the hand of Raphael of Urbino. Wherefore those Counts rightly hold it in supreme veneration, nor have they ever consented, for all the vast prices that have been offered to them by many Princes, to sell it to anyone.

For Bindo Altoviti, he made a portrait of him when he was a young man, which is held to be extraordinary; and likewise a picture of Our Lady, which he sent to Florence, and which is now in the Palace of Duke Cosimo, in the chapel of the new apartments, which were built and painted by me, where it serves as altar-piece. In it is painted a very old S. Anne, seated, and holding out to Our Lady her Son, the features of whose countenance, as well as the whole of His nude form, are so beautiful that with His smile He rejoices whoever beholds Him; besides which, Raphael depicted, in painting the Madonna, all the beauty that can be imparted to the aspect of a Virgin, with the complement of chaste humility in the eyes, honor in the brow, grace in the nose, and virtue in the mouth; not to mention that her raiment is such as to reveal infinite simplicity and dignity. And, indeed, I do not think that there is anything better to be seen than this whole work. There is a nude S. John, seated, with a female saint, who is likewise very beautiful; and for background there is a building, in which he painted a linen-covered window that gives light to the room wherein are the figures.

In Rome he made a picture of good size, in which he portrayed Pope Leo, Cardinal Giulio de' Medici, and Cardinal de' Rossi. In this the figures appear to be not painted, but in full relief; there is the pile of the velvet, with the damask of the Pope's vestments shining and rustling, the fur of the linings soft and natural, and the gold and silk so counterfeited that they do not seem to be in color, but real gold and silk. There is an illuminated book of parchment, which appears more real than the reality; and a little bell of wrought silver, which is more beautiful than words can tell. Among other things, also, is a ball of burnished gold on the Pope's chair, wherein are reflected, as if it were a mirror (such is its brightness), the light from the windows, the shoulders of the Pope, and the walls round the room. And all these things are executed with such diligence, that one may believe without any manner of doubt that no master is able, or is ever likely to be able, to do better. For this work the Pope was pleased to reward him very richly; and the picture is still to be seen in Florence, in the *guardaroba* of the Duke. In like manner he executed portraits of Duke Lorenzo and Duke Giuliano, with a perfect grace of coloring not achieved by any other than himself, which are in the possession of the heirs of Ottaviano de' Medici at Florence.

Thereupon there came to Raphael a great increase of glory, and likewise of rewards; and for this reason, in order to leave some memorial of himself, he caused a palace to be built in the Borgo Nuovo at Rome, which Bramante executed with castings. Now, the fame of this most noble craftsman, by reason of the aforesaid works and many others, having passed into France and Flanders, Albrecht Dürer, a most marvelous German painter, and an engraver of very beautiful copperplates, rendered tribute to Raphael out of his own works, and sent to him a portrait of himself, a head, executed by him in gouache on a cloth of fine linen, which showed the same on either side, the lights being transparent and obtained without lead-white, while the only grounding and coloring was done with water-colors, the white of the cloth serving for the ground of the bright parts. This work seemed to Raphael to be marvelous, and he sent him, therefore, many drawings executed by his own hand, which were received very gladly by Albrecht. That head was among the possessions of Giulio Romano, the heir of Raphael, in Mantua.

Raphael, having thus seen the manner of the engravings of Albrecht Dürer, and desiring on his own behalf to show what could be done with his work by such an art, caused Marc' Antonio Bolognese to make a very thorough study of the method; and that master became so excellent, that Raphael commissioned him to make prints of his first works, such as the drawing of the Innocents, a Last Supper, the Neptune, and the S. Cecilia being boiled in oil.

Raphael then painted for the Monastery of the Monks of Monte Oliveto, called S. Maria dello Spasmo, at Palermo, a panel-picture of Christ bearing the Cross, which is held to be a marvelous work. In this may be seen the impious ministers of the Crucifixion, leading Him with wrath and fury to His death on Mount Calvary; and Christ, broken with agony at the near approach of death, has fallen to the ground under the weight of the Tree of the Cross, and, bathed with sweat and blood, turns towards the Marys, who are in a storm of weeping. Moreover, there is seen among them Veronica, who stretches out her arms and offers Him a cloth, with an expression of the tenderest love, not to mention that the work is full of men-at-arms both on horseback and on foot, who are pouring forth from the gate of Jerusalem with the standards of justice in their hands, in various most beautiful attitudes. This panel, when completely finished, but not yet brought to its resting place, was very near coming to an evil end, for the story goes that after it had been put on shipboard, in order that it might be carried to Palermo, a terrible storm dashed against a rock the ship that was carrying it, in such a manner that the timbers broke asunder, and all the men were lost, together with the merchandise, save only the panel, which, safely packed in its case, was washed by the sea on to the shore of Genoa. There, having been fished up and drawn to land, it was found to be a thing divine, and was put into safekeeping; for it had remained undamaged and without any hurt or blemish, since even the fury of the winds and the waves of the sea had respect for the beauty of such a work. The news of this being then bruited abroad, the monks took measures to recover it, and no sooner had it been restored to them, by the favor of the Pope, than they gave satisfaction, and that liberally, to those who had rescued it. Thereupon it was once more put on board ship and brought at last to Sicily, where they set it up in Palermo; in which place it has more fame and reputation than the Mount of Vulcan itself.

While Raphael was engaged on these works, which, having to gratify great and distinguished persons, he could not refuse to undertake—not to mention that his own private interests prevented him from saying them nay—yet for all this he never ceased to carry on the series of pictures that he had begun in the Papal apartments and halls; wherein he always kept men who pursued the work from his own designs, while he himself, continually supervising everything, lent to so vast an enterprise the aid of the best efforts of which he was capable. No long time passed, therefore, before he threw open that apartment of the Borgia Tower in which he had painted a scene on every wall, two above the windows, and two others on the unbroken walls, the whole being wrought in such a manner that everything reveals spirit, feeling, and thought, and with such a harmony and unity of coloring that nothing better can be conceived. And since the ceiling of that apartment had been painted by Pietro Perugino, his master, Raphael would not destroy it, moved by respect for his memory and by the love that he bore to the man who had been the origin of the rank that he held in his art.

Such was the greatness of this master, that he kept designers all over Italy, at Pozzuolo, and even in Greece; and he was for ever searching out everything of the good that might help his art.

Now, continuing his work, he also painted a hall, wherein were some figures of the Apostles and other saints in tabernacles, executed *in terretta;* and there he caused to be made by Giovanni da Udine, his disciple, who has no equal in the painting of animals, all the animals that Pope Leo possessed, such as the chameleon, the civet cats, the apes, the parrots, the lions, the elephants, and other beasts even more strange. And besides embellishing the Palace greatly with grotesques and varied pavements, he also gave the designs for the Papal staircases, as well as for the *loggie* begun by the architect Bramante, but left unfinished on account of his death, and afterwards carried out with the new design and architecture of Raphael, who made for this a model of wood with better proportion and adornment than had been accomplished by Bramante. The Pope wishing to demonstrate the greatness and magnificence of his generous ambition, Raphael made the designs for the ornaments in stucco and for the scenes that were painted there, and likewise for the compartments; and as for the stucco and the grotesques, he placed at the head of that work Giovanni da Udine, and the figures he entrusted to Giulio Romano, although that master worked but little at them; and he also employed Giovanni Francesco, Il Bologna, Perino del Vaga, Pellegrino da Modena, Vincenzio da San Gimignano, and Polidoro da Caravaggio, with many other painters, who executed scenes and figures and other things that were required throughout that work, which Raphael caused to be completed with such perfection, that he even sent to Florence for pavements by the hand of Luca della Robbia. Wherefore it is certain that with regard to the paintings, the stucco ornaments, the arrangement, or any of the beautiful inventions, no one would be able to execute or even to imagine a more marvelous work; and its beauty was the reason that Raphael received the charge of all the works of painting and architecture that were in progress in the Palace.

He gave architectural designs for the Villa Madama of the Pope, and for many houses in the Borgo; in particular, for the Palace of Messer Giovanni Battista dall'Aquila, which was a very beautiful work. He also designed one for the Bishop of Troia, who had it built in the Via di S. Gallo at

Florence. For the Black Friars of S. Sisto in Piacenza, he painted the picture for their high altar, containing the Madonna with S. Sisto and S. Barbara, a truly rare and extraordinary work. He executed many pictures to be sent into France, and in particular, for the King, a S. Michael fighting with the Devil, which was held to be a marvelous thing. In this work he painted a fire-scarred rock, to represent the center of the earth, from the fissures of which were issuing sulphurous flames; and in Lucifer, whose scorched and burned limbs are painted with various tints of flesh-color, could be seen all the shades of anger that his venomous and swollen pride calls up against Him who overbears the greatness of him who is deprived of any kingdom where there might be peace, and doomed to suffer perpetual punishment. The opposite may be perceived in the S. Michael, clad in armor of iron and gold, who, although he is painted with a celestial air, yet has valor, force, and terror in his aspect, and has already thrown Lucifer down and hurled him backwards with his spear. In a word, this work was of such a kind that he won for it, and rightly, a most honorable reward from that King. He made portraits of Beatrice of Ferrara and other ladies, and in particular that of his own mistress, with an endless number of others.

Raphael was a very amorous person, delighting much in women, and ever ready to serve them; which was the reason that, in the pursuit of his carnal pleasures, he found his friends more complacent and indulgent toward him than perchance was right. Wherefore, when his dear friend Agostino Chigi commissioned him to paint the first loggia in his palace, Raphael was not able to give much attention to his work, on account of the love that he had for his mistress; at which Agostino fell into such despair, that he so contrived by means of others, by himself, and in other ways, as to bring it about, although only with difficulty, that this lady should come to live continually with Raphael in that part of the house where he was working; and in this manner the work was brought to completion. For this work he made all the cartoons, and he colored many of the figures in fresco with his own hand. Round these scenes he caused Giovanni da Udine to make a border of all kinds of flowers, foliage, and fruits, in festoons, which are as beautiful as they could be.

Meanwhile Raphael had risen to such greatness, that Leo X ordained that he should set to work on the Great Hall on the upper floor, wherein are the Victories of Constantine; and with this he made a beginning. A fancy likewise took the Pope to have some very rich tapestries made in gold and floss-silk; whereupon Raphael drew and colored with his own hand, of the exact form and size, all the cartoons, which were sent to Flanders to be woven; and the tapestries, when finished, were brought to Rome. This work was executed so marvelously, that it arouses astonishment in whoever beholds it, wondering how it could have been possible to weave the hair and beards in such detail, and to give softness to the flesh with mere threads; and it is truly rather a miracle than the work of human art, seeing that in these tapestries are animals, water, and buildings, all made in such a way that they seem to be not woven, but really wrought with the brush. The work cost 70,000 crowns, and it is still preserved in the Papal Chapel.

For Cardinal Colonna he painted a S. John on canvas, for which, on account of its beauty, that Cardinal had an extraordinary love; but happening to be attacked by illness, he was asked by Messer Jacopo da Carpi, the physician who cured him, to give it to him as a present; and because of this desire of Messer Jacopo, to whom he felt himself very deeply indebted, he gave it up. It is now in the possession of Francesco Benintendi, in Florence.

For Giulio de' Medici, Cardinal and Vice-Chancellor, he painted a panel-picture, to be sent into France, of the Transfiguration of Christ, at which he labored without ceasing, and brought it to the highest perfection with his own hand. In this scene he represented Christ Transfigured on Mount

Tabor, at the foot of which are the eleven Disciples awaiting Him. There may be seen a young man possessed by a spirit, who has been brought thither in order that Christ, after descending from the mountain, may deliver him; which young man stretches himself out in a distorted attitude, crying and rolling his eyes, and reveals his suffering in his flesh, his veins, and the beat of his pulse, all infected by that malignant spirit; and the color of his flesh, as he makes those violent and fearsome gestures, is very pale. This figure is supported by an old man, who, having embraced him and taken heart, with his eyes wide open and the light shining in them, is raising his brows and wrinkling his forehead, showing at one and the same time both strength and fear; gazing intently, however, at the Apostles, he appears to be encouraging himself by trusting in them. Among many women is one, the principal figure in that panel, who, having knelt down before the Apostles, and turning her head toward them, stretches her arms in the direction of the maniac and points out his misery; besides which the Apostles, some standing, some seated, and others kneeling, show that they are moved to very great compassion by such misfortune. And, indeed, he made therein figures and heads so fine in their novelty and variety, to say nothing of their extraordinary beauty, that it is the common opinion of all craftsmen that this work, among the vast number that he painted, is the most glorious, the most lovely, and the most divine. For whoever wishes to know how Christ Transfigured and made Divine should be represented in painting, must look at this work, wherein Raphael made Him in perspective over that mount, in a sky of exceeding brightness, with Moses and Elias, who, illumined by a dazzling splendor, burst into life in His light. Prostrate on the ground, in attitudes of great beauty and variety, are Peter, James, and John; one has his head to the earth, and another, shading his eyes with his hands, is defending himself from the rays and intense light of the splendor of Christ. He, clothed in snow-white raiment, with His arms outstretched and His head raised, appears to reveal the Divine essence and nature of all the Three Persons united and concentrated in Himself by the perfect art of Raphael, who seems to have summoned up all his powers in such a manner, in order to show the supreme force of his art in the countenance of Christ, that, after finishing this, the last work that he was to do, he never again touched a brush, being overtaken by death.

Now, having described the works of this most excellent craftsman, before I come to relate other particulars of his life and death, I do not wish to grudge the labor of saying something, for the benefit of the men of our arts, about the various manners of Raphael. He, then, after having imitated in his boyhood the manner of his master, Pietro Perugino, which he made much better in draftsmanship, coloring, and invention, believed that he had done enough; but he recognized, when he had reached a riper age, that he was still too far from the truth. For, after seeing the works of Leonardo da Vinci, who had no peer in the expressions of heads both of men and of women, and surpassed all other painters in giving grace and movement to his figures, he was left marveling and amazed; and in a word, the manner of Leonardo pleasing him more than any other that he had ever seen, he set himself to study it, and abandoning little by little, although with great difficulty, the manner of Pietro, he sought to the best of his power and knowledge to imitate that of Leonardo. But for all his diligence and study, in certain difficulties he was never able to surpass Leonardo; and although it appears to many that he did surpass him in sweetness and in a kind of natural facility, nevertheless he was by no means superior to him in that sublime groundwork of conceptions and that grandeur of art in which few have been the peers of Leonardo. Yet Raphael came very near to him, more than any other painter, and above all in grace of coloring. But to return to Raphael himself; in time he found himself very much hindered and impeded by the manner that he had adopted from Pietro when he was quite young, which he acquired with ease, since it was overprecise, dry, and feeble in draftsmanship. His being unable to forget it was the reason that he had great difficulty in learning the beauties of the nude and the methods of difficult foreshortenings from the cartoon that Michelangelo Buonarroti made for the Council Hall in Florence; and another might have lost heart, believing that he had been previously wasting his time, and would never have achieved, however lofty his genius, what Raphael accomplished. But he, having purged himself of Pietro's manner, and having thoroughly freed himself of it, in order to learn the manner of Michelangelo, so full of difficulties in every part, was changed, as it were, from a master once again into a disciple; and he forced himself with incredible study, when already a man, to do in a few months what might have called for the tender age at which all things are best acquired, and for a space of many years.

When Raphael resolved to set himself to change and improve his manner, he had never given his attention to nudes with that zealous study which is necessary, and had only drawn them from life in the manner that he had seen practiced by his master Pietro, imparting to them the grace that he had from nature. He then devoted himself to studying the nude and to comparing the muscles of anatomical subjects and of flayed human bodies with those of the living, which, being covered with skin, are not clearly defined, as they are when the skin has been removed; and going on to observe in what way they acquire the softness of flesh in the proper places, and how certain graceful flexures are produced by changing the point of view, and also the effect of inflating, lowering, or raising either a limb or the whole person, and likewise the concatenation of the bones, nerves, and veins, he became excellent in all the points that are looked for in a painter of eminence. Knowing, however, that in this respect he could never attain to the perfection of Michelangelo, he reflected, like a man of supreme judgment, that painting does not consist only in representing the nude human form, but has a wider field; that one can enumerate among the perfect painters those who express historical inventions well and with facility, and who show fine judgment in their fancies; and that he who, in the composition of scenes, can make them neither confused with too much detail nor poor with too little, but distributed with beautiful invention and order, may also be called an able and judicious craftsman. To this, as Raphael was well aware, may be added the enriching those scenes with a bizarre variety of perspectives, buildings, and landscapes, the method of clothing figures gracefully, the making them fade away sometimes in the shadows, and sometimes come forward into the light, the imparting of life and beauty to the heads of women, children, young men and old, and the giving them movement and boldness, according to necessity. He considered, also, how important is the furious flight of horses in battles, fierceness in soldiers, the knowledge how to depict all the sorts of animals, and above all the power to give such resemblance to portraits that they seem to be alive, and that it is known whom they represent; with an endless number of other things, such as the adornment of draperies, footwear, helmets, armor, women's headdresses, hair, beards, vases, trees, grottoes, rocks, fires, skies turbid or serene, clouds, rain, lightning, clear weather, night, the light of the moon, the splendor of the sun, and innumerable other things, which are called for every moment by the requirements of the art of painting. Pondering over these things, I say, Raphael resolved, since he could not approach Michelangelo in that branch of art to which he had set his hand, to seek to equal, and perchance to surpass him, in these others; and he devoted himself, therefore, not to imitating the manner of that master, but to the attainment of a catholic excellence in the other fields of art that have been described.

Raphael, then, having made this resolution, and having recognized that Fra Bartolommeo di San Marco had a passing good method of painting, well-grounded draftsmanship, and a pleasing manner of coloring, although at times, in order to obtain stronger relief, he made too much use of darks, took from him what appeared to him to suit his need and his fancy —namely, a middle course, both in drawing and in coloring; and mingling with that method certain others selected from the best work of other masters, out of many manners he made one, which was looked upon ever afterwards as his own, and which was and always will be vastly esteemed by all craftsmen. This was then seen perfected in the Sibyls and Prophets of the work that he executed, as has been related, in S. Maria della Pace; in the carrying out of which work he was greatly assisted by having seen the paintings of Michelangelo in the Chapel of the Pope. And if Raphael had remained content with this same manner, and had not sought to give it more grandeur and variety in order to prove that he had as good a knowledge of the nude as Michelangelo, he would not have lost a part of the good name that he had acquired; but the nudes that he made in that apartment of the Borgia Tower where there is the Burning of the Borgo, although they are fine, are not in every way excellent. In like manner, those that were painted likewise by him on the ceiling of the Palace of Agostino Chigi in the Trastevere did not give complete satisfaction, for they are wanting in that grace and sweetness which were peculiar to Raphael; the reason of which, in great part, was the circumstance that he had them colored by others after his design. However, repenting of this error, like a man of judgment, he resolved afterwards to execute by himself, without assistance from others, the panel-picture of the Transfiguration of Christ that is in S. Pietro a Montorio, wherein are all those qualities which, as has already been described, are looked for and required in a good picture. And if he had not employed in this work, as it were from caprice, printer's smoke-black, the nature of which, as has been remarked many times, is to become ever darker with time, to the injury of the other colors with which it is mixed, I believe that the picture would still be as fresh as when he painted it; whereas it now appears to be rather a mass of shadows than aught else.

I have thought fit, almost at the close of this Life, to make this discourse, in order to show with what labor, study, and diligence this honored craftsman always pursued his art; and even more for the sake of other painters, to the end that they may learn how to avoid those hindrances from which the wisdom and genius of Raphael were able to deliver him. I must add this as well, that every man should be satisfied and contented with doing that work to which he feels himself drawn by a natural inclination, and should not seek, out of emulation, to put his hand to that for which nature has not adapted him; for otherwise he will labor in vain, and often to his own shame and loss. Moreover, where striving is enough, no man should aim at super-striving, merely in order to surpass those who, by some great gift of nature, or by some special grace bestowed on them by God, have performed or are performing miracles in art; for the reason that he who is not suited to any particular work, can never reach, let him labor as he may, the goal to which another, with the assistance of nature, has attained with ease.

But now, having discoursed on these matters of art, perchance at greater length than was needful, let us return to the life and death of Raphael. He had a close friendship with Cardinal Bernardo Divizio of Bibbiena, who had importuned him for many years to take a wife of his choosing; and Raphael, while not directly refusing to obey the wishes of the Cardinal, had yet put the matter off, saying that he would rather wait till three or four years had passed. This term came upon Raphael when he was not expecting it, and he was reminded by the Cardinal of his promise; whereupon, seeing himself bound, like the courteous man that he was, he would not break his word, and thus accepted as his wife a niece of that Cardinal. And because he was always very ill content with this entanglement, he continued to delay the matter in such a way that many months passed without the marriage being brought to pass. But it was with no dishonorable motive that he did this, for, having been so many years in the service of the Court, and being the creditor of Leo for a good sum, it had been hinted to him that when the hall on which he was engaged was finished, the Pope proposed to reward him for his labors and abilities by giving him a red hat, of which he had already determined to distribute a good number, and some of them to men of less merit than Raphael.

Meanwhile, pursuing his amours in secret, Raphael continued to divert himself beyond measure with the pleasures of love; whence it happened that, having on one occasion indulged in more than his usual excess, he returned to his house in a violent fever. The physicians, therefore, believing that he had overheated himself, and receiving from him no confession of the excess of which he had been guilty, imprudently bled him, insomuch that he was weakened and felt himself sinking; for he was in need rather of restoratives. Thereupon he made his will: and first, like a good Christian, he sent his mistress out of the house, leaving her the means to live honorably. Next, he divided his possessions among his disciples, Giulio Romano, whom he had always loved dearly, and the Florentine Giovanni Francesco, called Il Fattore, with a priest of Urbino, his kinsman, whose name I do not know. Then he gave orders that some of his wealth should be used for restoring with new masonry one of the ancient tabernacles in S. Maria Ritonda, and for making an altar, with a marble statue of Our Lady, in that church, which he chose as his place of repose and burial after death; and he left all the rest to Giulio and Giovanni Francesco, appointing as executor of his will Messer Baldassarre da Pescia, then Datary to the Pope. Finally, he confessed and was penitent, and ended the course of his life at the age of thirty-seven, on the same day that he was born, which was Good Friday. And even as he embellished the world with his talents, so, it may be believed, does his soul adorn Heaven by its presence.

As he lay dead in the hall where he had been working, there was placed at his head the picture of the Transfiguration, which he had executed for Cardinal de' Medici; and the sight of that living picture, in contrast with the dead body, caused the hearts of all who beheld it to burst with sorrow. That work, in memory of the loss of Raphael, was placed by the Cardinal on the high altar of S. Pietro a Montorio; and on account of the nobility of his every action, it was held ever afterwards in great estimation. His body received that honorable burial which his noble spirit had deserved, for there was no craftsman who did not weep with sorrow and follow him to the grave. His death was also a great grief to the whole Court of the Pope, first because he had held in his lifetime the office of Groom of the Chamber, and likewise because he had been so dear to the Pope that his loss caused him to weep bitterly.

O happy and blessed spirit, in that every man is glad to speak of thee, to celebrate thy actions, and to admire every drawing that thou didst leave to us! When this noble craftsman died, the art of painting might well have died also, seeing that when he closed his eyes, she was left as it were blind. And now for us who have survived him, it remains to imitate the good, nay, the supremely excellent method bequeathed to us by him as a pattern, and, as is called for by his merit and our obligations, to hold a most grateful remembrance of this in our minds, and to pay the highest honor to his memory with our lips. For in truth we have from him art, coloring, and invention harmonized and brought to such a pitch of perfection as could scarcely be hoped for; nor may any intellect ever think to surpass him. And in addition to this benefit that he conferred on art, like a true friend to her, as long as he lived he never ceased to show how one should deal with great men, with those of middle station, and with the lowest. And, indeed, among his extraordinary gifts, I perceive one of such value that I for my part am amazed at it, in that Heaven gave him the power to produce in our art an effect wholly contrary to the nature of us painters, which was that our craftsmen—I do not mean only the lesser, but also those whose humor it was to be great persons; and of this humor art creates a vast number—while working in company with Raphael, felt themselves naturally united and in such accord, that all evil humors vanished at the sight of him, and every vile and base thought fell away from their minds. Such unity was never greater at any other time than his; and this happened because they were overcome both by his courtesy and by his art, and even more by the good disposition of his nature, which was so full of gentleness and so overflowing with loving-kindness, that it was seen that the very animals, not to speak of men, honored him. It is said that if any painter who knew him, and even any who did not know him, asked him for some drawing that he needed, Raphael would leave his own work in order to assist him. And he always kept a vast number of them employed, aiding them and teaching them with such a love as might have been the due rather of his own children than of fellow-craftsmen; for which reason he was never seen to go to Court without having with him, as he left his house, some fifty painters, all able and excellent, who kept him company in order to do him honor. In short, he lived not like a painter, but like a prince. Wherefore, O art of painting, thou couldst then esteem thyself indeed most blessed, in possessing a craftsman who, both with his genius and his virtues, exalted thee higher than Heaven! Truly happy mightest thou call thyself, in that thy disciples, following in the footsteps of so great a man, have seen how life should be lived, and how important is the union of art and virtue, which, wedded in Raphael, had strength to prevail on the magnificent Julius II and the magnanimous Leo X, exalted as they were in rank and dignity, to make him their most intimate friend and show him all possible generosity, insomuch that by their favor and by the wealth that they bestowed upon him, he was enabled to do vast honor both to himself and to art. Blessed, also, may be called all those who, employed in his service, worked under him, since whoever imitated him found that he had reached an honorable haven; and in like manner all those who imitate his labors in art will be honored by the world, even as, by resembling him in uprightness of life, they will win rewards from Heaven.

ANDREA DEL SARTO

[Andrea d'Agnolo di Francesco di Luca, known as Andrea del Sarto, was born in 1486 and died in 1531.]

AT length, after the Lives of many craftsmen who have been excellent, some in coloring, some in drawing, and others in invention, we have come to the most excellent Andrea del Sarto, in whose single person nature and art demonstrated all that painting can achieve by means of draftsmanship, coloring, and invention, insomuch that, if Andrea had possessed a little more fire and boldness of spirit, to correspond to his profound genius and judgment in his art, without a doubt he would have had no equal. But a certain timidity of spirit and a sort of humility and simplicity in his nature made it impossible that there should be seen in him that glowing ardor and that boldness which, added to his other qualities, would have made him truly divine in painting; for which reason he lacked those adornments and that grandeur and abundance of manners which have been seen in many other painters. His figures, however, for all their simplicity and purity, are well conceived, free from errors, and absolutely perfect in every respect. The expressions of his heads, both in children and in women, are gracious and natural, and those of men, both young and old, admirable in their vivacity and animation; his draperies are beautiful to a marvel, and his nudes very well conceived. And although his drawing is simple, all that he colored is rare and truly divine.

Andrea was born in Florence, in the year 1486, to a father who was all his life a tailor; whence he was always called

Andrea del Sarto* by everyone. Having come to the age of seven, he was taken away from his reading and writing school and apprenticed to the goldsmith's craft. But in this he was always much more willing to practice his hand in drawing, to which he was drawn by a natural inclination, than in using the tools for working in silver or gold; whence it came to pass that Gian Barile, a painter of Florence, but one of gross and vulgar taste, having seen the boy's good manner of drawing, took him under his protection, and, making him abandon his work as goldsmith, directed him to the art of painting. Andrea, beginning with much delight to practice it, recognized that nature had created him for that profession; and in a very short space of time, therefore, he was doing such things with colors as filled Gian Barile and the other craftsmen in the city with marvel. Now after three years, through continual study, he had acquired an excellent mastery over his work, and Gian Barile saw that by persisting in his studies the boy was likely to achieve an extraordinary success. Having therefore spoken of him to Piero di Cosimo, who was held at that time to be one of the best painters in Florence, he placed Andrea with Piero. And Andrea, as one full of desire to learn, labored and studied without ceasing; while nature, which had created him to be a painter, so wrought in him, that he handled and managed his colors with as much grace as if he had been working for fifty years. Wherefore Piero conceived an extraordinary love for him, feeling marvelous pleasure in hearing that when Andrea had any time to himself, particularly on feast days, he would spend the whole day in company with other young men, drawing in the Sala del Papa, wherein were the cartoons of Michelangelo and Leonardo da Vinci, and that, young as he was, he surpassed all the other draftsmen, both native and foreign, who were always competing there with one another.

Among these young men, there was one who pleased Andrea more than any other with his nature and conversation,

* The tailor's Andrew.

namely, the painter Franciabigio; and Franciabigio, likewise, was attracted by Andrea. Having become friends, therefore, Andrea said to Franciabigio that he could no longer endure the caprices of Piero, who was now old, and that for this reason he wished to take a room for himself. Hearing this, Franciabigio, who was obliged to do the same thing because his master Mariotto Albertinelli had abandoned the art of painting, said to his companion Andrea that he also was in need of a room, and that it would be to the advantage of both of them if they were to join forces. Having therefore taken a room on the Piazza del Grano, they executed many works in company; among others, the curtains that cover the panel-pictures on the high altar of the Servi; for which they received the commission from a sacristan very closely related to Franciabigio.

The men of that company in Florence which is called the Company of the Scalzo used to assemble at the head of the Via Larga, above the houses of the Magnificent Ottaviano de' Medici, and opposite to the garden of S. Marco, in a building dedicated to S. John the Baptist, which had been built in those days by a number of Florentine craftsmen, who had made there, among other things, an entrance-court of masonry with a loggia which rested on some columns of no great size. And some of them, perceiving that Andrea was on the way to becoming known as an excellent painter, and being richer in spirit than in pocket, determined that he should paint round that cloister twelve pictures in chiaroscuro—that is to say, in fresco with *terretta*—containing twelve scenes from the life of S. John the Baptist. Whereupon, setting his hand to this, he painted in the first the scene of S. John baptizing Christ, with much diligence and great excellence of manner, whereby he gained credit, honor, and fame to such an extent, that many persons turned to him with commissions for works, as to one whom they thought to be destined in time to reach that honorable goal which was foreshadowed by his extraordinary beginnings in his profession.

Not long after this he was commissioned to paint for a chapel in S. Gallo, the Church of the Eremite Observantines of the Order of S. Augustine, outside the Porta a S. Gallo, a panel-picture of Christ appearing in the garden to Mary Magdalene in the form of a gardener; which work, what with the coloring and a certain quality of softness and harmony, is sweetness itself, and so well executed, that it led to his painting two others not long afterwards for the same church, as will be related below. This panel is now in S. Jacopo tra Fossi, on the Canto degli Alberti, together with the two others.

After these works, Andrea and Franciabigio, leaving the Piazza del Grano, took new rooms in the Sapienza, near the Convent of the Nunziata; whence it came about that Andrea and Jacopo Sansovino, who was then a young man and was working at sculpture in the same place under his master Andrea Contucci, formed so warm and so close a friendship together, that neither by day nor by night were they ever separated one from another. Their discussions were for the most part on the difficulties of art, so that it is no marvel that both of them should have afterwards become most excellent, as is now being shown of Andrea and as will be related in the proper place of Jacopo.

There was at this same time in the Convent of the Servi, selling the candles at the counter, a friar called Fra Mariano dal Canto alla Macine, who was also sacristan; and he heard everyone extolling Andrea mightily and saying that he was by way of making marvelous proficience in painting. Whereupon he planned to fulfil a desire of his own without much expense; and so, approaching Andrea, who was a mild and guileless fellow, on the side of his honor, he began to persuade him under the cloak of friendship that he wished to help him in a matter which would bring him honor and profit and would make him known in such a manner, that he would never be poor any more. Now many years before, Alesso Baldovinetti had painted a Nativity of Christ in the first cloister of the Servi, on the wall that has the Annunciation behind it; and in the same cloister, on the other side, Cosimo Rosselli had begun a scene of S. Filippo, the founder of that Servite Order, assuming the habit. But Cosimo had not carried that scene to completion, because death came upon him at the very moment when he was working at it. The friar, then, being very eager to see the rest finished, thought of serving his own ends by making Andrea and Franciabigio, who, from being friends, had become rivals in art, compete with one another, each doing part of the work. This, besides effecting his purpose very well, would make the expense less and their efforts greater. Thereupon, revealing his mind to Andrea, he persuaded him to undertake that enterprise, by pointing out to him that since it was a public and much frequented place, he would become known on account of such a work no less by foreigners than by the Florentines; that he should not look for any payment in return, or even for an invitation to undertake it, but should rather pray to be allowed to do it; and that if he were not willing to set to work, there was Franciabigio, who, in order to make himself known, had offered to accept it and to leave the matter of payment to him. These incitements did much to make Andrea resolve to undertake the work, and the rather as he was a man of little spirit; and the last reference to Franciabigio induced him to make up his mind completely and to come to an agreement, in the form of a written contract, with regard to the whole work, on the terms that no one else should have a hand in it. The friar, then, having thus pledged him and given him money, demanded that he should begin by continuing the life of S. Filippo, without receiving more than ten ducats from him in payment of each scene; and he told Andrea that he was giving him even that out of his own pocket, and was doing it more for the benefit and advantage of the painter than through any want or need of the convent.

Andrea, therefore, pursuing that work with the utmost diligence, like one who thought more of honor than of profit, after no long time completely finished the first three scenes and unveiled them. These scenes brought extraordinary fame and honor to Andrea; and thus encouraged, he went on to paint two other scenes. Having thus finished that side of the cloister, and considering that if the honor was great, the payment was small, Andrea resolved to give up the rest of the work, however much the friar might complain. But the latter would not release him from his bond without Andrea first promising that he would paint two other scenes, at his own leisure and convenience, however, and with an increase of payment; and thus they came to terms.

Having come into greater repute by reason of these works, Andrea received commissions for many pictures and works of importance; among others, one from the General of the Monks of Vallombrosa, for painting an arch of the vaulting, with a Last Supper on the front wall, in the Refectory of the Monastery of S. Salvi, outside the Porta alla Croce. In four medallions on that vault he painted four figures, S. Benedict, S. Giovanni Gualberto, S. Salvi the Bishop, and S. Bernardo degli Uberti of Florence, a friar of that Order and a Cardinal; and in the center he made a medallion containing three faces, which are one and the same, to represent the Trinity. All this was very well executed for a work in fresco, and Andrea, therefore, came to be valued at his true worth in the art of painting.

Meanwhile the Servite friar had allotted to Franciabigio one of the scenes in the above-mentioned cloister; but that master had not yet finished making the screen, when Andrea, becoming apprehensive, since it seemed to him that Franciabigio was an abler and more dexterous master than himself in the handling of colors in fresco, executed, as it were out of rivalry, the cartoons for his two scenes, which he intended to paint on the angle between the side door of S. Bastiano and the smaller door that leads from the cloister into the Nunziata. Having made the cartoons, he set to work in fresco; and in the first scene he painted the Nativity of Our Lady, a composition of figures beautifully proportioned and grouped with great grace in a room, wherein some women who are friends and relatives of the newly delivered mother, having come to visit her, are standing about her, all clothed in such garments as were customary at that time, and other women of lower degree, gathered around the fire, are washing the new-born babe, while others are preparing the swathing-bands and doing other similar services. Among them is a little boy, full of life, who is warming himself at the fire, with an old man resting in a very natural attitude on a couch, and likewise some women carrying food to the mother who is in bed, with movements truly lifelike and appropriate. And all these figures, together with some little boys who are hovering in the air and scattering flowers, are most carefully considered in their expressions, their draperies, and every other respect, and so soft in color, that the figures appear to be of flesh and everything else rather real than painted.

In the other scene Andrea painted the three Magi from the East, who, guided by the Star, went to adore the Infant Jesus Christ. He represented them dismounted, as though they were near their destination; and that because there was only the space embracing the two doors to separate them from the Nativity of Christ which may be seen there, by the hand of Alesso Baldovinetti. In this scene Andrea painted the Court of those three Kings coming behind them, with baggage, much equipment, and many people following in their train, among whom, in a corner, are three persons portrayed from life and wearing the Florentine dress, one being Jacopo Sansovino, a full-length figure looking straight at the spectator, while another, with an arm in foreshortening, who is leaning against him and making a sign, is Andrea, the master of the work, and a third head, seen in profile behind Jacopo, is that of Ajolle, the musician. There are, in addition, some little boys who are climbing on the walls, in order to be able to see the magnificent procession and the fantastic animals that those three Kings have brought with them. This scene is quite equal in excellence to that mentioned above; nay, in both the one and the other he surpassed himself, not to speak of Franciabigio, who also finished his.

At this same time Andrea painted for the Abbey of S. Godenzo, a benefice belonging to the same friars, a panel which was held to be very well executed. And for the Friars of S. Gallo he made a panel-picture of Our Lady receiving the Annunciation from the Angel, wherein may be seen a very pleasing harmony of coloring, while the heads of some Angels accompanying Gabriel show a sweet gradation of tints and a perfectly executed beauty of expression in their features. Andrea then painted for Zanobi Girolami a picture with figures of no great size, wherein was a story of Joseph, the son of Jacob, which was finished by him with unremitting diligence, and therefore held to be a very beautiful painting. Meanwhile, thanks to his talent, he had become intimate with Giovanni Gaddi, afterwards appointed Clerk of the Chamber, who, always delighting in the arts of design, was then keeping Jacopo Sansovino continually at work. Being pleased, therefore, with the manner of Andrea, he caused him to paint a picture of Our Lady for himself, which was very beautiful, for Andrea painted various patterns and other ingenious devices round it, so that it was considered to be the most beautiful work that he had executed up to that time. After this he made for Giovanni di Paolo, the mercer, another picture of Our Lady, which, being truly lovely, gave infinite pleasure to all who saw it. And for Andrea Santini he executed another, containing Our Lady, Christ, S. John, and S. Joseph, all wrought with such diligence that the painting has always been esteemed in Florence as worthy of great praise.

All these works acquired such a name for Andrea in his city, that among the many, both young and old, who were painting at that time, he was considered one of the most excellent who were handling brushes and colors. Wherefore he found himself not only honored, but even, although he exacted the most paltry prices for his labors, in a condition to do something to help and support his family, and also to shelter himself from the annoyances and anxieties which afflict those of us who live in poverty. But he became enamored of a young woman, and a little time afterwards, when she had been left a widow, he took her for his wife; and then he had more than enough to do for the rest of his life, and much more trouble than he had suffered in the past, for the reason that, in addition to the labors and annoyances that such entanglements generally involve, he undertook others into the bargain, such as that of letting himself be harassed now by jealousy, now by one thing, and now by another.

But to return to the works of his hand, which were as rare as they were numerous: after those of which mention has been made above, he painted for a friar of S. Croce, of the Order of Minorites, who was then Governor of the Nunnery of S. Francesco in Via Pentolini, and delighted much in paintings, a panel-picture destined for the Church of those Nuns, of Our Lady standing on high upon an octagonal pedestal, at the corners of which are seated some Harpies, as it were in adoration of the Virgin; and she, using one hand to uphold her Son, who is clasping her most tenderly round the neck with His arms, in a very beautiful attitude, is holding a closed book in the other hand and gazing on two little naked boys, who, while helping her to stand upright, serve as ornaments about her person. This Madonna has on her right a beautifully painted S. Francis, in whose face may be seen the goodness and simplicity that truly belonged to that saintly man; besides which, the feet are marvelous, and so are the draperies, because Andrea always rounded off his figures with a very rich flow of folds and with certain most delicate curves, in such a way as to reveal the nude below. On her left hand she has a S. John the Evangelist, represented as a young man and in the act of writing his Gospel, in a very beautiful manner. In this work, moreover, over the building and the figures, is a film of transparent clouds, which appear to be really moving. This picture, among all Andrea's works, is held at the present day to be one of singular and truly rare beauty.

Now, while Andrea was adorning his city with these and other works, and his name was growing greater every day, the men of the Company of the Scalzo resolved that he should finish the work in their cloister, which he had formerly begun by painting the scene of the Baptism of Christ. Having resumed that work, therefore, more willingly, he executed two scenes there, with two very beautiful figures of Charity and Justice to adorn the door that leads into the building of the Company. In one of these scenes he represented S. John preaching to the multitude in a spirited attitude, lean in person, as befitted the life that he was leading, and with an expression of countenance filled with inspiration and thoughtfulness. Marvelous, likewise, are the variety and the vivacity of his hearers, some being shown in admiration, and all in astonishment, at hearing that new message and a doctrine so singular and never heard before. Even more did Andrea exert his genius in painting the same John baptizing with water a vast number of people, some of whom are stripping off their clothes, some receiving the baptism, and others, naked, waiting for him to finish baptizing those who are before them. In all of them Andrea showed a vivid emotion, with a burning desire in the gestures of those who are eager to be purified of their sins; not to mention that all the figures are so well executed in that chiaroscuro, that the whole has the appearance of a real and most lifelike scene in marble.

I will not refrain from saying that while Andrea was employed on these and other pictures, there appeared certain copper engravings by Albrecht Dürer, and Andrea made use of them, taking some of the figures and transforming them into his manner. And this has caused some people, while not saying that it is a bad thing for a man to make adroit use of the good work of others, to believe that Andrea had not much invention.

Andrea executed for Alessandro Corsini a picture of a Madonna seated on the ground with a Child in her arms, surrounded by many little boys, which was finished with beautiful art and with very pleasing color; and for a mercer, much his friend, who kept a shop in Rome, he made a most beautiful head. Giovan Battista Puccini of Florence, likewise, taking extraordinary pleasure in the manner of Andrea, commissioned him to paint a picture of Our Lady for sending into France; but it proved to be so fine that he kept it for himself, and would by no means send it. However, having been asked, while transacting the affairs of his business in France, to undertake to send choice paintings to that country, he caused Andrea to paint a picture of a Dead Christ surrounded by some Angels, who were supporting Him and contemplating with gestures of sorrow and compassion their Maker sunk to such a pass through the sins of the world. This work, when finished, gave no less satisfaction in France, whither it was sent, than it had done in Florence, insomuch that the King, kindled with even greater desire to have works by Andrea, gave orders that he should execute others; which was the reason that Andrea, encouraged by his friends, resolved to go in a short time to France.

But meanwhile the Florentines, hearing in the year 1515 that Pope Leo X wished to grace his native city with his presence, ordained for his reception extraordinary festivities and a sumptuous and magnificent spectacle, with so many arches, façades, temples, colossal figures, and other statues and ornaments, that there had never been seen up to that time anything richer, more gorgeous, or more beautiful; for there was then flourishing in that city a greater abundance of fine and exalted intellects than had ever been known at any other period. But what was admired more than everything else was the façade of S. Maria del Fiore, made of wood, and so well decorated with various scenes in chiaroscuro by our Andrea, that nothing more could have been desired. The architecture of this work was by Jacopo Sansovino, as were some scenes in bas-relief and many figures carved in the round; and it was declared by the Pope that this structure—which was designed by Lorenzo de' Medici, father of that Pontiff, when he was alive—could not have been more beautiful, even if it had been of marble. The same Jacopo made a horse similar to the one in Rome, which was held to be a miracle of beauty, on the Piazza di S. Maria Novella. An endless number of ornaments, also, were executed for the Sala del Papa in the Via della Scala, and that street was half filled with most beautiful scenes wrought by the hands of many craftsmen, but designed for the most part by Baccio Bandinelli. Wherefore, when Leo entered Florence, on the third day of September in the same year, this spectacle was pronounced to be the grandest that had ever been devised, and the most beautiful.

But to return now to Andrea: being again requested to make another picture for the King of France, in a short time he finished one wherein he painted a very beautiful Madonna, which was sent off immediately, the merchants receiving for it four times as much as they had paid. Now at that very time Pier Francesco Borgherini had caused to be made by Baccio d'Agnolo some paneling, chests, chairs, and a bed, all carved in walnut wood, for the furnishing of an apartment; wherefore, to the end that the paintings therein might be equal in excellence to the rest of the work, he commissioned Andrea to paint part of the scenes on these with figures of no great size, representing the acts of Joseph the son of Jacob, in competition with some of great beauty that had been executed by Granaccio and Jacopo da Pontormo. Andrea, then, devoting an extraordinary amount of time and diligence to the work, strove to bring it about that they should prove to be more perfect than those of the others mentioned above; in which he succeeded to a marvel, for in the variety of events happening in the stories he showed how great was his worth in the art of painting. So excellent were those scenes, that an attempt was made by Giovan Battista della Palla, on account of the siege of Florence, to remove them from the places where they were fixed, in order to send them to the King of France; but, since they were fixed in such a way that it would have meant spoiling the whole work, they were left where they were, together with a picture of Our Lady, which is held to be a very choice work.

After this Andrea executed a head of Christ, now kept by the Servite Friars on the altar of the Nunziata, of such beauty, that I for my part do not know whether any more beautiful image of the head of Christ could be conceived by the intellect of man. For the chapels in the Church of S. Gallo, outside the Porta S. Gallo, there had been painted, in addition to the two panel-pictures by Andrea, a number of others, which were not equal to his; wherefore, since there was a commission to be given for another, those friars contrived to persuade the owner of the chapel to give it to Andrea; and he, beginning it immediately, made therein four figures standing, engaged in a disputation about the Trinity. One of these is S. Augustine, who, robed as a Bishop and truly African in aspect, is moving impetuously toward S. Peter Martyr, who is holding up an open book in a proud and sublime attitude: and the head and figure of the latter are much extolled. Beside him is a S. Francis holding a book in one hand and pressing the other against his breast; and he appears to be expressing with his lips a glowing ardor that makes him almost melt away in the heat of the discussion. There is also a S. Laurence, who, being young, is listening, and seems to be yielding to the authority of the others. Below them are two figures kneeling, one a Magdalene with most beautiful draperies, whose countenance is a portrait of Andrea's wife; for in no place did he paint a woman's features without copying them from her, and if perchance it happened at times that he took them from other women, yet, from his being used to see her continually, and from the circumstance that he had drawn her so often, and, what is more, had her impressed on his mind, it came about that almost all the heads of women that he made resembled her. The other kneeling figure is a S. Sebastian, who, being naked, shows his back, which appears to all who see it to be not painted, but of living flesh. And indeed, among so many works in oils, this was held by craftsmen to be the best. It is now to be found in S. Jacopo tra Fossi on the Canto degli Alberti, together with others by the hand of the same master.

While Andrea was living poorly enough in Florence, engaged in these works, but without bettering himself a whit, the two pictures that he had sent to France had been duly considered in that country by King Francis I; and among many others which had been sent from Rome, from Venice, and from Lombardy, they had been judged to be by far the best. The King therefore praising them mightily, it was remarked to him that it would be an easy matter to persuade Andrea to come to France to serve his Majesty; which news was so agreeable to the King, that he gave orders that all that was necessary should be done, and that money for the journey should be paid to Andrea in Florence. Andrea then set out for France with a glad heart, taking with him his assistant Andrea Sguazzella; and, having arrived at last at the Court, they were received by the King with great kindness and rejoicing. Before the very day of his arrival had passed by, Andrea proved for himself how great were the courtesy and the liberality of that magnanimous King, receiving presents of money and rich and honorable garments. Beginning to work soon afterwards, he became so dear to the King and to all the Court, that he was treated lovingly by everyone, and it appeared to him that his departure from his country had brought him from one extreme of wretchedness to the other extreme of bliss. Among his first works was a portrait from life of the Dauphin, the son of the King, born only a few months before, and still in swaddling clothes; and when he took this to the King, he received a present of three hundred gold crowns. Then, continuing to work, he painted for the

King a figure of Charity, which was considered a very rare work and was held by that Sovereign in the estimation that it deserved. After that, his Majesty granted him a liberal allowance and did all that he could to induce Andrea to stay willingly with him, promising him that he should never want for anything; and this because he liked Andrea's resoluteness in his work, and also the character of the man, who was contented with everything. Moreover, giving great satisfaction to the whole Court, he executed many pictures and various other works; and if he had kept in mind the condition from which he had escaped and the place to which fortune had brought him, there is no doubt that he would have risen— to say nothing of riches—to a most honorable rank. But one day, when he was at work on a S. Jerome in Penitence for the mother of the King, there came to him some letters from Florence, written by his wife; and he began, whatever may have been the reason, to think of departing. He sought leave, therefore, from the King, saying that he wished to go to Florence, but would return without fail to his Majesty after settling some affairs; and he would bring his wife with him, in order to live more at his ease in France, and would come back laden with pictures and sculptures of value. The King, trusting in him, gave him money for that purpose; and Andrea swore on the Testament to return to him in a few months.

Thus, then, he arrived in Florence, and for several months blissfully took his joy of his fair lady, his friends, and the city. And finally, the time at which he was to return having passed by, he found in the end that what with building, taking his pleasure, and doing no work, he had squandered all his money and likewise that of the King. Even so he wished to return, but he was more influenced by the sighs and prayers of his wife than by his own necessities and the pledge given to the King, so that, in order to please his wife, he did not go back; at which the King fell into such disdain, that for a long time he would never again look with a favorable eye on any painter from Florence, and he swore that if Andrea ever came into his hands he would give him a very different kind of welcome, with no regard whatever for his abilities. And thus Andrea, remaining in Florence, and sinking from the highest rung of the ladder to the very lowest, lived and passed the time as best he could.

At that time the elder Bartolommeo Panciatichi, who was carrying on a great mercantile business in France, desiring to leave a memorial of himself in Lyons, ordered Baccio d'Agnolo to have a panel painted for him by Andrea, and to send it to him there; saying that he wanted the subject to be the Assumption of Our Lady, with the Apostles about the tomb. This work, then, Andrea carried almost to completion; but since the wood of the panel split apart several times, he would sometimes work at it, and sometimes leave it alone, so that at his death it remained not quite finished. Afterwards it was placed by the younger Bartolommeo Panciatichi in his house, as a work truly worthy of praise on account of the beautiful figures of the Apostles; not to speak of the Madonna, who is surrounded by a choir of little boys standing, while certain others are supporting her and bearing her upwards with extraordinary grace. And in the foreground of the panel, among the Apostles, is a portrait of Andrea, so natural that it seems to be alive. It is now at the villa of the Baroncelli, a little distance from Florence, in a small church built by Piero Salviati near his villa to do honor to the picture.

The same master painted for Zanobi Bracci, who much desired to have some work by his hand, for one of his apartments, a picture of Our Lady, in which she is on her knees, leaning against a rock, and contemplating Christ, who lies on a heap of drapery and looks up at her, smiling; while a S. John, who stands there, is making a sign to the Madonna, as if to say that her Child is the true Son of God. Behind these figures is a S. Joseph with his head resting on his hands, which are lying on a rock; and he appears to be filled with joy at seeing the human race become divine through that Birth.

Cardinal Giulio de' Medici having been commissioned by Pope Leo to see to the adorning with stucco and paintings of the ceiling in the Great Hall of Poggio a Caiano, a palatial villa of the Medici family, situated between Pistoia and Florence, the charge of arranging for that work and of paying out the money was given to the Magnificent Ottaviano de' Medici, as to a person who, not falling short of the standard of his ancestors, was well informed in such matters and a loving friend to all the masters of our arts, and delighted more than any other man to have his dwellings adorned with the works of the most excellent. Ottaviano ordained, therefore, although the commission for the whole work had already been given to Franciabigio, that he should have only a third, Andrea another, and Jacopo da Pontormo the last. But it was found impossible, for all the efforts that the Magnificent Ottaviano made to urge them on, and for all the money that he offered and even paid to them, to get the work brought to completion; and Andrea alone finished with great diligence a scene on one wall, representing Caesar being presented with tribute of all kinds of animals. The drawing for this work is in our book, with many others by his hand; it is in chiaroscuro, and is the most finished that he ever made. In this picture Andrea, in order to surpass Franciabigio and Jacopo, subjected himself to unexampled labor, drawing in it a magnificent perspective-view and a very masterly flight of steps, which formed the ascent to the throne of Caesar. And these steps he adorned with very well-designed statues, not being content with having proved the beauty of his genius in the variety of figures that are carrying on their backs all those different animals, such as the figure of an Indian who is wearing a yellow coat, and carrying on his shoulders a cage drawn in perspective with some parrots both within it and without, the whole being rarely beautiful; and such, also, as some who are leading Indian goats, lions, giraffes, panthers, lynxes, and apes, with Moors and other lovely things of fancy, all grouped in a beautiful manner and executed divinely well in fresco. On these steps, also, he made a dwarf seated and holding a box containing a chameleon, which is so well executed in all the deformity of its fantastic shape, that it is impossible to imagine more beautiful proportions than those that he gave it. But, as has been said, this work remained unfinished, on account of the death of Pope Leo; and although Duke Alessandro de' Medici had a great desire that Jacopo da Pontormo should finish it, he was not able to prevail on him to put his hand to it. And in truth it suffered a very grievous wrong in the failure to complete it, seeing that the hall, for one in a villa, is the most beautiful in the world.

After returning to Florence, Andrea painted a picture with a nude half-length figure of S. John the Baptist, a very beautiful thing, which he executed at the commission of Giovan Maria Benintendi, who presented it afterwards to the Lord Duke Cosimo.

While affairs were proceeding in this manner, Andrea, remembering sometimes his connection with France, sighed from his heart: and if he had hoped to find pardon for the fault he had committed, there is no doubt that he would have gone back. Indeed, to try his fortune, he sought to see whether his talents might be helpful to him in the matter. Thus he painted a picture of a half-naked S. John the Baptist, meaning to send it to the Grand Master of France, to the end that he might occupy himself with restoring the painter to the favor of the King. However, whatever may have been the reason, he never sent it after all, but sold it to the Magnificent Ottaviano de' Medici, who always valued it much as long as he lived.

Not long afterwards he was commissioned by Zanobi Bracci to paint a picture for Monsignore di San Biause,* which he executed with all possible diligence, hoping that it might enable him to regain the favor of King Francis, to

* Jacques de Beaune, Intendant of Finance under Francis I.

whose service he desired to return. Afterwards, in the year 1523, the plague came to Florence and also to some places in the surrounding country; and Andrea, in order to avoid that pestilence and also to do some work, went at the instance of Antonio Brancacci to the Mugello to paint a panel for the Nuns of S. Piero a Luco, of the Order of Camaldoli, taking with him his wife and a step-daughter, together with his wife's sister and an assistant. Living quietly there, then, he set his hand to the work. And since those venerable ladies showed more and more kindness and courtesy every day to his wife, to himself, and to the whole party, he applied himself with the greatest possible willingness to executing that panel, in which he painted a Dead Christ mourned by Our Lady, S. John the Evangelist, and the Magdalene, figures so lifelike, that they appear truly to have spirit and breath.

In this manner, then, Andrea passed without danger the time of the plague, and those nuns received from the genius of that great man such a work as can bear comparison with the most excellent pictures that have been painted in our day; wherefore it is no marvel that Ramazzotto, the captain of mercenaries of Scaricalasino, sought to obtain it on several occasions during the siege of Florence, in order to send it to his chapel in S. Michele in Bosco at Bologna.

Now Federigo II, Duke of Mantua, in passing through Florence on his way to make obeisance to Clement VII, saw over a door in the house of the Medici that portrait of Pope Leo between Cardinal Giulio de' Medici and Cardinal de' Rossi, which the most excellent Raphael of Urbino had formerly painted; and being extraordinarily pleased with it, he resolved, being a man who delighted in pictures of such beauty, to make it his own. And so, when he was in Rome and the moment seemed to him to have come, he asked for it as a present from Pope Clement, who courteously granted his request. Thereupon orders were sent to Florence to Ottaviano de' Medici, under whose care and government were Ippolito and Alessandro, that he should have it packed up and taken to Mantua. This matter was very displeasing to the Magnificent Ottaviano, who would never have consented to deprive Florence of such a picture, and he marveled that the Pope should have given it up so readily. However, he answered that he would not fail to satisfy the Duke; but that, since the frame was bad, he was having a new one made, and when it had been gilt he would send the picture with every possible precaution to Mantua. This done, Messer Ottaviano, in order to "save both the goat and the cabbage," as the saying goes, sent privately for Andrea and told him how the matter stood, and how there was no way out of it but to make an exact copy of the picture with the greatest care and send it to the Duke, secretly retaining the one by the hand of Raphael. Andrea, then, having promised to do all in his power and knowledge, caused a panel to be made similar in size and in every respect, and painted it secretly in the house of Messer Ottaviano. And to such purpose did he labor, that when it was finished even Messer Ottaviano, for all his understanding in matters of art, could not tell the one from the other, nor distinguish the real and true picture from the copy; especially as Andrea had counterfeited even the spots of dirt, exactly as they were in the original. And so, after they had hidden the picture of Raphael, they sent the one by the hand of Andrea, in a similar frame, to Mantua; at which the Duke was completely satisfied, and above all because the painter Giulio Romano, a disciple of Raphael, had praised it, failing to detect the trick. This Giulio would always have been of the same opinion, and would have believed it to be by the hand of Raphael, but for the arrival in Mantua of Giorgio Vasari, who, having been as it were the adoptive child of Messer Ottaviano, and having seen Andrea at work on that picture, revealed the truth. For Giulio making much of Vasari, and showing him, after many antiquities and paintings, that picture of Raphael's, as the best work that was there, Giorgio said to him, "A beautiful work it is, but in no way by the hand of Raphael." "What?" answered Giulio. "Should I not know it, when I recognize the very strokes that I made with my own brush?" "You have forgotten them," said Giorgio, "for this picture is by the hand of Andrea del Sarto; and to prove it, there is a sign (to which he pointed) that was made in Florence, because when the two were together they could not be distinguished." Hearing this, Giulio had the picture turned round, and saw the mark; at which he shrugged his shoulders and said these words, "I value it no less than if it were by the hand of Raphael—nay, even more, for it is something out of the course of nature that a man of excellence should imitate the manner of another so well, and should make a copy so like. It is enough that it should be known that Andrea's genius was as valiant in double harness as in single." Thus, then, by the wise judgment of Messer Ottaviano, satisfaction was given to the Duke without depriving Florence of so choice a work, which, having been presented to him afterwards by Duke Alessandro, he kept in his possession for many years; and finally he gave it to Duke Cosimo, who has it in his *guardaroba* together with many other famous pictures.

While Andrea was making this copy, he also painted for the same Messer Ottaviano a picture with only the head of Cardinal Giulio de' Medici, who afterwards became Pope Clement; and this head, which was similar to that by Raphael, and very beautiful, was presented eventually by Messer Ottaviano to old Bishop de' Marzi.

M. Jacopo, a Servite friar, in releasing and absolving a woman from a vow, had told her that she must have a figure of Our Lady painted over the outer side of that lateral door of the Nunziata which leads into the cloister; and therefore, finding Andrea, he said to him that he had this money to spend, and that although it was not much it seemed to him right, since the other works executed by Andrea in that place had brought him such fame, that he and no other should paint this one as well. Andrea, who was nothing if not an amiable man, moved by the persuasions of the friar and by his own desire for profit and glory, answered that he would do it willingly; and shortly afterwards, putting his hand to the work, he painted in fresco a most beautiful Madonna seated with her Son in her arms, and S. Joseph leaning on a sack, with his eyes fixed upon an open book. And of such a kind was this work, in draftsmanship, grace, and beauty of coloring, as well as in vivacity and relief, that it proved that he outstripped and surpassed by a great measure all the painters who had worked up to that time. Such, indeed, is this picture, that by its own merit and without praise from any other quarter it makes itself clearly known as amazing and most rare.

There was wanting only one scene in the cloister of the Scalzo for it to be completely finished; wherefore Andrea, who had added grandeur to his manner after having seen the figures that Michelangelo had begun and partly finished for the Sacristy of S. Lorenzo, set his hand to executing this last scene. In this, giving the final proof of his improvement, he painted the Birth of S. John the Baptist, with figures that were very beautiful and much better and stronger in relief than the others made by him before in the same place. Most beautiful, among others in this work, are a woman who is carrying the new-born babe to the bed on which lies S. Elizabeth, who is likewise a most lovely figure, and Zacharias, who is writing on a paper that he has placed on his knee, holding it with one hand and with the other writing the name of his son, and all with such vivacity, that he lacks nothing save the breath of life. Most beautiful, also, is an old woman who is seated on a stool, smiling with gladness at the delivery of the other aged woman, and revealing in her attitude and expression all that would be seen in a living person after such an event.

The Monks of S. Salvi had let many years pass by without thinking of having a beginning made with their Last Supper, which they had commissioned Andrea to execute at the time when he painted the arch with the four figures; but finally an

Abbot, who was a man of judgment and breeding, determined that he should finish that work. Thereupon Andrea, who had already pledged himself to it on a previous occasion, far from making any demur, put his hand to the task, and, working at it one piece at a time when he felt so inclined, finished it in a few months, and that in such a manner, that the work was held to be, as it certainly is, the most spontaneous and the most vivacious in coloring and drawing that he ever made, or that ever could be made. For, among other things, he gave infinite grandeur, majesty, and grace to all the figures, insomuch that I know not what to say of this Last Supper that would not be too little, it being such that whoever sees it is struck with amazement. Wherefore it is no marvel that on account of its excellence it was left standing amid the havoc of the siege of Florence, in the year 1529, at which time the soldiers and destroyers, by command of those in authority, pulled down all the suburbs outside the city, and all the monasteries, hospitals, and other buildings. These men, I say, having destroyed the Church and Campanile of S. Salvi, and beginning to throw down part of the convent, had come to the refectory where this Last Supper is, when their leader, seeing so marvelous a painting, of which he may have heard speak, abandoned the undertaking and would not let any more of that place be destroyed, reserving the task until such time as there should be no alternative.

Andrea then made a portrait from life of a steward of the Monks of Vallombrosa, who lived almost always in the country on the affairs of his monastery; and this portrait was placed under a sort of bower, in which he had made pergolas and contrivances of his own in various fanciful designs, so that it was buffeted by wind and rain, according to the pleasure of that steward, who was the friend of Andrea. And because, when the work was finished, there were some colors and lime left over, Andrea, taking a tile, called to his wife Lucrezia and said to her: "Come here, for these colors are left over, and I wish to make your portrait, so that all may see how well you have preserved your beauty even at your time of life, and yet may know how your appearance has changed, which will make this one different from your early portraits." But the woman, who may have had something else in her mind, would not stand still; and Andrea, as it were from a feeling that he was near his end, took a mirror and made a portrait of himself on that tile, of such perfection, that it seems alive and as real as nature; and that portrait is in the possession of the same Madonna Lucrezia, who is still living.

About the same time Giovan Battista della Palla, having bought all the sculptures and pictures of note that he could obtain, and causing copies to be made of those that he could not buy, had despoiled Florence of a vast number of choice works, without the least scruple, in order to furnish a suite of rooms for the King of France, which was to be richer in suchlike ornaments than any other in the world. And this man, desiring that Andrea should return to the service and favor of the King, commissioned him to paint two pictures. In one of these Andrea painted Abraham in the act of trying to sacrifice his son; and that with such diligence, that it was judged that up to that time he had never done anything better. This picture, having been bought by Filippo Strozzi after the death of Andrea and the capture of Battista, was presented by him to Signor Alfonso Davalos, Marchese del Vasto, who had it carried to the island of Ischia, near Naples, and placed in one of his apartments in company with other most noble paintings.

In the other picture Andrea painted a very beautiful Charity, with three little boys; and this was afterwards bought from the wife of Andrea, after his death, by the painter Domenico Conti, who sold it later to Niccolò Antinori, who treasures it as a rare work, as indeed it is.

During this time there came to the Magnificent Ottaviano de' Medici, seeing from that last picture how much Andrea had improved his manner, a desire to have a picture by his hand. Whereupon Andrea, who was eager to serve that lord, to whom he was much indebted, because he had always shown favor to men of lofty intellect, and particularly to painters, executed for him a picture of Our Lady seated on the ground with the Child riding astride on her knees, while He turns His head toward a little S. John supported by an old S. Elizabeth, a figure so natural and so well painted that she appears to be alive, even as every other thing is wrought with incredible diligence, draftsmanship, and art. Having finished this picture, Andrea carried it to Messer Ottaviano; but since that lord had something else to think about, Florence being then besieged, he told Andrea, while thanking him profoundly and making his excuses, to dispose of it as he thought best. To which Andrea made no reply but this: "The labor was endured for you, and yours the work shall always be." "Sell it," answered Messer Ottaviano, "and use the money, for I know what I am talking about." Andrea then departed and returned to his house, nor would he ever give the picture to anyone, for all the offers that were made to him; but when the siege was raised and the Medici back in Florence, he took it once more to Messer Ottaviano, who accepted it right willingly, thanking him and paying him double. The work is now in the apartment of his wife, Madonna Francesca, sister to the very reverend Salviati, who holds the beautiful pictures left to her by her magnificent consort in no less account than she does the duty of retaining and honoring his friends.

During the siege of Florence some captains had fled the city with the pay-chests; on which account Andrea was asked to paint on the façade of the Palace of the Podestà and in the Piazza not only those captains, but also some citizens who had fled and had been proclaimed outlaws. He said that he would do it; but in order not to acquire, like Andrea del Castagno, the name of Andrea degl'Impiccati, he gave it out that he was entrusting the work to one of his assistants, called Bernardo del Buda. However, having made a great enclosure, which he himself entered and left by night, he executed those figures in such a manner that they appeared to be the men themselves, real and alive. The soldiers, who were painted on the façade of the old Mercatanzia in the Piazza, near the Condotta, were covered with whitewash many years ago, that they might be seen no longer.

The siege being finished, Andrea was waiting for matters to mend, although with little hope that his French project would succeed, since Giovan Battista della Palla had been taken prisoner, when Florence became filled with soldiers and stores from the camp. Among those soldiers were some lansquenets sick of the plague, who brought no little terror into the city and shortly afterwards left it infected. Thereupon, either through this apprehension or through some imprudence in eating after having suffered much privation in the siege, one day Andrea fell grievously ill and took to his bed with death on his brow; and finding no remedy for his illness, and being without much attention—for his wife, from fear of the plague, kept as far away from him as she could—he died, so it is said, almost without a soul being aware of it; and he was buried by the men of the Scalzo with scant ceremony in the Church of the Servi, near his own house, in the place where the members of that Company are always buried.

The death of Andrea was a very great loss to the city and to art, because up to the age of forty-five, which he attained, he went on always improving from one work to another in such wise that, if he had lived longer, he would have continued to confer benefits on art; for the reason that it is better to go on making progress little by little, advancing with a firm and steady foot through the difficulties of art, than to seek to force one's intellect and nature in a single effort. Nor is there any doubt that if Andrea had stayed in Rome when he went there to see the works of Raphael and Michelangelo, and also the statues and ruins of that city, he would have enriched his manner greatly in the composition of scenes, and would one day have given more delicacy and greater force to his figures; which has never been thoroughly achieved save by one who has been some time in Rome, to study those works in detail and grow familiar with them. Having then from nature a sweet and gracious manner of drawing and great facility and vivacity of coloring, both in fresco-work and in oils, it is believed without a doubt that if he had stayed in Rome, he would have surpassed all the craftsmen of his time. But some believe that he was deterred from this by the abundance of works of sculpture and painting, both ancient and modern, that he saw in that city, and by observing the many young men, disciples of Raphael and of others, resolute in draftsmanship and working confidently and without effort, whom, like the timid fellow that he was, he did not feel it in him to excel. And so, not trusting himself, he resolved, as the best course for him, to return to Florence; where, reflecting little by little on what he had seen, he made such proficience that his works have been admired and held in price, and, what is more, imitated more often after his death than during his lifetime. Whoever has some holds them dear, and whoever has consented to sell them has received three times as much as was paid to him, for the reason that he never received anything but small prices for his works. In our book are many drawings by his hand, all good; but in particular there is one that is altogether beautiful, of the scene that he painted at Poggio, showing the tribute of all the animals from the East being presented to Caesar. This drawing, which is executed in chiaroscuro, is a rare thing, and the most finished that Andrea ever made; for when he drew natural objects for reproduction in his works, he made mere sketches dashed off on the spot, contenting himself with marking the character of the reality; and afterwards, when reproducing them in his works, he brought them to perfection. His drawings, therefore, served him rather as memoranda of what he had seen than as models from which to make exact copies in his pictures.

VERONESE

[*Paolo Cagliari, called, as a native of Verona, Veronese,
was born in 1528 and died in 1588.*]

PAOLO VERONESE is a painter in very good repute in Venice
at the present day, in that, although he is not yet more than
thirty years of age, he has executed many works worthy of
praise. This master, who was born at Verona to a stonecutter,
or, as they say in those parts, a stone-hewer, after having
learned the rudiments of painting from Giovanni Caroto of
Verona, painted in fresco the hall of the Paymaster and As-
sessor Portesco at Tiene, in the Vicentino; works executed
with good design and judgment and a beautiful manner. At
Maser, near Asolo in the Trevisano, he has painted the very
beautiful house of Signor Daniello Barbaro, Patriarch-elect
of Aquileia. At Verona, for the Refectory of S. Nazzaro, a
monastery of Black Friars, he has painted in a large picture
on canvas the supper that Simon the Leper gave to Our Lord,
when the woman of sin threw herself at His feet, with many
figures, portraits from life, and very rare perspective-views;
and under the table are two dogs so beautiful that they appear real and alive, and further away certain cripples executed excellently well.

By the hand of Paolo, in the Hall of the Council of Ten
at Venice, in an oval that is larger than certain others that are
there, placed, as the principal one, in the center of the ceiling,
is a Jove who is driving away the Vices, in order to signify
that that supreme and absolute tribunal drives away vice and
chastises wicked and vicious men. The same master painted
the ceiling of the Church of S. Sebastiano, which is a very

rare work, and the altar-piece of the principal chapel, together with some pictures that serve to adorn it, and likewise the doors of the organ; which are all pictures truly worthy of the highest praise. In the Hall of the Grand Council he painted a large picture of Frederick Barbarossa presenting himself to the Pope, with a good number of figures varied in their costumes and vestments, all most beautiful and representing worthily the Court of a Pope and an Emperor, and also a Venetian Senate, with many noblemen and Senators of that Republic, portrayed from life. In short, this work is such in its grandeur and design, and in the beauty and variety of the attitudes, that it is rightly extolled by everyone. After this scene, Paolo painted the ceilings of certain chambers, which are used by that Council of Ten, with figures in oils, which are much foreshortened and very rare.

In like manner, he painted in fresco the façade of the house of a merchant, which was a very beautiful work, on the road from S. Maurizio to S. Moisè; but the wind from the sea is little by little destroying it. For Camillo Trevisani, at Murano, he painted a loggia and an apartment in fresco, which were much extolled. And in S. Giorgio Maggiore at Venice, at the head of a large apartment, he painted in oils the Marriage of Cana in Galilee, which was a marvelous work for its grandeur, the number of figures, the variety of costumes, and the invention; and, if I remember right, there are to be seen in it more than one hundred and fifty heads, all varied and executed with great diligence.

The same Paolo was commissioned by the Procurators of S. Mark to paint certain angular medallions that are in the ceiling of the Nicene Library, which was left to the Signoria by Cardinal Bessarion, with a vast treasure of Greek books. Now the above-named lords, when they had the painting of that library begun, promised a prize of honor, in addition to the ordinary payment, to him who should acquit himself best in painting it; and the pictures were divided among the best painters that there were at that time in Venice. When the work was finished and the pictures painted had been very well considered, a chain of gold was placed round the neck of Paolo, he being the man who was judged to have done better than all the others. The picture that gave him the victory and the prize of honor was that wherein he painted Music, in which are depicted three very beautiful young women, one of whom, the most beautiful, is playing a great bass viol, looking down at the fingerboard of the instrument, the attitude of her person showing that her ear and her voice are fixed intently on the sound; and of the other two, one is playing a lute, and the other singing from a book. Near these women is a Cupid without wings, who is playing a harpsichord, signifying that Love is born from Music, or rather, that Love is always in company with Music; and, because he never parts from her, Paolo made him without wings. In the same picture he painted Pan, the God, according to the poets, of shepherds, with certain pipes made of the bark of trees, as it were consecrated to him as votive offerings by shepherds who have been victorious in playing them. Two other pictures Paolo painted in the same place; in one is Arithmetic, with certain Philosophers dressed in the ancient manner, and in the other is Honor, seated on a throne, to whom sacrifices are being offered and royal crowns presented. But, seeing that this young man is at this very moment at the height of his activity and not yet in his thirty-second year, I shall say nothing more of him for the present.

TINTORETTO

*[Jacopo di Battista Robusti, called Il Tintoretto, the little
dyer, because his father was a dyer, was born, probably,
in 1518 and died in 1594.]*

IN the city of Venice there lived, as he still does, a painter
called Jacopo Tintoretto, who has delighted in all the arts,
and particularly in playing various musical instruments, besides being agreeable in his every action, but in the matter of
painting swift, resolute, fantastic, and extravagant, and the
most extraordinary brain that the art of painting has ever
produced, as may be seen from all his works and from the
fantastic compositions of his scenes, executed by him in a
fashion of his own and contrary to the use of other painters.
Indeed, he has surpassed even the limits of extravagance with
the new and fanciful inventions and the strange vagaries of
his intellect, working at haphazard and without design, as if
to prove that art is but a jest. This master at times has left as
finished works sketches still so rough that the brush strokes
may be seen, done more by chance and vehemence than with
judgment and design. He has painted almost every kind of
picture in fresco and in oils, with portraits from life, and at
every price, insomuch that with these methods he has executed, as he still does, the greater part of the pictures painted
in Venice. And since in his youth he proved himself by
many beautiful works a man of great judgment, if only he had
recognized how great an advantage he had from nature, and
had improved it by reasonable study, as has been done by
those who have followed the beautiful manners of his predecessors, and had not dashed his work off by mere skill of

hand, he would have been one of the greatest painters that Venice has ever had. Not that this prevents him from being a bold and able painter, and delicate, fanciful, and alert in spirit.

Now, when it had been ordained by the Senate that Jacopo Tintoretto and Paolo Veronese, at that time young men of great promise, should each execute a scene in the Hall of the Great Council, and Orazio, the son of Titian, another, Tintoretto painted in his scene Frederick Barbarossa being crowned by the Pope, depicting there a most beautiful building, and about the Pontiff a great number of Cardinals and Venetian gentlemen, all portrayed from life, and at the foot the Pope's chapel of music. In all this he acquitted himself in such a manner, that the picture can bear comparison with those of the others.

Not long afterwards, another scene being required in that hall, Tintoretto so went to work with the aid of friends and other means, that it was given to him to paint; whereupon he executed it in such a manner that it was a marvel, and that it deserves to be numbered among the best things that he ever did, so powerful in him was his determination that he would equal, if not vanquish and surpass, his rivals who had worked in that place. In the principal chapel of S. Rocco he painted two pictures in oils as broad as the width of the whole chapel —namely, about twenty-four feet each. In one he depicted a view in perspective as of a hospital filled with beds and sick persons in various attitudes who are being healed by S. Rocco; and among these are some nude figures very well conceived, and a dead body in foreshortening that is very beautiful. In the other is a story likewise of S. Rocco, full of most graceful and beautiful figures, and such, in short, that it is held to be one of the best works that this painter has executed. In a scene of the same size, in the center of the church, he painted Jesus Christ healing the impotent man at the Pool of Bethesda, which is also a work held to be passing good.

In the Church of S. Maria dell'Orto, where, as has been

told above, Cristofano and his brother, painters of Brescia, painted the ceiling, Tintoretto has painted—that is, on canvas and in oils—the two walls of the principal chapel, which are forty-four feet in height from the vaulting to the cornice at the foot. In that which is on the right hand he has depicted Moses returning from the Mount, where he had received the Laws from God, and finding the people worshipping the Golden Calf; and opposite to that, in the other, is the Universal Judgment of the last day, painted with an extravagant invention that truly has in it something awesome and terrible, by reason of the diversity of figures of either sex and all ages that are there, with vistas and distant views of the souls of the blessed and the damned. There, also, may be seen the boat of Charon, but in a manner so different from that of others, that it is a thing beautiful and strange. If this fantastic invention had been executed with correct and well-ordered drawing, and if the painter had given diligent attention to the parts and to each particular detail, as he has done to the whole in expressing the confusion, turmoil, and terror of that day, it would have been a most stupendous picture. And whoever glances at it for a moment, is struck with astonishment; but, considering it afterwards minutely, it appears as if painted as a jest. The same master has painted in oils in that church, on the doors of the organ, Our Lady ascending the steps of the Temple, which is a highly finished work, and the best-executed and most gladsome picture that there is in that place. In the Sacristy of S. Sebastiano, in competition with Paolo Veronese, who executed many pictures on the ceiling and the walls of that place, he painted over the presses Moses in the Desert and other scenes. The same Tintoretto then painted for the altar of the Pietà, in S. Giobbe, three Marys, S. Francis, S. Sebastian, and S. John, with a piece of landscape; and, on the organ doors in the Church of the Servites, S. Augustine and S. Philip, and beneath them Cain killing his brother Abel. At the altar of the Sacrament in S. Felice, or rather, on the ceiling of the tribune, he painted the four

Evangelists; and in the lunette above the altar an Annunciation, in the other lunette Christ praying on the Mount of Olives, and on the wall the Last Supper that He had with His Apostles. And in S. Francesco della Vigna, on the altar of the Deposition from the Cross, there is by the same hand the Madonna in a swoon, with the other Marys and some Prophets.

In the Scuola of S. Marco, near SS. Giovanni e Polo, are four large scenes by his hand. In one of these is S. Mark, who, appearing in the air, is delivering one who is his votary from many torments that may be seen prepared for him with various instruments of torture, which being broken, the executioner was never able to employ them against that devout man; and in that scene is a great abundance of figures, foreshortenings, pieces of armor, buildings, portraits, and other suchlike things, which render the work very ornate. In the second is a tempest of the sea, and S. Mark, likewise in the air, delivering another of his votaries; but that scene is by no means executed with the same diligence as that already described. In the third is a storm of rain, with the dead body of another of S. Mark's votaries, and his soul ascending into Heaven; and there, also, is a composition of passing good figures. In the fourth, wherein an evil spirit is being exorcised, he counterfeited in perspective a great loggia, and at the end of it a fire that illumines it with many reflections. And in addition to those scenes there is on the altar a S. Mark by the same hand, which is a passing good picture.

These works, then, and many others that are here passed over, it being enough to have made mention of the best, have been executed by Tintoretto with such rapidity, that, when it was thought that he had scarcely begun, he had finished. And it is a notable thing that with the most extravagant ways in the world, he has always work to do, for the reason that when his friendships and other means are not enough to obtain for him any particular work, even if he had to do it, I do not say at a low price, but without payment or by force, in one way or another, do it he would. And it is not long since, Tintoretto having executed the Passion of Christ in a large picture in oils and on canvas for the Scuola of S. Rocco, the men of that Company resolved to have some honorable and magnificent work painted on the ceiling above it, and therefore to allot that commission to that one among the painters that there were in Venice who should make the best and most beautiful design. Having therefore summoned Joseffo Salviati, Federigo Zucchero, who was in Venice at that time, Paolo Veronese, and Jacopo Tintoretto, they ordained that each of them should make a design, promising the work to him who should acquit himself best in this. While the others, then, were engaged with all possible diligence in making their designs, Tintoretto, having taken measurements of the size that the work was to be, sketched a great canvas and painted it with his usual rapidity, without anyone knowing about it, and then placed it where it was to stand. Whereupon, the men of the Company having assembled one morning to see the designs and to make their award, they found that Tintoretto had completely finished the work and had placed it in position. At which being angered against him, they said that they had called for designs and had not commissioned him to execute the work; but he answered them that this was his method of making designs, that he did not know how to proceed in any other manner, and that designs and models of works should always be after that fashion, so as to deceive no one, and that, finally, if they would not pay him for the work and for his labor, he would make them a present of it. And after these words, although he had many contradictions, he so contrived that the work is still in the same place. In this canvas, then, there is painted a Heaven with God the Father descending with many Angels to embrace S. Rocco, and in the lowest part are many figures that signify, or rather, represent the other principal Scuole of Venice, such as the Carità, S. Giovanni Evangelista, the Misericordia, S. Marco, and S. Teodoro, all executed after his usual manner. But since it would be too long a task to enumerate all the pictures of Tintoretto, let it be enough to have spoken of the above-named works of that master, who is a truly able man and a painter worthy to be praised.

MICHELANGELO

*[Michelangelo di Lodovico di Leonardo Buonarroti
Simoni was born in 1475 and died in 1564.]*

WHILE the most noble and industrious spirits were striving,
by the light of the famous Giotto and of his followers, to give
to the world proof of their ability, the Ruler of Heaven in
His clemency sent down to earth a spirit with universal
ability in every art, who might be able, working by himself
alone, to show what manner of thing is the perfection of the
art of design in executing the lines, contours, shadows, and
high lights, so as to give relief to works of painting, and what
it is to work with correct judgment in sculpture, and how in
architecture it is possible to render habitations secure and
commodious, healthy and cheerful, well-proportioned, and
rich with varied ornaments. He was pleased, in addition, to
endow him with the true moral philosophy and with the ornament of sweet poesy, to the end that the world might choose
him and admire him as its highest exemplar in the life, works,
saintliness of character, and every action of human creatures,
and that he might be acclaimed by us as a being rather divine than human. And since He saw that in the practice of
these rare exercises and arts—namely, in painting, in sculpture, and in architecture—the Tuscan intellects have always
been exalted and raised high above all others, He chose to
give him Florence for his country.

There was born a son, then, in the Casentino, in the year
1475, under a fateful and happy star, from an excellent and
noble mother, to Lodovico di Leonardo Buonarroti Simoni,
a descendant, so it is said, of the most noble and most ancient

family of the Counts of Canossa. To that Lodovico, I say, who was in that year Podestà of the township of Chiusi and Caprese, near the Sasso della Vernia, where S. Francis received the Stigmata, in the Diocese of Arezzo, a son was born on the 6th of March, a Sunday, about the eighth hour of the night, to which son he gave the name Michelagnolo, because he wished to suggest that he was something celestial and divine beyond the use of mortals. Having finished his office as Podestà, Lodovico returned to Florence and settled in the village of Settignano, at a distance of three miles from the city, where he had a farm that had belonged to his forefathers; which place abounds with stone and is all full of quarries of grey-stone, which is constantly being worked by stonecutters and sculptors, who for the most part are born in the place. Michelagnolo was put out to nurse by Lodovico in that village with the wife of a stonecutter: wherefore the same Michelagnolo, discoursing once with Vasari, said to him jestingly, "Giorgio, if I have anything of the good in my brain, it has come from my being born in the pure air of your country of Arezzo, even as I also sucked in with my nurse's milk the chisels and hammer with which I make my figures." In time Lodovico's family increased, and, being in poor circumstances, with slender revenues, he set about apprenticing his sons to the Guilds of Silk and Wool. Michelagnolo, who by that time was well grown, was placed to be schooled in grammar with Maestro Francesco da Urbino; but, since his genius drew him to delight in design, all the time that he could snatch he would spend in drawing in secret, being scolded for this by his father and his other elders, and at times beaten, they perchance considering that to give attention to that art, which was not known by them, was a mean thing and not worthy of their ancient house.

At this time Michelagnolo had formed a friendship with Francesco Granacci, who, likewise a lad, had placed himself with Domenico Ghirlandaio in order to learn the art of painting; wherefore Granacci, loving Michelagnolo, and perceiving that he was much inclined to design, supplied him daily with drawings by Ghirlandaio, who at that time was reputed to be one of the best masters that there were not only in Florence, but throughout all Italy. Whereupon, the desire to work at art growing greater every day in Michelangelo, Lodovico, perceiving that he could not divert the boy from giving his attention to design, and that there was no help for it, and wishing to derive some advantage from it and to enable him to learn that art, resolved on the advice of friends to apprentice him with Domenico Ghirlandaio. Michelangelo, when he was placed with Domenico Ghirlandaio, was fourteen years of age. Now he who wrote his life after the year 1550, when I wrote these Lives the first time, has said that some persons, through not having associated with him, have related things that never happened, and have left out many that are worthy to be recorded, and has touched on this circumstance in particular, taxing Domenico with jealousy and saying that he never offered any assistance to Michelangelo; which is clearly false, as may be seen from an entry by the hand of Lodovico, the father of Michelangelo, written in one of Domenico's books, which book is now in the possession of his heirs. That entry runs thus: "1488, I record, this first day of April, that I, Lodovico di Leonardo di Buonarrota, placed Michelangelo my son with Domenico and David di Tommaso di Currado for the three years next to come, on these terms and conditions, that the said Michelangelo shall remain with the abovenamed persons for the said period of time, in order to learn to paint and to exercise that vocation; that the said persons shall have command over him; and that the same Domenico and David shall be bound to give him in those three years twenty-four florins of full weight, the first year six florins, the second year eight florins, and the third ten florins; in all, the sum of ninety-six *lire*." And next, below this, is another record, or rather, entry, also written in the hand of Lodovico: "The aforesaid Michelangelo has received of that sum, this sixteenth day of April, two gold florins in gold. I,

Lodovico di Leonardo, his father, have received twelve *lire* and twelve *soldi* as cash due to him." These entries I have copied from the book itself, in order to prove that all that was written at that time, as well as all that is about to be written, is the truth; nor do I know that anyone has been more associated with him than I have been, or has been a more faithful friend and servant to him, as can be proved even to one who knows not the facts, neither do I believe that there is anyone who can show a greater number of letters written by his own hand, or any written with greater affection than he has expressed to me. I have made this digression for the sake of truth, and it must suffice for all the rest of his Life. Let us now return to our story.

When the ability as well as the person of Michelangelo had grown in such a manner, that Domenico, seeing him execute some works beyond the scope of a boy, was astonished, since it seemed to him that he not only surpassed the other disciples, of whom he had a great number, but very often equaled the things done by himself as master, it happened that one of the young men who were learning under Domenico copied with the pen some draped figures of women from works by Ghirlandaio; whereupon Michelangelo took that drawing and with a thicker pen outlined one of those women with new lineaments, in the manner that it should have been in order to be perfect. And it is a marvelous thing to see the difference between the two manners, and the judgment and excellence of a mere lad who was so spirited and bold, that he had the courage to correct the work of his master. That sheet is now in my possession, treasured as a relic; and I received it from Granacci to put in my book of drawings together with others by the same hand, which I received from Michelangelo. In the year 1550, when Giorgio was in Rome, he showed it to Michelangelo, who recognized it and was pleased to see it again, saying modestly that he knew more of the art when he was a boy than he did at that time, when he was an old man.

Now it happened that when Domenico was at work on the great chapel of S. Maria Novella, one day that he was out Michelangelo set himself to draw the staging with some desks and all the appliances of art, and some of the young men who were working there. Whereupon, when Domenico had returned and seen Michelangelo's drawing, he said, "This boy knows more about it than I do."

At that time the Magnificent Lorenzo de' Medici kept the sculptor Bertoldo in his garden on the Piazza di S. Marco, not so much as custodian or guardian of the many beautiful antiques that he had collected and gathered together at great expense in that place, as because, desiring very earnestly to create a school of excellent painters and sculptors, he wished that these should have as their chief and guide the above-named Bertoldo, who was a disciple of Donatello. Bertoldo, although he was so old that he was not able to work, was nevertheless a well-practiced master and in much repute, not only because he had polished with great diligence the pulpits cast by his master Donatello, but also on account of many castings in bronze that he had executed himself, of battles and certain other small works, in the execution of which there was no one to be found in Florence at that time who surpassed him. Now Lorenzo, who bore a very great love to painting and to sculpture, was grieved that there were not to be found in his time sculptors noble and famous enough to equal the many painters of the highest merit and reputation, and he determined, as I have said, to found a school. To this end he besought Domenico Ghirlandaio that, if he had among the young men in his workshop any that were inclined to sculpture, he might send them to his garden, where he wished to train and form them in such a manner as might do honor to himself, to Domenico, and to the whole city. Whereupon there were given to him by Domenico as the best of his young men, among others, Michelangelo and Francesco Granacci; and they, going to the garden, found there that Torrigiano, a young man of the Torrigiani family, was executing in clay some figures in the round that had been given to him by Bertoldo. Michelangelo, seeing this, made some out of emulation; wherefore Lorenzo, seeing his fine spirit, always regarded him with much expectation. And he, thus encouraged, after some days set himself to counterfeit from a piece of marble an antique head of a Faun that was there, old and wrinkled, which had the nose injured and the mouth laughing. Michelangelo, who had never yet touched marble or chisels, succeeded so well in counterfeiting it, that the Magnificent Lorenzo was astonished; and then, perceiving that, departing from the form of the antique head, he had opened out the mouth after his own fancy and had made a tongue, with all the teeth showing, that lord, jesting pleasantly, as was his wont, said to him, "Surely you should have known that old folks never have all their teeth, and that some are always wanting." It appeared to Michelangelo, in his simplicity, both fearing and loving that lord, that he had spoken the truth; and no sooner had Lorenzo departed than he straightway broke one of the teeth and hollowed out the gum, in such a manner, that it seemed as if the tooth had dropped out. And then he awaited with eagerness the return of the Magnificent Lorenzo, who, when he had come and had seen the simplicity and excellence of Michelangelo, laughed at it more than once, relating it as a miracle to his friends. Moreover, having made a resolve to assist and favor Michelangelo, he sent for his father Lodovico and asked for the boy from him, saying that he wished to maintain him as one of his own children; and Lodovico gave him up willingly. Thereupon the Magnificent Lorenzo granted him a chamber in his own house and had him attended, and he ate always at his table with his own children and with other persons of quality and of noble blood who lived with that lord, by whom he was much honored. This was in the year after he had been placed with Domenico, when Michelangelo was about fifteen or sixteen years of age; and he lived in that house four years, which was until the death of the Magnificent Lorenzo in 1492. During that time, then, Michelangelo had five ducats a month from that lord as an allowance and also to help his father; and for his particular gratification Lorenzo gave him a violet cloak, and to his father an office in the Customs. Truth to tell, all the young men in the garden were salaried, some little and some much, by the liberality of that magnificent and most noble citizen, and rewarded by him as long as he lived.

At this time, at the advice of Poliziano, a man eminent in letters, Michelangelo executed from a piece of marble given to him by that lord the Battle of Hercules with the Centaurs, which was so beautiful that now, to those who study it from time to time, it appears as if by the hand not of a youth but of a master of repute, perfected by study and well practiced in that art. It is now in his house, treasured in memory of him by his nephew Leonardo as a rare thing, which indeed it is. That Leonardo, not many years since, had in his house in memory of his uncle a Madonna of marble in bas-relief by the hand of Michelangelo, little more than two feet in height, in which when a lad, at this same time, wishing to counterfeit the manner of Donatello, he acquitted himself so well that it seems as if by Donatello's hand, save that there may be seen in it more grace and more design. That work Leonardo afterwards gave to Duke Cosimo de' Medici, who treasures it as a unique thing.

Now, returning to the garden of the Magnificent Lorenzo: that garden was full of antiques and richly adorned with excellent pictures, all gathered together in that place for their beauty, for study, and for pleasure. Michelangelo always had the keys, and he was much more earnest than the others in his every action, and showed himself always alert, bold, and resolute. He drew for many months from the pictures of Masaccio in the Carmine, where he copied those works with so much judgment, that the craftsmen and all other men were astonished, in such sort that envy grew against him together with his fame. It is said that Torrigiano, after contracting a friendship with him, mocked him, being moved by envy at seeing him more honored than himself and more able in art, and struck him a blow of the fist on the nose with such force, that he broke and crushed it very grievously and marked him for life; on which account Torrigiano was banished from Florence.

When the Magnificent Lorenzo died, Michelangelo returned to his father's house in infinite sorrow at the death of so great a man, the friend of every talent. There he bought a great piece of marble, and from it carved a Hercules eight feet high, which stood for many years in the Palace of the Strozzi; this was esteemed an admirable work, and afterwards, in the year of the siege, it was sent into France to King Francis by Giovan Battista della Palla. It is said that Piero de' Medici, who had been left heir to his father Lorenzo, having long been intimate with Michelangelo, used often to send for him when he wished to buy antiques, such as cameos and other carved stones. One winter, when much snow fell in Florence, he caused him to make in his courtyard a statue of snow, which was very beautiful; and he honored Michelangelo on account of his talents in such a manner, that his father, beginning to see that he was esteemed among the great, clothed him much more honorably than he had been wont to do.

For the Church of S. Spirito in the city of Florence Michelangelo made a Crucifix of wood, which was placed, as it still is, above the lunette of the high altar; doing this to please the Prior, who placed rooms at his disposal, in which he was constantly flaying dead bodies, in order to study the secrets of anatomy, thus beginning to give perfection to the great knowledge of design that he afterwards acquired. It came about that the Medici were driven out of Florence, and a few weeks before that Michelangelo had gone to Bologna, and then to Venice, fearing, as he saw the insolence and bad government of Piero de' Medici, lest some evil thing might befall him from his being the servant of that family; but, not having found any means of living in Venice, he returned to Bologna.

There he had the misfortune to neglect, through lack of thought, when entering by the gate, to learn the countersign for going out again, a command having been issued at that time, as a precaution, at the desire of Messer Giovanni Bentivogli, that all strangers who had not the countersign should be fined fifty Bolognese *lire;* and having fallen into such a predicament, nor having the means to pay, Michelangelo by chance was seen by Messer Giovan Francesco Aldovrandi, one of the Sixteen of the Government, who had compassion on him, and, having made him tell his story, liberated him, and then kept him in his house for more than a year. One day Aldovrandi took him to see the tomb of S. Dominic, made by Giovanni Pisano and then by Maestro Niccolò dell'Arca, sculptors of olden days. In that work there were wanting a S. Petronio and an Angel holding a candelabrum, figures of about two feet, and Aldovrandi asked him if he felt himself able to make them; and he answered Yes. Whereupon he had the marble given to him, and Michelangelo executed them in such a manner, that they are the best figures that are there; and Messer Francesco Aldovrandi caused thirty ducats to be given to him for the two. Michelangelo stayed a little more than a year in Bologna, and he would have stayed there even longer, in order to repay the courtesy of Aldovrandi, who loved him both for his design and because, liking Michelangelo's Tuscan pronunciation in reading, he was pleased to hear from his lips the works of Dante, Petrarch, Boccaccio, and other Tuscan poets. But, since he knew that he was wasting his time, he was glad to return to Florence.

There he made for Lorenzo di Pier Francesco de' Medici a S. Giovannino of marble, and then set himself to make from another piece of marble a Cupid that was sleeping, of the size of life. This, when finished, was shown by means of Baldassarre del Milanese to Lorenzo di Pier Francesco as a beautiful thing, and he, having pronounced the same judgment, said to Michelangelo: "If you were to bury it under ground and then sent it to Rome treated in such a manner as to make it look old, I am certain that it would pass for an antique, and you would thus obtain much more for it than by selling it here." It is said that Michelangelo handled it in such a manner as to make it appear an antique; nor is there any reason to marvel at that, seeing that he had genius enough to do it, and even more. Others maintain that Milanese took it to Rome and buried it in a vineyard that he had there, and then sold it as an antique to Cardinal San Giorgio for two hundred ducats. Others, again, say that Milanese sold to the Cardinal one that Michelangelo had made for him, and that he wrote to Lorenzo di Pier Francesco that he should cause thirty crowns to be given to Michelangelo, saying that he had not received more for the Cupid, and thus deceiving the Cardinal, Lorenzo di Pier Francesco, and Michelangelo; but afterwards, having received information from one who had seen that the boy was fashioned in Florence, the Cardinal contrived to learn the truth by means of a messenger, and so went to work that Milanese's agent had to restore the money and take back the Cupid. That work, having come into the possession of Duke Valentino, was presented by him to the Marchioness of Mantua, who took it to her own country, where it is still to be seen at the present day. This affair did not happen without some censure attaching to Cardinal San Giorgio, in that he did not recognize the value of the work, which consisted in its perfection; for modern works, if only they be excellent, are as good as the ancient. What greater vanity is there than that of those who concern themselves more with the name than the fact? But of that kind of men, who pay more attention to the appearance than to the reality, there are some to be found at any time.

Now this event brought so much reputation to Michelangelo, that he was straightway summoned to Rome and engaged by Cardinal San Giorgio, with whom he stayed nearly a year, although, as one little conversant with our arts, he did not commission Michelangelo to do anything. The talent of Michelangelo was then clearly recognized by a Roman gentleman named Messer Jacopo Galli, an ingenious person, who caused him to make a Cupid of marble as large as life, and then a figure of a Bacchus ten palms high, who has a cup in the right hand, and in the left hand the skin of a tiger, with a bunch of grapes at which a little satyr is trying to nibble.

During his stay in Rome, Michelangelo made so much proficience in the studies of art, that it was a thing incredible to see his exalted thoughts and the difficulties of the manner exercised by him with such supreme facility; to the amazement not only of those who were not accustomed to see such things, but also of those familiar with good work, for the reason that all the works executed up to that time appeared as nothing in comparison with his. These things awakened in Cardinal di San Dionigi, called Cardinal de Rohan, a Frenchman, a desire to leave in a city so famous some worthy memorial of himself by the hand of so rare a craftsman; and he caused him to make a Pietà of marble in the round, which, when finished, was placed in the Chapel of the Vergine Maria della Febbre in S. Pietro.* Among the lovely things to be seen in the work, to say nothing of the divinely beautiful draperies, is the body of Christ; nor let anyone think to see greater beauty of members or more mastery of art in any body, or a nude with more detail in the muscles, veins, and nerves over the framework of the bones, nor yet a corpse more similar than this to a real corpse. Here is perfect sweetness in the expression of the head, harmony in the joints and attachments of the arms, legs, and trunk, and the pulses and veins so wrought, that in truth Wonder herself must marvel that the hand of a craftsman should have been able to execute so divinely and so perfectly, in so short a time, a work so admirable; and it is certainly a miracle that a stone without any shape at the beginning should ever have been reduced to such perfection as Nature is scarcely able to create in the flesh. Such were Michelangelo's love and zeal together in this work,

* St. Peter's.

that he left his name—a thing that he never did again in any other work—written across a girdle that encircles the bosom of Our Lady. And the reason was that one day Michelangelo, entering the place where it was set up, found there a great number of strangers from Lombardy, who were praising it highly, and one of them asked one of the others who had done it, and he answered, "Our Gobbo from Milan." Michelangelo stood silent, but thought it something strange that his labors should be attributed to another; and one night he shut himself in there, and, having brought a little light and his chisels, carved his name upon it.

From this work he acquired very great fame, and although certain persons, rather fools than otherwise, say that he has made Our Lady too young, are these so ignorant as not to know that unspotted virgins maintain and preserve their freshness of countenance a long time without any mark, and that persons afflicted as Christ was do the contrary? That circumstance, therefore, won an even greater increase of glory and fame for his genius than all his previous works.

Letters were written to him from Florence by some of his friends, saying that he should return, because it was not unlikely that he might obtain the spoiled block of marble lying in the Office of Works, which Piero Soderini, who at that time had been made Gonfalonier of the city for life, had very often talked of having executed by Leonardo da Vinci, and was then arranging to give to Maestro Andrea Contucci of Monte Sansovino, an excellent sculptor, who was seeking to obtain it. Now, however difficult it might be to carve a complete figure out of it without adding pieces (for which work of finishing it without adding pieces none of the others, save Buonarroti alone, had courage enough), Michelangelo had felt a desire for it for many years back; and, having come to Florence, he sought to obtain it. This block of marble was eighteen feet high, and from it, unluckily, one Maestro Simone da Fiesole had begun a giant, and he had managed to work so ill, that he had hacked a hole between the legs, and it was altogether misshapen and reduced to ruin, insomuch that the Wardens of Works of S. Maria del Fiore, who had the charge of the undertaking, had placed it on one side without troubling to have it finished; and so it had remained for many years past, and was likely to remain. Michelangelo measured it all anew, considering whether he might be able to carve a reasonable figure from that block by accommodating himself as to the attitude to the marble as it had been left all misshapen by Maestro Simone; and he resolved to ask for it from Soderini and the Wardens, by whom it was granted to him as a thing of no value, they thinking that whatever he might make of it would be better than the state in which it was at that time, seeing that neither in pieces nor in that condition could it be of any use to their building. Whereupon Michelangelo made a model of wax, fashioning in it, as a device for the Palace, a young David with a sling in his hand, to the end that, even as he had defended his people and governed them with justice, so those governing that city might defend her valiantly and govern her justly. And he began it in the Office of Works of S. Maria del Fiore, in which he made an enclosure of planks and masonry, thus surrounding the marble; and, working at it continuously without anyone seeing it, he carried it to perfect completion. The marble had already been spoilt and distorted by Maestro Simone, and in some places it was not enough to satisfy the wishes of Michelangelo for what he would have liked to do with it; and he therefore suffered certain of the first marks of Maestro Simone's chisel to remain on the extremity of the marble, some of which are still to be seen. And truly it was a miracle on the part of Michelangelo to restore to life a thing that was dead.

This statue, when finished, was of such a kind that many disputes took place as to how to transport it to the Piazza della Signoria. Whereupon Giuliano da San Gallo and his brother Antonio made a very strong framework of wood and suspended the figure from it with ropes, to the end that it might not hit against the wood and break to pieces, but might rather keep rocking gently; and they drew it with windlasses over flat beams laid upon the ground, and then set it in place. On the rope which held the figure suspended he made a slipknot which was very easy to undo but tightened as the weight increased, which is a most beautiful and ingenious thing; and I have in my book a drawing of it by his own hand—an admirable, secure, and strong contrivance for suspending weights.

It happened at this time that Piero Soderini, having seen it in place, was well pleased with it, but said to Michelangelo, at a moment when he was retouching it in certain parts, that it seemed to him that the nose of the figure was too thick. Michelangelo noticed that the Gonfalonier was beneath the Giant, and that his point of view prevented him from seeing it properly; but in order to satisfy him he climbed upon the staging, which was against the shoulders, and quickly took up a chisel in his left hand, with a little of the marble dust that lay upon the planks of the staging, and then, beginning to strike lightly with the chisel, let fall the dust little by little, nor changed the nose a whit from what it was before. Then, looking down at the Gonfalonier, who stood watching him, he said, "Look at it now." "I like it better," said the Gonfalonier, "you have given it life." And so Michelangelo came down, laughing to himself at having satisfied that lord, for he had compassion on those who, in order to appear full of knowledge, talk about things of which they know nothing.

When it was built up, and all was finished, he uncovered it, and it cannot be denied that this work has carried off the palm from all other statues, modern or ancient, Greek or Latin; and it may be said that neither the Marforio at Rome, nor the Tiber and the Nile of the Belvedere, nor the Giants of Monte Cavallo, are equal to it in any respect, with such just proportion, beauty and excellence did Michelangelo finish it. He received from Piero Soderini in payment for it four hundred crowns; and it was set in place in the year 1504.

In consequence of the fame that he thereby won as a sculptor, he made for the above-named Gonfalonier a most beautiful David of bronze, which Soderini sent to France; and at this time, also, he began, but did not finish, two medallions of marble—one for Taddeo Taddei, which is now in his house, and another that he began for Bartolommeo Pitti, which was presented by Fra Miniato Pitti of Monte Oliveto, a man with a rare knowledge in cosmography and many other sciences, and particularly in painting, to Luigi Guicciardini, who was much his friend. These works were held to be admirable in their excellence; and at this same time, also, he blocked out a statue of S. Matthew in marble in the Office of Works of S. Maria del Fiore, which statue, rough as it is, reveals its full perfection and teaches sculptors in what manner figures can be carved out of marble without their coming out misshapen, so that it may be possible to go on ever improving them by removing more of the marble with judgment, and also to draw back and change some part, according as the necessity may arise. He also made a medallion in bronze of a Madonna, which he cast in bronze at the request of certain Flemish merchants of the Moscheroni family, persons of high nobility in their own country, who paid him a hundred crowns for it, and sent it to Bruges.

There came to Agnolo Doni, a Florentine citizen and a friend of Michelangelo, who much delighted to have beautiful things both by ancient and by modern craftsmen, a desire to possess some work by Michelangelo; wherefore that master began for him a round picture containing a Madonna, who, kneeling on both knees, has an Infant in her arms and presents Him to Joseph, who receives Him. Here Michelangelo expresses in the turn of the head of the Mother of Christ and in the gaze of her eyes, which she keeps fixed on the supreme beauty of her Son, her marvelous contentment and her lovingness in sharing it with that saintly old man, who receives Him with equal affection, tenderness, and reverence, as may be seen very readily in his countenance, without considering it long. Nor was this enough for Michelangelo, who, the better to show how great was his art, made in the background of his work a number of nudes, some leaning, some standing, and some seated; and with such diligence and finish he executed this work, that without a doubt, of his pictures on panel, which indeed are but few, it is held to be the most finished and the most beautiful work that there is to be found. When it was completed, he sent it covered up to Agnolo's house by a messenger, with a note demanding seventy ducats in payment. It seemed strange to Agnolo, who was a careful person, to spend so much on a picture, although he knew that it was worth more, and he said to the messenger that forty was enough, which he gave to him. Thereupon Michelangelo sent them back to him, with a message to say that he should send back either one hundred ducats or the picture. Then Agnolo, who liked the work, said, "I will give him these seventy," but he was not content; indeed, angered by Agnolo's breach of faith, he demanded the double of what he had asked the first time, so that, if Agnolo wanted the picture, he was forced to send him a hundred and forty.

It happened that while Leonardo da Vinci, that rare painter, was painting in the Great Council Hall, as has been related in his Life, Piero Soderini, who was then Gonfalonier, moved by the great ability that he saw in Michelangelo, caused a part of that Hall to be allotted to him; which was the reason that he executed the other façade in competition with Leonardo, taking as his subject the War of Pisa. To this end Michelangelo was given a room in the Hospital of the Dyers at S. Onofrio, and there he began a vast cartoon, but would never consent that anyone should see it. And this he filled with naked men that were bathing in the River Arno on account of the heat, when suddenly the alarm sounded in the camp, announcing that the enemy were attacking; and, as the soldiers were springing out of the water to dress themselves, there could be seen, depicted by the divine hands of Michelangelo, some hastening to arm themselves in order to give assistance to their companions, others buckling on their cuirasses, many fastening other armor on their bodies, and a vast number beginning the fray and fighting on horseback. There were also many figures in groups, all sketched in various manners, some outlined with charcoal, some drawn with strokes, others stumped in and heightened with lead-white, Michelangelo desiring to show how much he knew in his profession. Wherefore the craftsmen were seized with admiration and astonishment, seeing the perfection of art revealed to them in that drawing by Michelangelo; and some who saw them, after beholding figures so divine, declare that there has never been seen any work, either by his hand or by the hands of others, no matter how great their genius, that can equal it in divine beauty of art. And, in truth, it is likely enough, for the reason that since the time when it was finished and carried to the Sala del Papa with great acclamation from the world of art and extraordinary glory for Michelangelo, all those who studied from that cartoon and drew those figures—as was afterwards the custom in Florence for many years both for strangers and for natives—became persons eminent in art, as we have since seen. The cartoon having thus become a school for craftsmen, it was taken into the Great Upper Hall in the house of the Medici; and this was the reason that it was left with too little caution in the hands of the craftsmen, insomuch that during the illness of Duke Giuliano, while no one was expecting such a thing, it was torn up and divided into many pieces, and scattered over various places.

The name of Michelangelo, by reason of the Pietà that he had made, the Giant in Florence, and the cartoon, had become so famous, that in the year 1503, Pope Alexander VI having died and Julius II having been elected, at which time Michelangelo was about twenty-nine years of age, he was summoned with much graciousness by Julius II, who wished to set him to make his tomb; and for the expenses of the journey a hundred crowns were paid to him by the Pope's representatives. Having made his way to Rome, he spent many months there before he was made to set his hand to any work. But finally the Pope's choice fell on a design that he had made for that tomb, an excellent testimony to the genius of Michelangelo, which in beauty and magnificence, abundance of ornamentation and richness of statuary, surpassed every ancient or imperial tomb. Whereupon Pope Julius took courage, and thus resolved to set his hand to make anew the Church of S. Pietro in Rome, in order to erect the tomb in it. And so Michelangelo set to work with high hopes; and, in order to make a beginning, he went to Carrara to excavate all the marble, with two assistants, receiving a thousand crowns on that account from Alamanno Salviati in Florence. There, in those mountains, he spent eight months without other moneys or supplies; and he had many fantastic ideas of carving great statues in those quarries, in order to leave memorials of himself, as the ancients had done before him, being invited by those masses of stone. Then, having picked out the due quantity of marbles, he caused them to be loaded on board ship at the coast and then conveyed to Rome, where they filled half the Piazza di S. Pietro, round about S. Caterina, and between the church and the corridor that goes to the Castello. In that place Michelangelo had prepared his room for executing the figures and the rest of the tomb; and, to the end that the Pope might be able to come at his convenience to see him at work, he had caused a drawbridge to be constructed between the corridor and that room, which led to a great intimacy between them. But in time these favors brought much annoyance and even persecution upon him, and stirred up much envy against him among his fellow-craftsmen.

Of this work Michelangelo executed during the lifetime and after the death of Julius four statues completely finished and eight only blocked out, as will be related in the proper place; and since the work was designed with extraordinary invention, we will describe here below the plan that he adopted. In order to produce an effect of supreme grandeur, he decided that it should be wholly isolated, so as to be seen from all four sides, each side in one direction being twenty-four feet and each in the other thirty-six, so that the proportions were a square and a half. It had a range of niches running right round the outer side, which were divided one from another by terminal figures clothed from the middle upwards, which with their heads supported the first cornice, and each terminal figure had bound to it, in a strange and bizarre attitude, a naked captive, whose feet rested on a projection of the base. These captives were all provinces subjugated by that Pontiff and rendered obedient to the Apostolic Church; and there were various other statues, likewise bound, of all the noble arts and sciences, which were thus shown to be subject to death no less than was that Pontiff, who made such honorable use of them. On the corners of the first cornice were to go four large figures, the Active and the Contemplative Life, S. Paul, and Moses. The structure rose above the cornice in steps gradually diminishing, with a frieze of scenes in bronze, and with other figures, children and ornaments all around, and at the summit, as a crown to the work, were two figures, one of which was Heaven, who, smiling, was supporting a bier on her shoulder, together with Cybele, the Goddess of Earth, who appeared to be grieving that she was left in a world robbed of all virtue by the death of such a man; and Heaven appeared to be smiling with gladness that his soul had passed to celestial glory. The work was so arranged that one might enter and come out again by the ends of the quadrangular structure, between the niches, and the interior curved in the form of an oval after the manner of a temple, in the center of which was the sarcophagus wherein was to be laid the dead body of that Pope. And, finally, there were to be in this whole work forty statues of marble, without counting the other scenes, children, and ornaments, the carvings covering the cornices, and the other architectural members of the work. Michelangelo ordained, to expedite the labor, that a part of the marbles should be conveyed to Florence, where he intended at times to spend the summer months in order to avoid the malaria of Rome; and there he executed one side of the work in many pieces, complete in every detail. In Rome he finished entirely with his own hand two of the captives, figures divinely beautiful, and other statues, than which none better have ever been seen; but in the end they were never placed in position, and those captives were presented by him to Ruberto Strozzi, when Michelangelo happened to be lying ill in his house; which captives were afterwards sent as presents to King Francis, and they are now at Ecouen in France. Eight statues, likewise, he blocked out in Rome, and in Florence he blocked out five and finished a Victory with a captive beneath, which are now in the possession of Duke Cosimo, having been presented by Michelangelo's nephew, Leonardo, to his Excellency, who has placed the Victory in the Great Hall of his Palace, which was painted by Vasari.

He finished the Moses, a statue in marble ten feet high, which no modern work will ever equal in beauty; and of the ancient statues, also, the same may be said. For, seated in an attitude of great dignity, he rests one arm on the Tables, which he holds with one hand, and with the other he holds his beard, which is long and waving, and carved in the marble in such sort, that the hairs—in which the sculptor finds such difficulty—are wrought with the greatest delicacy, soft, feathery, and detailed in such a manner, that one cannot but believe that his chisel was changed into a pencil. To say nothing of the beauty of the face, which has all the air of a true Saint and most dread Prince, you seem, while you gaze upon it, to wish to demand from him the veil wherewith to cover that face, so resplendent and so dazzling it appears to you, and so well has Michelangelo expressed the divinity that God infused in that most holy countenance. In addition, there are draperies carved out and finished with most beautiful curves of the borders; while the arms with their muscles, and the hands with their bones and nerves, are carried to such a pitch of beauty and perfection, and the legs, knees, and feet are covered with buskins so beautifully fashioned, and every part of the work is so finished, that Moses may be called now more than ever the friend of God, seeing that He has designed to assemble together and prepare his body for the Resurrection before that of any other, by the hands of Michelangelo. Well may the Hebrews continue to go there, as they do every Sabbath, both men and women, like flocks of starlings, to visit and adore that statue; for they will be adoring a thing not human but divine.

Finally all the agreements for this work were made, and the end came into view; and of the four sides one of the smaller ones was afterwards erected in S. Pietro in Vincola. It is said that while Michelangelo was executing the work, there came to the Ripa all the rest of the marbles for the tomb that had remained at Carrara, which were conveyed to the Piazza di S. Pietro, where the others were; and, since it was necessary to pay those who had conveyed them, Michelangelo went, as was his custom, to the Pope. But, his Holiness having on his hands that day some important business concerning Bologna, he returned to his house and paid for those marbles out of his own purse, thinking to have the order for them straightway from his Holiness. He returned another day to speak of them to the Pope, but found difficulty in entering, for one of the grooms told him that he had orders not to admit him, and that he must have patience. A Bishop then said to the groom, "Perhaps you do not know this man?" "Only too well do I know him," answered the groom; "but I am here to do as I am commanded by my superiors and by the Pope." This action displeased Michelangelo, and, considering that it was contrary to what he had experienced before, he said to the Pope's groom that he should tell his Holiness that from that time forward, when he should want him, it would be found that he had gone elsewhere; and then, having returned to his house, at the second hour of the night he set out on post-horses, leaving two servants to sell all the furniture of his house to the Jews and to follow him to Florence, whither he was bound. Having arrived at Poggibonzi, a place in the Florentine territory, and therefore safe, he stopped; and almost immediately five couriers arrived with letters from the Pope to bring him back. Despite their entreaties and also the letters, which ordered him to return to Rome under threat of punishment, he would not listen to a word; but finally the prayers of the couriers induced him to write a few words in reply to his Holiness, asking for pardon, but saying that he would never again return to his presence, since he had caused him to be driven away like a criminal, that his faithful service had not deserved such treatment, and that his Holiness should look elsewhere for someone to serve him.

After arriving at Florence, Michelangelo devoted himself during the three months that he stayed there to finishing the cartoon for the Great Hall, which Piero Soderini, the Gonfalonier, desired that he should carry into execution. During that time there came to the Signoria three Briefs commanding them to send Michelangelo back to Rome: wherefore he, perceiving this vehemence on the part of the Pope, and not trusting him, conceived the idea, so it is said, of going to Constantinople to serve the Grand Turk, who desired to secure him, by means of certain Friars of S. Francis, to build a bridge crossing from Constantinople to Pera. However, he was persuaded by Piero Soderini, although very unwilling, to go to meet the Pope as a person of public importance with the title of Ambassador of the city, to reassure him; and finally the Gonfalonier recommended him to his brother Cardinal Soderini for presentation to the Pope, and sent him off to Bologna, where his Holiness had already arrived from Rome. His departure from Rome is also explained in another way—namely, that the Pope became angered against Michelangelo, who would not allow any of his works to be seen; that Michelangelo suspected his own men, doubting (as happened more than once) that the Pope disguised himself and saw what he was doing on certain occasions when he himself was not at home or at work; and that on one occasion, when the Pope had bribed his assistants to admit him to see the chapel of his uncle Sixtus, which, as was related a little time back, he caused Buonarroti to paint, Michelangelo, having waited in hiding because he suspected the treachery of his assistants, threw planks down at the Pope when he entered the chapel, not considering who it might be, and drove him forth in a fury. It is enough for us to know that in the one way or the other he fell out with the Pope and then became afraid, so that he had to fly from his presence.

Now, having arrived in Bologna, he had scarcely drawn off his riding boots when he was conducted by the Pope's servants to his Holiness, who was in the Palazzo de' Medici; and he was accompanied by a Bishop sent by Cardinal Soderini, because the Cardinal, being ill, was not able to go himself. Having come into the presence of the Pope, Michelangelo knelt down, but his Holiness looked askance at him, as if in anger, and said to him, "Instead of coming yourself to meet us, you have waited for us to come to meet you!" meaning to infer that Bologna is nearer to Florence than Rome. Michelangelo, with a courtly gesture of the hands, but in a firm voice, humbly begged for pardon, saying in excuse that he had acted as he had done in anger, not being able to endure to be driven away so abruptly, but that, if he had erred, his Holiness should once more forgive him. The Bishop who had presented Michelangelo to his Holiness, making excuse for him, said to the Pope that such men were ignorant creatures, that they were worth nothing save in their own art, and that he should freely pardon him. The Pope, seized with anger, belabored the Bishop with a staff that he had in his hand, saying to him, "It is you that are ignorant, who level insults at him that we ourselves do not think of uttering"; and then the Bishop was driven out by the groom with fisticuffs. When he had gone, the Pope, having discharged his anger upon him, gave Michelangelo his benediction; and the master was detained in Bologna with gifts and promises, until finally his Holiness commanded him that he should make a statue of bronze in the likeness of Pope Julius, ten feet in height. In this work he showed most beautiful art in the attitude, which had an effect of much majesty and grandeur, and displayed richness and magnificence in the draperies, and in the countenance, spirit, force, resolution, and stern dignity; and it was placed in a niche over the door of S. Petronio. It is said that while Michelangelo was working at it, he received a visit from Francia, a most excellent goldsmith and painter, who wished to see it, having heard so much praise and fame of him and of his works, and not having seen any of them, so that agents had been set to work to enable him to see it, and he had obtained permission. Whereupon, seeing the artistry of Michelangelo, he was amazed: and then, being asked by Michelangelo what he thought of that figure, Francia answered that it was a most beautiful casting and a fine material. Wherefore Michelangelo, considering that he had praised the bronze rather than the workmanship, said to him, "I owe the same obligation to Pope Julius, who has given it to me, that you owe to the apothecaries who give you your colors for painting"; and in his anger, in the presence of all the gentlemen there, he declared that Francia was a fool. In the same connection, when a son of Francia's came before him and was announced as a very beautiful youth, Michelangelo said to him, "Your father's living figures are finer than those that he paints."

Michelangelo had the statue finished in clay before the Pope departed from Bologna for Rome, and his Holiness, having gone to see it, but not knowing what was to be placed in the left hand, and seeing the right hand raised in a proud gesture, asked whether it was pronouncing a benediction or a curse. Michelangelo answered that it was admonishing the people of Bologna to mind their behavior, and asked his Holiness to decide whether he should place a book in the left hand; and he said, "Put a sword there, for I know nothing of letters." The Pope left a thousand crowns in the bank of M.

Anton Maria da Lignano for the completion of the statue, and at the end of the sixteen months that Michelangelo toiled over the work it was placed on the frontispiece in the façade of the Church of S. Petronio, as has been related; and we have also spoken of its size. This statue was destroyed by the Bentivogli, and the bronze was sold to Duke Alfonso of Ferrara, who made with it a piece of artillery called La Giulia; saving only the head, which is to be found in his *guardaroba*.

When the Pope had returned to Rome and Michelangelo was at work on the statue, Bramante, the friend and relative of Raphael of Urbino, and for that reason little the friend of Michelangelo, perceiving that the Pope held in great favor and estimation the works that he executed in sculpture, was constantly planning with Raphael in Michelangelo's absence to remove from the mind of his Holiness the idea of causing Michelangelo, after his return, to devote himself to finishing his tomb; saying that for a man to prepare himself a tomb during his own lifetime was an evil augury and a hurrying on of his death. And they persuaded his Holiness that on the return of Michelangelo, he should cause him to paint in memory of his uncle Sixtus the vaulting of the chapel that he had built in the Palace. In this manner it seemed possible to Bramante and other rivals of Michelangelo to draw him away from sculpture, in which they saw him to be perfect, and to plunge him into despair, they thinking that if they compelled him to paint, he would do work less worthy of praise, since he had no experience of colors in fresco, and that he would prove inferior to Raphael, and, even if he did succeed in the work, in any case it would make him angry against the Pope; so that in either event they would achieve their object of getting rid of him. And so, when Michelangelo returned to Rome, the Pope was not disposed at that time to finish his tomb, and requested him to paint the vaulting of the chapel. Michelangelo, who desired to finish the tomb, believing the vaulting of that chapel to be a great and difficult labor, and considering his own want of practice in colors, sought by every means to shake such a burden from his shoulders, and proposed Raphael for the work. But the more he refused, the greater grew the desire of the Pope, who was headstrong in his undertakings, and, in addition, was being spurred on anew by the rivals of Michelangelo, and especially by Bramante; so that his Holiness, who was quick-tempered, was on the point of becoming enraged with Michelangelo. Whereupon Michelangelo, perceiving that his Holiness was determined in the matter, resolved to do it; and the Pope commanded Bramante to erect the scaffolding from which the vaulting might be painted. Bramante made it all supported by ropes, piercing the vaulting; which having perceived, Michelangelo inquired of Bramante how he was to proceed to fill up the holes when he had finished painting it, and he replied that he would think of that afterwards, and that it could not be done otherwise. Michelangelo recognized that Bramante was either not very competent for such a work or else little his friend, and he went to the Pope and said to him that the scaffolding was not satisfactory, and that Bramante had not known how to make it; and the Pope answered, in the presence of Bramante, that he should make it after his own fashion. And so he commanded that it should be erected upon props so as not to touch the walls, a method of making scaffoldings for vaults that he taught afterwards to Bramante and others, whereby many fine works have been executed. Thus he enabled a poor creature of a carpenter, who rebuilt the scaffolding, to dispense with so many of the ropes, that, after selling them (for Michelangelo gave them to him), he made up a dowry for his daughter.

He then set his hand to making the cartoons for that vaulting; and the Pope decided, also, that the walls which the masters before him in the time of Sixtus had painted should be scraped clean, and decreed that he should have fifteen thousand ducats for the whole cost of the work; which price was fixed through Giuliano da San Gallo. Thereupon, forced by the magnitude of the undertaking to resign himself to obtaining assistance, Michelangelo sent for men to Florence; and he determined to demonstrate in such a work that those who had painted there before him were destined to be vanquished by his labors, and also resolved to show to the modern craftsmen how to draw and paint. Having begun the cartoons, he finished them; and the circumstances of the work spurred him to soar to great heights, both for his own fame and for the welfare of art. And then, desiring to paint it in fresco colors, and not having any experience of them, there came from Florence to Rome certain of his friends who were painters, to the end that they might give him assistance in such a work, and also that he might learn from them the method of working in fresco, in which some of them were well-practiced; and among these were Granaccio, Giuliano Bugiardini, Jacopo di Sandro, the elder Indaco, Agnolo di Donnino, and Aristotile. Having made a commencement with the work, he caused them to begin some things as specimens; but, perceiving that their efforts were very far from what he desired, and not being satisfied with them, he resolved one morning to throw to the ground everything that they had done. Then, shutting himself up in the chapel, he would never open to them, nor even allowed himself to be seen by them when he was at home. And so, when the jest appeared to them to be going too far, they resigned themselves to it and returned in shame to Florence. Thereupon Michelangelo, having made arrangements to paint the whole work by himself, carried it well on the way to completion with the utmost solicitude, labor, and study; nor would he ever let himself be seen, lest he should give any occasion to compel him to show it, so that the desire in the minds of everyone to see it grew greater every day.

Pope Julius was always very desirous to see any undertakings that he was having carried out, and therefore became more eager than ever to see this one, which was hidden from him. And so one day he resolved to go to see it, but was not admitted, for Michelangelo would never have consented to show it to him; out of which affair arose the quarrel that has been described, when he had to depart from Rome because he would not show his work to the Pope. Now, when a third of the work was finished (as I ascertained from him in order to clear up all doubts), it began to throw out certain spots of mould, one winter that the north wind was blowing. The reason of this was that the Roman lime, which is made of travertine and white in color, does not dry very readily, and, when mixed with pozzolana, which is of a tawny color, makes a dark mixture which, when soft, is very watery; and when the wall has been well soaked, it often breaks out into an efflorescence in the drying; and thus this salt efflorescence of moisture came out in many places, but in time the air consumed it. Michelangelo was in despair over this, and was unwilling to continue the work, asking the Pope to excuse him, since he was not succeeding; but his Holiness sent Giuliano da San Gallo to see him, and he, having told him whence the defect arose and taught him how to remove the spots of mould, encouraged him to persevere.

Now, when he had finished half of it, the Pope, who had subsequently gone to see it several times (mounting certain ladders with the assistance of Michelangelo), insisted that it should be thrown open, for he was hasty and impatient by nature, and could not wait for it to be completely finished and to receive, as the saying is, the final touch. No sooner was it thrown open than all Rome was drawn to see it, and the Pope was the first, not having the patience to wait until the dust caused by the dismantling of the scaffolding had settled. Thereupon Raphael of Urbino, who was very excellent in imitation, after seeing it straightway changed his manner, and without losing any time, in order to display his ability, painted the Prophets and Sibyls; and at the same time Bramante sought to have the other half of the chapel entrusted by the Pope to Raphael. Which hearing, Michelangelo complained of Bramante, and revealed to the Pope without any reserve many faults both in his life and in his architectural works; of which last, in the building of S. Pietro, as was seen afterwards, Michelangelo became the corrector. But the Pope, recognizing more clearly every day the ability of Michelangelo, desired that he should continue the work, judging, after he had seen it uncovered, that he could make the second half considerably better; and so in twenty months he carried that work to perfect completion by himself alone, without the assistance even of anyone to grind his colors. Michelangelo complained at times that on account of the haste that the Pope imposed on him he was not able to finish it in his own fashion, as he would have liked; for his Holiness was always asking him importunately when he would finish it. On one occasion, among others, he replied, "It will be finished when I shall have satisfied myself in the matter of art." "But it is our pleasure," answered the Pope, "that you should satisfy us in our desire to have it done quickly"; and he added, finally, that if Michelangelo did not finish the work quickly he would have him thrown down from the scaffolding. Whereupon Michelangelo, who feared and had good reason to fear the anger of the Pope, straightway finished all that was wanting, without losing any time, and, after taking down the rest of the scaffolding, threw it open to view on the morning of All Saints' Day, when the Pope went into the chapel to sing Mass, to the great satisfaction of the whole city. Michelangelo desired to retouch some parts *"a secco,"* as the old masters had done on the scenes below, painting backgrounds, draperies, and skies in ultramarine, and ornaments in gold in certain places, to the end that this might produce greater richness and a more striking effect; and the Pope, having learned that this ornamentation was wanting, and hearing the work praised so much by all who had seen it, wished him to finish it; but, since it would have been too long a labor for Michelangelo to rebuild the scaffolding, it was left as it was. His Holiness, often seeing Michelangelo, would say to him that the chapel should be enriched with colors and gold, since it looked poor. And Michelangelo would answer familiarly,

"Holy Father, in those times men did not bedeck themselves with gold, and those that are painted there were never very rich, but rather holy men, on which account they despised riches."

For this work Michelangelo was paid by the Pope three thousand crowns on several occasions, of which he had to spend twenty-five on colors. The work was executed with very great discomfort to himself, from his having to labor with his face upwards, which so impaired his sight that for a time, which was not less than several months, he was not able to read letters or look at drawings save with his head backwards. And to this I can bear witness, having painted five vaulted chambers in the great apartments in the Palace of Duke Cosimo, when, if I had not made a chair on which I could rest my head and lie down at my work, I would never have finished it; even so, it has so ruined my sight and injured my head, that I still feel the effects, and I am astonished that Michelangelo endured all that discomfort so well. But in truth, becoming more and more kindled every day by his fervor in the work, and encouraged by the proficience and improvement that he made, he felt no fatigue and cared nothing for discomfort.

The distribution of this work is contrived with six pendentives on either side, with one in the center of the walls at the foot and at the head, and on these he painted Sibyls and Prophets, twelve feet in height; in the center of the vault the history of the world from the Creation down to the Deluge and the Drunkenness of Noah, and in the lunettes all the Genealogy of Christ. In these compartments he used no rule of perspectives in foreshortening, nor is there any fixed point of view, but he accommodated the compartments to the figures rather than the figures to the compartments, being satisfied to execute those figures, both the nude and the draped, with the perfection of design, so that another such work has never been and never can be done, and it is scarcely possible even to imitate his achievement.

Besides this, in order to display the perfection of art and also the greatness of God, he painted in a scene God dividing Light from Darkness, wherein may be seen His Majesty as He rests self-sustained with the arms outstretched, and reveals both love and power. In the second scene he depicted with most beautiful judgment and genius God creating the Sun and Moon, in which He is supported by many little Angels, in an attitude sublime and terrible by reason of the foreshortenings in the arms and legs. In the same scene Michelangelo depicted Him after the Blessing of the Earth and the Creation of the Animals, when He is seen on that vaulting as a figure flying in foreshortening; and wherever you go throughout the chapel, it turns constantly and faces in every direction. So, also, in the next scene, where He is dividing the Water from the Earth; and both these are very beautiful figures and refinements of genius such as could be produced only by the divine hands of Michelangelo. He then went on, beyond that scene, to the Creation of Adam, wherein he figured God as borne by a group of nude Angels of tender age, which appear to be supporting not one figure only, but the whole weight of the world; this effect being produced by the venerable majesty of His form and by the manner of the movement with which He embraces some of the little Angels with one arm, as if to support Himself, and with the other extends the right hand toward Adam, a figure of such a kind in its beauty, in the attitude, and in the outlines, that it appears as if newly fashioned by the first and supreme Creator rather than by the brush and design of a mortal man. Beyond this, in another scene, he made God taking our mother Eve from Adam's side, in which may be seen those two nude figures, one as it were dead from his being the thrall of sleep, and the other become alive and filled with animation by the blessing of God. Very clearly do we see from the brush of this most gifted craftsman the difference that there is between sleep and wakefulness, and how firm and stable, speaking humanly, the Divine Majesty may appear.

Next to this there follows the scene when Adam, at the persuasion of a figure half woman and half serpent, brings death upon himself and upon us by the Forbidden Fruit; and there, also, are seen Adam and Eve driven from Paradise. In the figure of the Angel is shown with nobility and grandeur the execution of the mandate of a wrathful Lord, and in the attitude of Adam the sorrow for his sin together with the fear of death, as likewise in the woman may be seen shame, abasement, and the desire to implore pardon, as she presses the arms to the breast, clasps the hands palm to palm, and sinks the neck into the bosom, and also turns the head toward the Angel, having more fear of the justice of God than hope in His mercy. Nor is there less beauty in the story of the sacrifice of Cain and Abel, wherein are some who are bringing up the wood, some who are bent down and blowing at the fire, and others who are cutting the throat of the victim; which certainly is all executed with not less consideration and attention than the others. He showed the same art and the same judgment in the story of the Deluge, wherein are seen various deaths of men, who, terrified by the horror of those days, are striving their utmost in different ways to save their lives. For in the faces of those figures may be seen life a prey to death, not less than fear, terror, and disregard of everything; and compassion is visible in many that are assisting one another to climb to the summit of a rock in search of safety, among them one who, having embraced one half dead, is striving his utmost to save him, than which Nature herself could show nothing better. Nor can I tell how well expressed is the story of Noah, who, drunk with wine, is sleeping naked, and has before him one son who is laughing at him and two who are covering him up—a scene incomparable in the beauty of the artistry, and not to be surpassed save by himself alone.

Then, as if his genius had taken courage from what it had achieved up to that time, it soared upwards and proved itself even greater in the five Sibyls and seven Prophets that are painted there, each ten feet or more in height. In all these are well-varied attitudes, beautiful draperies, and different vestments; and all, in a word, are wrought with marvelous invention and judgment, and to him who can distinguish their expressions they appear divine. Jeremiah is seen with the legs crossed, holding one hand to the beard, and resting that elbow on the knee; the other hand rests in his lap, and he has the head bowed in a manner that clearly demonstrates the melancholy, cogitation, anxious thought and bitterness of soul that his people cause him. Equally fine, also, are two little children that are behind him, and likewise the first Sibyl, beyond him in the direction of the door, in which figure, wishing to depict old age, in addition to enveloping her in draperies, he sought to show that her blood is already frozen by time; besides which, since her sight has become feeble, he has made her as she reads bring the book very close to her eyes. Beyond this figure follows the Prophet Ezekiel, an old man, who has a grace and a movement that are most beautiful, and is much enveloped in draperies, while with one hand he holds a roll of prophecies, and with the other uplifted, turning his head, he appears to be about to utter great and lofty words; and behind him he has two boys who hold his books. Next to him follows a Sibyl, who is doing the contrary to the Erythraean Sibyl that we described above, for, holding her book away from her, she seeks to turn a page, while with one knee over the other she sits sunk within herself, pondering gravely over what she is to write; and then a boy who is behind her, blowing on a burning brand, lights her lamp. This figure is of extraordinary beauty in the expression of the face, in the headdress, and in the arrangement of the draperies; besides which she has the arms nude, which are equal to the other parts. Beyond this Sibyl he painted the Prophet Joel, who, sunk within himself, has taken a scroll and reads it with great attention and appreciation: and from his aspect it is so clearly evident that he is satisfied with that which he finds written there, that he looks like a living person who has applied his thoughts intently to some matter. Over the door of the chapel, likewise, he placed the aged Zaccharias, who, seeking through his written book for something that he cannot find, stands with one leg on high and the other low; and, while the ardor of the search after something that he cannot find causes him to stand thus, he takes no notice of the discomfort that he suffers in such a posture. This figure is very beautiful in its aspect of old age, and somewhat full in form, and has draperies with few folds, which are most beautiful. In addition, there is another Sibyl, who is next in the direction of the altar on the other side, displaying certain writings, and, with her boys in attendance, is no less worthy of praise than are the others. Beyond her is the Prophet Isaiah, who, wholly absorbed in his own thoughts, has the legs crossed over one another, and, holding one hand in his book to mark the place where he was reading, has placed the elbow of the other arm upon the book, with the cheek pressed against the hand; and, being called by one of the boys that he has behind him, he turns only the head, without disturbing himself otherwise. Whoever shall consider his countenance, shall see touches truly taken from Nature herself, the true mother of art, and a figure which, when well studied in every part, can teach in liberal measure all the precepts of the good painter. Beyond this Prophet is an aged Sibyl of great beauty, who, as she sits, studies from a book in an attitude of extraordinary grace, not to speak of the beautiful attitudes of the two boys that are about her. Nor may any man think with all his imaginings to be able to attain to the excellence of the figure of a youth representing Daniel, who, writing in a great book, is taking certain things from other writings and copying them with extraordinary attention; and as a support for the weight of the book Michelangelo painted a boy between his legs, who is upholding it while he writes, all which no brush held by a human hand, however skilful, will ever be able to equal. And so, also, with the beautiful figure of the Libyan Sibyl, who, having written a great volume drawn from many books, is in an attitude of womanly grace, as if about to rise to her feet; and in one and the same movement she makes as if to rise and to close the book—a thing most difficult, not to say impossible, for any other but the master of the work.

And what can be said of the four scenes at the corners, on the spandrels of that vaulting; in one of which David, with all the boyish strength that he can exert in the conquest of a giant, is cutting off his head, bringing marvel to the faces of some soldiers who are about the camp. And so, also, do men marvel at the beautiful attitudes that Michelangelo depicted in the story of Judith, at the opposite corner, in which may be seen the trunk of Holofernes, robbed of life but still quivering, while Judith is placing the lifeless head in a basket on the head of her old serving-woman, who, being tall in stature, is stooping to the end that Judith may be able to reach up to her and adjust the weight well; and the servant, while upholding the burden with her hands, seeks to conceal it, and, turning her head toward the trunk, which, although dead, draws up an arm and a leg and makes a noise in the tent, she shows in her expression fear of the camp and terror of the dead body—a picture truly full of thought. But more beautiful and more divine than this or any of the others is the story of the Serpents of Moses, which is above the left-hand corner of the altar; for the reason that in it is seen the havoc wrought by death, the rain of serpents, their stings and their bites, and there may also be perceived the serpent of brass that Moses placed upon a pole. In this scene are shown vividly the various deaths that those die who are robbed of all hope by the bite of the serpents, and one sees the deadly venom causing vast numbers to die in terror and convulsions, to say nothing of the rigid legs and twisted arms of those who remain in the attitudes in which they were struck down, unable to move, and the marvelous heads that are shrieking and thrown backwards in despair. Not less beautiful than all these are those who, having looked upon the serpent, and feeling their pains alleviated by the sight of it, are gazing on it with profound emotion; and among them is a woman who is supported by another figure in such a manner that the assistance rendered to her by him who upholds her is no less manifest than her pressing need in such sudden alarm and hurt. In the next scene, likewise, in which Ahasuerus, reclining in a bed, is reading his chronicles, are figures of great beauty, and among them three figures eating at a table, which represent the council that was held for the deliverance of the Jewish people and the hanging of Haman. The figure of Haman was executed by Michelangelo in an extraordinary manner of foreshortening, for he counterfeited the trunk that supports his person, and that arm which comes forward, not as painted things but as real and natural, standing out in relief, and so also that leg which he stretches outwards and other parts that bend inwards: which figure, among all that are beautiful and difficult, is certainly the most beautiful and the most difficult.

It would take too long to describe all the beautiful fantasies in the different actions in the part where there is all the Genealogy of the Fathers, beginning with the sons of Noah, to demonstrate the Genealogy of Jesus Christ, in which figures is a variety of things that it is not possible to enumerate, such as draperies, expressions of heads, and an infinite number of novel and extraordinary fancies, all most beautifully considered. Nothing there but is carried into execution with genius: all the figures there are masterly and most beautifully foreshortened, and everything that you look at is divine and beyond praise. And who will not be struck dumb with admiration at the sight of the sublime force of Jonah, the last figure in the chapel, wherein by the power of art the vaulting, which in fact springs forward in accord with the curve of the masonry, yet, being in appearance pushed back by that figure, which bends inwards, seems as if straight, and, vanquished by the art of design with its lights and shades, even appears in truth to recede inwards?

When the work was thrown open, the whole world could be heard running up to see it, and, indeed, it was such as to make everyone astonished and dumb. Wherefore the Pope, having been magnified by such a result and encouraged in his heart to undertake even greater enterprises, rewarded Michelangelo liberally with money and rich gifts: and Michelangelo would say at times of the extraordinary favors that the Pope conferred upon him, that they showed that he fully recognized his worth, and that, if by way of proving his friendliness he sometimes played him strange tricks, he would heal the wound with signal gifts and favors. As when, Michelangelo once demanding from him leave to go to Florence for the festival of S. John, and asking money for that purpose, the Pope said, "Well, but when will you have this chapel finished?" "As soon as I can, Holy Father." The Pope, who had a staff in his hand, struck Michelangelo, saying, "As soon as I can! As soon as I can! I will soon make you finish it!" Whereupon Michelangelo went back to his house to get ready to go to Florence; but the Pope straightway sent Cursio, his Chamberlain, to Michelangelo with five hundred crowns to pacify him, fearing lest he might commit one of his caprices, and Cursio made excuse for the Pope, saying that such things were favors and marks of affection. And Michelangelo, who knew the Pope's nature and, after all, loved him, laughed over it all, for he saw that in the end everything turned to his profit and advantage, and that the Pontiff would do anything to keep a man such as himself as his friend.

When the chapel was finished, before the Pope was overtaken by death, his Holiness commanded Cardinal Santiquattro and Cardinal Aginense, his nephew, in the event of his death, that they should cause his tomb to be finished, but on a smaller scale than before. To this work Michelangelo set himself once again, and so made a beginning gladly with the tomb, hoping to carry it once and for all to completion without so many impediments; but he had from it ever afterwards vexations, annoyances, and travails, more than from any other work that he did in all his life, and it brought upon him for a long time, in a certain sense, the accusation of being ungrateful to that Pope, who had so loved and favored him. Thus, when he had returned to the tomb, and was working at it continually, and also at times preparing designs from which he might be able to execute the façades of the chapel, envious Fortune decreed that that memorial, which had been begun with such perfection, should be left unfinished. For at that time there took place the death of Pope Julius, and the work was abandoned on account of the election of Pope Leo X, who, being no less splendid than Julius in mind and spirit, had a desire to leave in his native city (of which he was the first Pope), in memory of himself and of a divine craftsman who was his fellow-citizen, such marvels as only a mighty Prince like himself could undertake. Wherefore he gave orders that the façade of S. Lorenzo, a church built by the Medici family in Florence, should be erected for him, which was the reason that the work of the tomb of Julius was left unfinished; and he demanded advice and designs from Michelangelo, and desired that he should be the head of that work. Michelangelo made all the resistance that he could, pleading that he was pledged in the matter of the tomb to Santiquattro and Aginense, but the Pope answered him that he was not to think of that, and that he himself had already seen to it and contrived that Michelangelo should be released by them; promising, also, that he should be able to work in Florence, as he had already begun to do, at the figures for that tomb. All this was displeasing to the Cardinals, and also to Michelangelo, who went off in tears.

Many and various were the discussions that arose on this subject, on the ground that such a work as that façade should have been distributed among several persons, and in the matter of the architecture many craftsmen flocked to Rome to see the Pope, and made designs; Baccio d'Agnolo, Antonio da San Gallo, Andrea Sansovino and Jacopo Sansovino, and the gracious Raphael of Urbino, who was afterwards summoned to Florence for that purpose at the time of the Pope's visit. Thereupon Michelangelo resolved to make a model and not to accept anyone beyond himself as his guide or superior in the architecture of such a work; but this refusal of assistance was the reason that neither he nor any other executed the work, and that those masters returned in despair to their customary pursuits. Michelangelo, going to Carrara, had an order authorizing that a thousand crowns should be paid to him by Jacopo Salviati; but on his arrival Jacopo was shut up in his room on business with some citizens, and Michelangelo, refusing to wait for an audience, departed without saying a word and went straightway to Carrara. Jacopo heard of Michelangelo's arrival, and, not finding him in Florence, sent him a thousand crowns to Carrara. The messenger demanded that Michelangelo should write him a receipt, to which he answered that the money was for the expenses of the Pope and not for his own interest, and that the messenger might take it back, but that he was not accustomed to write out quittances or receipts for others; whereupon the other returned in alarm to Jacopo without a receipt.

While Michelangelo was at Carrara and was having marble quarried for the tomb of Julius, thinking at length to finish it, no less than for the façade, a letter was written to him saying that Pope Leo had heard that in the mountains of Pietrasanta near Seravezza, in the Florentine dominion, at the summit of the highest mountain, which is called Monte Altissimo, there were marbles of the same excellence and beauty as those of Carrara. This Michelangelo already knew, but it seems that he would not take advantage of it because of his friendship with the Marchese Alberigo, Lord of Carrara, and, in order to do him a good service, chose to quarry those of Carrara rather than those of Seravezza; or it may have been that he judged it to be a long undertaking and likely to waste much time, as indeed it did. However, he was forced to go to Seravezza, although he pleaded in protest that it would be more difficult and costly, as in truth it was, especially at the beginning, and, moreover, that the report about the marble was perhaps not true; but for all that the Pope would not hear a word of objection. Thereupon it was decided to make a road for several miles through the mountains, breaking down rocks with hammers and pickaxes to obtain a level, and sinking piles in the marshy places; and there Michelangelo spent many years in executing the wishes of the Pope. Finally five columns of the proper size were excavated, one of which is on the Piazza di S. Lorenzo in Florence, and the others are on the seashore. And for this reason the Marchese Alberigo, who saw his business ruined, became the bitter enemy of Michelangelo, who was not to blame. Michelangelo, in addition to these columns, excavated many other marbles there, which are still in the quarries, abandoned there for more than thirty years. But at the present day Duke Cosimo has given orders for the road to be finished, of which there are still two miles to make over very difficult ground, for the transportation of these marbles, and also a road from another quarry of excellent marble that was discovered at that time by Michelangelo, in order to be able to finish many beautiful undertakings.

Michelangelo having gone back to Florence, he lost much time now in one thing and now in another. And he made at that time for the Palace of the Medici a model for the knee-shaped windows of those rooms that are at the corner, where Giovanni da Udine adorned the chamber in stucco and painting, which is a much extolled work; and he caused to be made for them by the goldsmith Piloto, but under his own direction, those jalousies of perforated copper, which are certainly admirable things. Michelangelo consumed many years in quarrying marbles, although it is true that while they were being excavated he made models of wax and other things for the work. But this undertaking was delayed so long, that the money assigned by the Pope for the purpose was spent on the war in Lombardy; and at the death of Leo the work was left unfinished, nothing being accomplished save the laying of a foundation in front to support it, and the transportation of a large column of marble from Carrara to the Piazza di S. Lorenzo.

The death of Leo completely dismayed the craftsmen and the arts both in Rome and in Florence; and while Adrian VI was alive Michelangelo gave his attention in Florence to the tomb of Julius. But after the death of Adrian, Clement VII was elected, who was no less desirous than Leo and his other predecessors to leave his fame established by the arts of architecture, sculpture, and painting. At this time, which was the year 1525, Giorgio Vasari was taken as a little boy to Florence by the Cardinal of Cortona, and placed with Michelangelo to learn art. But Michelangelo was then summoned to Rome by Pope Clement VII, who had made a beginning with the library of S. Lorenzo and also the new sacristy, in which he proposed to place the marble tombs that he was having made for his forefathers; and he resolved that Vasari should go to work with Andrea del Sarto until he should himself be free again, and went in person to Andrea's workshop to present him.

Michelangelo departed for Rome in haste, harassed once again by Francesco Maria, Duke of Urbino, the nephew of Pope Julius, who complained of him, saying that he had received sixteen thousand crowns for the above-named tomb, yet was living a life of pleasure in Florence; and he threatened in his anger that, if Michelangelo did not give his attention to the work, he would make him rue it. Having arrived in Rome, Pope Clement, who wished to make use of him, advised him to draw up his accounts with the agents of the Duke, believing that after all that he had done he must be their creditor rather than their debtor; and so the matter rested. After discussing many things together, they resolved to finish completely the library and new sacristy of S. Lorenzo in Florence. Michelangelo therefore departed from Rome, and raised the cupola that is now to be seen, causing it to be wrought in various orders of composition; and he had a ball with seventy-two faces made by the goldsmith Piloto, which is very beautiful. It happened, while Michelangelo was raising the cupola, that he was asked by some friends, "Should you not make your lantern very different from that of Filippo Brunelleschi?" And he answered them, "Different it can be made with ease, but better, no." He made four tombs in that sacristy, to adorn the walls and to contain the bodies of the fathers of the two Popes, the elder Lorenzo and his brother Giuliano, and those of Giuliano, the brother of Leo, and of Duke Lorenzo, his nephew. And since he wished to execute the work in imitation of the old sacristy that Filippo Brunelleschi had built, but with another manner of ornamentation, he made in it an ornamentation in a composite order, in a more varied and more original manner than any other master at any time, whether ancient or modern, had been able to achieve, for in the novelty of the beautiful cornices, capitals, bases, doors, tabernacles, and tombs, he departed not a little from the work regulated by measure, order, and rule, which other men did according to a common use and after Vitruvius and the antiquities, to which he would not conform. That license has done much to give courage to those who have seen his methods to set themselves to imitate him, and new fantasies have since been seen which have more of the grotesque than of reason or rule in their ornamentation. Wherefore the craftsmen owe him an infinite and everlasting obligation, he having broken the bonds and chains by reason of which they had always followed a beaten path in the execution of their works. And even more did he demonstrate and seek to make known such a method afterwards in the library of S. Lorenzo, at the same place; in the beautiful distribution of the windows, in the pattern of the ceiling, and in the marvelous entrance of the vestibule. Nor was there ever seen a more resolute grace, both in the whole and in the parts, as in the consoles, tabernacles, and cornices, nor any staircase more commodious; in which last he made such bizarre breaks in the outlines of the steps, and departed so much from the common use of others, that everyone was amazed.

At this time he sent his disciple Pietro Urbano of Pistoia

to Rome to carry to completion a nude Christ holding the Cross, a most admirable figure, which was placed beside the principal chapel of the Minerva, at the commission of Messer Antonio Metelli. About the same time there took place the sack of Rome and the expulsion of the Medici from Florence; by reason of which upheaval those who governed the city of Florence resolved to rebuild the fortifications, and therefore made Michelangelo Commissary General over all that work. Whereupon he made designs and caused fortifications to be built for several parts of the city, and finally encircled the hill of San Miniato with bastions, which he made not with sods of earth, wood, and bundles of brushwood, as is generally done, but with a stout base of chestnut, oak, and other good materials interwoven, and in place of sods he took unbaked bricks made with tow and the dung of cattle, squared with very great diligence. And for this reason he was sent by the Signoria of Florence to Ferrara, to inspect the fortifications of Duke Alfonso I, and so also his artillery and munitions; where he received many courtesies from that lord, who besought him that he should do something for him with his own hand at his leisure, and Michelangelo promised that he would. After his return, he was continually engaged in fortifying the city, but, although he was thus occupied, nevertheless he kept working at a picture of a Leda for that Duke, painted with his own hand in distemper colors, which was a divine thing, as will be related in the proper place; also continuing the statues for the tombs of S. Lorenzo, but in secret. At this time Michelangelo spent some six months on the hill of San Miniato in order to press on the fortification of that hill, because if the enemy became master of it, the city was lost; and so he pursued these undertakings with the utmost diligence.

At this same time he continued the work in the abovementioned sacristy, in which were seven statues that were left partly finished and partly not. With these, and with the architectural inventions of the tombs, it must be confessed that he surpassed every man in these three professions; to which testimony is borne by the statues of marble, blocked out and finished by him, which are to be seen in that place. One is Our Lady, who is in a sitting attitude, with the right leg crossed over the left and one knee placed upon the other, and the Child, with the thighs astride the leg that is uppermost, turns in a most beautiful attitude toward His Mother, hungry for her milk, and she, while holding Him with one hand and supporting herself with the other, bends forward to give it to Him; and although the figure is not equal in every part, and it was left rough and showing the marks of the gradine, yet with all its imperfections there may be recognized in it the full perfection of the work. Even more did he cause everyone to marvel by the circumstance that in making the tombs of Duke Giuliano and Duke Lorenzo de' Medici he considered that earth alone was not enough to give them honorable burial in their greatness, and desired that all the phases of the world should be there, and that their sepulchers should be surrounded and covered by four statues; wherefore he gave to one Night and Day, and to the other Dawn and Twilight; which statues, most beautifully wrought in form, in attitude, and in the masterly treatment of the muscles, would suffice, if that art were lost, to restore her to her pristine luster. There, among the other statues, are the two Captains, armed; one the pensive Duke Lorenzo, the very presentment of wisdom, with legs so beautiful and so well wrought, that there is nothing better to be seen by mortal eye; and the other is Duke Giuliano, so proud a figure, with the head, the throat, the setting of the eyes, the profile of the nose, the opening of the mouth, and the hair all so divine, to say nothing of the hands, arms, knees, feet, and, in short, every other thing that he carved therein, that the eye can never be weary or have its fill of gazing at them; and, of a truth, whoever studies the beauty of the buskins and the cuirass, believes it to be celestial rather than mortal. But what shall I say of the Dawn, a nude woman, who is such as to awaken melancholy in the soul and to render impotent the style of sculpture? In her attitude may be seen her effort, as she rises, heavy with sleep, and raises herself from her downy bed; and it seems that in awakening she has found the eyes of that great Duke closed in death, so that she is agonized with bitter grief, weeping in her own unchangeable beauty in token of her great sorrow. And what can I say of the Night, a statue not rare only, but unique? Who is there who has ever seen in that art in any age, ancient or modern, statues of such a kind? For in her may be seen not only the stillness of one sleeping, but the grief and melancholy of one who has lost a great and honored possession; and we must believe that this is that night of darkness that obscures all those who thought for some time, I will not say to surpass, but to equal Michelangelo in sculpture and design. In that statue is infused all the somnolence that is seen in sleeping forms; wherefore many verses in Latin and rhymes in the vulgar tongue were written in her praise by persons of great learning, such as these, of which the author is not known—

> The Night that here thou seest, in graceful guise
> Thus sleeping, by an Angel's hand was carved
> In this pure stone; but sleeping, still she lives.
> Awake her if thou doubtest, and she'll speak.

To which Michelangelo, speaking in the person of Night, answered thus—

> Happy am I to sleep, and still more blest
> To be of stone, while grief and shame endure;
> To see, nor feel, is now my utmost hope,
> Wherefore speak softly, and awake me not.

Truly, if the enmity that there is between Fortune and Genius, between the envy of the one and the excellence of the other, had not prevented such a work from being carried to completion, Art was like to prove to Nature that she surpassed her by a great measure in every conception.

While Michelangelo was laboring with the greatest solicitude and love at these works, there came in 1529 the siege of Florence, which hindered their completion only too effectually, and was the reason that he did little or no more work upon them, the citizens having laid upon him the charge of fortifying not only the hill of S. Miniato, but also the city, as we have related. And thus, having lent a thousand crowns to that Republic, and being elected one of the Nine, a military Council appointed for the war, he turned all his mind and soul to perfecting those fortifications. But in the end, when the enemy had closed round the city, and all hope of assistance was failing little by little, and the difficulties of maintaining the defense were increasing, and it appeared to Michelangelo that he was in a sorry pass with regard to his personal safety, he determined to leave Florence and make his way to Venice, without making himself known to anyone on the road. He set out secretly, therefore, by way of the hill of S. Miniato, without anyone knowing of it, taking with him Antonio Mini, his disciple, and the goldsmith Piloto, his faithful friend; and each of them carried a number of crowns on his person, sewn into his quilted doublet. Having arrived in Ferrara, they rested there; and it happened that on account of the alarm caused by the war and the league of the Emperor and the Pope, who were besieging Florence, Duke Alfonso d'Este was keeping strict watch in Ferrara, and required to be secretly informed by the hosts who gave lodging to travelers of the names of all those who lodged with them from one day to another; and he caused a list of all foreigners, with their nationality, to be brought to him every day. It came to pass, then, that when Michelangelo had dismounted with his companions, intending to stay there without revealing himself, this became known in that way to the Duke, who was very glad, because he had already become his friend. That Prince was a man of lofty mind, delighting constantly in persons of ability all his life long, and he straightway sent some of the first men of his Court with orders to conduct him in the name of his Excellency to the Palace, where the Duke was, to remove thither his horses and all his baggage, and to give him a handsome lodging in that Palace. Michelangelo, finding himself in the power of another, was constrained to obey and to make the best of a bad business, and he went with those courtiers to the Duke, but without removing his baggage from the inn. Thereupon the Duke, after first complaining of his reserve, gave him a great reception; and then, making him rich and honorable presents, he sought to detain him in Ferrara with the promise of a fine salary. He, having his mind set on something else, would not consent to remain; but the Duke again made him a free offer of all that was in his power, praying him that he should at least not depart as long as the war continued. Whereupon Michelangelo, not wishing to be outdone in courtesy, thanked him warmly, and, turning toward his two companions, said that he had brought twelve thousand crowns to Ferrara, and that, if the Duke had need of them, they were at his disposal, together with himself. The Duke then took him through the Palace to divert him, as he had done on another occasion, and showed him all the beautiful things that he had there, including a portrait of himself by Titian, which was much commended by Michelangelo. However, his Excellency was not able to keep him in the Palace, for he insisted on returning to the inn; wherefore the host who was lodging him received from the Duke a great abundance of things wherewith to do him honor, and also orders that at his departure he should not accept anything for his lodging. From Ferrara he made his way to Venice, where many gentlemen sought to become known to him; but he, who always had a very poor opinion of their knowledge of his profession, departed from the Giudecca, where he had his lodging. There, so it is said, he made for that city at that time, at the request of the Doge Gritti, a design for the bridge of the Rialto, which was very rare in invention and in ornamentation.

Michelangelo was invited with great insistence to go back to his native country, being urgently requested not to abandon his undertaking there, and receiving a safe-conduct; and finally, vanquished by love of her, he returned, but not without danger to his life. At this time he finished the Leda that he was painting, as has been related, at the request of Duke Alfonso; and it was afterwards taken to France by Antonio Mini, his disciple. And at this same time he saved the campanile of S. Miniato, a tower which sorely harassed the enemy's forces with its two pieces of artillery, so that their artillerists, having set to work to batter it with heavy cannon, had half ruined it, and were like to destroy it completely, when Michelangelo protected it so well with bales of wool and stout mattresses suspended by cords, that it is still standing.

When peace had been made, Baccio Valori, the Pope's Commissioner, received orders to have some of the most partisan citizens arrested and imprisoned in the Bargello, and the same tribunal sought out Michelangelo at his house; but he, fearing that, had fled secretly to the house of one who was much his friend, where he remained hidden many days. Finally, when the first fury had abated, Pope Clement, remembering the ability of Michelangelo, caused a diligent search to be made for him, with orders that nothing should be said to him, but rather that his former appointments should be restored to him, and that he should attend to the work of S. Lorenzo, over which he placed as proveditor M. Giovan Battista Figiovanni, the old servant of the Medici family and Prior of S. Lorenzo. Thus reassured, Michelangelo, in order to make Baccio Valori his friend, began a figure six feet high in marble, which was an Apollo drawing an arrow from his quiver, and carried it almost to completion. It is now in the apartment of the Prince of Florence, and is a very rare work, although it is not completely finished.

At this time a certain gentleman was sent to Michelangelo

by Duke Alfonso of Ferrara, who, having heard that the master had made some rare work for him with his own hand, did not wish to lose such a jewel. Having arrived in Florence and found Michelangelo, the envoy presented to him letters of recommendation from that lord; whereupon Michelangelo, receiving him courteously, showed him the Leda embracing the Swan that he had painted, with Castor and Pollux issuing from the Egg, in a large picture executed in distemper, as it were with the breath. The Duke's envoy, thinking from the praise that he heard everywhere of Michelangelo that he should have done something great, and not recognizing the excellence and artistry of that figure, said to Michelangelo: "Oh, this is but a trifle." Michelangelo, knowing that no one is better able to pronounce judgment on works than those who have had long practice in them, asked him what was his vocation. And he answered, with a sneer, "I am a merchant"; believing that he had not been recognized by Michelangelo as a gentleman, and as it were making fun of such a question, and at the same time affecting to despise the industry of the Florentines. Michelangelo, who had understood perfectly the meaning of his words, at once replied: "You will find you have made a bad bargain this time for your master. Get you gone out of my sight."

Now in those days Antonio Mini, his disciple, who had two sisters waiting to be married, asked him for the Leda, and he gave it to him willingly, with the greater part of the designs and cartoons that he had made, which were divine things, and also two chests full of models, with a great number of finished cartoons for making pictures, and some of works that had been painted. When Antonio took it into his head to go to France, he carried all these with him; the Leda he sold to King Francis by means of some merchants, and it is now at Fontainebleau, but the cartoons and designs were lost, for he died there in a short time, and some were stolen; and so our country was deprived of all these valuable labors, which was an incalculable loss. The cartoon of the Leda has since come back to Florence, and Bernardo Vecchietti has it; and so also four pieces of the cartoons for the chapel, with nudes and Prophets, brought back by the sculptor Benvenuto Cellini, and now in the possession of the heirs of Girolamo degli Albizzi.

It became necessary for Michelangelo to go to Rome to see Pope Clement, who, although angry with him, yet, as the friend of every talent, forgave him everything, and gave him orders that he should return to Florence and have the library and sacristy of S. Lorenzo completely finished; and, in order to shorten that work, a vast number of statues that were to be included in it were distributed among other masters. Two he allotted to Tribolo, one to Raffaello da Montelupo, and one to Fra Giovanni Agnolo, the Servite friar, all sculptors; and he gave them assistance in these, making rough models in clay for each of them. Whereupon they all worked valiantly, and he, also, caused work to be pursued on the library, and thus the ceiling was finished in carved woodwork, which was executed after his models by the hands of the Florentines Carota and Tasso, excellent carvers and also masters of carpentry; and likewise the shelves for the books, which were executed at that time by Battista del Cinque and his friend Ciappino, good masters in that profession. And in order to give the work its final perfection there was summoned to Florence the divine Giovanni da Udine, who, together with others his assistants and also some Florentine masters, decorated the tribune with stucco; and they all sought with great solicitude to give completion to that vast undertaking.

Now, just as Michelangelo was about to have the statues carried into execution, at that very time the Pope took it into his head to have him near his person, being desirous to have the walls of the Chapel of Sixtus* painted, where Michelangelo had painted the vaulting for Julius II, his nephew. On the principal wall, where the altar is, Clement wished him to paint the Universal Judgment, to the end that he might dis-

* The Sistine Chapel.

play in that scene all that the art of design could achieve, and opposite to it, on the other wall, over the principal door, he had commanded that he should depict the scene when Lucifer was expelled for his pride from Heaven, and all those Angels who sinned with him were hurled after him into the center of Hell. While Michelangelo was directing the preparation of the designs and cartoons of the Last Judgment on the first wall, he never ceased for a single day to be at strife with the agents of the Duke of Urbino, by whom he was accused of having received sixteen thousand crowns from Julius II for the tomb. This accusation was more than he could bear, and he desired to finish the work some day, although he was already an old man, and he would have willingly stayed in Rome to finish it, now that he had found, without seeking it, such a pretext for not returning any more to Florence, since he had a great fear of Duke Alessandro de' Medici, whom he regarded as little his friend; for, when the Duke had given him to understand through Signor Alessandro Vitelli that he should select the best site for the building of the castle and citadel of Florence, he answered that he would not go save at the command of Pope Clement.

Finally an agreement was formed in the matter of the tomb, that it should be finished in the following manner: there was no longer to be an isolated tomb in a rectangular shape, but only one of the original façades, in the manner that best pleased Michelangelo, and he was to be obliged to place in it six statues by his own hand. In this contract that was made with the Duke of Urbino, his Excellency consented that Michelangelo should be at the disposal of Pope Clement for four months in the year, either in Florence or wherever he might think fit to employ him. But, although it seemed to Michelangelo that at last he had obtained some peace, he was not to be quit of it so easily, for Pope Clement, desiring to see the final proof of the force of his art, kept him occupied with the cartoon of the Judgment. However, contriving to convince the Pope that he was thus engaged, at the same time he kept working in secret, never relaxing his efforts, at the statues that were going into the above-named tomb.

In the year 1534 came the death of Pope Clement, whereupon the work of the library and sacristy in Florence, which had remained unfinished in spite of all the efforts made to finish it, was stopped. Then, at length, Michelangelo thought to be truly free and able to give his attention to finishing the tomb of Julius II. But Paul III, not long after his election, had him summoned to his presence, and, besides paying him compliments and making him offers, requested him to enter his service and remain near his person. Michelangelo refused, saying that he was not able to do it, being bound by contract to the Duke of Urbino until the tomb of Julius should be finished. The Pope flew into a rage and said: "I have had this desire for thirty years, and now that I am Pope do you think I shall not satisfy it? I shall tear up the contract, for I am determined to have you serve me, come what may." Michelangelo, hearing this resolution, was tempted to leave Rome and in some way find means to give completion to the tomb; however, fearing, like a wise man, the power of the Pope, he resolved to try to keep him pacified with words, seeing that he was so old, until something should happen. The Pope, who wished to have some extraordinary work executed by Michelangelo, went one day with ten Cardinals to visit him at his house, where he demanded to see all the statues for the tomb of Julius, which appeared to him marvelous, and particularly the Moses, which figure alone was said by the Cardinal of Mantua to be enough to do honor to Pope Julius. And after seeing the designs and cartoons that he was preparing for the wall of the chapel, which appeared to the Pope to be stupendous, he again besought Michelangelo with great insistence that he should enter his service, promising that he would persuade the Duke of Urbino to content himself with three statues, and that the others should be given to other excellent masters to execute after his models. Whereupon, his Holiness having arranged this with the agents of the Duke, a new contract was made, which was confirmed by the Duke; and Michelangelo of his own free will bound himself to pay for the other three statues and to have the tomb erected, depositing for this purpose in the bank of the Strozzi one thousand five hundred and eighty ducats. This he might have avoided, and it seemed to him that he had truly done enough to be free of such a long and troublesome undertaking; and afterwards he caused the tomb to be erected in S. Pietro in Vincola in the following manner. He erected the lower base, which was all carved, with four pedestals which projected outwards as much as was necessary to give space for the captive that was originally intended to stand on each of them, instead of which there was left a terminal figure; and since the lower part had thus a poor effect, he placed at the feet of each terminal figure a reversed console resting on the pedestal. Those four terminal figures had between them three niches, two of which (those at the sides) were round, and were to have contained the Victories. Instead of the Victories, he placed in one Leah, the daughter of Laban, to represent the Active Life, with a mirror in her hand to signify the consideration that we should give to our actions, and in the other hand a garland of flowers, to denote the virtues that adorn our life during its duration, and make it glorious after death; and the other figure was her sister Rachel, representing the Contemplative Life, with the hands clasped and one knee bent, and on the countenance a look as of ecstasy of spirit. These statues Michelangelo executed with his own hand in less than a year. In the center is placed, upon a dado of marble, the gigantic and most beautiful statue of Moses. Truly this whole work has turned out very well, but not by a great measure as it had been planned in the original design.

Michelangelo resolved, since he could not do otherwise, to serve Pope Paul, who allowed him to continue the work as ordered by Clement, without changing anything in the inventions and the general conception that had been laid before him, thus showing respect for the genius of that great man,

for whom he felt such reverence and love that he sought to
do nothing but what pleased him; of which a proof was soon
seen. His Holiness desired to place his own arms beneath the
Jonah in the chapel, where those of Pope Julius II had previously been put; but Michelangelo, being asked to do this,
and not wishing to do a wrong to Julius and Clement, would
not place them there, saying that they would not look well;
and the Pope, in order not to displease him, was content to
have it so, having recognized very well the excellence of such
a man, and how he always followed what was just and honorable without any adulation or respect of persons—a thing
that the great are wont to experience very seldom. Michelangelo, then, caused a projection of well-baked and chosen
bricks to be carefully built on the wall of the above-named
chapel (a thing which was not there before), and contrived
that it should overhang one foot from above, so that neither
dust nor any other dirt might be able to settle upon it. But
I will not go into the particulars of the invention and composition of this scene, because so many copies of it, both
large and small, have been printed, that it does not seem
necessary to lose time in describing it. It is enough for us
to perceive that the intention of this extraordinary man has
been to refuse to paint anything but the human body in its
best proportioned and most perfect forms and in the greatest
variety of attitudes, and not this only, but likewise the play
of the passions and contentments of the soul, being satisfied
with justifying himself in that field in which he was superior
to all his fellow-craftsmen, and to lay open the way of the
grand manner in the painting of nudes, and his great knowledge in the difficulties of design; and, finally, he opened out
the way to facility in this art in its principal province, which
is the human body, and, attending to this single object, he
left on one side the charms of coloring and the caprices and
new fantasies of certain minute and delicate refinements which
many other painters, perhaps not without some show of reason, have not entirely neglected. For some, not so well

grounded in design, have sought with variety of tints and shades of coloring, with various new and bizarre inventions, and, in short, with the other method, to win themselves a place among the first masters; but Michelangelo, standing always firmly rooted in his profound knowledge of art, has shown to those who know enough how they should attain to perfection.

But to return to the story: Michelangelo had already carried to completion more than three-fourths of the work, when Pope Paul went to see it. And Messer Biagio da Cesena, the master of ceremonies, a person of great propriety, who was in the chapel with the Pope, being asked what he thought of it, said that it was a very disgraceful thing to have made in so honorable a place all those nude figures showing their nakedness so shamelessly, and that it was a work not for the chapel of a Pope, but for a bagnio or tavern. Michelangelo was displeased at this, and, wishing to revenge himself, as soon as Biagio had departed he portrayed him from life, without having him before his eyes at all, in the figure of Minos with a great serpent twisted round the legs, among a heap of Devils in Hell; nor was Messer Biagio's pleading with the Pope and with Michelangelo to have it removed of any avail, for it was left there in memory of the occasion, and it is still to be seen at the present day.

It happened at this time that Michelangelo fell no small distance from the staging of this work, and hurt his leg; and in his pain and anger he would not be treated by anyone. Now there was living at this same time the Florentine Maestro Baccio Rontini, his friend, an ingenious physician, who had a great affection for his genius; and he, taking compassion on him, went one day to knock at his door. Receiving no answer either from the neighbors or from him, he so contrived to climb by certain secret ways from one room to another, that he came to Michelangelo, who was in a desperate state. And then Maestro Baccio would never abandon him or take himself off until he was cured.

Having recovered from this injury, he returned to his labor, and, working at it continually, he carried it to perfect completion in a few months, giving such force to the paintings in the work, that he justified the words of Dante: Dead are the dead, the living seem to live. And here, also, may be seen the misery of the damned and the joy of the blessed. Wherefore, when this Judgment was thrown open to view, it proved that he had not only vanquished all the earlier masters who had worked there, but had sought to surpass the vaulting that he himself had made so famous, excelling it by a great measure and outstripping his own self. For he imagined to himself the terror of those days, and depicted, for the greater pain of all who have not lived well, the whole Passion of Christ, causing various naked figures in the air to carry the Cross, the Column, the Lance, the Sponge, the Nails, and the Crown of Thorns, all in different attitudes, executed to perfection in a triumph of facility over their difficulties. In that scene is Christ seated, with a countenance proud and terrible, turning toward the damned and cursing them; not without great fear in Our Lady, who, hearing and beholding that vast havoc, draws her mantle close around her. There are innumerable figures, Prophets and Apostles, that form a circle about Him, and in particular Adam and S. Peter, who are believed to have been placed there, one as the first parent of those thus brought to judgment, and the other as having been the first foundation of the Christian Church; and at His feet is a most beautiful S. Bartholomew, who is displaying his flayed skin. There is likewise a nude figure of S. Laurence; besides which, there are multitudes of Saints without number, both male and female, and other figures, men and women, around Him, near or distant, who embrace one another and make rejoicing, having received eternal blessedness by the grace of God and as the reward of their works. Beneath the feet of Christ are the Seven Angels with the Seven Trumpets described by S. John the Evangelist, who, as they sound the call to judgment, cause the hair of all who behold them to stand on end at the terrible wrath that their countenances reveal. Among others are two Angels that have each the Book of Life in the hands: and near them, on one side, not without beautiful consideration, are seen the Seven Mortal Sins in the forms of Devils, assailing and striving to drag down to Hell the souls that are flying toward Heaven, all with very beautiful attitudes and most admirable foreshortenings. Nor did he hesitate to show to the world, in the resurrection of the dead, how they take to themselves flesh and bones once more from the same earth, and how, assisted by others already alive, they go soaring toward Heaven, whence succor is brought to them by certain souls already blessed; not without evidence of all those marks of consideration that could be thought to be required in so great a work. For studies and labors of every kind were executed by him, which may be recognized throughout the whole work without exception; and this is manifested with particular clearness in the bark of Charon, who, in an attitude of fury, strikes with his oars at the souls dragged down by the Devils into the bark, after the likeness of the picture that the master's best-beloved poet, Dante, described.

Nor would it be possible to imagine how much variety there is in the heads of those Devils, which are truly monsters from Hell. In the sinners may be seen sin and the fear of eternal damnation; and, to say nothing of the beauty of every detail, it is extraordinary to see so great a work executed with such harmony of painting, that it appears as if done in one day, and with such finish as was never achieved in any miniature. And, of a truth, the terrible force and grandeur of the work, with the multitude of figures, are such that it is not possible to describe it, for it is filled with all the passions known to human creatures, and all expressed in the most marvelous manner. For the proud, the envious, the avaricious, the wanton, and all the other suchlike sinners can be distinguished with ease by any man of fine perception, because in figuring them Michelangelo observed every rule of

Nature in the expressions, in the attitudes, and in every other natural circumstance; a thing which, although great and marvelous, was not impossible to such a man, for the reason that he was always observant and shrewd and had seen men in plenty, and had acquired by commerce with the world that knowledge that philosophers gain from cogitation and from writings. Wherefore he who has judgment and understanding in painting perceives there the most terrible force of art, and sees in those figures such thoughts and passions as were never painted by any other but Michelangelo. So, also, he may see there how the variety of innumerable attitudes is accomplished, in the strange and diverse gestures of young and old, male and female; and who is there who does not recognize in these the terrible power of his art, together with the grace that he had from Nature, since they move the hearts not only of those who have knowledge in that profession, but even of those who have none? There are foreshortenings that appear as if in relief, a harmony of painting that gives great softness, and fineness in the parts painted by him with delicacy, all showing in truth how pictures executed by good and true painters should be; and in the outlines of the forms turned by him in such a way as could not have been achieved by any other but Michelangelo, may be seen the true Judgment and the true Damnation and Resurrection. This is for our art the exemplar and the grand manner of painting sent down to men on earth by God, to the end that they may see how Destiny works when intellects descend from the heights of Heaven to earth, and have infused in them divine grace and knowledge. This work leads after it bound in chains those who persuade themselves that they have mastered art; and at the sight of the strokes drawn by him in the outlines of no matter what figure, every sublime spirit, however mighty in design, trembles and is afraid. And while the eyes gaze at his labors in this work, the senses are numbed at the mere thought of what manner of things all other pictures, those painted and those still unpainted, would appear if placed in comparison with such perfection. Truly blessed may he be called, and blessed his memories, who has seen this truly stupendous marvel of our age! Most happy and most fortunate Paul III, in that God granted that under thy protection should be acquired the renown that the pens of writers shall give to his memory and thine! How highly are thy merits enhanced by his genius! And what good fortune have the craftsmen had in this age from his birth, in that they have seen the veil of every difficulty torn away, and have beheld in the pictures, sculptures, and architectural works executed by him all that can be imagined and achieved!

He toiled eight years over executing this work, and threw it open to view in the year 1541, I believe, on Christmas day, to the marvel and amazement of all Rome, nay, of the whole world; and I, who was that year in Venice, and went to Rome to see it, was struck dumb by its beauty.

Pope Paul, as has been related, had caused a chapel called the Pauline to be erected on the same floor by Antonio da San Gallo, in imitation of that of Nicholas V; and in this he resolved that Michelangelo should paint two great pictures with two large scenes. In one he painted the Conversion of S. Paul, with Jesus Christ in the air and a multitude of nude Angels making most beautiful movements, and below, all dazed and terrified, Paul fallen from his horse to the level of the ground, with his soldiers about him, some striving to raise him up, and others, struck with awe by the voice and splendor of Christ, are flying in beautiful attitudes and marvelous movements of panic, while the horse, taking to flight, appears to be carrying away in its headlong course him who seeks to hold it back; and this whole scene is executed with extraordinary design and art. In the other picture is the Crucifixion of S. Peter, who is fixed, a nude figure of rare beauty, upon the cross; showing the ministers of the crucifixion, after they have made a hole in the ground, seeking to raise the cross on high, to the end that he may remain crucified with his feet in the air; and there are many remarkable and beautiful considerations. Michelangelo, as has been said elsewhere, gave his attention only to the perfection of art, and therefore there are no landscapes to be seen there, nor trees, nor buildings, nor any other distracting graces of art, for to these he never applied himself, as one, perchance, who would not abase his great genius to such things. These, executed by him at the age of seventy-five, were his last pictures, and, as he used himself to tell me, they cost him much fatigue, for the reason that painting, and particularly working in fresco, is no art for men who have passed a certain age. Michelangelo arranged that Perino del Vaga, a very excellent painter, should decorate the vaulting with stucco and with many things in painting, after his designs, and such, also, was the wish of Pope Paul III; but the work was afterwards delayed, and nothing more was done, even as many undertakings are left unfinished, partly by the fault of want of resolution in the craftsmen, and partly by that of Princes little zealous in urging them on.

Pope Paul had made a beginning with the fortifying of the Borgo, and had summoned many gentlemen, together with Antonio da San Gallo, to a conference; but he wished that Michelangelo also should have a part in this, knowing that the fortifications about the hill of S. Miniato in Florence had been constructed under his direction. After much discussion, Michelangelo was asked what he thought; and he, having opinions contrary to San Gallo and many others, declared them freely. Whereupon San Gallo said to him that his arts were sculpture and painting, and not fortification. Michelangelo replied that of sculpture and painting he knew little, but of fortification, what with the thought that he had devoted to it for a long time, and his experience in what he had done, it appeared to him that he knew more than either Antonio or any of his family; showing him in the presence of the company that he had made many errors in that art. Words rising high on either side, the Pope had to command silence; but no long time passed before Michelangelo brought a design for all the fortifications of the Borgo, which laid open the way for all that has since been ordained and executed; and this was the reason that the great gate of S. Spirito, which was approaching completion under the direction of San Gallo, was left unfinished.

The spirit and genius of Michelangelo could not rest without doing something; and, since he was not able to paint, he set to work on a piece of marble, intending to carve from it four figures in the round and larger than life, including a Dead Christ, for his own delight and to pass the time, and because, as he used to say, the exercise of the hammer kept him healthy in body. This Christ, taken down from the Cross, is supported by Our Lady, by Nicodemus, who bends down and assists her, planted firmly on his feet in a forceful attitude, and by one of the Marys, who also gives her aid, perceiving that the Mother, overcome by grief, is failing in strength and not able to uphold Him. Nor is there anywhere to be seen a dead form equal to that of Christ, who, sinking with the limbs hanging limp, lies in an attitude wholly different, not only from that of any other work by Michelangelo, but from that of any other figure that was ever made. A laborious work is this, a rare achievement in a single stone, and truly divine; but, as will be related hereafter, it remained unfinished, and suffered many misfortunes, although Michelangelo had intended that it should serve to adorn his own tomb, at the foot of that altar where he thought to place it.

It happened in the year 1546 that Antonio da San Gallo died; whereupon, there being now no one to direct the building of S. Pietro, many suggestions were made by the superintendents to the Pope as to who should have it. Finally his Holiness, inspired, I believe, by God, resolved to send for Michelangelo. But he, when asked to take Antonio's place, refused it, saying, in order to avoid such a burden, that architecture was not his proper art; and in the end, entreaties not availing, the Pope commanded that he should accept it, whereupon, to his great displeasure and against his wish, he was forced to undertake that enterprise. And one day among others that he went to S. Pietro to see the wooden model that San Gallo had made, and to examine the building, he found there the whole San Gallo faction, who, crowding before Michelangelo, said to him in the best terms at their command that they rejoiced that the charge of the building was to be his, and that the model was a field where there would never be any want of pasture. "You speak the truth," answered Michelangelo, meaning to infer, as he declared to a friend, that it was good for sheep and oxen, who knew nothing of art. And afterwards he used to say publicly that San Gallo had made it wanting in lights, that it had on the exterior too many ranges of columns one above another, and that, with its innumerable projections, pinnacles, and subdivisions of members, it was more akin to the German manner than to the good method of the ancients or to the gladsome and beautiful modern manner; and, in addition to this, that it was possible to save fifty years of time and more than three hundred thousand crowns of money in finishing the building, and to execute it with more majesty, grandeur, and facility, greater beauty and convenience, and better ordered design. This he afterwards proved by a model that he made, in order to bring it to the form in which the work is now seen constructed; and thus he demonstrated that what he said was nothing but the truth. This model cost him twenty-five crowns, and was made in a fortnight; that of San Gallo, as has been related, cost four thousand, and took many years to finish. From this and other circumstances it became evident that that Church was but a shop and a business for making money, and that it would be continually delayed, with the intention of never finishing it, by those who had undertaken it as a means of profit.

Such methods did not please our upright Michelangelo, and in order to get rid of all these people, while the Pope was forcing him to accept the office of architect to the work, he said to them openly one day that they should use all the assistance of their friends and do all that they could to prevent him from entering on that office, because, if he were to undertake such a charge, he would not have one of them about the building. Which words, spoken in public, were taken very ill, as may be believed, and were the reason that they conceived a great hatred against him, which increased every day as they saw the whole design being changed, both within and without, so that they would scarcely let him live, seeking out daily new and various devices to harass him, as will be related in the proper place. Finally the Pope issued a *Motu-proprio* creating him head of that construction, with full authority, and giving him power to do or undo whatever he chose, and to add, take away, or vary anything at his pleasure; and he decreed that all the officials employed in the work should be subservient to his will. Whereupon Michelangelo, seeing the great confidence and trust that the Pope placed in him, desired, in order to prove his generosity, that it should be declared in the *Motu-proprio* that he was serving in the construction for the love of God and without any reward. It is true that the Pope had formerly granted to him the ferry over the river at Piacenza, which yielded him about six hundred crowns; but he lost it at the death of Duke Pier Luigi Farnese, and in exchange for it he was given a Chancellery at Rimini, a post of less value. About that he showed no concern; and, although the Pope sent him money several times by way of salary, he would never accept it, to which witness is borne by Messer Alessandro Ruffini, Chamberlain to the Pope at that time, and by M. Pier Giovanni Aliotti, Bishop of Forlì. Finally the model that had been made by Michelangelo was approved by the Pope; which model diminished S. Pietro in size, but gave it greater grandeur, to the satisfaction of all those who have judgment, although some who profess to be good judges, which in fact they are not, do not approve of it. He found that the four principal piers built by Bramante, and left by Antonio da San Gallo, which had to support the weight of the tribune, were weak;

and these he partly filled up, and beside them he made two
winding or spiral staircases, in which is an ascent so easy that
the beasts of burden can climb them, carrying all the materials to the very top, and men on horseback, likewise, can
go up to the uppermost level of the arches. The first cornice
above the arches he constructed of travertine, curving in a
round, which is an admirable and graceful thing, and very
different from any other; nor could anything better of that
kind be done. He also made a beginning with the two great
recesses of the transepts; and whereas formerly, under the
direction of Bramante, Baldassarre, and Raphael, as has been
related, eight tabernacles were being made on the side toward
the Camposanto, and that plan was afterwards followed by
San Gallo, Michelangelo reduced these to three, with three
chapels in the interior, and above them a vaulting of travertine, and a range of windows giving a brilliant light, which
are varied in form and of a sublime grandeur. But, since these
things are in existence, and are also to be seen in engraving,
not only those of Michelangelo, but those of San Gallo as
well, I will not set myself to describe them, for it is in no
way necessary. Let it suffice to say that he set himself, with
all possible diligence, to cause the work to be carried on in
those parts where the building was to be changed in design,
to the end that it might remain so solid and stable that it
might never be changed by another.

The Roman people, with the sanction of that Pope, had
a desire to give some useful, commodious, and beautiful form
to the Campidoglio, and to furnish it with colonnades, as-
cents, and inclined approaches with and without steps, and
also with the further adornment of the ancient statues that
were already there, in order to embellish that place. For this
purpose they sought the advice of Michelangelo, who made
them a most beautiful and very rich design, in which, on the
side where the Senatore stands, toward the east, he arranged
a façade of travertine, and a flight of steps that ascends from
two sides to meet on a level space, from which one enters into

the center of the hall of that Palace, with rich curving wings adorned with balusters that serve as supports and parapets. And there, to enrich that part, he caused to be placed on certain bases the two ancient figures in marble of recumbent River Gods, each eighteen feet high, and of rare workmanship, one of which is the Tiber and the other the Nile; and between them, in a niche, is to go a Jove. On the southern side, where there is the Palace of the Conservatori, in order that it might be made rectangular, there followed a rich and well-varied façade, with a loggia at the foot full of columns and niches, where many ancient statues are to go; and all around are various ornaments, doors, windows, and the like, of which some are already in place. On the other side from this, toward the north, below the Araceli, there is to follow another similar façade; and before it, toward the west, is to be an ascent of baston-like steps, which will be almost level, with a border and parapet of balusters; here will be the principal entrance, with a colonnade, and bases on which will be placed all that wealth of noble statues in which the Campidoglio is now so rich. In the middle of the Piazza, on a base in the form of an oval, is placed the famous bronze horse on which is the statue of Marcus Aurelius, which the same Pope Paul caused to be removed from the Piazza di Laterano, where Sixtus IV had placed it. This edifice is now being made so beautiful that it is worthy to be numbered among the finest works that Michelangelo has executed, and it is being carried to completion at the present day under the direction of M. Tommaso de' Cavalieri, a Roman gentleman who was, and still is, one of the greatest friends that Michelangelo ever had.

Pope Paul III had caused San Gallo, while he was alive, to carry forward the Palace of the Farnese family, but the great upper cornice, to finish the roof on the outer side, had still to be constructed, and his Holiness desired that Michelangelo should execute it from his own designs and directions. Michelangelo, not being able to refuse the Pope, who so esteemed and favored him, caused a model of wood to be made, twelve feet in length, and of the size that it was to be; and this he placed on one of the corners of the Palace, so that it might show what effect the finished work would have. It pleased his Holiness and all Rome, and that part of it has since been carried to completion which is now to be seen, proving to be the most varied and the most beautiful of all that have ever been known, whether ancient or modern. On this account, after San Gallo was dead, the Pope desired that Michelangelo should have charge of the whole construction as well; and there he made the great marble window with the beautiful columns of variegated marble, which is over the principal door of the Palace, with a large escutcheon of great beauty and variety, in marble, of Pope Paul III, the founder of that Palace. Within the Palace he continued, above the first range of the court, the two other ranges, with the most varied, graceful, and beautiful windows, ornaments and upper cornice that have ever been seen, so that, through the labors and the genius of that man that court has now become the most handsome in Europe. He widened and enlarged the Great Hall, and set in order the front vestibule, and caused the vaulting of that vestibule to be constructed in a new variety of curve, in the form of a half oval.

Now in that year there was found at the Baths of Antoninus a mass of marble fourteen feet in every direction, in which there had been carved by the ancients a Hercules standing upon a mound, who was holding the Bull by the horns, with another figure assisting him, and around that mound various figures of Shepherds, Nymphs, and different animals—a work of truly extraordinary beauty, showing figures so perfect in one single block without any added pieces, which was judged to have been intended for a fountain. Michelangelo advised that it should be conveyed into the second court, and there restored so as to make it spout water in the original manner; all which advice was approved, and the work is still being restored at the present day with great diligence, by order of the Farnese family, for that purpose. At that time, also, Michelangelo made a design for the building of a bridge across the River Tiber in a straight line with the Farnese Palace, to the end that it might be possible to go from that palace to another palace and gardens that they possessed in the Trastevere, and also to see at one glance in a straight line from the principal door which faces the Campo di Fiore, the court, the fountain, the Strada Giulia, the bridge, and the beauties of the other garden, even to the other door which opened on the Strada di Trastevere—a rare work, worthy of that Pontiff and of the judgment, design, and art of Michelangelo.

In the year 1547 died Sebastiano Viniziano, the Friar of the Papal Signet-office; and, Pope Paul proposing that the ancient statues of his Palace should be restored, Michelangelo willingly favored the Milanese sculptor Guglielmo della Porta, a young man of promise, who had been recommended by the above-named Fra Sebastiano to Michelangelo, who, liking his work, presented him to Pope Paul for the restoration of those statues. And the matter went so far forward that Michelangelo obtained for him the Signet-office, and he then set to work on restoring the statues, some of which are to be seen in that Palace at the present day. But Guglielmo, forgetting the benefits that he had received from Michelangelo, afterwards became one of his opponents.

In the year 1549 there took place the death of Pope Paul III; whereupon, after the election of Pope Julius III, Cardinal Farnese gave orders for a grand tomb to be made for his kinsman Pope Paul by the hand of Fra Guglielmo, who arranged to erect it in S. Pietro, below the first arch of the new church, beneath the tribune, which obstructed the floor of the church, and was, in truth, not the proper place. Michelangelo advised, most judiciously, that it could not and should not stand there, and the Frate, believing that he was doing this out of envy, became filled with hatred against him; but afterwards he recognized that Michelangelo had spoken the truth, and that the fault was his, in that he had had the opportunity and had not finished the work, as will be related in another place. And to this I can bear witness, for the reason that in the year 1550 I had gone by order of Pope Julius III to Rome to serve him (and very willingly, for love of Michelangelo), and I took part in that discussion. Michelangelo desired that the tomb should be erected in one of the niches, where there is now the Column of the Possessed, which was the proper place, and I had so gone to work that Julius III was resolving to have his own tomb made in the other niche with the same design as that of Pope Paul, in order to balance that work; but the Frate, who set himself against this, brought it about that his own was never finished after all, and that the tomb of the other Pontiff was also not made; which had all been predicted by Michelangelo.

In the same year Pope Julius turned his attention to having a chapel of marble with two tombs constructed in the Church of S. Pietro a Montorio for Cardinal Antonio di Monte, his uncle, and Messer Fabiano, his grandfather, the first founder of the greatness of that illustrious house. For this work Vasari having made designs and models, Pope Julius, who always esteemed the genius of Michelangelo and loved Vasari, desired that Michelangelo should fix the price between them; and Vasari besought the Pope that he should prevail upon him to take it under his protection. Now Vasari had proposed Simone Mosca for the carvings of this work, and Raffaello da Montelupo for the statues; but Michelangelo advised that no carvings of foliage should be made in it, not even in the architectural parts of the work, saying that where there are to be figures of marble there must not be any other thing. On which account Vasari feared that the work should be abandoned, because it would look poor; but in fact, when he saw it finished, he confessed that Michelangelo had shown great judgment.

At that time Vasari was with Michelangelo every day; and one morning the Pope in his kindness gave them both leave that they might visit the Seven Churches on horseback (for it was Holy Year), and receive the Pardon in company. Whereupon, while going from one church to another, they had many useful and beautiful conversations on art and every industry, and out of these Vasari composed a dialogue, which will be published at some more favorable opportunity, together with other things concerning art. In that year Pope Julius III confirmed the *Motu-proprio* of Pope Paul III with regard to the building of S. Pietro; and although much evil was spoken to him of Michelangelo by the friends of the San Gallo faction, in the matter of the construction of S. Pietro, at that time the Pope would not listen to a word, for Vasari had demonstrated to him (as was the truth) that Michelangelo had given life to the building, and also persuaded his Holiness that he should do nothing concerned with design without the advice of Michelangelo. This promise the Pope kept ever afterwards, for neither at the Vigna Julia did he do anything without his counsel, nor at the Belvedere, where there was built the staircase that is there now, in place of the semicircular staircase that came forward, ascending in eight steps, and turned inwards in eight more steps, erected in former times by Bramante in the great recess in the center of the Belvedere. And Michelangelo designed and caused to be built the very beautiful quadrangular staircase, with balusters of peperino-stone, which is there at the present day.

Vasari had finished in that year the printing of his work, the Lives of the Painters, Sculptors, and Architects, in Florence. Now he had not written the Life of any living master, although some who were old were still alive, save only of Michelangelo; and in the book were many records of circumstances that Vasari had received from his lips, his age and his judgment being the greatest among all the craftsmen. Giorgio therefore presented the work to him, and he received it very gladly.

Before the beginning of the year 1551, the San Gallo faction arranged a conspiracy against Michelangelo, whereby

the Pope was to hold an assembly in S. Pietro, and to sum-
mon together the superintendents and all those who had the
charge of the work, in order to show to the Pope, by means of
false calumnies, that Michelangelo had ruined that building,
because, he having already built the apse of the King, where
there are the three chapels, and having executed these with
the three windows above, they, not knowing what was to be
done with the vaulting, with feeble judgment had given the
elder Cardinal Salviati and Marcello Cervini, who afterwards became Pope, to understand that S. Pietro was being
left with little light. Whereupon, all being assembled, the
Pope said to Michelangelo that the deputies declared that the
apse would give little light, and he answered: "I would like
to hear these deputies speak in person." Cardinal Marcello
replied: "We are here." Then Michelangelo said to him:
"Monsignore, above these windows, in the vaulting, which is
to be made of travertine, there are to be three others." "You
have never told us that," said the Cardinal. And Michelangelo answered: "I am not obliged, nor do I intend to be
obliged, to say either to your Highness or to any other person
what I am bound or desirous to do. Your office is to obtain
the money and to guard it from thieves, and the charge of
the design for the building you must leave to me." And then,
turning to the Pope, he said: "Holy Father, you see what my
gains are, and that if these fatigues that I endure do not profit
me in my mind, I am wasting my time and my work." The
Pope, who loved him, laid his hands on his shoulders, and
said: "You shall profit both in mind and in body; do not
doubt it." Michelangelo having thus been able to get rid of
those persons, the Pope came to love him even more; and he
commanded him and Vasari that on the day following they
should both present themselves at the Vigna Julia, in which
place his Holiness had many discussions with him, and they
carried that work almost to the condition of perfect beauty in
which it now is; nor did the Pope discuss or do anything in

the matter of design without Michelangelo's advice and judgment.

In the year 1554, I returned to Florence to re-enter the service of Duke Cosimo. The departure of Vasari grieved Michelangelo, and likewise Giorgio, for the reason that Michelangelo's adversaries kept harassing him every day, now in one way and now in another; wherefore they did not fail to write to one another daily. And in April of the same year, Vasari giving him the news that Leonardo, the nephew of Michelangelo, had had a male child, that they had accompanied him to baptism with an honorable company of most noble ladies, and that they had revived the name of Buonarroto, Michelangelo answered in a letter to Vasari in these words:

"Dear Friend Giorgio,

"I have had the greatest pleasure from your letter, seeing that you still remember the poor old man, and even more because you were present at the triumph which, as you write, you witnessed in the birth of another Buonarroto; for which intelligence I thank you with all my heart and soul. But so much pomp does not please me, for man should not be laughing when all the world is weeping. It seems to me that Leonardo should not make so much rejoicing over a new birth, with all that gladness which should be reserved for the death of one who has lived well. Do not marvel if I delay to answer; I do it so as not to appear a merchant. As for the many praises that you send me in your letter, I tell you that if I deserved a single one of them, it would appear to me that in giving myself to you body and soul, I had truly given you something, and had discharged some infinitesimal part of the debt that I owe you; whereas I recognize you every hour as my creditor for more than I can repay, and, since I am an old man, I can now never hope to be able to square the account in this life, but perhaps in the next. Wherefore I pray you have patience, and remain wholly yours. Things here are much as usual."

Already, in the time of Paul III, Duke Cosimo had sent Tribolo to Rome to see if he might be able to persuade Michelangelo to return to Florence, in order to give completion to the Sacristy of S. Lorenzo. But Michelangelo excused himself because, having grown old, he could not support the burden of such fatigues, and demonstrated to him with many reasons that he could not leave Rome. Whereupon Tribolo finally asked him about the staircase of the library of S. Lorenzo, for which Michelangelo had caused many stones to be prepared, but there was no model of it nor any certainty as to the exact form, and, although there were some marks on a pavement and some other sketches in clay, the true and final design could not be found. However, no matter how much Tribolo might beseech him and invoke the name of the Duke, Michelangelo would never answer a word save that he remembered nothing of it. Orders were given to Vasari by Duke Cosimo that he should write to Michelangelo, requesting him to write saying what final form that staircase was to have; in the hope that through the friendship and love that he bore to Vasari, he would say something that might lead to some solution and to the completion of the work. Vasari wrote to Michelangelo the mind of the Duke, saying that the execution of all that was to be done would fall to him; which he would do with that fidelity and care with which, as Michelangelo knew, he was wont to treat such of his works as he had in charge. Wherefore Michelangelo sent the directions for making the above-named staircase in a letter by his own hand on the 28th of September, 1555.

"MESSER GIORGIO, DEAR FRIEND,

"Concerning the staircase for the library, of which so much has been said to me, you may believe that if I could remember how I had designed it, I would not need to be entreated.

There does, indeed, come back to my mind, like a dream, a certain staircase; but I do not believe that it is exactly the one which I conceived at that time, because it comes out so stupid. However, I will describe it here. Take a quantity of oval boxes, each one palm in depth, but not of equal length and breadth. The first and largest place on the pavement at such a distance from the wall of the door as may make the staircase easy or steep, according to your pleasure. Upon this place another, which must be so much smaller in every direction as to leave on the first one below as much space as the foot requires in ascending; diminishing and drawing back the steps one after another toward the door, in accord with the ascent. And the diminution of the last step must reduce it to the proportion of the space of the door. The said part of the staircase with the oval steps must have two wings, one on one side and one on the other, with corresponding steps but not oval. Of these the central flight shall serve as the principal staircase, and from the center of the staircase to the top the curves of the said wings shall meet the wall; but from the center down to the pavement they shall stand, together with the whole staircase, at a distance of about three palms from the wall, in such a manner that the basement of the vestibule shall not be obstructed in any part, and every face shall be left free. I am writing nonsense; but I know well that you will find something to your purpose."

Michelangelo also wrote to Vasari in those days that Julius III being dead, and Marcellus elected, the faction that was against him, in consequence of the election of the new Pontiff, had again begun to harass him. Which hearing, and not liking these ways, the Duke caused Giorgio to write and tell him that he should leave Rome and come to live in Florence, where the Duke did not desire more than his advice and designs at times for his buildings, and that he would receive from that lord all that he might desire, without doing anything with his own hand. But then, Marcellus being dead, and Paul IV having been elected, by whom once again numerous offers had been made to him from the very beginning, when he went to kiss his feet, the desire to finish the building of S. Pietro, and the obligation by which he thought himself bound to that task, kept him back; and, employing certain excuses, he wrote to the Duke that for the time being he was not able to serve him, and to Vasari a letter in these very words:

"MESSER GIORGIO, MY DEAR FRIEND,

"I call God to witness how it was against my will and under the strongest compulsion that I was set to the building of S. Pietro in Rome by Pope Paul III, ten years ago. Had they continued to work at that building up to the present day, as they were doing then, I would now have reached such a point in the undertaking that I might be thinking of returning home; but for want of money it has been much retarded, and is still being retarded at the time when it has reached the most laborious and difficult stage, insomuch that to abandon it now would be nothing short of the greatest possible disgrace and sin, losing the reward of the labors that I have endured in those ten years for the love of God. I have made you this discourse in answer to your letter, and also because I have a letter from the Duke that has made me marvel much that his Excellency should have deigned to write so graciously; for which I thank God and his Excellency to the best of my power and knowledge. I wander from the subject, because I have lost my memory and my wits, and writing is a great affliction to me, for it is not my art. The conclusion is this: to make you understand what would be the result if I were to abandon the construction and depart from Rome; firstly, I would please a number of thieves, and secondly, I would be the cause of its ruin, and perhaps, also, of its being suspended for ever."

Continuing to write to Giorgio, Michelangelo said to him, to excuse himself with the Duke, that he had a house and many convenient things at his disposal in Rome, which were worth thousands of crowns, in addition to being in danger of his life from disease of the kidneys, colic, and the stone, as happens to every old person, and as could be proved by Maestro Realdo, his physician, from whom he congratulated himself on having his life, after God; that for these reasons he was not able to leave Rome, and, finally, that he had no heart for anything but death. Meanwhile he gave his attention to working at many parts of S. Pietro, in order so to fix the form that it might never again be changed. During this time certain persons had informed him that Pope Paul IV was minded to make him alter the façade of the chapel where the Last Judgment is, because, he said, those figures showed their nakedness too shamelessly. When, therefore, the mind of the Pope was made known to Michelangelo, he answered: "Tell the Pope that it is no great affair, and that it can be altered with ease. Let him put the world right, and every picture will be put right in a moment."

Michelangelo was employed in the time of Pope Paul IV on many parts of the fortifications of Rome, and also by Salustio Peruzzi, to whom that Pope, as has been related elsewhere, had given the charge of executing the great portal of the Castello di S. Angelo, which is now half ruined; and he occupied himself in distributing the statues of that work, examining the models of the sculptors, and correcting them. At that time the French army approached near to Rome, and Michelangelo thought that he was like to come to an evil end together with that city; whereupon he resolved to fly from Rome and went secretly to the mountains of Spoleto, where he visited certain seats of hermits.

Michelangelo used to work almost every day, as a pastime, at that block with the four figures of which we have already spoken; which block he broke into pieces at this time for these reasons, either because it was hard and full of emery, and the chisel often struck sparks from it, or it may have been that the judgment of the man was so great that he was never content with anything that he did. A proof that this is true is that there are few finished statues to be seen out of all that he executed in the prime of his manhood, and that those completely finished were executed by him in his youth; and the others, with the exception of the Dukes Giuliano and Lorenzo, Night, Dawn, and Moses, with the other two, the whole number of these statues not amounting in all to eleven, the others, I say, were all left unfinished, and, moreover, they are many, Michelangelo having been wont to say that if he had had to satisfy himself in what he did, he would have sent out few, nay, not one. For he had gone so far with his art and judgment, that, when he had laid bare a figure and had perceived in it the slightest degree of error, he would set it aside and run to lay his hand on another block of marble, trusting that the same would not happen to the new block; and he often said that this was the reason that he gave for having executed so few statues and pictures.

There had entered into the service of Paul IV, and also into the charge of the building of S. Pietro, the architect Pirro Ligorio, and he was now once more harassing Michelangelo, going about saying that he had sunk into his second childhood. Wherefore, angered by such treatment, he would willingly have returned to Florence, and, having delayed to return, he was again urged in letters by Giorgio, but he knew that he was too old, having now reached the age of eighty-one. Writing at that time to Vasari by his courier, and sending him various spiritual sonnets, he said that he was come to the end of his life, that he must be careful where he directed his thoughts, that by reading he would see that he was at his last hour, and that there arose in his mind no thought upon which was not graved the image of death; and in one letter he said:

"It is God's will, Vasari, that I should continue to live in misery for some years. I know that you will tell me that I am an old fool to wish to write sonnets, but since many say that

I am in my second childhood, I have sought to act accordingly. By your letter I see the love that you bear me, and you may take it as certain that I would be glad to lay these feeble bones of mine beside those of my father, as you beg me to do; but by departing from here I would be the cause of the utter ruin of the building of S. Pietro, which would be a great disgrace and a very grievous sin. However, when it is so firmly established that it can never be changed, I hope to do all that you ask me, if it be not a sin to keep in anxious expectation certain gluttons that await my immediate departure."

Michelangelo by this time was reduced to a feeble condition, and it was evident that little was being done in S. Pietro, now that he had carried on a great part of the frieze of the windows within, and of the double columns without, which curve above the great round cornice where the cupola is to be placed, as will be related; and he was exhorted and urged by his greatest friends, such as the Cardinal of Carpi, Messer Donato Giannotti, Francesco Bandini, Tommaso de' Cavalieri, and Lottino that, since he saw the delay in the raising of the cupola, he should at least make a model of it. He stayed many months without making up his mind to this, but in the end he made a beginning, and then little by little constructed a small model in clay, from which, as an exemplar, and from the plans and profiles that he had drawn, it might be possible afterwards to make a larger one of wood. This, having made a beginning with it, he caused to be constructed in little more than a year by Maestro Giovanni Franzese, with much study and pains; and he made it on such a scale that the smaller proportions of the model, measured by the old Roman palm, corresponded with complete exactness to those of the large work.

The completion of this model caused the greatest satisfaction not only to all his friends, but to all Rome, the form of the building having been thus settled and established. It then came to pass that Paul IV died, and after him was elected Pius IV, who, while causing the building of the little palace in the wood of the Belvedere to be continued by Pirro Ligorio, who remained architect to the Palace, made many gracious offers and advances to Michelangelo. The *Motu-proprio* originally received by Michelangelo from Paul III, and then from Julius III and Paul IV, in respect of the building of S. Pietro, he confirmed in his favor, and he restored to him a part of the revenues and allowances taken away by Paul IV, employing him in many of his works of building; and in his time he caused the construction of S. Pietro to be carried on vigorously.

The same year Duke Cosimo went to Rome with the Lady Duchess Leonora, his consort, and Michelangelo, after the Duke's arrival, went straightway to see him. The Duke, after receiving him with many endearments, caused him, out of respect for his great genius, to sit by his side, and with much familiarity talked to him of all that he had caused to be done in painting and sculpture at Florence, and also of all that he was minded to have done, and in particular of the Hall; and Michelangelo again encouraged and reassured him in that matter, lamenting, since he loved that Lord, that he was not young enough to be able to serve him. His Excellency said that he had discovered the way to work porphyry, a thing which Michelangelo could not believe, and the Duke therefore sent him the head of Christ wrought by the sculptor Francesco del Tadda, at which he was astonished. He visited the Duke several times the while that he stayed in Rome, to his vast satisfaction, and wrote to Vasari that it vexed him to be old and infirm, for he would have liked to do something for that Lord, but he was going about trying to buy some beautiful antique to send to him in Florence.

Being requested at this time by the Pope for a design for the Porta Pia, Michelangelo made three, all fantastic and most beautiful, of which the Pope chose the least costly for putting into execution; and it is now to be seen erected there, with much credit to him. Perceiving the inclination of the Pope, and hoping that he would restore the other gates of Rome, he made many other designs for him; and he did the like, at the request of the same Pontiff, in the matter of the new Church of S. Maria degli Angeli in the Baths of Diocletian, in order to convert them into a temple for the use of Christians. A design by his hand prevailed over many others made by excellent architects, being executed with such beautiful considerations for the convenience of the Carthusian Friars, who have now carried it almost to completion, that it caused his Holiness and all the prelates and lords of the Court to marvel at the judgment of the lovely conceptions that he had drawn, availing himself of all the skeleton of those baths, out of which was seen formed a most beautiful temple, with an entrance surpassing the expectations of all the architects; from which he acquired infinite praise and honor.

Michelangelo had been seventeen years in the construction of S. Pietro, and several times the deputies had tried to remove him from that position, but they had not succeeded, and they were seeking to oppose him in every matter now with one vexatious pretext and now with another, hoping that out of weariness, being now so old that he could do no more, he would retire before them. But Michelangelo attended constantly to establishing it securely with directions, doubting on account of those envious persecutions lest it might come to be changed after his death; so that at the present day it is strong enough to allow the vaulting to be raised with perfect security. Moreover, Pius IV, living after him, commanded the superintendents of construction that nothing of what Michelangelo had directed should be changed; and with even greater authority his successor, Pius V, caused it to be carried out, who, lest disorder should arise, insisted that the designs made by Michelangelo should be carried into execution with the utmost fidelity, so that, when the architects Pirro Ligorio and Jacopo Vignuola were in charge of it, and Pirro wished presumptuously to disturb and alter those directions, he was removed with little honor, and only Vignuola remained.

But to return to Michelangelo: I must relate that about a year before his death, Vasari secretly prevailed upon Duke Cosimo de' Medici to persuade the Pope by means of Messer Averardo Serristori, his Ambassador, that, since Michelangelo was much reduced, a diligent watch should be kept on those who were about him to take care of him, or who visited him at his house, and that, in the event of some sudden accident happening to him, such as might well happen to an old man, he should make arrangements for his property, designs, cartoons, models, money, and all his other possessions at the time of his death, to be set down in an inventory and placed in security, for the sake of S. Pietro, so that, if there were things pertaining to that building, and also to the sacristy, library, and façade of S. Lorenzo, they might not be taken away, as is often wont to happen; and in the end, all this being duly carried out, such diligence had its reward. Leonardo, the nephew of Michelangelo, was desirous to go during the coming Lent to Rome, as one who guessed that he was now come to the end of his life; and at this Michelangelo was content. When, therefore, he fell sick of a slow fever, he straightway caused Daniello to write to Leonardo that he should come; but the illness grew worse, although Messer Federigo Donati, his physician, and his other attendants were about him, and with perfect consciousness he made his will in three sentences, leaving his soul in the hands of God, his body to the earth, and his substance to his nearest relatives, and enjoining on his friends that, at his passing from this life, they should recall to him the agony of Jesus Christ. And so at the twenty-third hour of the seventeenth day of February, in the year 1564, he breathed his last, to go to a better life.

Michelangelo was much inclined to the labors of art, seeing that everything, however difficult, succeeded with him, he having had from nature a genius very apt and ardent in these most noble arts of design. Moreover, in order to be entirely perfect, innumerable times he made anatomical studies, dissecting men's bodies in order to see the principles of their construction and the concatenation of the bones, muscles, veins, and nerves, the various movements and all the postures of the human body; and not of men only, but also of animals, and particularly of horses, which last he much delighted to keep. Of all these he desired to learn the principles and laws in so far as touched his art, and this knowledge he so demonstrated in the works that fell to him to handle, that those who attend to no other study than this do not know more. He so executed his works, whether with the brush or with the chisel, that they are almost inimitable, and he gave to his labors, as has been said, such art and grace, and a loveliness of such a kind, that (be it said without offense to any) he surpassed and vanquished the ancients; having been able to wrest things out of the greatest difficulties with such facility, that they do not appear wrought with effort, although whoever draws his works after him finds enough in imitating them.

The genius of Michelangelo was recognized in his lifetime, and not, as happens to many, after death, for it has been seen that Julius II, Leo X, Clement VII, Paul III, Julius III, Paul IV, and Pius IV, all supreme Pontiffs, always wished to have him near them, and also, as is known, Suleiman, Emperor of the Turks, Francis of Valois, King of France, the Emperor Charles V, the Signoria of Venice, and finally, as has been related, Duke Cosimo de' Medici; all offering him honorable salaries, for no other reason but to avail themselves of his great genius. This does not happen save to men of great worth, such as he was; and it is evident and well known that all these three arts were so perfected in him, that it is not found that among persons ancient or modern, in all the many years that the sun has been whirling round, God has granted this to any other but Michelangelo. He had imagination of such a kind, and so perfect, and the things conceived by him in idea were such, that often, through not being able to express with the hands conceptions so terrible and grand, he abandoned his works—nay, destroyed many of them; and I know that a little before he died he burned a great number of designs, sketches, and cartoons made with his own hand, to the end that no one might see the labors endured by him and his methods of trying his genius, and that he might not appear less than perfect. Of such I have some by his hand, found in Florence, and placed in my book of drawings; from which, although the greatness of that brain is seen in them, it is evident that when he wished to bring forth Minerva from the head of Jove, he had to use Vulcan's hammer. Thus he used to make his figures in the proportion of nine, ten, and even twelve heads, seeking nought else but that in putting them all together there should be a certain harmony of grace in the whole, which nature does not present; saying that it was necessary to have the compasses in the eyes and not in the hand, because the hands work and the eye judges; which method he used also in architecture.

No one should think it strange that Michelangelo delighted in solitude, he having been one who was enamored of his art, which claims a man, with all his thoughts, for herself alone. For all this, he prized the friendship of many great persons and of learned and ingenious men, at convenient times; and these he maintained. Thus the great Cardinal Ippolito de' Medici loved him greatly, and, having heard that a Turkish horse that he possessed pleased Michelangelo because of its beauty, it was sent as a present to him by the liberality of that lord, with ten mules laden with fodder, and a serving-man to attend to it; and Michelangelo accepted it willingly. The illustrious Cardinal Pole was much his friend, Michelangelo being enamored of his goodness and his talents; also Cardinal Farnese, and Santa Croce, which latter afterwards became Pope Marcellus, Cardinal Ridolfi, Cardinal Maffeo, Monsignor Bembo, Carpi, and many other cardinals, bishops, and prelates, whom it is not necessary to name. Others were Monsignor Claudio Tolomei, the Magnificent Messer Ottaviano de' Medici, his gossip, whose son he held at baptism, and Messer Bindo Altoviti; M. Lorenzo Ridolfi, M. Annibale Caro, and M. Giovan Francesco Lottini of Volterra. But infinitely more than any of the others he loved M. Tommaso de' Cavalieri, a Roman gentleman, for whom, being a young man and much inclined to these arts, he made, to the end that he might learn to draw, many most superb drawings of divinely beautiful heads, designed in black and red chalk; and then he drew for him a Ganymede rapt to Heaven by Jove's Eagle, a Tityus with the Vulture devouring his heart, the Chariot of the Sun falling with Phaëthon into the Po, and a Bacchanal of children, which are all in themselves most rare things, and drawings the like of which have never been seen. Michelangelo made a life-size portrait of Messer Tommaso in a cartoon, and neither before nor afterwards did he take the portrait of anyone, because he abhorred executing a resemblance to the living subject, unless it were of extraordinary beauty. These drawings, on account of the great delight that M. Tommaso took in them, were the reason that he afterwards obtained a good number, miraculous things, which Michelangelo once drew for Fra Sebastiano Viniziano, who carried them into execution; and in truth he rightly treasures them as relics, and he has courteously given craftsmen access to them.

Duke Cosimo de' Medici possesses many designs, sketches, and cartoons by the hand of Michelangelo, and likewise the statue of Victory with a captive beneath, ten feet in height, and four captives in the rough which serve to teach us how to carve figures from the marble by a method secure from any chance of spoiling the stone; which method is as follows. You take a figure in wax or some other solid material, and lay it horizontally in a vessel of water, which water being by its nature flat and level at the surface, as you raise the said figure little by little from the level, so it comes about that the more salient parts are revealed, while the lower parts—those, namely, on the under side of the figure—remain hidden, until in the end it all comes into view. In the same manner must figures be carved out of marble with the chisel, first laying bare the more salient parts, and then little by little the lower parts; and this method may be seen to have been followed by Michelangelo in the above-mentioned captives, which his Excellency wishes to be used as exemplars for his Academicians.

Michelangelo loved his fellow-craftsmen, and held intercourse with them, as with Jacopo Sansovino, Rosso, Pontormo, Daniello da Volterra, and Giorgio Vasari of Arezzo, to which last he showed innumerable kindnesses; and he was the reason that Giorgio gave his attention to architecture, intending to make use of him some day, and he readily conferred and discussed matters of art with him. Those who say that he was not willing to teach are wrong, because he was always willing with his intimates and with anyone who asked him for counsel; and I have been present on many such occasions, but of these, out of consideration, I say nothing, not wishing to reveal the deficiencies of others. It may be urged that he had bad fortune with those who lived with him in his house, which was because he hit upon natures little able to imitate him. If he had found a nature after his heart, as he told me several times, in spite of his age he would often have made anatomical studies, and would have written upon them, for the benefit of his fellow-craftsmen; for he was disappointed by several. But he did not trust himself, through not being able to express himself in writing as he would have liked, because he was not practiced in diction, although in the prose of his letters he explained his conceptions very well in a few words. He much delighted in readings of the poets in the vulgar tongue, and particularly of Dante, whom he much admired, imitating him in his conceptions and inventions; and so with Petrarch, having delighted to make madrigals and sonnets of great weight, upon which commentaries have been written.

Michelangelo sent a vast number by his own hand—receiving answers in rhyme and in prose—to the most illustrious Marchioness of Pescara,* of whose virtues he was enamored, and she likewise of his; and she went many times to Rome from Viterbo to visit him, and Michelangelo designed for her a Dead Christ in the lap of Our Lady, with two little Angels, all most admirable, and a Christ fixed on the Cross, who, with the head uplifted, is recommending His Spirit to the Father, a divine work; and also a Christ with the Woman of Samaria at the well. He much delighted in the sacred Scriptures, like the excellent Christian that he was; and he held in great veneration the works written by Fra Girolamo Savonarola, because he had heard the voice of that friar in the pulpit. He greatly loved human beauty for the sake of imitation in art, being able to select from the beautiful the most beautiful, for without this imitation no perfect work can be done; but not with lascivious and disgraceful thoughts, as he proved by his way of life, which was very frugal. Thus, when he was young, all intent on his work, he contented himself with a little bread and wine, and this he continued when old until the time when he was painting the Judgment in the Chapel, taking his refreshment in the evening when he had finished the day's work, but always very frugally. And, although he was rich, he lived like a poor man, nor did any friend ever eat at his table, or rarely; and he would not accept presents from anyone, because it appeared to him that if anyone gave him something, he would be bound to him for ever. This sober life kept him very active and in want of very little sleep, and often during the night, not being able to sleep, he would rise to labor with the chisel; having made a cap of thick paper, and over the center of his head he kept a lighted candle, which in this way threw light over where he was working without encumbering his hands. Vasari, who had seen the cap several times, reflecting that he did not use wax, but candles of pure goat's tallow, which are excellent, sent him four bundles of these, which weighed forty pounds. And

* Vittoria Colonna.

his servant with all courtesy carried them to him at the second hour of the evening, and presented them to him; but Michelangelo refused them, declaring that he did not want them; and then the servant said: "They have broken my arms on the way between the bridge and here, and I shall not carry them back to the house. Now here in front of your door there is a solid heap of mud; they will stand in it beautifully, and I will set them all alight." Michelangelo said to him: "Put them down here, for I will not have you playing pranks at my door."

He told me that often in his youth he slept in his clothes, being weary with labor and not caring to take them off only to have to put them on again later. There are some who have taxed him with being avaricious, but they are mistaken, for both with works of art and with his substance he proved the contrary, having given away so many things for which he could have obtained thousands of crowns. What better proof can I give than this, that I know from personal experience that he made many designs and went to see many pictures and buildings, without demanding any payment? But let us come to the money earned by him by the sweat of his brow, not from revenues, not from traffickings, but from his own study and labor. Can he be called avaricious who succored many poor persons, as he did, and secretly married off a good number of girls, and enriched those who served him and assisted him in his works, as with his servant Urbino, whom he made a very rich man? This Urbino was his man of all work, and had served him a long time; and Michelangelo said to him: "If I die, what will you do?" And he answered: "I will serve another master." "You poor creature," said Michelangelo, "I will save you from such misery"; and presented two thousand crowns to him in one sum, an act such as is generally left to Caesars and Pontiffs. To his nephew, moreover, he gave three and four thousand crowns at a time, and at the end he left him ten thousand crowns, besides the property in Rome.

Michelangelo was a man of tenacious and profound memory, so that, on seeing the works of others only once, he remembered them perfectly, and could avail himself of them in such a manner, that scarcely anyone has ever noticed it; nor did he ever do anything that resembled another thing by his hand, because he remembered everything that he had done. In his youth, being once with his painter-friends, they played for a supper for him who should make a figure most completely wanting in design and clumsy, after the likeness of the puppet-figures which those make who know nothing, scrawling upon walls; and in this he availed himself of his memory, for he remembered having seen one of those absurdities on a wall, and drew it exactly as if he had had it before him, and thus surpassed all those painters—a thing difficult for a man so steeped in design, and accustomed to choice works, to come out of with credit. He was full of disdain, and rightly, against anyone who did him an injury, but he was never seen to run to take revenge; nay, rather, he was most patient, modest in all his ways, very prudent and wise in his speech, with answers full of weight, and at times sayings most ingenious, amusing, and acute. He said many things that have been written down by me, of which I shall include only a few, because it would take too long to give them all. To a citizen who found him by Or San Michele in Florence, where he had stopped to gaze at Donatello's statue of S. Mark, and who asked him what he thought of that figure, Michelangelo answered that he had never seen a figure that had more of the air of a good man than that one, and that, if S. Mark was like that, one could give credence to what he had written. Being shown a drawing by a boy then beginning to learn to draw, who was recommended to him, some persons excusing him because it was not long since he had applied himself to art, he replied: "That is evident." He said a similar thing to a painter who had painted a Pietà, and had not acquitted himself well: "It is indeed a pitiful thing to see." Being asked by a friend what he thought of one who had counterfeited in marble some of the most celebrated antique figures, and boasted that in his imitations he had surpassed the antiques by a great measure, Michelangelo replied: "He who goes behind others can never go in front of them, and he who is not able to work well for himself cannot make good use of the works of others." Passing by S. Giovanni in Florence, he was asked his opinion of those doors, and he answered: "They are so beautiful that they would do well at the gates of Paradise." He went to see a work of sculpture which was about to be sent out because it was finished, and the sculptor was taking much trouble to arrange the lights from the windows, to the end that it might show up well; whereupon Michelangelo said to him: "Do not trouble yourself; the important thing will be the light of the Piazza"; meaning to imply that when works are in public places, the people must judge whether they are good or bad. A painter had executed a scene, and had copied many things from various other works, both drawings and pictures, nor was there anything in that work that was not copied. It was shown to Michelangelo, who, having seen it, was asked by a very dear friend what he thought of it, and he replied: "He has done well, but I know not what this scene will do on the day of Judgment, when all bodies shall recover their members, for there will be nothing left of it." A priest, his friend, said to him: "It is a pity that you have not taken a wife, so that you might have had many children and left them all your honorable labors." And Michelangelo replied: "I have only too much of a wife in this art of mine, who has always kept me in tribulation, and my children shall be the works that I may leave, which, even if they are naught, will live a while. Woe to Lorenzo Ghiberti, if he had not made the gates of S. Giovanni, for his children and grandchildren sold or squandered all that he left, but the gates are still standing." Vasari, sent by Julius III to Michelangelo's house for a design at the first hour of the night, found him working at the Pietà in marble that he broke. Michelangelo, recognizing him by the knock at the door, left his work and took a lamp in his hand; Vasari explained what he wanted, whereupon Michelangelo sent Urbino upstairs for the design, and then they entered into another conversation. Meanwhile Vasari turned his eyes to examine a leg of the Christ at which he was working, seeking to change it; and, in order to prevent Vasari from seeing it, he let the lamp fall from his hand, and they were left in darkness. He called to Urbino to bring a light, and meanwhile came forth from the enclosure where the work was, and said: "I am so old that death often pulls me by the cloak, that I may go with him, and one day this body of mine will fall like the lamp, and the light of my life will be spent."

Now, to be brief, I must record that the master's constitution was very sound, for he was lean and well knit together with nerves, and although as a boy he was delicate, and as a man he had two serious illnesses, he could always endure any fatigue and had no infirmity, save that in his old age he suffered from dysuria and from gravel, which in the end developed into the stone; wherefore for many years he was syringed by the hand of Maestro Realdo Colombo, his very dear friend, who treated him with great diligence. He was of middle stature, broad in the shoulders, but well proportioned in all the rest of the body. In his latter years he wore buskins of dogskin on the legs, next to the skin, constantly for whole months together, so that afterwards, when he sought to take them off, on drawing them off the skin often came away with them. Over the stockings he wore boots of cordwain fastened on the inside, as a protection against damp. His face was round, the brow square and spacious, with seven straight lines, and the temples projected considerably beyond the ears; which ears were somewhat on the large side, and stood out from the cheeks. The body was in proportion to the face, or rather on the large side; the nose somewhat flattened; having been broken, as was said, by Torrigiano; the eyes rather on the small side, of the color of horn, spotted with bluish and yellowish gleams; the eyebrows with few hairs, the lips thin, with the lower lip rather thicker and projecting a little, the chin well shaped and in proportion with the rest, the hair black, but mingled with white hairs, like the beard, which was not very long, forked, and not very thick.

Truly his coming was to the world, as I said at the beginning, an exemplar sent by God to the men of our arts, to the end that they might learn from his life the nature of noble character, and from his works what true and excellent craftsmen ought to be. And I, who have to praise God for infinite blessings, as is seldom wont to happen with men of our profession, count it among the greatest blessings that I was born at the time when Michelangelo was alive, that I was thought worthy to have him as my master, and that he was so much my friend and intimate, as everyone knows, and as the letters written by him to me, now in my possession, bear witness; and out of love for truth, and also from the obligation that I feel to his loving kindness, I have contrived to write many things of him, and all true, which many others have not been able to do.

TITIAN

[*Tiziano di Gregorio di Conte de' Vecelli, called by
English-speaking people Titian of Cadore, was born
between 1488 and 1490; died in 1576.*]

TITIAN was born at Cadore, a little township situated on the
Piave and five miles distant from the pass of the Alps, from
the family of the Vecelli, one of the most noble in that place.
At the age of ten, having a fine spirit and a lively intelligence,
he was sent to Venice to the house of an uncle, an honored
citizen, who, perceiving the boy to be much inclined to painting, placed him with Gian Bellini, an excellent painter very
famous at that time. Under his discipline, attending to design, he soon showed that he was endowed by nature with
all the gifts of intellect and judgment that are necessary for
the art of painting; and since at that time Gian Bellini and the
other painters of that country, from not being able to study
ancient works, were much—nay, altogether—given to copying
from the life whatever work they did, and that with a dry,
crude, and labored manner, Titian also for a time learned that
method. But having come to about the year 1507, Giorgione
da Castelfranco, not altogether liking that mode of working,
began to give to his pictures more softness and greater relief,
with a beautiful manner; nevertheless he used to set himself
before living and natural objects and counterfeit them as well
as he was able with colors, and paint them broadly with tints
crude or soft according as the life demanded, without doing
any drawing, holding it as certain that to paint with colors
only, without the study of drawing on paper, was the true and
best method of working, and the true design. For he did not

perceive that for him who wishes to distribute his compositions and accommodate his inventions well, it is necessary that he should first put them down on paper in several different ways, in order to see how the whole goes together, for the reason that the idea is not able to see or imagine the inventions perfectly within herself, if she does not reveal and demonstrate her conception to the eyes of the body, that these may assist her to form a good judgment. Besides which, it is necessary to give much study to the nude, if you wish to comprehend it well, which you will never do, nor is it possible, without having recourse to paper; and to keep always before you, while you paint, persons naked or draped, is no small restraint, whereas, when you have formed your hand by drawing on paper, you then come little by little with greater ease to carry your conceptions into execution, designing and painting together. And so, gaining practice in art, you make both manner and judgment perfect, doing away with the labor and effort wherewith those pictures were executed of which we have spoken above, not to mention that by drawing on paper, you come to fill the mind with beautiful conceptions, and learn to counterfeit all the objects of nature by memory, without having to keep them always before you or being obliged to conceal beneath the glamour of coloring the painful fruits of your ignorance of design, in the manner that was followed for many years by the Venetian painters, Giorgione, Palma, Pordenone, and others, who never saw Rome or any other works of absolute perfection.

Titian, then, having seen the method and manner of Giorgione, abandoned the manner of Gian Bellini, although he had been accustomed to it for a long time, and attached himself to that of Giorgione; coming in a short time to imitate his works so well, that his pictures at times were mistaken for works by Giorgione, as will be related below. Then, having grown in age, practice, and judgment, Titian executed many works in fresco, which cannot be enumerated in order, being dispersed over various places; let it suffice that they were

such, that the opinion was formed by many experienced
judges that he would become, as he afterwards did, a most
excellent painter. At the time when he first began to follow
the manner of Giorgione, not being more than eighteen years
of age, he made the portrait of a gentleman of the Barberigo
family, his friend, which was held to be very beautiful, the
likeness of the flesh-coloring being true and natural, and all
the hairs so well distinguished one from another, that they
might have been counted, as also might have been the stitches
in a doublet of silvered satin that he painted in that work. In
short, it was held to be so well done, and with such diligence,
that if Titian had not written his name on a dark ground, it
would have been taken for the work of Giorgione.

Meanwhile Giorgione himself had executed the principal
façade of the House of the German Merchants in Venice, and
by means of Barberigo there were allotted to Titian certain
scenes on the same building, above the Merceria. After which
work he painted a large picture with figures of the size of life,
which is now in the hall of M. Andrea Loredano, who dwells
near S. Marcuola. In that picture is painted Our Lady going
into Egypt, in the midst of a great forest and certain landscapes that are very well done, because Titian had given his
attention for many months to such things, and had kept in his
house for that purpose some Germans who were excellent
painters of landscapes and verdure. In the wood in that picture, likewise, he painted many animals, which he portrayed
from the life; and they are truly natural, and almost alive. Next,
in the house of M. Giovanni D'Anna, a Flemish gentleman
and merchant, his gossip, he made his portrait, which has all
the appearance of life, and also an "Ecce Homo" with many
figures, which is held by Titian himself and by others to be
a very beautiful work. The same master painted a picture of
Our Lady with other figures the size of life, of men and children, all portrayed from the life and from persons of that
house. Then in the year 1507, while the Emperor Maximilian
was making war on the Venetians, Titian, according to his

own account, painted an Angel Raphael with Tobias and a dog in the Church of S. Marziliano, with a distant landscape, where, in a little wood, S. John the Baptist is praying on his knees to Heaven, whence comes a radiance that illumines him; and this work it is thought that he executed before he made a beginning with the façade of the House of the German Merchants. Concerning which façade, many gentlemen, not knowing that Giorgione was not working there any more and that Titian was doing it, who had uncovered one part, meeting with Giorgione, congratulated him in friendly fashion, saying that he was acquitting himself better in the façade toward the Merceria than he had done in that which is over the Grand Canal. At which circumstance Giorgione felt such disdain, that until Titian had completely finished the work and it had become well known that the same had done that part, he would scarcely let himself be seen; and from that time onward he would never allow Titian to associate with him or be his friend.

In the year after, 1508, Titian published in wood-engraving the Triumph of Faith, with an infinity of figures; our first Parents, the Patriarchs, the Prophets, the Sibyls, the Innocents, the Martyrs, the Apostles, and Jesus Christ borne in Triumph by the four Evangelists and the four Doctors, with the Holy Confessors behind. In that work Titian displayed boldness, a beautiful manner, and the power to work with facility of hand; and I remember that Fra Sebastiano del Piombo, conversing of this, said to me that if Titian had been in Rome at that time, and had seen the works of Michelangelo, those of Raphael, and the ancient statues, and had studied design, he would have done things absolutely stupendous, considering the beautiful mastery that he had in coloring, and that he deserved to be celebrated as the finest and greatest imitator of Nature in the matter of color in our times, and with the foundation of the grand method of design he might have equaled Raphael and Michelangelo. At Padua, in the Church of S. Antonio, he executed likewise in fresco some stories of the actions of that Saint, and for that of S. Spirito he painted a little altar-piece with a S. Mark seated in the midst of certain Saints, in whose faces are some portraits from life done in oils with the greatest diligence; which picture many have believed to be by the hand of Giorgione. Then, a scene having been left unfinished in the Hall of the Great Council through the death of Giovanni Bellini, wherein Frederick Barbarossa is kneeling at the door of the Church of S. Marco before Pope Alexander IV, who places his foot on Barbarossa's neck, Titian finished it, changing many things, and making there many portraits from life of his friends and others; for which he was rewarded by receiving from the Senate an office in the House of the German Merchants, called the Senseria, which yields three hundred crowns a year. That office those Signori are accustomed to give to the most excellent painter of their city, on the condition that he shall be obliged from time to time to paint the portrait of their Prince or Doge, at his election, for the price of only eight crowns, which the Prince himself pays to him; which portrait is afterwards kept, in memory of him, in a public place in the Palace of S. Marco.

In the year 1514 Duke Alfonso of Ferrara had caused a little chamber to be decorated, and had commissioned Dosso, the painter of Ferrara, to execute in certain compartments stories of Aeneas, Mars, and Venus, and in a grotto Vulcan with two smiths at the forge; and he desired that there should also be there pictures by the hand of Gian Bellini. Bellini painted on another wall a vat of red wine with some Bacchanals around it, and Satyrs, musicians, and other men and women, all drunk with wine, and near them a nude and very beautiful Silenus, riding on his ass, with figures about him that have the hands full of fruits and grapes; which work was in truth executed and colored with great diligence, insomuch that it is one of the most beautiful pictures that Gian Bellini ever painted, although in the manner of the draperies there is a certain sharpness after the German manner (nothing, indeed, of any account), because he imitated a picture by the Fleming Albrecht Dürer, which had been brought in those days to Venice and placed in the Church of S. Bartolommeo, a rare work and full of most beautiful figures painted in oils.

That work he was not able to finish completely, because he was old, and Titian, as the most excellent of all the others, was sent for to the end that he might finish it; wherefore, being desirous to acquire excellence and to make himself known, he executed with much diligence two scenes that were wanting in that little chamber. In the first is a river of red wine, about which are singers and musicians, both men and women, as it were drunk, and a naked woman who is sleeping, so beautiful that she might be alive, together with other figures; and on this picture Titian wrote his name. In the other, which is next to it and seen first on entering, he painted many little boys and Loves in various attitudes, which much pleased that lord, as also did the other picture; but most beautiful of all is one of those boys who is making water into a river and is reflected in the water, while the others are around a pedestal that has the form of an altar, upon which is a statue of Venus with a sea-conch in the right hand, and Grace and Beauty about her, which are very lovely figures and executed with incredible diligence. On the door of a press, likewise, Titian painted an image of Christ from the waist upwards, marvelous, nay, stupendous, to whom a base Hebrew is showing the coin of Caesar; which image, and also other pictures in that little chamber, our best craftsmen declare to be the finest and best executed that Titian has ever done, and indeed they are most rare. Wherefore he well deserved to be most liberally recompensed and rewarded by that lord, whom he portrayed excellently well with one arm resting on a great piece of artillery; and he also made a portrait of Signora Laura, who afterwards became the wife of the Duke, which is a stupendous work. And, in truth, gifts have great potency with those who labor for the love of art, when they are uplifted by the liberality of Princes.

Having then returned to Venice, Titian painted on a canvas in oils, for the father-in-law of Giovanni da Castel Bolognese, a naked shepherd and a country girl who is offering him some pipes, that he may play them, with a most beautiful landscape; which picture is now at Faenza, in the house of the said Giovanni. He then executed for the high altar in the Church of the Friars Minors, called the Cà Grande, a picture of Our Lady ascending into Heaven, and below her the twelve Apostles, who are gazing upon her as she ascends; but of this work, from its having been painted on cloth, and perhaps not well kept, there is little to be seen. For the Chapel of the Pesari family, in the same church, he painted in an altar-piece the Madonna with the Child in her arms, a S. Peter and a S. George, and about them the patrons of the work, kneeling and portrayed from life; among whom are the Bishop of Paphos and his brother, then newly returned from the victory which that Bishop won against the Turks. For the little Church of S. Niccolò, in the same convent, he painted in an altar-piece S. Nicholas, S. Francis, S. Catharine, and also a nude S. Sebastian, portrayed from life and without any artifice that can be seen to have been used to enhance the beauty of the limbs and trunk, there being nothing there but what he saw in the work of nature, insomuch that it all appears as if stamped from the life, so flesh-like it is and natural; but for all that it is held to be beautiful, as is also very lovely the Madonna with the Child in her arms at whom all those figures are gazing. The subject of that picture was drawn on wood by Titian himself, and then engraved by others and printed. For the Church of S. Rocco, after the works described above, he painted a picture of Christ with the Cross on His shoulder, and about His neck a cord that is drawn by a Hebrew; and that figure, which many have believed to be by the hand of Giorgione, is now the object of the greatest devotion in Venice, and has received in alms more crowns than Titian and Giorgione ever gained in all their lives. Then he was invited to Rome by

Bembo, whom he had already portrayed, and who was at that time Secretary to Pope Leo X, to the end that he might see Rome, Raphael of Urbino, and others; but Titian delayed the visit so long from one day to another, that Leo died, and Raphael in 1520, and after all he never went. For the Church of S. Maria Maggiore he painted a picture with S. John the Baptist in the Desert among some rocks, an Angel that appears as if alive, and a little piece of distant landscape with some trees upon the bank of a river, all full of grace.

He made portraits from life of the Prince Grimani and Loredano, which were held to be admirable; and not long afterwards of King Francis, when he departed from Italy in order to return to France. And in the year when Andrea Gritti was elected Doge, Titian painted his portrait, which was a very rare thing, in a picture wherein are Our Lady, S. Mark, and S. Andrew with the countenance of that Doge; which picture, a most marvelous work, is in the Sala del Collegio. He has also painted portraits, in addition to those of the Doges named above (being obliged, as has been related, to do it), of others who have been Doges in their time: Pietro Lando, Francesco Donato, Marcantonio Trevisano, and Veniero. But by the two Doges and brothers Priuli he has been excused recently, because of his great age, from that obligation. Before the sack of Rome there had gone to live in Venice Pietro Aretino, a most famous poet of our times, and he became very much the friend of Titian and Sansovino; which brought great honor and advantage to Titian, for the reason that the poet made him known wherever his pen reached, and especially to Princes of importance, as will be told in the proper place.

Meanwhile, to return to Titian's works, he painted the altar-piece for the altar of S. Piero Martire in the Church of SS. Giovanni e Paolo, depicting therein that holy martyr larger than life, in a forest of very great trees, fallen to the ground and assailed by the fury of a soldier, who has wounded him so grievously in the head, that as he lies but half alive there is seen in his face the horror of death, while in another friar who runs forward in flight may be perceived the fear and terror of death. In the air are two nude Angels coming down from a flash of Heaven's lightning, which gives light to the landscape, which is most beautiful, and to the whole work besides, which is the most finished, the most celebrated, the greatest, and the best conceived and executed that Titian has as yet ever done in all his life. This work being seen by Gritti, who was always very much the friend of Titian, as also of Sansovino, he caused to be allotted to him a great scene of the rout of Ghiaradadda, in the Hall of the Great Council. In it he painted a battle with soldiers in furious combat, while a terrible rain falls from Heaven; which work, wholly taken from life, is held to be the best of all the scenes that are in that Hall, and the most beautiful. And in the same Palace, at the foot of a staircase, he painted a Madonna in fresco. Having made not long afterwards for a gentleman of the Contarini family a picture of a very beautiful Christ, who is seated at table with Cleophas and Luke, it appeared to that gentleman that the work was worthy to be in a public place, as in truth it is. Wherefore having made a present of it, like a true lover of his country and of the commonwealth, to the Signoria, it was kept a long time in the apartments of the Doge; but at the present day it is in a public place, where it may be seen by everyone, in the Salotta d'Oro in front of the Hall of the Council of Ten, over the door.

It is said that in the year 1530, the Emperor Charles V being in Bologna, Titian was invited to that city by Cardinal Ippolito de' Medici, through the agency of Pietro Aretino. There he made a most beautiful portrait of his Majesty in full armor, which so pleased him, that he caused a thousand crowns to be given to Titian; but of these he was obliged afterwards to give the half to the sculptor Alfonso Lombardi, who had made a model to be reproduced in marble.

Having returned to Venice, Titian found that a number of gentlemen, who had taken Pordenone into their favor, praising much the works executed by him on the ceiling of the Sala de' Pregai and elsewhere, had caused a little altar-piece to be allotted to him in the Church of S. Giovanni Elemosinario, to the end that he might paint it in competition with Titian, who for the same place had painted a short time before the said S. Giovanni Elemosinario in the habit of a Bishop. But, for all the diligence that Pordenone devoted to that altar-piece, he was not able to equal or even by a great measure to approach to the work of Titian. Next, Titian executed a most beautiful altar-picture of an Annunciation for the Church of S. Maria degli Angeli at Murano, but he who had caused it to be painted not being willing to spend five hundred crowns upon it, which Titian was asking, by the advice of Messer Pietro Aretino he sent it as a gift to the above-named Emperor Charles V, who, liking that work vastly, made him a present of two thousand crowns; and where that picture was to have been placed, there was set in its stead one by the hand of Pordenone. Nor had any long time passed when Charles V, returning to Bologna for a conference with Pope Clement, at the time when he came with his army from Hungary, desired to be portrayed again by Titian. Before departing from Bologna, Titian also painted a portrait of the above-named Cardinal Ippolito de' Medici in Hungarian dress, and in a smaller picture the same man in full armor; both which portraits are now in the *guardaroba* of Duke Cosimo. At that same time he executed a portrait of Alfonso Davalos, Marchese del Vasto, and one of the above-named Pietro Aretino, who then contrived that he should become the friend and servant of Federigo Gonzaga, Duke of Mantua, with whom Titian went to his States and there painted a portrait of him, which is a living likeness, and then one of the Cardinal, his brother. These finished, he painted, for the adornment of a room among those of Giulio Romano, twelve figures from the waist upwards of the twelve Caesars, very beautiful, beneath each of which the said Giulio afterwards painted a story from their lives.

In Cadore, his native place, Titian has painted an altar-picture wherein are Our Lady, S. Tiziano the Bishop, and a portrait of himself kneeling. In the year when Pope Paul III went to Bologna, and from there to Ferrara, Titian, having gone to the Court, made a portrait of that Pope, which was a very beautiful work, and from it another for Cardinal S. Fiore; and both these portraits, for which he was very well paid by the Pope, are in Rome, one in the *guardaroba* of Cardinal Farnese, and the other in the possession of the heirs of the above-named Cardinal S. Fiore, and from them have been taken many copies, which are dispersed throughout Italy. At this same time, also, he made a portrait of Francesco Maria, Duke of Urbino, which was a marvelous work; wherefore M. Pietro Aretino on this account celebrated him in a sonnet. There are in the *guardaroba* of the same Duke, by the hand of Titian, two most lovely heads of women, and a young recumbent Venus with flowers and certain light draperies about her, very beautiful and well finished; and, in addition, a figure of S. Mary Magdalene with the hair all loose, which is a rare work. There, likewise, are the portraits of Charles V, King Francis as a young man, Duke Guidobaldo II, Pope Sixtus IV, Pope Julius II, Paul III, the old Cardinal of Lorraine, and Suleiman Emperor of the Turks; which portraits, I say, are by the hand of Titian, and most beautiful.

In the year 1541 Titian painted for the Friars of S. Spirito, in Venice, the altar-piece of their high altar, figuring in it the Descent of the Holy Spirit upon the Apostles, with a God depicted as of fire, and the Spirit as a Dove; which altar-piece becoming spoiled in no long time, after having many disputes with those friars he had to paint it again, and it is that which is over the altar at the present day. For the Church of S. Nazzaro in Brescia he executed the altar-piece of the high altar in five pictures; in the central picture is Jesus Christ returning to life, with some soldiers around, and at the sides are S. Nazzaro, S. Sebastian, the Angel Gabriel, and the

Virgin receiving the Annunciation. In a picture for the wall at the entrance of the Duomo of Verona, he painted an Assumption of Our Lady into Heaven, with the Apostles on the ground, which is held to be the best of the modern works in that city. In the year 1541 he made the portrait of Don Diego di Mendoza, at that time Ambassador of Charles V in Venice, a whole-length figure and standing, which was very beautiful; and from this Titian began what has since come into fashion, the making of certain portraits of full length. In the same manner he painted that of the Cardinal of Trento, then a young man, and for Francesco Marcolini the portrait of Messer Pietro Aretino, but this last was by no means as beautiful as one of that poet, likewise by the hand of Titian, which Aretino himself sent as a present to Duke Cosimo de' Medici, to whom he sent also the head of Signor Giovanni de' Medici, the father of the said Lord Duke. That head was copied from a cast taken from the face of that lord when he died at Mantua, which was in the possession of Aretino; and both these portraits are in the *guardaroba* of the same Lord Duke, among many other most noble pictures.

The same year, Vasari having been thirteen months in Venice to execute a ceiling for Messer Giovanni Cornaro, and some works for the Company of the Calza, Sansovino, who was directing the construction of S. Spirito, had commissioned him to make designs for three large pictures in oils which were to go into the ceiling, to the end that he might execute them in painting; but, Vasari having afterwards departed, those three pictures were allotted to Titian, who executed them most beautifully, from his having contrived with great art to make the figures foreshortened from below upwards. In one is Abraham sacrificing Isaac, in another David severing the neck of Goliath, and in the third Abel slain by his brother Cain. About the same time Titian painted a portrait of himself, in order to leave that memory of himself to his children.

The year 1546 having come, he went at the invitation of

Cardinal Farnese to Rome, where he found Vasari, who, having returned from Naples, was executing the Hall of the Cancelleria for the above-named Cardinal; whereupon, Titian having been recommended by that lord to Vasari, Giorgio kept him company lovingly in taking him about to see the sights of Rome. And then, after Titian had rested for some days, rooms were given to him in the Belvedere, to the end that he might set his hand to painting once more the portrait of Pope Paul, of full length, with one of Farnese and one of Duke Ottavio, which he executed excellently well and much to the satisfaction of those lords. At their persuasion he painted, for presenting to the Pope, a picture of Christ from the waist upwards in the form of an "Ecce Homo," which work, whether it was that the works of Michelangelo, Raphael, Polidoro, and others had made him lose some force, or for some other reason, did not appear to the painters, although it was a good picture, to be of the same excellence as many others by his hand, and particularly his portraits. Michelangelo and Vasari, going one day to visit Titian in the Belvedere, saw in a picture that he had executed at that time a nude woman representing Danaë, who had in her lap Jove transformed into a rain of gold; and they praised it much, as one does in the painter's presence. After they had left him, discoursing of Titian's method, Buonarroti commended it not a little, saying that his coloring and his manner much pleased him, but that it was a pity that in Venice men did not learn to draw well from the beginning, and that those painters did not pursue a better method in their studies. "For," he said, "if this man had been in any way assisted by art and design, as he is by nature, and above all in counterfeiting the life, no one could do more or work better, for he has a fine spirit and a very beautiful and lively manner." And in fact this is true, for the reason that he who has not drawn much nor studied the choicest ancient and modern works, cannot work well from memory by himself or improve the things that he copies from life, giving them the grace and perfection wherein art goes beyond the scope of nature, which generally produces some parts that are not beautiful.

Titian finally departed from Rome, with many gifts received from those lords. Arriving in Florence, and seeing the rare works of that city, he was amazed by them no less than he had been by those of Rome. And besides that, he visited Duke Cosimo, who was at Poggio a Caiano, offering to paint his portrait; to which his Excellency did not give much heed, perchance in order not to do a wrong to the many noble craftsmen of his city and dominion.

Then, having arrived in Venice, Titian finished for the Marchese del Vasto an Allocution (for so they called it) made by that lord to his soldiers; and after that he took the portrait of Charles V, that of the Catholic King, and many others. These works finished, he painted a little altar-piece of the Annunciation for the Church of S. Maria Nuova in Venice; and then, employing the assistance of his young men, he executed a Last Supper in the refectory of SS. Giovanni e Paolo, and for the high altar of the Church of S. Salvadore an altar-piece in which is a Christ Transfigured on Mount Tabor, and for another altar in the same church a Madonna receiving the Annunciation from the Angel. But these last works, although there is something of the good to be seen in them, are not much esteemed by him, and have not the perfection that his other pictures have. And since the works of Titian are without number, and particularly the portraits, it is almost impossible to make mention of them all; wherefore I shall speak only of the most remarkable, but without order of time, it being of little import to know which was first and which later. Several times, as has been related, he painted the portrait of Charles V, and in the end he was summoned for that purpose to the Court, where he portrayed him as he was in those his later years; and the work of Titian so pleased that all-conquering Emperor, that after he had once seen it he would not be portrayed by other painters. Each time that he painted him, he received a thousand crowns of gold as a present, and he was made by his Majesty a Chevalier, with a revenue of two hundred crowns on the Chamber of Naples. In like manner, when he portrayed Philip, King of Spain, the son of Charles, he received from him a fixed allowance of two hundred crowns more; insomuch that, adding those four hundred to the three hundred that he has on the House of the German Merchants from the Signori of Venice, he has without exerting himself a fixed income of seven hundred crowns every year. Of the same Charles V and King Philip Titian sent portraits to the Lord Duke Cosimo, who has them in his *guardaroba*. He portrayed Ferdinand, King of the Romans, who afterwards became Emperor, and both his sons, Maximilian, now Emperor, and his brother. He also portrayed Queen Maria, and, for the Emperor Charles V, the Duke of Saxony when he was a prisoner. But what a waste of time is this? There has been scarce a single lord of great name, or Prince, or great lady, who has not been portrayed by Titian, a painter of truly extraordinary excellence in this field of art. He painted portraits of King Francis I of France, as has been related, Francesco Sforza, Duke of Milan, the Marquis of Pescara, Antonio da Leva, Massimiano Stampa, Signor Giovan Battista Castaldo, and other lords without number.

In like manner, besides the works mentioned above, at various times he has executed many others. In Venice, by order of Charles V, he painted in a great altar-piece the Triune God enthroned, Our Lady and the Infant Christ, with the Dove over Him, and the ground all of fire, signifying Love; and the Father is surrounded by fiery Cherubim. On one side is the same Charles V, and on the other the Empress, both clothed in linen garments, with the hands clasped in the attitude of prayer, among many Saints; all which was after the command of the Emperor, who, at that time at the height of his victories, began to show that he was minded to retire from the things of this world, as he afterwards did, in order to die like a true Christian, fearing God and desirous of his own salvation. Which picture the Emperor said to Titian that he wished to place in the monastery wherein afterwards he finished the course of his life; and since it is a very rare work, it is expected that it may soon be published in engravings. The same Titian executed for Queen Maria a Prometheus who is bound to Mount Caucasus and torn by Jove's Eagle, a Sisyphus in Hell who is toiling under his stone, and Tityus devoured by the Vulture. These her Majesty received, excepting the Prometheus, and with them a Tantalus of the same size (namely, that of life), on canvas and in oils. He executed, also, a Venus and Adonis that are marvelous, she having swooned, and the boy in the act of rising to leave her, with some dogs about him that are very natural. On a panel of the same size he represented Andromeda bound to the rock, and Perseus delivering her from the Sea-Monster, than which picture none could be more lovely; as is also another of Diana, who, bathing in a fount with her Nymphs, transforms Actaeon into a stag. He also painted Europa passing over the sea on the back of the Bull. All these pictures are in the possession of the Catholic King, held very dear for the vivacity that Titian has given to the figures with his colors, making them natural and as if alive.

It is true, however, that the method of work which he employed in these last pictures is no little different from the method of his youth, for the reason that the early works are executed with a certain delicacy and a diligence that are incredible, and they can be seen both from near and from a distance, and these last works are executed with bold strokes and dashed off with a broad and even coarse sweep of the brush, insomuch that from near little can be seen, but from a distance they appear perfect. This method has been the reason that many, wishing to imitate him therein and to play the practiced master, have painted clumsy pictures; and this happens because, although many believe that they are done without effort, in truth it is not so, and they deceive themselves, for it is known that they are painted over and over again, and that he returned to them with his colors so many times, that the labor may be perceived. And this method, so used, is judicious, beautiful, and astonishing, because it makes pictures appear alive and painted with great art, but conceals the labor.

Titian painted recently in a picture six feet high and eight feet broad, Jesus Christ as an Infant in the lap of Our Lady and adored by the Magi, with a good number of figures of two feet each, which is a very lovely work, as is also another picture that he himself copied from that one and gave to the old Cardinal of Ferrara. Another picture, in which he depicted Christ mocked by the Jews, which is most beautiful, was placed in a chapel of the Church of S. Maria delle Grazie, in Milan. For the Queen of Portugal he painted a picture of a Christ scourged by Jews at the Column, a little less than the size of life, which is very beautiful. For the high altar of S. Domenico, at Ancona, he painted an altar-piece with Christ on the Cross, and at the foot Our Lady, S. John, and S. Dominic, all most beautiful, and executed in his later manner with broad strokes, as has just been described above. And by the same hand, in the Church of the Crocicchieri at Venice, is the picture that is on the altar of S. Lorenzo, wherein is the martyrdom of that Saint, with a building full of figures, and S. Laurence lying half upon the gridiron, in foreshortening, with a great fire beneath him, and about it some who are kindling it. And since he counterfeited an effect of night, there are two servants with torches in their hands, which throw light where the glare of the fire below the gridiron does not reach, which is piled high and very fierce. Besides this, he depicted a lightning flash, which, darting from Heaven and cleaving the clouds, overcomes the light of the fire and that of the torches, shining over the Saint and the other principal figures, and, in addition to those three lights, the figures that he painted in the distance at the windows of the building have the light of lamps and candles that are near them; and all, in short, is executed with beautiful art, judgment, and genius. In the Church of S. Sebastiano, on the altar of S. Niccolò, there is by the hand of the same Titian a little altar-piece of a S. Nicholas who appears as if alive, seated in a chair painted in the likeness of stone, with an Angel that is holding his miter; which work he executed at the commission of Messer Niccolò Crasso, the advocate. Titian afterwards painted, for sending to the Catholic King, a figure of S. Mary Magdalene from the middle of the thighs upwards, all disheveled; that is, with the hair falling over the shoulders, about the throat, and over the breast, the while that, raising the head with the eyes fixed on Heaven, she reveals remorse in the redness of the eyes, and in her tears repentance for her sins. Wherefore the picture moves mightily all who behold it; and, what is more, although she is very beautiful, it moves not to lust but to compassion. This picture, when it was finished, so pleased Silvio Badoer, a Venetian gentleman, that in order to have it, being one who takes supreme delight in painting, he gave Titian a hundred crowns: wherefore Titian was forced to paint another, which was not less beautiful, for sending to the above-named Catholic King. He also portrayed Bembo another time (namely, after he became a Cardinal), Fracastoro, and Cardinal Accolti of Ravenna.

In addition to the works described and many others of less merit executed by this man, which are omitted for the sake of brevity, he has in his house, sketched in and begun, the following: the Martyrdom of S. Laurence, similar to that described above, and destined by him for sending to the Catholic King. He also began, many years ago, for Alfonso I, Duke of Ferrara, a picture of a nude young woman bowing before Minerva, with another figure at the side, and a sea in the center of which, in the distance, is Neptune in his car; but through the death of that lord, after whose fancy the work was being executed, it was not finished, and remained with Titian.

All these works, I say, he has executed, with many others

that I omit in order not to be wearisome, up to his present age of about seventy-six years. Titian has been very sound in health, and as fortunate as any man of his kind has ever been; and he has not received from Heaven anything save favors and blessings. In his house at Venice have been all the Princes, men of letters and persons of distinction who have gone to that city or lived there in his time, because, in addition to his excellence in art, he has shown great gentleness, beautiful breeding, and most courteous ways and manners. He has had in Venice some competitors, but not of much worth, so that he has surpassed them easily with the excellence of his art and with his power of attaching himself and making himself dear to the men of quality. He has earned much, for he has been very well paid for his works; but it would have been well for him in these his last years not to work save as a pastime, so as not to diminish with works of less excellence the reputation gained in his best years, when his natural powers were not declining and drawing toward imperfection. When Vasari, the writer of this history, was at Venice in the year 1566, he went to visit Titian, as one who was much his friend, and found him at his painting with brushes in his hand, although he was very old; and he had much pleasure in seeing him and discoursing with him.

Titian, then, having adorned with excellent pictures the city of Venice, nay, all Italy and other parts of the world, deserves to be loved and revered by the craftsmen, and in many things to be admired and imitated, as one who has executed and is still executing works worthy of infinite praise, which shall endure as long as the memory of illustrious men may live.

SANSOVINO

[Jacopo d'Antonio di Jacopo Tatti, called Jacopo Sansovino, was born in 1486 and died in 1570.]

THE family of the Tatti in Florence is recorded in the books of the Commune from the year 1300, because, having come from Lucca, a very noble city of Tuscany, it was always abundant in industrious and honored men, and they were most highly favored by the House of Medici. Of this family was born Jacopo, of whom we are writing in this place; and he was born from Antonio, a most excellent person, and from his wife Francesca, in the month of January, 1486. In the first years of his boyhood he was set, as is usual, to learn his letters; and, after beginning to show in these vivacities of brain and readiness of spirit, not long afterwards he applied himself of his own accord to drawing, giving evidence in a certain sort that nature was inclining him much more to this kind of work than to letters, for the reason that he went very unwillingly to school and learned much against his will the rudiments of grammar. His mother, whom he resembled very strongly, perceiving this and fostering his genius, gave him assistance, causing him to be taught design in secret, because she loved the thought that her son should be a sculptor, perchance in emulation of the then rising glory of Michelangelo Buonarroti, who at that time was still very young: and also moved by a certain fateful augury, in that Michelangelo and this Jacopo had been born in one and the same street. Now the boy, after some time, was placed to learn the trade of a merchant; in which, delighting even less than in letters, he did and said so much, that he obtained leave from his father to attend without hindrance to that toward which he was urged by nature.

There had come to Florence at that time Andrea Contucci of Monte Sansovino, a township near Arezzo, risen to great fame in our day from having been the birthplace of Pope Julius III; which Andrea, having acquired in Italy and in Spain the name of the best sculptor and architect that there was in art after Michelangelo, was staying in Florence in order to execute two figures in marble that were to be placed over that door of the Temple of S. Giovanni which faces toward the Misericordia. To him Jacopo was entrusted to be taught the art of sculpture. Whereupon Andrea, having recognized how excellent in sculpture the young man was destined to become, did not fail to teach him with all possible care all those things which might make him known as his disciple. And so, loving him very dearly, and doing his best for him with much affection, and being loved by the young man with equal tenderness, people judged that the pupil would not only become as excellent as his master, but would by a great measure surpass him. And such were the reciprocal friendliness and love between these two, as it were between father and son, that Jacopo in those early years began to be called no longer Tatti, but Sansovino, and so he has always been, and always will be.

Now, Jacopo beginning to exercise his hand, he was so assisted by Nature in the things that he did, that, although at times he did not use much study and diligence in his work, nevertheless in what he did there could be seen facility, sweetness, grace, and a certain delicacy very pleasing to the eyes of craftsmen, insomuch that his every sketch, rough study, and model has always had a movement and a boldness that Nature is wont to give to but few sculptors. Moreover, the friendship and intercourse that Andrea del Sarto and Jacopo Sansovino had with each other in their childhood, and then in their youth, assisted not a little both the one and the other, for they followed the same manner in design and had the same grace in execution, one in painting and the other in sculpture, and, conferring together on the problems of art, and Jacopo making models of figures for Andrea, they gave one another very great assistance. And that this is true a proof is that in the altar-piece of S. Francesco, belonging to the Nuns of the Via Pentolini, there is a S. John the Evangelist which was copied from a most beautiful model in clay that Sansovino made in those days in competition with Baccio da Montelupo.

Becoming known to all the craftsmen of Florence, and being considered a young man of fine parts and excellent character, Jacopo was invited by Giuliano da San Gallo, architect to Pope Julius II, to Rome, vastly to his satisfaction; and then, taking extraordinary pleasure in the ancient statues that are in the Belvedere, he set himself to draw them. Whereupon Bramante, who was likewise architect to Pope Julius, holding the first place at that time and dwelling in the Belvedere, having seen some drawings by this young man, and a nude recumbent figure of clay in full-relief, holding a vessel to contain ink, which he had made, liked them so much that he took him under his protection and ordered him to make a large copy in wax of the Laocoön, which he was having copied also by others, in order to take a cast in bronze—namely, by Zaccheria Zacchi of Volterra, the Spaniard Alonzo Berughetta, and Vecchio of Bologna. These, when all were finished, Bramante caused to be seen by Raphael of Urbino, in order to learn which of the four had acquitted himself best; whereupon it was judged by Raphael that Sansovino, young as he was, had surpassed the others by a great measure. Then, by the advice of Cardinal Domenico Grimani, orders were given to Bramante that he should have Jacopo's copy cast in bronze; and so the mould was made, and the work, being cast in metal, came out very well. And afterwards, having been polished, it was given to the Cardinal, who held it as long as he lived not less dear than if it had been the antique; and when he came to die, he left it as a very rare thing to the most Serene Signoria of Venice, which, after having kept it many years in the press of the Hall of the Council of Ten, finally in the year 1534 presented it to the Cardinal of Lorraine, who took it to France.

While Sansovino was acquiring greater fame every day in Rome with his studies in art, being held in much consideration, Giuliano da San Gallo, who had been keeping him in his house in the Borgo Vecchio, fell ill; and when he departed from Rome in a litter, in order to go to Florence for a change of air, a room was found for Jacopo by Bramante, likewise in the Borgo Vecchio, in the Palace of Domenico della Rovere, Cardinal of San Clemente, where Pietro Perugino was also dwelling, who at that time was painting for Pope Julius the vaulting of the chamber in the Borgia Tower. Whereupon Pietro, having seen the beautiful manner of Sansovino, caused him to make many models in wax for himself, and among them a Christ taken down from the Cross in the round, with many ladders and figures, which was a very beautiful thing. This and other things of the same sort, and models of various fantasies, were all collected afterwards by M. Giovanni Gaddi, and they are now in his house on the Piazza di Madonna in Florence. And these works were the reason that Sansovino became very intimately associated with Maestro Luca Signorelli, the painter of Cortona, with Bramantino da Milano, with Bernardino Pinturicchio, with Cesare Cesariano, who was in repute at that time for his commentaries on Vitruvius, and with many other famous and beautiful intellects of that age. Bramante, then, desiring that Sansovino should become known to Pope Julius, arranged to have some antiques restored by him; whereupon Jacopo, setting to work, displayed such diligence and so much grace in restoring them, that the Pope and all who saw them judged that nothing better could be done. These praises so spurred Sansovino to surpass himself, that, having given himself beyond measure to his studies, and being, also, somewhat delicate in constitution and suffering from some excess such as young men commit, he became so ill that he was forced for the sake of his life to return to Florence, where, profiting by his native air, by the advantage of his youth, and by the diligence and care of the physicians, in a short time he completely recovered. Now Messer Piero Pitti was arranging at that time to have a Madonna of marble made for that façade of the Mercato Nuovo in Florence where the clock is, and it appeared to him, since there were in Florence many young men of ability and also old masters, that the work should be given to that one among them who might make the best model. Whereupon one was given to Baccio da Montelupo to execute, one to Zaccheria Zacchi of Volterra, who had likewise returned to Florence the same year, another to Baccio Bandinelli, and yet another to Sansovino; and when these were placed in comparison, the honor and the work were given by Lorenzo di Credi, an excellent painter and a person of judgment and probity, and likewise by the other judges, craftsmen, and connoisseurs, to Sansovino. But, although the work was therefore allotted to him, nevertheless so much delay was caused in procuring and conveying the marble for him, by the envious machinations of Averardo da Filicaia, who greatly favored Bandinelli and hated Sansovino, that he was ordered by certain other citizens, having perceived that delay, to make one of the large Apostles in marble that were going into the Church of S. Maria del Fiore. Wherefore, having made the model of a S. James (which model, when the work was finished, came into the possession of Messer Bindo Altoviti), he began that figure and, continuing to work at it with all diligence and study, he carried it to completion so perfectly, that it is a miraculous figure and shows in all its parts that it was wrought with incredible study and care, the draperies, arms, and hands being undercut and executed with such art and such grace, that there is nothing better in marble to be seen. Thus, Sansovino showed in what way undercut draperies should be executed, having made these so delicate and so natural, that in some places he reduced the marble to the thickness that is seen in real folds and in the edges and hems of the borders of draperies; a difficult method, and one demanding much time and patience if you wish that it should so succeed as to display the perfection of art. These works caused Sansovino to be held by the men of art and by all Florence to be a most excellent and gracious master; on which account Giovanni Bartolini, having caused a house to be built in his garden of Gualfonda, desired that Sansovino should make for him a young Bacchus in marble, of the size of life. Whereupon the model for this was made by Sansovino, and it pleased Giovanni so much, that he had him supplied with the marble, and Jacopo began it with such eagerness, that his hands and brain flew as he worked. This work, I say, he studied in such a manner, in order to make it perfect, that he set himself to portray from the life, although it was winter, an assistant of his called Pippo del Fabbro, making him stand naked a good part of the day. Which Pippo would have become a capable craftsman, for he was striving with every effort to imitate his master; but, whether it was the standing naked with the head uncovered at that season, or that he studied too much and suffered hardships, before the Bacchus was finished he went mad, copying the attitudes of that figure. And this he showed one day that it was raining in torrents, when, Sansovino calling out "Pippo!" and he not answering, the master afterwards saw him mounted on the summit of a chimney on the roof, wholly naked and striking the attitude of his Bacchus. At other times, taking a sheet or other large piece of cloth, and wetting it, he would wrap it round his naked body, as if he were a model of clay or rags, and arrange the folds; and then, climbing up to some extraordinary place, and settling himself now in one attitude and now in another, as a Prophet, an Apostle, a soldier, or something else, he would have himself portrayed, standing thus for a period of two hours without speaking, not otherwise than as if he had been a motionless statue. Many other amusing follies of that kind poor Pippo played, but above all he was never able to forget the

Bacchus that Sansovino had made, save only when he died, a few years afterwards.

But to return to the statue; when it was carried to completion, it was held to be the most beautiful work that had ever been executed by a modern master, seeing that in it Sansovino overcame a difficulty never yet attempted, in making an arm raised in the air and detached on every side, which holds between the fingers a cup all cut out of the same marble with such delicacy, that the attachment is very slight, besides which the attitude is so well conceived and balanced on every side, and the legs and arms are so beautiful and so well proportioned and attached to the trunk, that to the eye and to the touch the whole seems much more like living flesh; insomuch that the fame that it has from all who see it is well deserved, and even more.

In the year 1514, when festive preparations of great richness were to be made in Florence for the coming of Pope Leo X, orders were given by the Signoria and by Giuliano de' Medici that many triumphal arches of wood should be made in various parts of the city. Whereupon Sansovino not only executed the designs for many of these, but himself undertook in company with Andrea del Sarto to construct the façade of S. Maria del Fiore all of wood, with statues, scenes, and architectural orders. His Holiness having then determined that the façade of S. Lorenzo should be executed in marble, the while that Raphael of Urbino and Michelangelo were expected from Rome, Sansovino, by order of the Pope, made a design for it; which giving much satisfaction, Baccio d'Agnolo was commissioned to make a model of it in wood, which proved very beautiful. Meanwhile, Michelangelo had made another, and he and Sansovino were ordered to go to Pietrasanta; where, finding much marble, but difficult to transport, they lost so much time, that when they returned to Florence they found the Pope departed for Rome. Whereupon, both following after him with their models, each by himself, Jacopo arrived at the very moment when Michelangelo's model was being shown to his Holiness in the Torre Borgia; but he did not succeed in obtaining what he hoped, because, whereas he believed that he would at least make under Michelangelo part of the statues that were going into that work, the Pope having spoken of it to him and Michelangelo having given him so to understand, he perceived on arriving in Rome that Michelangelo wished to be alone in the work. Nevertheless, having made his way to Rome and not wishing to return to Florence without any result, he resolved to remain in Rome and there give his attention to sculpture and architecture. And so, having undertaken to execute for the Florentine Giovan Francesco Martelli a Madonna in marble larger than life, he made her most beautiful, with the Child in her arms; and this was placed upon an altar within the principal door of S. Agostino.

At this time, with the favor of Pope Leo, the Florentine colony had bestirred itself out of emulation of the Germans, Spaniards, and Frenchmen, who had either begun or finished the churches of their colonies in Rome, and had begun to perform their solemn offices in those already built and adorned; and the Florentines had sought leave likewise to build a church for themselves. For which the Pope having given instructions to Lodovico Capponi, the Consul of the Florentine colony at that time, it was determined that behind the Banchi, at the beginning of the Strada Giulia, on the bank of the Tiber, an immense church should be built, to be dedicated to S. John the Baptist; which might surpass in magnificence, grandeur, cost, ornamentation, and design, the churches of all the other colonies. There competed, then, in making designs for this work, Raphael of Urbino, Antonio da San Gallo, Baldassarre da Siena, and Sansovino; and the Pope, when he had seen all their designs, extolled as the best that of Sansovino, because, besides other things, he had made at each of the four corners of that church a tribune, and a larger tribune in the center, after the likeness of the plan that Sebastiano Serlio placed in his second book on Architecture.

Whereupon, all the heads of the Florentine colony concurring
with the will of the Pope, with much approval of Sansovino,
the foundations were begun for a part of that church, altogether one hundred and seventy-six feet in length. But, there
being not enough space, and yet wishing to make the façade
of the church in line with the houses of the Strada Giulia,
they were obliged to stretch out into the stream of the Tiber
at least one hundred and twenty feet; which pleasing many
of them, because the grandeur as well as the cost was increased by making the foundations in the river, work was begun on this, and they spent upon it more than forty thousand
crowns, which would have been enough to build half the
masonry of the church.

In the meantime Sansovino, who was the head of this construction, while the foundations were being laid little by little,
had a fall and suffered a serious injury; and after a few days
he had himself carried to Florence for treatment, leaving the
charge of laying the rest of the foundations to Antonio da
San Gallo. But no long time passed before the Florentine
colony, having lost by the death of Leo so great a support
and so splendid a Prince, abandoned the building for the
duration of the life of Pope Adrian VI. Then, Clement having been elected, it was ordained, in order to pursue the same
order and design, that Sansovino should return and carry on
that construction in the same manner wherein he had first
arranged it; and so a beginning was made once more with
the work. Meanwhile, Sansovino undertook to make the tomb
of the Cardinal of Aragon and that of Cardinal Aginense;
and he had caused work to be begun on the marbles for the
ornaments, and had made many models for the figures, and
already Rome was in his hands, and he was executing many
works of the greatest importance for all those lords, having
been recognized by three Pontiffs, and especially by Pope
Leo, who presented him with a knighthood of S. Pietro,
which he sold during his illness, doubting lest he might die;
when God, in order to chastise that city and abate the pride

of the inhabitants of Rome, permitted that Bourbon should come with his army on the 6th of May, 1527, and that the whole city should be sacked and put to fire and sword.

In that ruin, besides many other beautiful intellects that came to an evil end, Sansovino was forced to his great loss to depart from Rome and to fly to Venice, intending from there to pass into France to enter the service of the King, whither he had been already invited. But, halting in that city in order to make himself ready and provide himself with many things, for he was despoiled of everything, it was announced to the Prince Andrea Gritti, who was much the friend of every talent, that Jacopo Sansovino was there. Whereupon there came to Gritti a desire to speak with him, because at that very time Cardinal Domenico Grimani had given him to understand that Sansovino would have been the man for the cupolas of S. Marco, their principal church, which, because of age and of weak foundations, and also from their being badly secured with chains, were all opening out and threatening to fall; and so he had him summoned. After many courtesies and long discussions, he said to Sansovino that he wished, or rather, prayed him, that he should find a remedy for the ruin of those tribunes; which Sansovino promised to do, and to put it right. And so, having agreed to do the work, he caused it to be taken in hand; and, having contrived all the scaffoldings in the interior and made supports of beams after the manner of stars, he propped in the central hollow of woodwork all the timbers that sustained the vault of each tribune, and encircled them on the inner side with curtains of woodwork, going on then to bind them on the outer side with chains of iron, to flank them with new walls, and to make at the foot new foundations for the piers that supported them, insomuch that he strengthened them vastly and made them for ever secure. By doing which he caused all Venice to marvel, and not only satisfied Gritti, but also—which was far more—rendered his ability so clearly manifest to that most illustrious Senate, that when the work

was finished, the Protomaster to the Lords Procurators of
S. Mark being dead, which is the highest office that those
lords give to their architects and engineers, they gave it to
him with the usual house and a passing handsome salary.
Whereupon Sansovino, having accepted it most willingly and
freed his mind of all doubt, became the head of all their
constructions, with honor and advantage for himself.

Having then entered on that office, he began to occupy
himself with every care, both with regard to buildings and
in the management of the papers and of the books that he
held by virtue of his office, acquitting himself with all possible
diligence in the affairs of the Church of S. Marco, of the
Commissions, which are a great number, and of the many
other matters that are in the charge of those Procurators; and
he showed extraordinary lovingness toward those Signori, in
that, having turned his whole attention to benefiting them
and to directing their affairs to the aggrandizement, embellish-
ment, and ornamentation of the church, the city, and the
public square (a thing never yet done by any other in that
office), he provided them with various advantages, profits,
and revenues by means of his inventions, with his ingenuity
of brain and readiness of spirit, yet always with little or no
expense to the Signori themselves. Among which benefits, one
was this; in the year 1529 there were between the two columns in the Piazza some butchers' stalls, and also between
the one column and the other many wooden cabins to accommodate persons in their natural necessities—a thing most
filthy and disgraceful, both for the dignity of the Palace and
of the Piazza Pubblica, and for the strangers who, coming
into Venice by way of S. Giorgio, saw first of all on arrival
that filthiness. Jacopo, after demonstrating to the Prince Gritti
the honorable and profitable nature of his design, caused
those stalls and cabins to be removed; and, placing the stalls
where they now are and making certain places for the sellers
of herbs, he obtained for the Procurators an additional revenue of seven hundred ducats, embellishing at the same time

the Piazza and the city. Not long afterwards, having perceived that in the Merceria (on the way to the Rialto, near the Clock), by removing a house that paid a rent of twenty-six ducats, a street could be made leading into the Spadaria, whereby the rent of the houses and shops all around would be increased, he threw down that house and increased their revenues by one hundred and fifty ducats a year. Besides this, by placing on that site the hostelry of the Pellegrino and another in the Campo Rusolo, he brought them in another four hundred ducats. He obtained for them similar benefits by the buildings in the Pescaria, and, on divers other occasions, by many houses and shops and other places belonging to those Signori, at various times; insomuch that the Procurators, having gained by his care a revenue of more than two thousand ducats, have been rightly moved to love him and to hold him dear.

Not long afterwards, by order of the Procurators, he set his hand to the very rich and beautiful building of the Library opposite to the Palazzo Pubblico, with such a variety of architecture (for it is both Doric and Corinthian), and such a wealth of carvings, cornices, columns, capitals, and half-length figures throughout the whole work, that it is a marvel; and all without any sparing of expense, since it is full of the richest pavements, stucco-work and scenes throughout the halls of that place, and public staircases adorned with various pictures, not to speak of the appurtenances and rich ornaments that it has at the principal door of entrance, which give it majesty and grandeur, demonstrating the ability of Sansovino. Which method of building was the reason that in that city, into which there had not entered up to that time any other method but that of building their houses and palaces in one and the same order, each man always continuing the same things with the same measurements and ancient use, without varying according to the sites as they found them, or according to convenience; it was the reason, I say, that buildings both public and private began to be erected with new designs and better order, and according to the ancient teaching of Vitruvius; and that work, in the opinion of those who are good judges and have seen many parts of the world, is without any equal.

He then built the Palace of Messer Giovanni Delfino, situated on the Grand Canal on the other side from the Rialto, opposite to the Riva del Ferro, at a cost of thirty thousand ducats. He built, likewise, that of Messer Leonardo Moro at S. Girolamo, a work of great cost, which has almost the appearance of a castle. And he erected the Palace of Messer Luigi de' Garzoni, wider by thirteen paces in every direction than is the House of the German Merchants, with so many conveniences, that water runs through the whole building, which is adorned with four most beautiful figures by Sansovino; which palace is at Ponte Casale, in the neighborhood of Venice. But the most beautiful is the Palace of Messer Giorgio Cornaro on the Grand Canal, which, without any doubt surpassing the others in convenience, majesty, and grandeur, is considered perhaps the finest that there is in Italy. He also built (to have done with speaking of private edifices) the Scuola or Confraternity of the Misericordia, a vast work costing one hundred and thirty thousand crowns, which, when carried to completion, will prove to be the most superb edifice in Italy. And his work, also, is the Church of S. Francesco della Vigna, where the Frati de' Zoccoli have théir seat, a work of great size and importance; but the façade was by another master. The Loggia about the Campanile of S. Marco, in the Corinthian Order, was from his design, with a very rich ornament of columns, and with four niches, in which are four supremely beautiful figures in bronze, little less than the size of life, which are by his hand, together with various scenes and figures in bas-relief. That work makes a most beautiful base to the said campanile, which has a thickness, on one of the sides, of thirty-five feet, which is about the extent of Sansovino's ornamentation. In height, from the ground to the cornice where are the windows of the bells, it is one hundred and sixty feet; from the level of that cornice to the other above it, where the corridor is, twenty-five feet; and the other dado above has a height of twenty-eight feet and a half. From that level of the corridor up to the pyramid is sixty feet; at the summit of which spire, the little square, upon which rests the Angel, is six feet high, and the said Angel, which turns with every wind, is ten feet high; insomuch that the whole height comes to be two hundred and ninety-two feet.

But the finest, richest, and strongest of his edifices is the Mint of Venice, all of iron and stone, for there is not in it one single piece of wood, in order to render it absolutely safe from fire. And the interior is distributed with such order and convenience for the sake of the many artificers, that there is not in any part of the world a treasury better ordered, or with greater strength, than that one, which he built entirely in the Rustic Order and very beautiful; which method, not having been used before in that city, caused the inhabitants to marvel not a little. He also erected in the Rialto, on the Grand Canal, the new vaults, with such good design, that almost every day there assembles there a very convenient market of townsmen and of other persons who flock to that city. And a very marvelous thing and new was that which he did for the Tiepoli at the Misericordia, in that, they having on the canal a great palace with many regal chambers, and the whole building being badly founded in the water, so that it was likely enough that in a few years the edifice would fall to the ground, Sansovino rebuilt all the foundations in the canal below the palace with very large stones, maintaining the house on its feet with a marvelous support of props, while the owners lived in their house with perfect security.

Nor for all this, while he has given his attention to so many buildings, has he ever ceased to occupy himself every day for his own delight with vast and beautiful works of sculpture, in marble and in bronze. Over the door of S. Marco he made a Madonna of marble, the size of life, which is held to be a very beautiful thing; and at the entrance to the sacristy of that place there is by his hand the door of bronze divided into two most beautiful parts, with stories of Jesus Christ all in half-relief and wrought excellently well. And over the door of the Arsenal he made a very beautiful Madonna, who is holding her Son in her arms, of marble. All which works not only have given luster and adornment to that Republic, but also have caused Sansovino to be better known every day as a most excellent craftsman, and loved and honored by the magnificent liberality of those Signori, and likewise by the other craftsmen, every work of sculpture and architecture that has been executed in that city in his time being referred to him. And in truth the excellence of Jacopo has well deserved that he should be held in the first rank among the craftsmen of design in that city, and that his talents should be loved and revered by all without exception, both nobles and plebeians, for the reason that, besides other things, as has been told, with his judgment and knowledge he has brought it about that the city has been made almost entirely new and has learned the true and good method of building.

Jacopo was in body of ordinary stature, without any fat, and he walked with the person upright. He was white in complexion, with the beard red; and in his youth he was very graceful and handsome, and therefore much beloved by various women of some importance. After he became old, he had a venerable presence, with a beautiful white beard, and walked like a young man, insomuch that he was still very strong and healthy and could see every least thing, however distant it might be, without spectacles, and when writing he kept his head erect, not bending over at all as is done by others. He delighted to dress handsomely, and was always very neat in his person; and he always took pleasure in women down to extreme old age, and much loved to talk of them. In his youth, by reason of his excesses, he was not very robust; but when he had become old he never suffered any illness, insomuch that for a period of fifty years, although at times he felt indisposed, he would never avail himself of any physician; nay, having had an apoplectic stroke for the fourth time at the age of eighty-four, he recovered by staying only two months in bed in a very dark and warm place, despising medicines. He had so good a stomach, that he was not afraid of anything, making no distinction between food that might be good and food that might be harmful; and in summer he lived almost entirely on fruits, eating very often as many as three cucumbers at a time, and half a citron, in his extreme old age. As for his qualities of mind, he was very prudent and foresaw future events in the matters of the present, weighing them against the past; and he was zealous in his affairs, not considering any fatigue, and never left his business to follow pleasures. He discoursed well and with many words upon no matter what subject that he understood, giving many illustrations with much grace; on which account he was very dear both to the great and to the small, and to his friends. And in his last years he had a memory still very fresh, and remembered in detail his childhood, the sack of Rome, and many things, fortunate or unfortunate, that he experienced in his time. He was courageous, and from his youth took delight in contending with those greater than himself, because, he used to say, by contending with the great a man advances, but against the little he lowers himself. He esteemed honor above everything in the world, wherefore in his affairs he was most loyal and a man of his word, and so pure in heart, that no offer, however great, could have corrupted him, although he was put to the test several times by his Signori, who for this and for other qualities regarded him not as their protomaster or minister, but as a father and brother, honoring him for his goodness, which was in no way feigned, but real. He was liberal with every man, and so loving toward his relatives, that he deprived himself of many comforts in order to assist them; although he lived always in repute and honor, as one who was observed by everyone. At times he let himself be overcome by anger, which was very great in him, but it soon passed; and very often with a few humble words you could make the tears come to his eyes. He had a surpassing love for the art of sculpture; such a love, indeed, that, to the end that it might be dispersed widely in various parts, he formed many disciples, making as it were a seminary of that art in Italy.

Now this man, having thus become celebrated in sculpture and in architecture a master without a rival, and having lived in the grace of mankind and also of God, who bestowed upon him the genius that made him illustrious, as has been related, when he had come to the age of eighty-four, feeling somewhat weary in body, took to his bed in order to rest; in which having lain without any kind of suffering, although he strove to rise and dress himself as if well, for a period of a month and a half, failing little by little, he asked for the Sacraments of the Church, which having received, while still hoping to live a few years, he sank gradually and died on the 2nd of November in the year 1570; and although in his old age he had run the whole course of nature, yet his death was a grief to all Venice.

THE AUTHOR TO
THE ARTISTS

Postscript to the Second Edition

HONORED and noble craftsmen, for whose profit and advantage, chiefly, I set myself a second time to so long a labor, I now find that by the favor and assistance of the Divine Grace I have accomplished in full that which at the beginning of this, my present task, I promised myself to do. For which result rendering thanks first to God and afterwards to my lords, who have granted me the facilities whereby I have been able to do this advantageously, I must then give repose to my weary pen and brain, which I shall do as soon as I shall have made some brief observations. If, then, it should appear to anyone that in my writing I have been at times rather long and even somewhat prolix, let him put it down to this, that I have sought as much as I have been able to be clear, and before any other thing to set down my story in such a manner that what has not been understood the first time, or not expressed satisfactorily by me, might be made manifest at any cost. And if what has been said once has been at times repeated in another place, the reasons for this have been two—first, that the matter that I was treating required it, and then that during the time when I rewrote and reprinted the work I broke off my writing more than once for a period not of days merely but of months, either for journeys or because of a superabundance of labors, works of painting, designs, and buildings; besides which, for a man like myself (I confess it freely) it is almost impossible to avoid every error. To those to whom it might appear that I have overpraised any craftsmen, whether old or modern, and who, comparing the old with those of the present age, might laugh at them, I know not what else to answer save that my intention has always been to praise not absolutely but, as the saying is, relatively, having regard to place, time, and other similar circumstances; and in truth, although Giotto, for example, was much extolled in his day, I know not what would have been said of him, as of other old masters, if he had lived in the time of Michelangelo, whereas the men of this age, which is at the topmost height of perfection, would not be in the position that they are if those others had not first been such as they were before us. In short, let it be believed that what I have done in praising or censuring I have done not with any ulterior object, but only to speak the truth or what I have believed to be the truth. But one cannot always have the goldsmith's balance in the hand, and he who has experienced what writing is, and particularly when one has to make comparisons, which are by their very nature odious, or to pronounce judgments, will hold me excused; and I know only too well how great have been the labors, hardships, and moneys that I have devoted over many years to this work. Such, indeed, and so many, have been the difficulties that I have experienced therein, that many a time I would have abandoned it in despair, if the succor of many true and good friends, to whom I shall always be deeply indebted, had not given me courage and persuaded me to persevere, they lending me all the loving aids that have been in their power, of notices, advices, and comparisons of various things, about which, although I had seen them, I was not a little perplexed and dubious. Those aids, indeed, have been such, that I have been able to lay bare the pure truth and bring this work into the light of day, in order to revive the memory of so many rare and extraordinary intellects, which was almost entirely buried, for the benefit of those who shall come after us. In doing which I have found no little assistance, as has been told elsewhere, in the writings of Lorenzo Ghiberti, Domenico Ghirlandaio, and Raphael of Urbino; but although I have lent them willing faith, nevertheless I have always sought to verify their statements by a sight of the works, for the reason that long practice teaches a diligent painter to be able to recognize the various manners of craftsmen not otherwise than a learned and well-practiced chancellor knows the various and diverse writings of his equals, or anyone the characters of his nearest and most familiar friends and relatives.

Now, if I have achieved the end that I have desired, which has been to benefit and at the same time to delight, that will be a supreme satisfaction to me, and, even if it be otherwise, it will be a contentment for me, or at least an alleviation of pain, to have endured fatigue in an honorable work such as should make me worthy of pity among all choice spirits, if not of pardon. But to come at last to the end of this long discourse; I have written as a painter and with the best order and method that I have been able, and, as for language, in that which I speak, whether it be Florentine or Tuscan, and in the most easy and facile manner at my command, leaving the long and ornate periods, choice words, and other ornaments of learned speech and writing, to such as have not, as I have, a hand rather for brushes than for the pen, and a head rather for designs than for writing. And if I have scattered throughout the work many terms peculiar to our arts, of which perchance it has not occurred to the brightest and greatest lights of our language to avail themselves, I have done this because I could do no less and in order to be understood by you, my craftsmen, for whom, chiefly, as I have said, I set myself to this labor. For the rest, then, I having done all that I have been able, accept it willingly, and expect not from me what I know not and what is not in my power; satisfying yourselves of my good intention, which is and ever will be to benefit and please others.

The twenty-fifth of August, 1567. Giorgio Vasari